TURKEY BEFORE AND AFTER ATATÜRK

BOOKS OF RELATED INTEREST

TURKEY
Identity, Democracy, Politics
Edited by Sylvia Kedourie

TURKEY IN EUROPE
Charles Eliot

ISRAEL, TURKEY AND GREECE
Uneasy Relations in the East Mediterranean
Amikam Nachmani

THE KURDISH QUESTION AND TURKEY
An Example of a Trans-state Ethnic Conflict
Kemal Kırışcı and Gareth M. Winrow

ANGLO-OTTOMAN ENCOUNTERS IN THE AGE OF REVOLUTION
The Collected Essays of Alan Cunningham, Volume 1
Edited by Edward Ingram

EASTERN QUESTIONS IN THE NINETEENTH CENTURY
The Collected Essays of Alan Cunningham, Volume 2
Edited by Edward Ingram

ARABIC POLITICAL MEMOIRS AND OTHER STORIES
Elie Kedourie

DEMOCRACY AND ARAB POLITICAL CULTURE
Elie Kedourie

THE GREAT POWERS AND THE END OF THE OTTOMAN EMPIRE
Edited by Marian Kent

MIDDLE EASTERN STUDIES
A Thirty Volume Index 1964–1994
Compiled by Frances A.S. Perry

THE EMERGENCE OF THE ARAB MOVEMENTS
Eliezer Tauber

TURKEY BEFORE AND AFTER ATATÜRK

Internal and External Affairs

Edited by

Sylvia Kedourie

FRANK CASS
LONDON • PORTLAND, OR

First published in 1999 in Great Britain by
FRANK CASS PUBLISHERS
Newbury House, 900 Eastern Avenue
London, IG2 7HH

and in the United States of America by
FRANK CASS PUBLISHERS
c/o ISBS, 5804 N.E. Hassalo Street
Portland, Oregon 97213-3644

Copyright © 1999 Frank Cass Publishers

Website: http://www.frankcass.com

British Library Cataloguing in Publication Data

Turkey before and after Atatürk : internal and external
affairs
1. Turkey – History 2. Turkey – Foreign relations – Europe
I. Kedourie, Sylvia
956.1

ISBN 0-7146-4947-3 (cloth)
ISBN 0-7146-8006-0 (paper)

Library of Congress Cataloging-in-Publication Data

Turkey before and after Atatürk : internal and external affairs /
edited by Sylvia Kedourie.
p.   cm.
Includes bibliographical references and index.
ISBN 0-7146-4947-3 (cloth). – ISBN 0-7146-8006-0 (pbk.)
1. Turkey–Politics and goverment–20th century. 2. Turkey–
Foreign relations. I. Kedourie, Sylvia.
DR576.T863   1998   98-31627
956.1'02-dc21   CIP

This group of studies first appeared as a special issue of *Middle Eastern Studies*,
Vol.34, No.4, October 1998 (ISSN 0026-3206), published by Frank Cass.

Printed in Great Britain by
Antony Rowe Ltd., Chippenham, Wilts.

Contents

Foreword

At first sight it may seem strange that a collection of academic studies on Turkey before and after Atatürk should refer only in passing to the founder of the Turkish republic. One explanation may be that the changes wrought by Mustafa Kemal Atatürk, which were officially described, and were seen by contemporaries, as a revolution, have, like revolutions elsewhere, changed aspect in retrospect and now appear as an episode in the history of the Turkish people and state, an episode amply prepared by precursors and assimilated by successors to the slow-moving evolution of their society. But the researches, which have borne fruit in this volume, suggest another reason why scholars of Turkey's recent past and present need not have Atatürk constantly in their sights.

Mustafa Kemal Paşa as he then was, led a national movement of resistance to the designs of ethnic adversaries, who were threatening the largely Turkish-speaking Muslim population of Anatolia and eastern Thrace with the loss of their land. He frustrated these designs by reassembling the Ottoman army, which the Allies had defeated in the First World War. After he had led this army to victory, he employed its commanders and civil officials, who, like them, had formerly served the Ottoman state, to govern the republic of which he became the founding father and first president. Although the Republican People's Party, which he fashioned as his political instrument, had a monopoly of power, and was influenced by totalitarian parties first in Bolshevik Russia, and then in Italy, Germany and elsewhere in Europe, Atatürk's republic was not a fully-fledged totalitarian state. The French Revolution remained a more potent source of inspiration than the Bolshevik Revolution and subsequent radical ideologies. Atatürk created the framework of an orderly independent state, within whose secure frontiers, proponents and opponents of contemporary Western secular ideologies – liberalism, Marxism, solidarism, fascism – argued their cases with a vigour which survived periodic, and usually measured, repression, and which left its mark on government policies. The ferment of ideas permitted and utilized by the Kemalist regime, to the extent it saw fit, is illustrated by the studies in this collection by Asım Karaömerlioğlu on the cult of the peasant which was promoted by People's Houses and which inspired the establishment of the Village Institutes in the 1930s and '40s, and by Mustafa Türkeş on the *Kadro* movement, launched by ex-Marxists and *Marxisants* also in the early 1930s, to urge the planned development of the country by a cadre of committed radical reformers, negotiating a third way between socialism and capitalism. The debate encompassed an elite educated in Western knowledge and aware of Western thought and experience, while excluding 'orientals' for whom traditional Islamic knowledge provided a frame of reference. But as Islamic officialdom – the hierarchy of *müftüs* [muftis], largely inherited from the Ottoman state – hastened to submit to the secular republic, popular resistance to the cultural revolution, imposed by Atatürk and his regime, could find leaders only among the small fry of provincial *hocas* [khodjas] and *şeyhs* [sheykhs]. The data presented in this volume by Gavin Brockett show both the extent and the sporadic, disorganized and doomed nature of what the Kemalist regime called 'reactionary incidents'.

However, the forces which the regime sought to control have survived to this day, as three papers in this collection make clear. Ethnic Turkish nationalism has spilled out of the civic mould shaped for it by Atatürk in his enlightened moments and has found an expression in the Nationalist Action Party, which has latterly tried to combine it with Islamic sentiment in the framework of the 'Turkish-Islamic synthesis', an ideology which received some official encouragement after the 1980 military coup. Burak Arıkan charts the progress of the party as it tried to steer by the incompatible beacons of ethnic exclusiveness, Islamic religious inclusiveness, and more universal democratic values. Metin Heper, an expert on the Turkish tradition of a strong state, joins forces with Fuat Keyman in explaining how and why this traditional strong state is showing weakness in its dealings with political parties more notable for promoting the interests of their clients than for advocating distinct policies. Meltem Müftüler-Bac sheds light on the relationship between domestic politics and foreign policy with regard to the possibility of Turkey's accession as a full member of the European Union. Atattürk was well aware of the link, as witness his insistence that a country's foreign policy should be consistent with its domestic political organisation. Müftüler-Bac sees both cultural and political obstacles on Turkey's path to Europe: the history of antagonism between Christendom and Islam, and the shortcomings of Turkish democracy, as measured by the standards of the European Union. Turkey's disagreements with Greece, particularly over Cyprus, constitute an additional difficulty. All these problems have antecedents.

Hasan Ünal's minutely researched examination of the Ottoman reaction to Bulgaria's unilateral declaration of independence in 1908 shows how carefully Turkish statesmen sought to balance their relations with the Balkan states. The task was made more difficult by the difference in approach between the Young Turk revolutionaries and the grand viziers they put in power. In 1908 old-fashioned prudence won the day. But the revolutionaries' ill-considered decision to take up the Italian challenge in

Libya in 1911 contributed to the loss of all Ottoman possessions west of the Maritza in the disastrous Balkan wars of 1912–13, and this in turn encouraged the Young Turk leader Enver Paşa to enter the First World War on the side of Germany in 1914. Hakan Kırımlı, in the first of his two studies, describes a little-known episode at the beginning of the war when a small group of Ukrainian nationalists made their way to Istanbul with the hope of enlisting Ottoman aid for a landing on the shores of their *terra irredenta*. For once, Enver turned away from a proffered adventure. But after the Russian Revolution, the Ottoman government was quick to see the advantages of an independent Ukraine, and diplomatic relations were established with Ukrainian authorities, whose composition and area of jurisdiction were in a state of constant flux. In his second essay, Kırımlı tells the tragicomic story of the Ukrainian mission in Istanbul. After the Ottoman defeat in 1918, this mission dealt with an impotent Ottoman government, Allied occupation authorities which gave precedence to the White Russian opponents of the Bolsheviks, and the Greek Patriarchate with its own nationalist agenda. Kırımlı stresses the significance of the two episodes as precursors of the relationship which is currently developing between Turkey and newly-independent Ukraine. But there are other instances of continuity. Thus Ahmed Fend (who later took the surname Tek), the first Ottoman consul-general in the capital of the German-sponsored Ukrainian state towards the end of the Great War, went on to become an Ottoman minister under Allied occupation in Istanbul, then an envoy of the Kemalist regime in Paris, a minister in Ankara and, finally, an ambassador of the Turkish republic in several countries. The fact that a bankrupt Ottoman foreign ministry in Allied-occupied Istanbul still had a research department which weighed up the implications of dealing with Ukrainian nationalists points to the seriousness which characterised Ottoman foreign policy and which the republic inherited.

An episode in the life of another notable survivor, the Ottoman diplomat and poet Abdülhak Hamid (Tarhan), is the subject of the essay by Syed Tanvir Wasti who tells the story of Hamid's short service as Ottoman consul in Bombay. Hamid, the son of an Ottoman diplomat, spent much of his life in Paris, London, where he married an Englishwoman, Brussels, where he acquired a Belgian wife, and on other foreign postings. His verse dramas, written in the high Ottoman language incomprehensible to Turks today, sought to recreate the works of Shakespeare, Racine and Corneille in an oriental setting. After the demise of the Ottoman state, the government of the republic awarded him a civil pension, and augmented it by having him elected as deputy for Istanbul, a sinecure which he kept until his death at the age of 85. Despite its radical discourse, the Kemalist regime made such room as it could for cultured gentlemen of the old Ottoman-European school.

In the opening paper in the collection, Christopher Clay assembles data on emigration from the Black Sea coast and eastern Anatolia in the 1880s and '90s and produces evidence of distress in these parts of the Ottoman state after the disastrous war with Russia in 1877–8. Historians dealing with the anti-Armenian pogroms of the 1890s have concentrated on the role of Armenian nationalist revolutionaries and the response of the Ottoman government and the Great Powers. Christopher Clay renders a useful service by drawing attention to the important economic component of intercommunal conflict.

There are no Armenians left today in eastern Turkey, where peace is now troubled by the armed campaign of radical Kurdish nationalists grouped in the Kurdistan Workers Party (PKK). The PKK problem and its effect on Turkey's domestic politics and relations with Western democracies are touched upon in the studies of Karaömerlioğlu and Müftüler-Bac in this collection. The Turkish government is currently making much of the economic causes of the disaffection of its citizens of Kurdish origin and is trying to direct investment to the area. It is well to be reminded, therefore, that distress is no stranger to this geographically ill-favoured region. There are similar parts of the world where people stay only as long, as they have no means of leaving, and where government-sponsored industrial development leads to the construction of 'cathedrals in the desert' (to borrow a term from the Italian Mezzogiorno), while improved communications serve only to accelerate emigration.

Thus all the papers in this collection, even where they deal with half-forgotten historical incidents, touch on matters of current concern. In 1998 Turkey marked the 60th anniversary of the death of Atatürk and the 75th of the establishment of the republic. It has chosen 1999 to celebrate the 700th anniversary of the foundation of the Ottoman state. Turkey, to use a phrase much in vogue today, is making peace with its history. This second collection of articles on Turkey edited by Sylvia Kedourie, drawing together past and present, comes at an opportune time with its scholarly contribution to the important process of peace-making and consequent restructuring which the Turkish republic is undergoing as it moves into maturity.

ANDREW MANGO
September 1998

Labour Migration and Economic Conditions in Nineteenth-Century Anatolia

CHRISTOPHER CLAY

The economic and social history of Anatolia in the nineteenth century, or indeed in any other part of the Ottoman period, remains largely unwritten, despite the existence of a growing number of interesting articles and monographs which throw light on particular aspects of it.[1] Indeed the depth of our ignorance is such that it is not so much a matter of questions remaining unanswered, as of the questions themselves still being unformulated. One issue that one would have thought would have been the subject of vigorous debate is the extent to which economic conditions in the rural areas and small towns of central and eastern Anatolia contributed to the great outburst of intercommunal conflict in 1894–95 known as the Armenian Massacres. In fact writing on the massacres has focused almost entirely on the political and moral aspects of what occurred, even though the most accessible primary source, the British government's Blue Books, are studded with suggestive references to underlying economic problems in the districts where trouble occurred.

For most of Anatolia except for its western fringes the economic and political changes of the mid- and late nineteenth century – the growing involvement of the Ottoman Empire with the emergent world economy and the increased centralization of government – seem to have brought harm rather than benefits. And especially was this so in eastern Anatolia which, for the purposes of this article is defined as the six so-called 'Armenian' *vilâyets* of the 1890s (Sivas, Mamuretülaziz, Erzurum, Bitlis, Diyarbekır and Van), together with the northern portion of Aleppo and the *vilâyet* of Trabzon which stretched along the eastern half of the southern shore of the Black Sea.[2] Those parts of this region which did have access to outside markets, that is the districts along the Black Sea coast, had little to export, whilst the vast land-locked interior which was almost without roads, let alone railways, lacked the means to export the agricultural and mineral goods it was capable of producing in large quantities. Imported manufactures, on the other hand, which had a more favourable value to weight ratio, were able to penetrate in significant quantities. The result was a persistently adverse balance of trade,

MAP

ANATOLIAN *VILÁYETS*, 1890 (AFTER CUINET)

RUMELIA

BLACK SEA

TRANSCAUCASIA

PERSIA

Istanbul

KASTAMONU

Samsun

TRABZON

Trabzon

ERZURUM

VAN

BITLIS

Bursa

BURSA

ANKARA

SIVAS

M-ÜL-AZIZ

DIYARBEKIR

Izmir

IZMIR

KONYA

ADANA

ALEPPO

Aleppo

0   100   200km

▬▬▬ Area defined as "eastern Anatolia"
      for the purposes of the article

even when invisibles (such as the earnings of the transit trade from Persia) are taken into account. Even more serious was the heavy burden of taxation and the drain of tax revenue year after year to Istanbul, unbalanced by any compensating government expenditure (other than on administration), save here and there at a few military centres such as Erzurum. The result was a chronically, and progressively more deeply, depressed regional economy, in which most, if not quite all,[3] forms of economic activity other than subsistence agriculture were constricted by lack of markets and continuous deflation. Eastern Anatolia was thus unable to provide an adequate livelihood for its steadily increasing numbers, especially in such pockets of dense population as the Black Sea littoral and the plains around Harput and Muş, giving rise to desperate impoverishment and forcing those who could to seek work elsewhere.[4]

That this situation was already in the process of development by the 1860s is clear from the very detailed British consular reports of that decade. At that stage, however, things were not nearly as bad as they were to become by the later 1880s and early 1890s. Various factors contributed to the worsening of an already bad situation. These included the effects of the war of 1877–78 and the famine of 1879–80 which followed it, and viciously deflationary changes to the currency imposed by the central government (also in 1879–80) without any heed for their social consequences. They also included a heavy fall in the prices of products that *could* be got to market in response to changes taking place in the wider international economy. Also there was an increased tax burden, and a substantial reduction in the value of remittances received from those who found employment outside the region. A full analysis of the east Anatolian economy in the later nineteenth century is, however, beyond the scope of a single essay. In the present piece it is therefore intended to concentrate upon the last of these factors, which preliminary indications suggest was one of the most important variables determining the economic (and social) fortunes of the region.

Certainly there was no doubt in the minds of the British consular representatives in the East of the significance of the money sent or brought home by the tens of thousands of labourers and artisans who went to find work elsewhere. Repeatedly in their reports they stressed its significance in introducing some liquidity into a region that was constantly being drained of specie by a chronically unfavourable balance of payments. Without it, they reported, peasant families would be even less able to meet their fiscal obligations than they were already, purchasing power for goods and services of whatever nature would be yet further reduced, and the means would cease to be available to pay for even the very modest quantity of goods which the eastern provinces imported from outside.[5] It is the argument of what follows that in the 1860s out-migration and remittances were on a very large scale, large enough to bring considerable relief to the regional economy. However in the following decades both contracted sharply, and it will be suggested that the scale of the contraction was large enough on its own considerably to exacerbate the parlous economic situation which had come to prevail in the East (and indeed probably in most of Anatolia) c.1890, and which provided the context in which the Armenian massacres occurred. It seems probable that deteriorating economic conditions lay behind the apparently increasingly predatory behaviour of the nomadic and semi-nomadic Kurds towards the settled population (especially its Christian elements), about which so many complaints reached the ears of the British consuls. Even more certainly the desperate poverty of the mass of the sedentary population of whatever religion produced an increasingly powerful resentment against those who controlled the retail trade and local money lending, almost all of whom were Armenian Christians – a feeling which in turn, whether spontaneously or not, eventually extended to the Armenian community as a whole.

Migration out of eastern Anatolia in search of better opportunities elsewhere was nothing new in the period with which we are concerned. For those living along the Black Sea coast, or having relatively easy access to it, Istanbul must always have been the main destination and certainly there were both Greeks and Armenians from Trabzon in the capital as early as 1540.[6] However for those living further south, in the deep interior, reaching the Ottoman capital involved an intimidatingly long and difficult overland journey. It is therefore probable that before the second quarter of the nineteenth century Diyarbekır, and above all Aleppo, beckoned much more strongly. South eastern Anatolia, as far off as Erzurum and Van, was one of the main areas upon which the latter drew to maintain and increase its population, and not only Armenian and Turkish speaking Muslim villagers, but also Kurdish and Turcoman tribesmen, were to be found there in considerable numbers throughout the seventeenth and eighteenth centuries. Of one particular group of seventy seven Armenians from Sasun, the mid seventeenth century sources cited by Bruce Masters specifically record that they had left their villages because the land there could no longer support them.[7]

In the mid, and even the later, nineteenth century both Diyarbekır and Aleppo still attracted migrants from the interior regions of eastern Anatolia. In 1880 Nestorians from the region south east of Lake Van were reported as customarily going to both places for employment on a seasonal basis, and in the previous October a petition from the Gregorian Armenian community of Aleppo to the British ambassador in Istanbul bore 1250 'signatures' of people who claimed to be natives of 'Saroun' (= Sasun?), Muş, Van, Arapkir and elsewhere.[8] Some years later, moreover, in 1896 many Armenian Christians in the villages near Van itself were in great distress because they had been unable to go to work in Diyarbekır as usual.[9] However even if the damage done to the textile industries of these two cities by western import competition has apparently been much exaggerated, changing patterns of trade must have greatly reduced the employment opportunities they could offer compared to earlier times, and thus their relative attractiveness to migrants.[10]

We shall see that from the 1860s onwards a number of quite new destinations for migrant labour were beginning to open up. All the same, however, there is no doubt that when, around or perhaps rather before the middle of the nineteenth century, the scale of the outward migration from the East increased very substantially,[11] it came to be heavily concentrated on Istanbul. The latter had long been by far the largest urban centre in the Ottoman world, but in the nineteenth century a variety of factors combined to enhance its relative importance. In particular there was the growing centralization of political authority there from Mahmut II's reign onwards; the expansion in the size of the central bureaucracy as the reform movement got underway; and the expenditure in the capital of funds derived from foreign borrowing and of the increased tax revenues collected in the provinces that resulted from these developments. All this gave a great boost to the economy of a city whose principal *raison d'être* was as a seat of government, and where an extraordinarily high proportion of the population derived its livelihood directly or indirectly from the government. The huge influx of foreign soldiers, sailors and their hangers-on in the Crimean War of the mid-1850s also temporarily created boom conditions with a correspondingly increased demand for labour, as did the redevelopment of large parts of the city in the wake of the enormously destructive fires of 1865 in Stambul and 1870 in Pera. In addition the early 1870s, especially 1871–73, saw a tremendous surge of business confidence in the capital, in part fuelled by the government's foreign borrowing, with numerous new banks and other enterprises, many with western participation, being set on foot. Despite rather poor trading conditions a great deal of money was being made out of financial dealings with the Porte, and many large residential and commercial building projects were being undertaken, especially in and around Pera.[12]

The population of the city was clearly growing strongly, especially during the mid-nineteenth century decades, rising from around 400,000 in the 1840s to over 800,000 in the 1880s, although interpretation of the published data to arrive at more precise figures is fraught with difficulties.[13] Given the unsatisfactory state of public health, and the low expectation of life that accompanied it, this growth could only have come from immigration. Undoubtedly immigrants to Istanbul came from all parts of the Empire, and indeed at certain periods from outside it as well, but at least by the period with which this article is concerned two particular regions, which shared a number of the same geographical, economic and social characteristics, seem to have contributed a disproportionately large number. One of these was the East and South East of Anatolia, and the other was Rumelia, especially western Rumelia, that is the provinces of Manastir, Yanya and Işkodra. There were, of course, a variety of other areas in the Ottoman world from which there was significant rural-urban migration. However for most of them there was a sufficiently attractive and accessible 'local' metropolis which was able to absorb a majority of those who had to, or wished to, leave their villages.[14] Thus from the Hauran such people went mainly to Damascus; from Mount Lebanon they went to Beirut; and from the Aegean Islands and from south western and western Anatolia, from at least as far inland as Konya, to Izmir. A relatively small proportion of them, therefore, ended up in the capital.

Of the two areas from which Istanbul drew most heavily for its immigrants, Rumelia was clearly both much closer and had a larger population. However, the inhabitants of the Balkans had a much wider choice of emigration opportunities than did those from the East. The prosperous port city of Salonica was reasonably accessible, and from it a short sea journey would take them not only to Istanbul but also the whole Marmara region including Bursa, as well as to İzmir and the districts along the coast and inland from it where export orientated commercial agriculture was developing rapidly by the 1860s. They could also go north to Serbia and Rumania. They were thus less heavily dependent on the capital as an outlet than the Easterners came to be.[15]

The existence in Istanbul by the 1860s and later of a disproportionately large number of immigrants from the geographically very distant eastern Anatolia was remarked upon by numerous contemporaries. It has also attracted the attention of a number of historians, as has the tendency for particular types of employment to be dominated by men from particular localities. Thus at least until 1896 the famous *hamals* tended to be Armenians from the Van region, *kayıkçıs* were mostly Greeks and Lazes from the Black Sea coast, cooks and watchmen came from Sivas, whilst Georgian speaking Muslims from near the Russian border were frequently found as attendants in the *hamams* and there was even supposed to be a village which supplied the best coffee-makers. In addition large numbers of Christians, Greek and Armenian, found employment in construction, the workshops of the traditional manufacturing sector, in building and in petty huckstering and retailing.[16]

What made possible, or at least facilitated, this flow of population from the Far East of Anatolia to Istanbul was the enormous expansion of shipping services along the Black Sea coast, from the mid 1830s onwards increasingly in the form of steamers. According to figures collected by the British consul, the volume of shipping clearing the port of Trabzon rose from an average of 15,225 tons a year in the early 1830s to 61,664 tons a year twenty years later, 177,861 tons a year in the early 1870s and 483,732 tons a year in the early 1890s.[17] By 1882 the steamships of five different companies called weekly at Trabzon, and steamship clearances which had already approached 300 a year before the end of the 1860s were nearly 400 yearly. Between 1888 and 1891 clearances were well over 500 a year! Samsun was also extremely well served, whilst by 1870 even Giresun had four steamers a week in each direction and Ordu three. Certainly all these were primarily freight carrying vessels but, in addition to a limited number of cabin passengers carried in some comfort, most of them also took much larger numbers (up to several hundred per voyage) who endured spartan conditions huddled on the decks. With so many sailings, those arriving at the ports would not have had to wait any length of time for a steamer, and once on board, depending on the schedule of the particular ship, would have been in Istanbul after only a few more days.[18]

As for the cost, the price of a deck passage must surely have come down substantially between the 1830s and about 1850, but thereafter it fluctuated considerably in response to the degree of competition prevailing between shipping companies. In the late 1860s a cartel formed by the Austrian, Turkish, French and Russian operators succeeded in keeping rates relatively high, a single ticket from Trabzon to Istanbul costing the equivalent of LT 1.21 per head in 1867. In the early 1880s LT 1.1 seems to have been the norm, but in 1884 in response to increased competition from British ships it fell to only half that, whilst in 1894 there was a sharp reduction from a high LT 1.375 to less than LT 1.[19] The cost of travelling from Samsun does not emerge from the Consular Reports but must have been lower. Even the cheapest of those fares were not insignificant when they are compared with the net incomes of peasant farmers or wage earners in the East, but they were easily within the ability of a family to save or borrow in order to send one of its members off to the capital.

Once travel by sea from the Black Sea ports to Istanbul became readily and cheaply available, migration thither from the interior districts of eastern Anatolia became a great deal easier. Instead of a walk of up to 2,000 km. or more over paths and rough tracks, which would have taken a minimum of seven or eight weeks, the journey could be made in less than half the time. From most of the area that was to become the *vilâyets* of Sivas, Mamuretülaziz, and even from Diyarbekır, the most accessible port was Samsun, whereas from Erzurum, Muş, Bitlis and Van, Trabzon was nearer.[20] Loaded pack animals travelling as part of a caravan could cover the distance from Bitlis and Van to Erzurum in nine and twelve days respectively in the early 1890s, whilst from Erzurum to Trabzon (327 km) took a further ten days, although the second half of the journey would have been slower before the opening of a proper road some twenty years before. A few years earlier the completion of another road from Harput to Sivas was said to have reduced the journey time from the first named to Samsun from twenty to thirteen days. Small groups of men on foot carrying little save food for their journey could presumably have travelled more quickly.[21] All told, therefore, the entire journey from (say) Van to the capital (over 750 km. by land and a further 1,240 km. by sea) might take as little as three weeks, whilst from Erzurum it could be done in two or even less.

The increased employment opportunities in Istanbul, and the much reduced journey times from eastern Anatolia resulting from the development of regular steamer services along the Black Sea coast, together seem to have turned what had been a regular but fairly small movement of labour into a substantial torrent. It also made feasible, possibly for the first time, migration of labour not only on a permanent or semi-permanent basis, but also on a seasonal one. It became practicable for men to spend the autumn and winter months earning a wage in Istanbul, and the spring and summer working on a family holding located along the upper Euphrates or in the vicinity of Lake Van. Others apparently went in the spring to work in the market gardens and farms in the countryside surrounding the city and returned home in the autumn.[22] Amongst those actually in Istanbul long-stay migrants must have far outnumbered seasonal workers, but in any particular year a majority, and sometimes a very large majority, of those travelling were seasonal workers. Variations in the demand for labour in the capital, as one would expect, seem to have affected seasonal (and therefore usually casual) workers more acutely than those with regular employment, so that the numbers of men travelling on a seasonal basis fluctuated more violently than the comings and goings of long-stay workers.

As for those who left the region for longer periods, probably few if any departed intending to stay away permanently, although the high death rate in the unhealthy city environment must have ensured that significant proportion never returned for that reason alone. Some, for whatever reason, remained in Istanbul indefinitely but it seems to be the case that eight to ten years represented a typical period of residence for a long-term migrant.[23] Those who survived long enough seem to have gone back to their home villages very occasionally for long visits, and eventually to have returned there for good, the more fortunate and successful with sufficient money saved to buy some land. European observers repeatedly commented on these patterns of behaviour and the employment records of manual staff working for the Imperial Ottoman Bank bear them out, at least in part.[24] Whether the families these long-stay migrants left behind were normally their *own* wives and children, or their parents and siblings, is a question, and there may have been differences in this respect between the practice in different parts of the region and between different communities. Thus, for the Muslims of Rize, McCarthy found no evidence in the demographic record that those leaving had wives in their villages to whom they periodically returned, whilst the British consul at Erzurum remarked that emigration of young men from Harput to Istanbul and elsewhere led to the avoidance of early and imprudent marriages. On the other hand, according to Karpat, *gurbetçis* [temporary migrants] from the Black Sea coast were usually married, and Lynch noted that those going from Van usually left brides behind.[25] Whether there was any significant movement of females to match that of males seems extremely doubtful, although when movement from eastern Anatolia to the capital was halted by the government in the autumn of 1894 some of those prevented from travelling were said to have been the *wives* of men working in Istanbul who had been intending to join their husbands.[26]

From the economic point of view the important thing about these migratory movements, at least as far as the East was concerned, was that excess labour was siphoned out of the region, and purchasing power was transmitted back from Istanbul and the other places where the out-migrants found employment. Nevertheless, how large a proportion of the population of the East travelled outside the region in search of work at some time in their lives, and what proportion might have been absent at any one time, it is impossible to know. In any event the sources make it quite clear that migrant labour did not derive in equal proportions from all areas and all communities. Some sent a much higher percentage of their young men than did others, either because a local tradition of migration had become established at some stage or because of a particularly acute mismatch between population and the locally available resources, as seems to have been the case in the *cazas* of Egin and Arapkir (Mamuretülaziz), and some of the districts south of Lake Van. Apart from the districts just mentioned others which seem to have provided particularly large numbers of emigrants were the fertile but densely populated plains of Harput and Muş, and the narrow coastal strip between the Black Sea and the mountains which lay along its southern shore. Also, whilst there is no question that both Christians and Muslims went to Istanbul and elsewhere in search of work, the number of the former who did so, if not absolutely greater was certainly greater in relation to their total numbers, if only because conscription took off many young Muslims who might otherwise have become migrant workers. There was therefore much variation across the region. However in some limited districts the proportion of the entire adult male population away at any particular point in time might be very high indeed, approaching or even exceeding the one quarter to one third figure suggested for some districts of Manastir *sancak* in Rumelia in 1869. Thus slightly earlier in the century as many as ten per cent of the male population of some Muslim villages in the Rize area left in only two years as a combined result of migration and conscription, whilst the well informed British consul Palgrave thought (c. 1870) that emigration was reducing 'the efficient', that is able-bodied, male population of Van, Kayseri and other districts by five or six per cent a year. In 1880 it could be said of Egin and Arapkir that there was hardly a family not represented by at least one member in the capital and, doubtless with some exaggeration, that few save women, children and old men were to be met with in the streets in either place. According to Cuinet, writing in 1890, 12,000–15,000 of the 131,400 Armenians of both sexes registered as living in the *vilâyet* of Bitlis (that is the equivalent to one-fifth or one quarter of the males), were at that time actually in Istanbul or elsewhere. And from one single Christian village in the plain of Muş in 1896 no fewer than a hundred men had gone to Istanbul leaving their women and children behind.[27]

As for the absolute numbers travelling from the East to Istanbul in search of work, in 1867 Palgrave reckoned that departures from Trabzon by sea for the capital were 30,000 to 35,000 yearly and from Samsun a further 20,000, 'most of them workers, porters and the like ... in search of employment'. And he added that the numbers had been running at this level for several years past, and had been even higher at the time of the Crimean War. This author has found no comparable estimate for any earlier year, but the number of passengers leaving Trabzon in 1862 just on British ships, which were neither as numerous nor as regular as French, Austrian, Russian or Ottoman ones, are certainly compatible with Palgrave's global figure for 1867, and indeed with an even higher one, 40,000 or more.[28] However, neither in the 1860s nor later were Trabzon and Samsun the only ports sending migrant workers to Istanbul. Rize, at this particular time, may have been despatching them eastwards to Transcaucasia rather than westwards, and smaller ports such as Ünye and Tirebolu probably provided relatively few.[29] On the other hand we have noticed above that by 1870 numerous steamers called at Ordu, and especially at Giresun, and both were certainly the embarkation point for considerable numbers. Almost nothing emerges about how many used the former, but the latter was linked by a track of sorts (and later a road) to the inland district of Şebinkarahisar whose inhabitants had a notoriously high propensity to seek work elsewhere. In 1879, when the numbers leaving the other Black Sea ports were a very great deal lower than they had been twelve years earlier, 6,553 passengers left Giresun by steamer alone, most of them, although not all, bound for Istanbul.[30] Altogether these other ports must therefore have added substantially to the combined total of 50,000–55,000 which, according to Palgrave, left Trabzon and Samsun for the capital, and probably we should be justified in adding as many as 20,000 more on account of them. We arrive, therefore, at a grand total of 70,000–75,000 annually travelling by sea to Istanbul from eastern Anatolia in 1867 and for some years previously.

Of course the accuracy of the passenger figures just cited, and of the much more detailed ones available for later years,[31] is a question. However we may note that one observer (in 1870) believed that many more people travelled on the Black Sea ships than actually paid for tickets.[32] The figures provided by the shipping companies to the British and French consuls, and from which they compiled their statistics, are therefore likely to have been rather, and perhaps substantially, *below* the true totals. Against this must be set the fact that inevitably at least some passengers were travelling for purposes other than work (for instance the haj), and that others did not go the whole way to Istanbul but disembarked at intermediate ports. However, one particular group who are irrelevant for our purposes, and whose inclusion would have artificially inflated the figures for the movement of labour, that is Ottoman soldiers being transferred to and from the eastern garrisons, are invariably mentioned separately in the sources and have been eliminated. The 1867 estimate of 70,000–75,000 travelling westwards from the Black sea ports in search of employment is thus likely to be somewhere near the truth.

Even this figure, however, does not provide a full account of labour migration from the East in the direction of Istanbul because of the certainty that some at least continued to make their way there the entire distance on foot. Yet it seems reasonable to believe that by the start of the last third of the nineteenth century it was relatively few. Certainly it cost less in money terms: c.1880 it may have been possible to get all the way to or from the East on foot spending only some Ps 40–45 (LT 0.4 – LT 0.45) for food and lodging in each direction, when the steamer ticket from Trabzon alone cost Ps 110 (LT 1.1).[33] But the longer time required meant a loss of earnings, so that in the end it was not necessarily really cheaper by a very large margin, and it may have been significantly more dangerous. It is true that two of the three Kurdish labourers employed by Cyrus Hamlin at the time of the building of Robert College (1869–71) returned to their homes 'beyond the Euphrates' on foot. But the detail in which Hamlin recounted their story suggests that he thought it unusual, and when Captain Burnaby discussed his forthcoming journey from Istanbul to Van with an Armenian priest in 1876, he was told that 'hardly anyone' went the whole distance by land and that he would do better to take the ship to Trabzon. Certainly a quarter of a century later, when the government expelled many Armenian workers from Istanbul in 1896, European observers took it for granted that they were bundled onto shipboard for their return to the East rather than despatched along the roads.[34]

Finally, if we are to try to assess the economic importance to the Anatolian East of the out-migration of labour, we must also try to bring destinations other than Istanbul and its environs into the equation. As noted above, a number of new opportunities were becoming available by the 1860s. There were, for instance, a number of quite separate areas elsewhere in Anatolia where the commercial farming of export crops required an increasing number of labourers, especially at peak seasons. One of these was the Izmir region, but most authorities agreed that in this case the main sources of migrant labour were the Aegean islands and the nearby regions in the direction of the Anatolian plateau. Some Easterners probably made their way there, although I have found no references to them having done so which suggests that their numbers were not large. Another area of expanding commercial agriculture was around Bursa, and there, according to the British consul Sandison, Kurds and Lazes (the former from along the Euphrates, the latter from 'beyond Trebizond') already comprised the bulk of the migrant labour force before the end of the 1850s. Their numbers must have become quite considerable with the passage of time, but the vast majority surely travelled via the Black Sea ports and Istanbul and will thus have already been counted. On the other hand those who went to the third area of commercial crop production, the Çukurova, will equally certainly have gone direct by land so that they at least must be added to the total already arrived at. However the main development of the Çukurova came later in the century, and even in the later 1860s the number of workers able to find employment in the region is likely to have been quite small.[35]

Another new destination of the 1860s was Egypt, where the expansion of cotton growing in the Nile Delta from the time of the American Civil War onwards pulled in workers both from Upper Egypt and from countries to the North East. It is unclear how many went there from the area with which we are concerned, but some certainly did.[36] A final set of new possibilities was created by the development of Russia's Transcaucasian provinces, especially by the construction of railways and the growth of towns there. Some of the movement of Ottoman Christians across the border was inspired by religious or political motives. Indeed in the aftermath of the 1877–78 war, and again as inter-communal tensions worsened in the mid-1890s, most of it may have been in response to such factors. However earlier on economic motives seem to have predominated. Greek villagers from around Gümüşhane are described as having customarily gone to Russia for seasonal work each spring, 'their district offering but few agricultural resources'. However, it was not *only* Christians who went to seek employment in Transcaucasia, for in 1872 the British vice-consul at

Trabzon noted that both Christians and Muslims were going there to work at railway building, and on other enterprises. For 1867 Palgrave estimated the number of those going from Trabzon to Russia via Batum and Poti at 24,000 and others must certainly be added for Rize, and perhaps for some of the more westerly ports as well. If we make some allowance for these, and for the fact that some Ottomans also reached Transcaucasia across the land frontier, a minimum figure of 30,000 travelling to Russia in 1867 seems likely.[37] In all, therefore, in that a year *at least* 100,000 people went from the East either to Istanbul or to Russia to find work. To this something more must be added for those who went south-westwards by land to the Çukurova and to Aleppo, as well as for those who reached Egypt. The numbers were unquestionably far smaller, but if we add a further 15,000 to account both for them we shall surely not be exaggerating. Altogether, therefore, out-migration in 1867 cannot (on the basis of Palgrave's figures) have been less than 110,000–120,000, and might have been significantly more. However how much of this was permanent or semi-permanent migration, and how much merely seasonal, is an issue to which we must now turn.

Unfortunately there is no published information available on the number of those of East Anatolian origin living in Istanbul, Aleppo, Transcaucasia or elsewhere. In the case of Istanbul, however, there are some population data which provide us with at least some help, although we may remember the comment of Ahmet Vefik in 1870 that 'the industrial population of [the] capital is so floating and variable as to make it most difficult for anyone to lay down its numbers'.[38] According to the censuses of 1844 and 1857 the number of *bekârs*, or temporarily resident bachelors, living in the city, increased from 75,748 at the former date to 94,119 at the latter. This last figure represented 39.5 per cent of the recorded male population of the city, and although large is very likely to have been an *under*estimate. In any event it must have increased substantially over the next decade since the generation or so after the Crimean War saw a huge growth of Istanbul's total population, much or most of it deriving from the arrival of temporary migrants from the provinces.[39] Any 1867 figure for the successors of those counted as *bekârs* in the two censuses just cited can only be guesswork but it would surely have been at least 120,000, even without making any allowance for under-enumeration. The true number, even excluding seasonal workers who are clearly not included in the various counts of the city's population, must have been significantly higher. Of course not all of them came from the East of Anatolia for we have seen that there was a substantial inflow to the capital from other areas, but there is every reason to think (for reasons indicated elsewhere)[40] that Easterners were by far the largest single group. It should also be remembered that not all of those who took ship from the Black Sea ports actually found work in Istanbul itself, and that a proportion went on to the developing villages along the Bosphorus not then counted as part of the city, into the surrounding countryside, or to Tekirdağ, Ismit and (as we have already noted) Bursa. Some, if not very many, may even have gone as far as the hinterland of Izmir. For a total of all those from the East in Istanbul and the Marmara region as a whole, living there on a semi-permanent basis but retaining contact with their home villages, 100,000 is probably a very *conservative* estimate.

However, unless the number was *far* higher, which does not really seem likely, it follows that in a year like 1867 when perhaps as many as 75,000 people travelled to Istanbul by sea from the Eastern Black Sea ports to find work, the great majority of those making the journey must have been short stay or seasonal migrants. It is simply not possible that the comings and goings of a population of around 100,000 long-stay migrants, even if it was growing very fast, could have accounted for more than a small part of this movement. How many arrivals per annum would have been required to 'support' the long-stay colony in Istanbul and the Marmara region obviously depends on one's assumptions about the size of that colony, its rate of growth, prevailing mortality rates and the average length of the period spent away from the East. The number, however, is unlikely much to have exceeded 20,000. It therefore follows that of the 70,000–75,000 people who were arriving annually from the East in the mid 1860s somewhere between 50,000 and 60,000 were seasonal workers who would return again after only a few months.

As for the number of East Anatolians in Transcaucasia, all we have to guide us is our estimate of at least 30,000 departures a year based on Palgrave's 1867 estimate for Trabzon alone. The sources also leave the impression that the average length of stay was much shorter than in Istanbul. Even so, however, the number of those there at any one time in the late 1860s cannot have been less than 30,000–35,000. In fact it may well have been nearer 40,000.

The main reason why workers were attracted to Istanbul from other regions of the Empire was first and foremost because the level of money wages was higher there. A good deal of scattered information is available on wages in the late Ottoman period, but, although it has not yet been subjected to analysis in a way which is helpful in the present context, there is no doubt about the existence of wide regional disparities.[41] Thus, for the years immediately on either side of 1870, daily rates in the capital for ordinary unskilled labour seem on average to have been at least one third higher than those prevailing at Trabzon. British consular officials recorded that such people could earn from Ps 6 to Ps 9 and Ps 10 a day in Istanbul, according to whether they were rated as third, second or first class labourers, compared to a *maximum* of Ps 5–6 in the Black Sea port. For skilled or semi-skilled building workers such as masons, carpenters and painters the differentials were greater still. However both wages and prices at Trabzon and elsewhere on the Black Sea coast were themselves higher than those prevailing in the interior regions of the East, again by as much as a third according to consul Palgrave. This is an assessment which is in part confirmed by reports that in 1866 gangs of workmen in the Ergani mines were paid from Ps 3 to Ps 5 a day, whilst 'ordinary workmen' in Diyarbekır received Ps 4 a day; that in 1879 (by which time there had been some upward movement because of the Russo-Turkish war) mining labourers in Konya *vilâyet* received Ps 5 a day; and by information from Kayseri in 1880 that the unskilled rate was Ps 4–5 per day.[42]

The difference between the level of wages in Istanbul and those regions in which so many of the migrant workers had their homes was thus considerably more than one third, perhaps as much as double, whilst it is likely that work was more continuously available in the capital so that actual earnings would have been larger by an even wider margin. Of course the cost of living was higher in the capital, but the migrant labourers lived lives of such intense frugality, living in communal lodgings and eating the cheapest of foods, that it does not seem likely that this factor was sufficient to offset the higher money wages. In any event, the other reason which drove labourers from the East to seek work outside the region was not so much that wages were so low within it but that for most of them paid work was simply not available at any wage, least of all during the winter months. In the villages there were few opportunities, whilst in many of the towns much of what work there was seems to have been taken up by recently arrived immigrant groups from Russia who were flooding into the Empire in the 1860s and later, many of whom were 'settled' or, as it often amounted to, left to survive as best they could, in eastern Anatolia. Most of the *hamals* in Trabzon in the late 1860s and early 1870s, for instance, were Circassians and Nogay Tartars.[43] It was this absolute shortage of employment in the East which explains the continuance of an outward movement to places where the wage differential was very much less marked than in the case of Istanbul, or indeed hardly existed at all. Thus throughout the early 1870s daily wage rates at Aleppo were no higher than they were at Trabzon, that is a maximum of Ps 6, whilst in the Çukurova they were usually less and in some years much less, as the still small and inelastic market for labour was repeatedly swamped by more people seeking seasonal work than could be employed at the wages usually prevailing.[44]

All the contemporary foreign observers who commented on the phenomenon of migrant labour agreed that those who left the East to find work elsewhere sent back or took back to their home villages a considerable part of what they earned. The money saved was either hoarded until required, or was lent out in diminutive loans at high rates of interest but doubtless often on very dubious security. Much of it was in due course literally carried back to the East by men returning temporarily or permanently to their villages. Hamlin's Kurds, dressed as beggars so as to avoid unwelcome attention, wore concealed leather girdles in which to hide the gold coins they were taking home. But it also seems that long-stay workers remitted their savings indirectly, between their home visits. The more successful and affluent may have used the *sarrafs* to do this but probably most entrusted their money to someone they thought they could trust who *was* travelling. Thus in December 1894, 15 Armenians from the Dersim who were working in Aleppo between them gave LT 90 (an average of LT 6 each) to a young man who was accompanying a trading caravan returning to their home district, only to have it stolen by one of the muleteers. The probability that men journeying back to eastern Anatolia were carrying money doubtless explains many of the often murderous assaults on humble people using the roads in that region, which became especially numerous in periods when law and order were poorly maintained such as the few years after 1878 and again towards the middle of the 1890s. The seven Armenian labourers of Toprakkale killed by a band of Kurds in June 1895, soon after they had crossed the frontier from Russia where they had been working, provide one example among many from that period.[45]

Without any direct evidence it is difficult to know how much the average migrant worker sent or took home. However, in the case of those in Istanbul, unskilled casual labourers earning the rate ascribed to those of the first class, that is Ps 10 per day, and working for 250 days a year,[46] would have earned a total of Ps 2,500, that is LT 25 a year. This is reasonably well in line with the estimate of the British consul in Manastir that migrant workers from his district earned an average of LS 12/LT 13.2 during the six summer months when days were longer and working would have been more continuous than during the winter. No doubt some of the long-stay migrants, such as those employed as field labourers on farms in the countryside, did not earn as much as Ps 2,500 a year – around Bursa in 1860 ordinary field labourers earned Ps 8 to Ps 10 a day in summer, but only half that rate in winter. However, many certainly earned considerably more. On the one hand they included a significant number who already possessed or came to acquire some skills, particularly in the building trades as carpenters, bricklayers, masons and so on,[47] even the lowest class of whom earned Ps 15 a day according to a British consular report of 1872. *Hamals*, of whom there were many thousands, were paid by the job rather than the day, and were supposed to do substantially better than ordinary labourers, as also were *kayıkçıs* who were likewise very numerous.[48] On the other hand it also seems reasonable to assume that many, although obviously not all, of those engaged in craft and retailing activities, made more than manual labourers. As for those few who somehow secured regular employment with a foreign firm, they might be paid up to twice as much as a casual labourer could expect to earn, even in the absence of any particular skills. Thus the Armenian *hommes de peine*, most of them from the province of Sivas,[49] employed by the Imperial Ottoman Bank at its *siège central* in Galata, normally started at either LT 36 or LT 48 a year, on top of which they received an annual bonus of LT 3 or more every 31 December, and wage increases every few years.[50] To assume average gross earnings of LT 10.5 in six months for seasonal workers (more of whom in the case of Istanbul came for the winter than for the summer) seems reasonable, but LT 25 in a full year for long-stay migrants at a time when employment was abundant is clearly too low. Somewhat more, possibly LT 27.50.[50] will therefore be a better basis for our calculations. Bearing in mind that those working in Istanbul were exempted from taxes which had to be paid even by extremely poor people in the provinces, and the extreme frugality of the migrant worker living away from his family, it seems reasonable to suppose that one third (more or less) of these gross earnings could be saved for remission to the East.[51] It follows, therefore, that on average those away from home for only short periods, that is seasonal workers, took back about LT 3.5 a year per head, whilst long-stay workers were able to remit LT 9 a year each. If anything these estimations probably err on the side of caution.[52]

Those working in Transcaucasia probably made slightly less than those who went to Istanbul. An estimate deriving from 1880 suggests that the 4500 or so Nestorians from the Urmia region of Persia who went to Russia to work as day labourers or artizans in Tiflis and the Caucasus earned around LS 100,000 a year, or just over LS 22/LT 24.2 per head. Wage levels in Transcaucasia were probably somewhat higher in 1880 than they had been ten or twelve years before, so this information suggests that average remittances by those going to Russia would have been less, perhaps by ten per cent, than the level we have just suggested for Istanbul. Another estimate, again for rather later on, was that the 60,000 seasonal workers from Azerbaijan who crossed into Russia every year c.1900 took home 30 Rubles a head, the equivalent of LS 3.16 or LT 3.48 each.[53]

We can now proceed to making rough estimates for the total amounts taken or sent back to eastern Anatolia by those working outside the region. As may be seen in Table 1, in the case of Istanbul and nearby places, on the basis of a long-stay colony of 100,000 remitting an average of LT 9 per annum each and 55,000 seasonal workers taking back LT 3.5 each, we arrive at a total of LT 900,000 + LT 192,500 = (in round figures) LT 1.11

TABLE 1

ESTIMATES OF REMITTANCES TO EASTERN ANATOLIA
BY MIGRANT WORKERS

(1) c.1867

	Number of workers	Remittances per head	Total remittances
Istanbul and Marmara region			
Long-stay workers	100,000	LT 9	LT 900,000
Seasonal workers	55,000	3.5	192,500
Transcaucasia			
Long stay workers	22,500	8.1	182,250
Seasonal workers	12,500	3.15	39,375
Other places			
Çukurova, Aleppo, Egypt etc.	?	?	100,000
Total			LT 1,414,125

(2) Early 1890s

	Number of workers	Remittances per head	Total remittances
Istanbul and Marmara region			
Long-stay workers	67,000	LT 6.75	LT 452,250
Seasonal workers	18,000	2.625	47,250
Transcaucasia			(
Long-stay workers	?	?	(110,000
Seasonal workers	?	?	(
Other places			
Çukurova, Aleppo, Egypt etc.	?	?	100,000
United States of America	4,000	22	88,000
Total			LT 797,500

Sources: See text of article and references there given.

million. For those going to Russia, assuming as plausible 'guestimates' 22,500 long-stay workers remitting LT 8.1 per annum each, and 12,500 seasonal workers taking back LT 3.15, we must add a further LT 182,250 + LT 39,375 = LT 221,625, or let us say LT 220,000 in round figures. And finally we must add something for those in the Çukurova, in Aleppo, in Egypt and anywhere else. Here, particularly, we are in the dark, both in terms of numbers and the likely size of the average remittance, but if we add a further LT 100,000 we shall surely once again be erring on the side of caution.

On fairly conservative assumptions, both in respect of the number of migrants and of the average remittance per capita, the total of remittances to eastern Anatolia on account of migrant labour alone around 1867 must, therefore, have been at least LT 1.42 million, and may well have been more. Of course the total value of funds returned to the region by 'exiles' living outside it would have been larger because there were also the profits of the numerous Armenian traders and shopkeepers of eastern origin who carried on business in towns all over the Empire, part of which were often used to buy land, build fine houses and finance comfortable retirements in their home towns and villages. Both Kayseri and Arapkir were particularly noted for the number of merchants they produced, whilst Egin was famous as the original home of many *sarrafs* and bankers whose splendid mansions gave it a highly distinctive appearance.[54] The profits of trade and finance should not be forgotten, but they will not be considered here because our concern is with the economic and social significance of labour migration rather than with mercantile endeavour or total capital flows. The question of how significant to the economy and society of the East remittances of LT 1.42 million may have been is one to which we shall return at the end of this article.[55]

The year 1867 does, however, seem to have represented a high water mark in the flow of labour from east to west. Late in 1869 Mr. Watson of the British Embassy in Istanbul wrote that the labour market there was overstocked by the number of arrivals from the East,[56] and by the early 1870s there was no doubt that the number of workers departing from the Black Sea ports had stabilized at a much lower level. As may be seen from Table 2, over the years 1869–76, passenger departures from Trabzon, which in 1867 had been 30,00–35,000 for Istanbul alone, averaged only half as many (17,401 p.a.) for both Istanbul *and* Russia.[57] It is true that the former figure was for departures by steam and sail, and the latter by steamers only. However it is not possible that the difference can be accounted for by an increase in passengers travelling by sailing ships, since the numbers of these clearing Trabzon were diminishing rapidly: indeed in the years 1873–75 there were respectively only 27,25 and nine of them.[58] At first the reduction in the number of those travelling would have mostly been accounted for by

TABLE 2

STEAMSHIP PASSENGERS AT THE PORT OF TRABZON
1869–90

	Departures	Arrivals
1869	18,932	12,950
1870	19,133	15,582
1871	13,630	15,210
1872	18,623	15,840
1873	16,179	21,585
1874	19,163	19,584
1875	16,146	16,043
1876	8,141	18,894
1877	3,445	5,978
1878	4,964	8,464
1879	15,340	13,582
1880	12,302	11,042
1881	16,393	14,955
1882	9,731	11,780
1883	12,163	11,421
1884	12,654	14,444
1885	23,962	14,487
1886	15,912	15,027
1887	24,765	16,964
1888	20,688	16,650
1889	19,813	16,670
1890	13,040	16,630

These figures exclude soldiers and 'religious'.

Sources: Ministère des Affaires Étrangères (Paris), CCC Trébizonde 9: états de navigations/états
maritimes. MAE (Nantes), Trébizonde 82: états du commerce de Trébizonde.

fewer seasonal migrants, but in 1871 and especially in 1873 substantially
more men returned from Istanbul than departed thither suggesting the
beginnings of a shrinkage in the permanent colony of long-stay migrants.
Given the relatively small contribution to total remittances contributed by
the seasonal migrants, however, these developments may not have greatly
affected the scale of the former before the onset of the great crisis of the
Ottoman state in the autumn of 1875.

Thereafter, however, there can be no question but that it did so very
seriously. During the crisis years of state bankruptcy, war, a depreciating
paper currency and general economic crisis (1876–79), the Trabzon
passenger figures show that movement of labour to Istanbul fell to very low
levels. Indeed in these years those returning (33,336) outnumbered those
leaving (16,550) by two to one And although after the period of acute
upheaval had run its course the number of departures recovered partially, at
an average of only just over 13,000 a year for 1879–84 they did not even

reach the level of 1869–75, let alone that of 1867. In 1882, indeed, recorded departures by steamship were down to no more than 9731. In 1885, and again in 1887–89, it is true that the figures were much higher, but even so (bearing in mind that some uncertain proportion of them will have been going to Russia), those bound for Istanbul must have been more than a third fewer than in 1867. In any event the upsurge was only temporary and the number of passenger departures had subsided again by 1890, the last year in our continuous series Some kind of confirmation of the very low figure for the years around 1882–83, and so by extension for the rest of the series cited in Table 2, is the information relating to the latter year from a different source that individual travellers on the road between Erzurum and Trabzon numbered about 10,000 in each direction, most of them 'labourers proceeding to or returning from Constantinople and other countries where they find work'.[59] As for the other Black Sea ports we are, it is true, almost without information, but Cuinet's figure for the number of passengers clearing Samsun (by steam *and* sail) in 1889–90 suggests that departures had declined by at least as large a proportion there as at Trabzon.[60] In addition the generally very low level of movement is confirmed by a comment of the vice-consul at Van in his report for 1888 that, on account of adverse economic conditions in the capital, what he described as the surplus inhabitants of the district where he was stationed were beginning to give up their annual exodus thither. Another comment, in 1893, again from Van, that 'there is now much less of temporary immigration or moving to Constantinople for the purpose of earning a small competence than formerly', confirms that matters had not improved five years later. The large total (21,264) recorded the following year (1894), seems to have been occasioned by the prospect of an exceptional demand for labour to repair the damage caused by the great earthquake which had struck in July, destroying part of the Grand Bazaar and causing extensive damage elsewhere in the city.[61] On the basis of total departures from Trabzon by steamer in 1883–90 and 1894, it appears that between the mid 1880s and the mid 1890s the number going to Istanbul from all the Black Sea ports taken together must have averaged around 30,000 a year.[62] And if for some years in the later 1880s it had been rather more than this average, for a considerable period in the later 1870s and early 1880s it had been much less.

The most serious aspect of the post-war situation in Istanbul, as far as the villagers of eastern Anatolia were concerned, was the permanently reduced employment prospects there. The boom years of the later 1860s, and to a lesser extent of the early 1870s, never returned, and for a generation the economy of the capital was more or less chronically depressed, deprived as it was of the stimulus imparted by a net import of foreign capital which had characterized the years of heavy government borrowing abroad. Many of its formerly wealthy inhabitants had been impoverished by the bankruptcy of 1875, the depreciation of the *kaime* and the loss of much of Rumelia. There seem to be no figures available for the foreign trade of the capital distinct from those for the Empire as a whole, but there is no doubt that for most of the period between the late 1870s and the mid 1890s it was languishing badly. There were various reasons for this but the most important was said to be Istanbul's progressive loss of its entrepôt functions in respect of other parts of the Near East, as direct commercial links were developed between the countries of Western Europe and such provincial ports as Salonica, Beirut, Basra and Bushire. This had been going on since before the Russo-Turkish war and as a result goods which had once passed over the wharves of Istanbul no longer came anywhere near it, and profits which had once accrued to its merchants were lost, so that more and more firms went out of business or moved away.[63]

Year after year the combined effects of a stagnant or declining foreign trade, falling commodity prices and deteriorating terms of trade, and a succession of political crises in Egypt, the Balkans or elsewhere, conspired to lower the level of business activity in general. Thus the Director General of the Imperial Ottoman Bank apologized to his superiors for the disappointing financial results achieved during 1884 which, he said, were the inevitable result 'de l'état languissant dans lequel notre place végète depuis tant d'années'. The next year (1885) he told them that 'toutes les branches du commerce ont été cruellement éprouvées, et notre place a eu à déplorer un grand nombre de suspensions de paiements et de faillites de maisons de commerce et de banque'. 1886 was even worse, and 1887 little better. A few years later the Bank's internal Annual Reports were repeating a similar litany of gloom. 1891 was not a good year, but in 1892 business stagnation was even more complete with no real improvement in 1893, whilst in the following April the statisticians calculated that in just over four years the prices of six major Ottoman export commodities, upon which the prosperity of a significant sector of the commercial community depended, had fallen by proportions ranging from 15 per cent in the case of wool to no less than 83 per cent in that of raisins![64] In view of all this it is not surprising to learn that the population of the city was almost static between 1885 and 1906,[65] and that building activity, which was of particular importance in employing migrant labour, was at a considerably lower ebb than it had been before 1875. There were few redevelopments of any importance during the last quarter of the century. In Pera the construction of grandiose apartment buildings gave way to the building of much more modest row houses, whilst the neglect of routine maintenance by even the well-to-do long remained all too evident.[66]

What made the problem of finding employment in Istanbul particularly difficult for outsiders was that the local supply of labour had been largely increased by the huge influx of refugees from Rumelia in 1877–78. Most of these people were eventually resettled in Anatolia, but a proportion of them took up permanent residence in the capital where, according to a contemporary observer, they 'eked out a precarious existence by casual labour in an over-stocked market'. Their numbers, moreover, were continually recruited in the years that followed by a stream of Muslims obliged to abandon their homes in the new Balkan states by the hostility of their Christian rulers.[67] It was, therefore, not just that the casual and labouring jobs, skilled and unskilled, which had been available in such numbers to migrants from eastern Anatolia (and elsewhere) in the later 1860s were less numerous in the 1880s, but that a large proportion of that lesser number was now taken up by the refugees.

The action of the Porte in ordering the provincial authorities to halt the movement of labour to Istanbul in the autumn of 1894, when as we have seen, on account of the recent earthquake, more men than usual were making their way thither, needs to be seen in this context. Coming at a time of increasing government anxiety about Armenian separatism and just after the suppression of the Sasun rebellion, it might be supposed that official motives for this action were strictly political. However it does not seem that it was directed only against Armenians travelling to Istanbul, for the reports of the British consuls refer to 'poor people' being stopped without distinction of community. It therefore appears likely that the government's concern was as much socio-economic as it was political, in that it feared that the prospects of additional employment in site clearance and rebuilding would suck in far more labour than could actually be employed that way, which would have resulted in the creation of a potentially dangerous pool of unemployed and discontented people at the heart of the Empire.[68] Some indication of how fierce the competition for jobs in the capital had become by the last decade of the century is provided by the comments of foreign observers on the events which followed the seizure of the Imperial Ottoman Bank by Armenian terrorists in August 1896. Sir Charles Eliot commented, *à propos* the *hamals* of Istanbul, that Kurds and Armenians were 'competitors and rivals' in what he termed the carrying trade of the city. There must therefore be a strong suspicion that the bloodthirstiness of those 'Lazes and other wild Asiatics', who played so prominent a part in hunting down and killing Armenians in the streets, owed a good deal to the knowledge that they were destroying not only the despised *gâvur* but also rivals for scarce employment. Certainly most of the Armenians killed, according to Mr Herbert of the British Embassy, were migrant labourers who earned their living as porters, dock labourers, office caretakers and the like, whilst Sir Edwin Pears reported that gangs of assassins were recruited by the circulation of rumours that if the Armenians could be got rid of their jobs would become available 'for Turks and Kurds from the interior'. And in the event it became notorious that most of the employment vacancies that resulted both from the 5,000–6,000 casualties of the massacre, and from the sending of thousands more Armenians back to their homes in the East, *were* taken up by Muslims from the same region.[69]

In view of all this it is not surprising to find contemporary comment confirming that, for many people at least, wages in Istanbul in the late nineteenth century were falling. In 1883 a consular report described labour in the capital as being 'plentiful and cheap', while in 1891 vice-consul Fitzmaurice remarked from Van on the reduced level of remittances that were the result of the lower wages that those who had gone to Istanbul to work were now able to earn.[70] There seems to be no confirmation, moreover, for the finding of Boratav and his collaborators that the war years of the late 1870s had seen a sufficiently large upward movement in money wages for their level to have remained well above that of the earlier period, despite fifteen or more years of decline in the 1880s and 1890s. Whether or not the procedure adopted by these authors is appropriate to the purposes of their article, which is to throw light on the movement of Ottoman wages *in general*, it cannot reveal much about their course in any *particular* place – and least of all in the capital which is very poorly represented in the data available to them.[71] Certainly the very large increase in the supply of labour in Istanbul as a result of the influx of refugees from Rumelia makes it unlikely that wage rates increased in terms of silver, although what happened to nominal wage payments in the years of monetary disorder (1876–79) when *kaime* drove all forms of metallic currency almost entirely out of circulation for ordinary day-to-day purposes is still obscure. Besides, in view of the economic conditions prevailing in the capital at this time, whatever the decline in wage *rates*, it is likely that total earnings fell even more markedly because of less continuous working. By the same token the profits obtained in the craft, petty retailing and service activities pursued by so many long-stay migrants, and about which even less is known than about wages, are also likely to have declined.

It might have been supposed that the economic development of Russian Transcaucasia, which was accelerating from the 1880s onwards, would have provided the people of eastern Anatolia with at least a partial compensation for the decreasing opportunities and declining wages they encountered in Istanbul, but in fact it does not seem to have done so. The repeated references in the consular Trade Reports of the later 1860s and early 1870s to labourers going to Russia, cease in the following decade.[72] On the one hand it seems that the improvement in the means of communication, both within Transcaucasia itself and to the north of the Caucasus, made it possible for labour from southern Russia to reach the region and work there on a seasonal basis in a way that had not been possible earlier on.[73] On the other hand much the most important focus of development was the city of Baku and its oil fields, and these were of much easier access (across the Caspian Sea) from northern Iran than from the main emigrant areas of Anatolia. It was therefore primarily the Iranian rather than the Ottoman rural poor who satisfied the demands of the expanding Transcaucasian economy for foreign labour in the years 1880 to 1914.[74] Certainly some movement from eastern Anatolia to Russia in search of jobs continued, and still did so in the early twentieth century when Louis Rambert commented on men from Tirebolu and other parts of the Black Sea coast going to work in the tobacco plantations of the Caucasus.[75] However in the early 1890s, as the Ottoman authorities became increasingly concerned about the infiltration of Armenian terrorists from across the border with Russia, they took to refusing re-admission to those who left their territory and wanted to return, which was obviously a discentive to seasonal or temporary migration. The sharp rise in the number of Armenians leaving for Russia from 1893 onwards, on which the British consular officials remarked, was primarily a movement of entire families who had sold or abandoned their land and houses and did not intend to return.[76] The availability of work on the Kars railway, which was under construction in the mid 1890s, was doubtless an encouragement for them to go, but the main reason was the deteriorating political situation as a result of which many no longer felt safe in their own homes. The fact that considerable numbers were also reported as going to Iran, where the prospects of making a living can hardly have been any better than in the districts from which they came, confirms this conclusion.[77]

According to the Russian census of 1897 there were then 86,323 Ottoman subjects living in the governorates of the Caucasus region (mostly in Kars, Kuban and Kutaiss), but the large number of females in this population (32,273 out of 86,323) suggests that most of it was accounted for by the recently arrived Armenian family groups just referred to. However, some indication of the number of temporary and seasonal workers is provided by the 21,777 surplus of males over females. In fact it is likely that many of these too were unattached young men who had also recently left Ottoman territory not intending to return, but even if this were not so it still seems an inescapable conclusion that the total of temporary and seasonal workers was lower in 1897 than it had been thirty years before. In all likelihood it was much lower.[78]

If Transcaucasia was unable to provide compensation for shrinking opportunities in Istanbul in the 1880s and 1890s, nor was Aleppo whose economy was not particularly prosperous in the last two decades of the century and which for part of them was deeply in the doldrums.[79] The Çukurova, on the other hand, *was* providing an increasingly important outlet. Here, as we have seen, expansion in the cultivated area, and the commercial production of cotton and grain, had begun somewhat earlier, but development was accelerating markedly in the 1880s and 1890s. Increases to the permanently settled population of a formerly very sparsely inhabited area derived mainly from the settlement of former nomads and Muslim refugees from outside the Empire, but there also grew up a demand for extra labour at the busy seasons of the year. This was met by a growing supply of seasonal agricultural workers, with different groups (or possibly the same groups) of men from the North and North East appearing south of the mountains in time for the spring ploughing, summer harvesting and so on. Those arriving for the harvest of 1891 were described as being Armenians and Kurds, and the heavy dependence of the Çukurova economy upon them was made manifest a few years later. In the spring of 1896, in the aftermath of the wave of massacres that had afflicted much of the region from which they came, none appeared, and the result was a heavy drop in that year's harvest of both grain and cotton. There was also a movement, particularly of Armenians, into the towns of the area, of which Adana was much the most important, and which accordingly developed as an essentially Armenian settlement. However the spring migrants of 1891, referred to above, reportedly numbered only 5000 or so. It does not seem, therefore, that the demand for labour in the Çukurova was yet large enough to compensate for the reduced opportunities elsewhere. Besides the very short seasons during which labour was required may have limited the districts from which it was worth men's while making the journey there – in 1909 those coming to bring in the barley harvest were said to have travelled only from the Maraş area. With no possibility of travelling any way other than on foot it would have taken longer to get from Van to Adana than from Van to Istanbul.[80]

Nor, finally, was Armenian migration to the United States of America, which came mainly from the Harput area, yet of much significance in an economic sense, for no more than 1,500 people had gone there by the end of the 1880s. As the numbers increased the British vice consul at Harput revised his estimate of the moneys being sent back across the Atlantic rapidly upwards from LS 30,000/LT 33,000 in 1888 to as much as LS 80,000/LT 88,000 in 1892, but even this latter figure could only make up for a small part of the reduced flow of remittances that were the result of declining numbers of migrant labourers leaving eastern Anatolia as a whole and the lower wages they were earning.[81]

How these various developments of the period after the Russo-Turkish War affected the total value of the funds remitted to eastern Anatolia by migrant workers it is impossible to measure with any pretence at accuracy. Nevertheless their impact must have been very substantial. Let us assume (on the basis of the figures for the flow of migrant labour cited above) that by the early 1890s the size of the long-stay colony in Istanbul and its general environs was smaller by one third than it had been c.1867, and that the number of seasonal migrants was down by two thirds. Also that there had been a reduction in average remittance per head of 25 per cent. As is shown in Table 1, we would then have 67,000 long-stay workers remitting LT 6.75 per annum each, and 18,000 seasonal migrants remitting LT 2.625, *i.e.* LT 452, 250 + LT 47,250 = LT 499,500. Let us also assume that remittances from Transcaucasia were only half what they had been in 1867, that is LT 110,000. Thirdly let us assume that an increased flow of earnings from those going to the Çukurova offset a decline in remittances from Aleppo and elsewhere, so that the 1867 figure of LT 100,000 for the various 'other' destinations remains appropriate. Finally we may add in the LS 80,000/LT 88,000 suggested by the consul at Harput for remittances from the United States for 1892. We will then arrive at a *very* roughly estimated grand total of LT 797,500 (let us call it LT 800,000) a year for remittances into eastern Anatolia in the early 1890s by those finding work outside it. This is only just over half (about 56 per cent) of the LT 1.42 million estimated for c.1867. And just as the earlier set of estimates probably erred on the side of caution in arriving at a figure for the value of remittances in 1867, so these are more likely to have understated than overstated the extent to which they had fallen in the following quarter of a century.

Finally we have to address the question of what a fall in the value of remittances from around LT 1.42 million to only LT 800,000 a year would have actually meant for the economy and society of the Anatolian East. No statistics for the gross regional product are available, nor in a context in which so much economic activity was subsistence based would they tell us much if they were. There are, however figures for the amounts due in taxation from the various *vilâyets*. For 1866–67 the total liability for direct taxation of the four huge *vilâyets* of Diyarbekır, Erzurum, Sivas and Trabzon which then accounted for most of the East as we have defined it,[82] may be estimated at LT 954,600. By 1889/90 the corresponding figure for the seven smaller *vilâyets* into which the four had been divided was LT 1,675,000, with the amounts actually collected probably being slightly less in each case.[83] It appears therefore that at the earlier date our estimate for the remittances from migrant labour were sufficient to pay the direct taxes due from the eastern *vilâyets* one and a half times over, whereas by the early 1890s they were scarcely enough to cover half of it. Since there is no reason to suppose that there was any improvement in the region's balance of visible trade (rather the contrary), and there was certainly no significant increase in government spending or any large imports of capital, most of the shortfall must necessarily have been squeezed from the consumption of a population already desperately poor, or found by the progressive realization of what few capital assets the population possessed. Nor can there be any doubt of the adverse effects of this on the regional economy. Most obviously demand, and thus the prices, of goods marketed locally (including those of the livestock products of the pastoral Kurds) were forced downwards. The already very limited opportunities for paid employment were further reduced, and the dependence of villagers and townsmen alike on the credit provided by shopkeepers and money-lenders was progressively increased.

The tensions which produced widespread and often sanguinary outbursts of popular rage amongst Muslims against the Armenians in the east (and other parts) of Anatolia in the mid-1890s were not, of course, purely economic in origin. But like other episodes of inter-communal violence, for instance in Mount Lebanon and Damascus in 1860, and the Druze rebellion in the Hauran in 1895–96, there is good reason to think that economic factors played an important role. The present article has focused on only one aspect, albeit an important one, of the socio-economic history of eastern Anatolia in the second half of the nineteenth century. There are plenty of other aspects which require investigation before we can fully understand the background to those dreadful events, and without such an understanding little progress is likely to be made in understanding why events in the east took the course they actually did.

NOTES

1. It is impracticable to provide an adequate introduction to the relevant literature in the present context, but a starting place is provided by H. Inalcik and D. Quataert (eds.), *An Economic and Social History of the Ottoman Empire 1300–1914* (Cambridge, 1994) of which Part IV relates to the nineteenth century. As the title suggests, this work is not just about Anatolia, but there is much about Anatolia in it and it has an excellent bibliography.
2. The general situation outlined below probably applied also in the Central Anatolian *vilâyets* of Kastamonu, Ankara and Konya: these, however, are less well documented in the sources utilized for this article. For the extent of the various *vilâyets*, see the map on p.2.
3. For the textile industries of the region's towns which still had markets outside the region, and which even underwent some expansion at certain periods, see D. Quataert, *Ottoman Manufacturing in the Age of the Industrial Revolution* (Cambridge, 1993), esp. pp.61–71.
4. The brief characterization of the economy of Eastern Anatolia in the preceding and succeeding paragraphs derives mainly from the British consular reports. A full version of the argument involved will be the subject of another essay.
5. Accounts and Papers (hereafter A and P) 1867 LXVII (Erzurum Consular), pp.446 and 451; 1884–85 LXXIX (Trebizond Consular), p.644, 656–7; 1891 LXXXVIII (Erzurum Consular), p.346. 1892 LXXXIV (Kharput Consular), p.616. 1898 CVI (Turkey No.1), p.207. In the last of these Vice-Consul Crowe quotes an Armenian villager in the plain of Muş as saying that 'whilst at Constantinople he could support his family by his earnings ... and pay his taxes, but since his return he could not make ends meet.'

6. N. Todorov, *The Balkan City 1400–1900* (Seattle, 1983), p.57.
7. B. Masters, *The Origins of Western Dominance in the Middle East* (New York and London, 1988), pp.84–6. A. Marcus, *The Middle East on the Eve of Modernity* (New York, 1989), pp.20–1, 30–1, 36, 55; see also his 'Patterns of migration to Ottoman Aleppo in the 17th and 18th centuries', *International Journal of Turkish Studies*, Vol. 4, No.1 (1987). A.K. Sanjian, *The Armenian Communities in Syria under Ottoman Domination* (Cambridge, Mass., 1965), pp.46–50.
8. A and P 1880 LXXX (Turkey No.4), p.804; and 1881, C (Turkey No.6), p.719.
9. A and P 1896 XCVI (Turkey No.8), p.742.
10. The population of Aleppo seems to have dropped in the mid-nineteenth century, but to have recovered somewhat by 1890; that of Diyarbekır dropped heavily between c.1840 and 1890. C. Issawi, *The Fertile Crescent 1800–1914* (New York and Oxford, 1988), pp.28–9; and his *The Economic History of Turkey 1800–1914* (Chicago and London, 1980), p.34.
11. K.H. Karpat, *The Gecekondu. Rural Migration and Urbanization* (Cambridge, 1976), p.54. Idem, *Ottoman Population 1830–1914* (Madison, 1985), p.103. See also A and P 1887 LXXXVI (Van and Hekkari Consular), pp.542–3: this reference suggests that significant migration from Van to Istanbul began in the 1850s.
12. S.T. Rosenthal, *The Politics of Dependency: Urban Reform in Istanbul* (Westport, 1980), pp.11–16. Z. Çelik, *The Remaking of Istanbul* (Seattle and London, 1986), pp.55–72, 135. N. Senior, *A Journal kept in Turkey and Greece* (London, 1859), pp.133–4. A and P 1874 LXVII (Constantinople Consular), pp.869–71.
13. S.J. and E.K. Shaw, *A History of the Ottoman Empire and Modern Turkey* (2 vols., Cambridge, 1976–77), II, p.241. The main problem of interpretation arises out of doubt as to exactly which districts are included. See Karpat, *Ottoman Population*, p.103.
14. Historically, as noted above, south-eastern Anatolia had had two such local metropolises in the form of Aleppo and Diyarbekır, but by the second half of the nineteenth century neither were able to absorb sufficient numbers to prevent large-scale migration to more distant destinations.
15. A and P 1870 LXVI (Industrial Classes), pp.558–68, 571. 1871 LXVIII (Industrial Classes, Further Reports), pp.771, 774, 776 and 830. See also M. Palairet, 'The migrant workers of the Balkans and their villages' in K. Roth (ed.), *Handwork in Mittel-und Südosteuropa* (Munich, 1987).
16. See particularly D. Quataert, *Social Disintegration and Popular Resistance in the Ottoman Empire 1881–1908* (New York and London, 1983), pp.97–100. Karpat, *Gecekondu*, pp.51–5. See also Odysseus (Sir C. Eliot), *Turkey in Europe* (London, 1908), pp.410–11. Sir E. Pears, *Turkey and its People* (London 1912), pp.52, 175–6. A and P 1873 LXV (Trebizond Consular), p.488; 1881 C (Turkey No.6), p.716.
17. Public Record Office, London (hereafter PRO), FO 526/12, f.496.
18. A and P 1868–69 LX (Trebizond Consular), p.442; 1870 LXIV (Anatolian Coast Consular), pp.537, 538; 1883 LXXIV (Trebizond Consular), pp.557–8, 584. 1890 LXXVII (Trebizond Consular), p.327; 1891 LXXXVIII (*idem.*), pp.258–9; 1892 LXXXIV (idem), pp.549–50. A detailed account of a voyage made in 1876 on a Russian ship going from Poti westwards along the Black Sea Coast may be read in J. Bryce, *Transcaucasia and Ararat* (London, ed. of 1896). pp.383–411. When Burnaby arrived in Trabzon early in 1877 he was able to board a steamer immediately and was in Istanbul in three days: F. Burnaby, *On Horseback through Asia Minor* (Oxford, 1996), p.324.
19. A and P 1868–69 LIX (Trebizond, Sivas etc. Consular), p.350. 1870 LXIV (Trebizond Consular), pp.573–4; 1884–85 LXXIX (idem), p.692; 1895 C (idem), p.814.
20. A and P 1868–69 LXI (Trebizond, Sivas etc. Consular), p.358, 392–5; 1868–69 LX (Trebizond Consular), pp.445–6; 1898 XCIX (Trebizond and Sivas Consular). p.269.
21. A and P 1884–85 LXXII (Erzurum Consular), p.658; 1892 LXXXIV (Erzurum Consular). p.529. The journey between Erzurum and Trabzon, or vice-versa, *could* be done in eight days, or even six, by a mounted party: H.F.B. Lynch, *Armenia. Travels and Studies* (2 vols., London, 1901), II, pp.226, 237, 244.
22. PRO, FO 195/771, Reply of Consul-Gen. Cumberbatch to circular enquiry, C'ple. 31 July 1863.

23. A and P 1884–85 LXXIX (Trebizond Consular). p.644. V. Cuinet, *La Turquie d'Asie* (4 vols., Paris, 1890), II, p.648. Sir T. Waugh, *Turkey Yesterday, Today and Tomorrow* (London, 1930), p.74.

24. Banque Ottomane, Bulgur Palas Archives (BPA): Volume entitled 'Personnel du siège central' (destroyed in 1986, but photocopies in the author's possession). This recorded, amongst other matters, *congés accordés* to the many Armenian manual workers from the East employed by the Bank and which varied in duration from two or three months to several years. In most cases they were only taken once or twice during a period of ten to fifteen years' employment.

25. J. McCarthy, 'Age, family and migration in nineteenth century Black Sea provinces of the Ottoman Empire', *International Journal for Middle Eastern Studies*, Vol.10 (1971), p.320. Karpat, *Gecekondu*, p.54 and n.18. Lynch, *Armenia*, II, p.92. A and P 1867 LXVIII (Kurdistan Consular), p.193. According to Consul Stuart long-term emigrants from the Yanya region of western Rumelia were usually married: A and P.1871 LXVIII (Industrial Classes, Further Reports), p.771. See also Palairet, 'Migrant workers', pp.42–3.

26. A and P 1896 XCVI (Turkey No.6), p.213.

27. A and P 1870 LXVI (Industrial Classes), p.558. 1870 LXVII (Land Tenure), pp.838–9. 1881 C (Turkey No.6), p.716. 1884 LXXXI (Erzurum Consular), p.225. 1898 CVI (Turkey No.1), p.207. Cuinet, *Turquie d'Asie*, II, pp.526–8. McCarthy, *IJMES* 10 (1979), p.320. See also Palairet, 'Migrant workers', pp.24–5.

28. A and P 1868–69 LIX (Trebizond, Sivas etc. Consular), p.391. PRO, FO 526/6.

29. Ünye had one steamer a week in 1869 and at least some passenger traffic. A and P 1870 LXIV (Anatolian Coast Consular), pp.534–5.

30. A and P 1870 LXIV (Anatolian Coast Consular), pp.537–9. 1880 LXXIV (Trebizond Consular), p.703.

31. See Table 2 on p.20 above.

32. H.J. Van Lennep, *Travels in Little-Known Parts of Asia Minor* (2 vols., London, 1870), p.33.

33. The amount cited was what the government gave demobilized soldiers for the purpose of returning home: A and P 1880 LXXII (Turkey No.23), p.821. (I owe this reference to Paul Brandon). For the cost of a steamer ticket, see above p.7.

34. C. Hamlin, *My Life and Times* (4th ed., London, n.d.), pp.459–64. Burnaby, *Asia Minor*, p.13. Anon., 'The Constantinople massacre', *Contemporary Review*, Vol.LXX (1896), p.462.

35. On the commercialization of agriculture in the İzmir region, see R. Kasaba, *The Ottoman Empire and the World Economy* (Albany, 1988), Ch.4; and his 'Migrant labour in Western Anatolia 1750–1850', in C. Keyder and F. Tabak, *Landholding and Commercial Agriculture in the Middle East* (Albany, 1991). On the Bursa area, see PRO, FO 78/1450, Agricultural Report for the district of Brussa for 1858, ff. 74–5. FO 78/1609, similar report for 1860, f. 55.

36. A and P 1867 LXVII (Erzurum Consular), p.451. 1884–85 LXXIX (Trebizond Consular), p.656.

37. PRO, FO 195/1238, Biliotti to Malet, Trebizond, 24 April 1879. A and P 1868–69 LXI (Trebizond, Sivas etc. Consular), pp.391, 403. 1873 LXVII (Trebizond Consular), p.698. 1874 LXVII (idem), p.965. 1875 LXXVI (idem), p.98. 1876 LXXV (idem), p.363.

38. Cited in A and P 1870 LXVI (Industrial Classes), p.549.

39. Karpat, *Ottoman Population*, p.103.

40. See above. p.6.

41. C. Issawi, *Turkey*, pp.37–42. K. Boratav, A. Gündüz Ökçün and Ş. Pamuk, 'Ottoman wages and the world economy, 1839–1913', *Review*, Vol.VIII, No.3 (1985), pp.379–405.

42. A and P 1870 LXVI (Industrial Classes), pp.550–1. 1871 LXVIII (Industrial Classes, Further Reports), pp.725–9, 733–4. 1872 LXII (idem), pp.549–50. 1867 LXVIII (Kurdistan Consular), p.192. 1868–69 (Trebizond Consular), p.444. 1874 LXVII (Trebizond Consular), p.965. 1880 LXXXII (Turkey No.23), pp.707–8. 1881 C (Turkey No.6), p.729.

43. PRO, FO 195/771. Consul Taylor's reply to circular about cotton cultivation, Diyarbekır, 18 July 1863. A and P 1868–69 LIX (Trebizond, Sivas etc. Consular), p.342. 1870 LXVII Part II (Land Tenure), p.838. 1871 LXVIII (Industrial Classes, Further Reports), p.723.

44. A and P 1872 LVII (Aleppo Consular), pp.284, 291. 1873 LXIV (idem), pp.770, 782. 1874

LXVII (idem), pp.770, 782. 1874 LXVII (idem), pp.283, 295–6. 1875 LXXVII (idem), pp.359, 371. 1876 LXXV (idem), pp.255, 267.

45. Hamlin, *Life and Times*, p.463. A and P 1871 LXVIII (Industrial Classes, Further Reports), p.730. 1884–85 LXXIX (Erzurum Consular), pp.644, 656–7. 1896 XCVI (Turkey No.6), pp.278–9, 404.

46. 250 days a year seems more realistic than the 300 a year used by Consul Palgrave in his calculations of total earnings in A and P 1871 LXVIII (Industrial Classes, Further Reports), pp.726–7. Hamlin says that in the winter of 1869–70, during the building of Robert College, 'there were often three, four or five working days in each week'. *Life and Times*, p.460.

47. In the building of Robert College (1869–71) half the masons employed were Greek, the other half Armenians from Van. Hamlin, *Life and Times*, pp.458–9.

48. PRO, FO 78/1609. Bursa agricultural report for 1860, f.55. FO 195/774, similar report for 1864, f.376 v. A and P 1870 LXVI (Industrial Classes), p.558. 1871 LXVIII (Industrial Classes, Further Reports), pp.725, 728. 1872 LXII (idem), pp.549–50. H.O. Dwight, *Constantinople and Its Problems* (London and Edinburgh, 1901), p.152.

49. By contrast equivalent employees at the Bank's Stambul branch were mostly from Muş. BPA, Volume entitled 'Registre du personnel des agences A' (destroyed in 1986 but photocopies in the author's possession).

50. BPA, 'Personnel du siège central' (destroyed in 1986, but photocopies in the author's possession).

51. Some support for this assumption derives for the calculations of Consul Palgrave in A and P 1871 LXVIII (Industrial Classes, Further Reports), pp.726–32. According to a 1909 study of workers in the Baku oilfields roughly 30 per cent of earnings were remitted or saved: cited in A. Altstadt-Mirhadi, 'The Azerbaijani Turkish community of Baku before World War I' (unpublished PhD thesis, University of Chicago, 1983), pp.146 *et seq.*

52. Sir Edwin Pears, who lived most of his adult life in Istanbul, stated that Armenian workers often remitted as much as three quarters of their wages to their families. This does not seem credible, but he may have had in mind domestic servants and others who received free board and lodging as part of their total remuneration and would not therefore have needed to spend much of their cash earnings. Sir E. Pears, *Life of Abdul Hamid* (London, 1917), p.254. Another long time resident of Istanbul provides calculations which imply that Armenian *hamal*s saved over half their earnings, but this also seems too high. Dwight, *Constantinople*, p.152. Around 1970 Turkish migrant workers in the EEC saved about half of their net earnings: T. Çiller, 'The Economics of Exporting Labour to the EEC: A Turkish Perspective' in E. Kedourie (ed.), *The Middle Eastern Economy* (London, 1977), p.183, n.8.

53. A and P 1881 C (Turkey No.5), p.402. M.L. Entner, *Russo-Persian Commercial Relations, 1828–1914* (Gainesville, 1965), p.60.

54. Cuinet, *Turquie d'Asie*, II, p.364. A and P 1881 C (Turkey No.6), p.716. 1897 CI (Turkey No.7), p.575.

55. See below pp.27–8.

56. A and P 1870 LXVI (Industrial Classes), p.555.

57. At this time only Russian and Ottoman ships went eastwards from Trabzon as well as westwards. Between them they carried an average of some 9,700 passengers a year outbound from Trabzon during 1869–76, so it may be arbitrarily but reasonably supposed that half of these, say 4850 out of the 17,401 leaving Trabzon in total, went to Russia rather than to Istanbul: see sources to Table 2 on p.20.

58. A and P 1874 LXVII (Trebizond Consular), p.979. 1875 LXXVI (idem), p.99. 1876 (idem), p.364.

59. A and P 1884 LXXXIII (Trebizond to Erzurum Road), p.176.

60. Cuinet, *Turquie d'Asie*, I, p.99. By this time scarcely any sailing vessels called at Trabzon.

61. A and P 1889 LXXXI Erzurum Consular), p.44. 1894 LXXXVIII (Erzurum Consular), p.476. 1896 XCVI (Turkey No.6), p.213.

62. Average of all steamer departures from Trabzon 1883–90 and 1894 = 18,251 p.a. Deduct half of those using Russian ships (2,265 p.a.) = 15,986. Add 40 per cent of Trabzon for Samsun (6,400 p.a.) and the other ports (6,400 p.a.) = 28,786 p.a.

63. A and P 1880 LXXV (Constantinople Consular), pp.252–3. 1883 LXXIV (idem), pp.179–83. 1887 LXXXVI (idem), p.598. 1889 LXXXI (idem), p.76.
64. Archives Nationales (Paris), 207AQ/122 169–71: Rapports Généraux for 1884–7, and 1891–3.
65. S.J. Shaw, 'The Population of Istanbul in the Nineteenth Century', *IJMES*, Vol.10 (1979), p.266.
66. Çelik, *Remaking of Istanbul*, pp.72, 137. Sir R. Graves, *Storm Centres of the Near East* (London, 1933), p.22.
67. Karpat, *Ottoman Population*, pp.75, 103–5; and see his 'The Social and Political Foundations of Nationalism in South East Europe after 1878', in R. Melville and H.-J. Schröder, *Die Berliner Kongress von 1878* (Wiesbaden, 1982), pp.397–9, 494–5. Graves, *Storm Centres*, p.23.
68. A and P 1896 XCVI (Turkey No.6), pp.198–9, 213.
69. A and P 1897 CI (Turkey No.1), pp.337–8. Eliot, *Turkey in Europe*, p.410. Sir E. Pears, *Forty Years in Constantinople* (London, 1916), pp.161–2.
70. A and P 1883 LXXIV (Constantinople Consular), p.196. 1892 LXXXIV (Erzurum Consular), p.530.
71. Boratav *et al.*, 'Ottoman wages', esp. pp.391, 402–3.
72. The last such reference was in 1881. A and P 1882 LXX (Trebizond Consular), p.768.
73. A and P 1894 LXXXVIII (Batum Consular), p.611. 1896 LXXXVIII (idem), p.334. Labour seems generally to have been cheap and abundant in the Russian provinces north west of the Caucasus:- A and P 1892 LXXXIII (Taganrog Agriculture), p.746. 1893/4 XCVI (idem), p.110. 1894 LXXXVII (Taganrog Consular), p.549.
74. C. Issawi, *The Economic History of Iran 1800–1914* (Chicago and London, 1971), pp.50–2. Entner, *Commercial Relations*, pp.59–61. According to the Russian census of 1897 there were nearly 25,000 Persian subjects in Baku but only a few hundred Ottoman ones: *Premier Recensement Général de la Population de l'Empire de Russie*, redigé par N. Troinitsky (2 Parts, St Petersburg, 1905) Table XIA.
75. L. Rambert, *Notes et Impressions de Turquie* (Geneva and Paris, 1926), p.148.
76. According to Consul Graves at Erzurum even individual men going to Russia 'nominally' to seek seasonal work often did not return: A and P 1896 XCV (Turkey No.3), p.899.
77. A and P 1896 XCVI (Turkey No.6), pp.58, 101, 187, 214, 242, 313–14 and 368. 1896 XCV (Turkey No.3), p.877. 1897 CI (Turkey No.3), p.410; and ibid (Turkey No.7), p.560.
78. *Premier Recensement Général*, Tables XI and XIA.
79. Quataert, *Ottoman Manufacturing*, pp.76–9. See also the comments of the British Consul on economic conditions in Aleppo with reference to 1882, 1883, 1888, 1889 and 1893. A and P 1883 LXXIII (Aleppo Consular), p.119. 1884 LXXX (idem), p.593. 1889 LXXXI (idem), pp.19–21. 1890 LXXVII (idem), pp.372–3. 1894 LXXXVIII (idem), p.414.
80. J. Hinderink and M.B. Kiray, *Social Stratification as an Obstacle to Development* (New York, 1970), pp.11–15. B.N. Şimşir, *British Documents on Ottoman Armenians III. 1891–95* (Ankara, 1989), p.38. A and P 1897 XCIV (Aleppo and Adana Consular), p.183. C.J. Walker, *Armenia. The Survival of a Nation* (London, 1990), p.183.
81. R. Mirak, 'Armenian emigration to the United States to 1915: leaving the old country', *Journal of Armenian Studies*, Vol.I, No.1 (1975), pp.13–15. A and P 1891 LXXXVIII (Erzurum Consular), pp.346, 349. 1892 LXXXIV (Kharput Consular), p.616. 1893–94 XCVII (Erzurum Consular), p.392. By 1912, however, Armenian emigrants to USA were remitting around £3000 *a week* to Harput alone: BPA, letter from Mamuretülaziz branch enclosed in BIO London to *direction générale* in C'ple, 20 Nov. 1912, Correspondence Reçue, Londres, Vol.10.
82. See the map on p.2.
83. The 1866–67 estimate derives from details found in Archives Nationales (Paris), 207 AQ/232 D2: budget documents for 1292 (1876–77); and A and P 1870 LXV (Mr Barron's Report on the Taxation of Turkey), pp.574, 589, 619. For 1890, see *Turquie d'Asie*, I pp.39–40, 177–8; II 348–9, 657; III 445, 554–5, and 685.

The Indian Sojourn of Abdülhak Hâmid

SYED TANVIR WASTI

One of the many introspective and interesting passages in the autobiography of Abdülhak Hâmid[1] is where he lists the multitude of people, starting from his immediate circle of family and friends and extending as far as Shakespeare and Hafiz, who have provided inspiration for or have had some effect on his prolific literary output. If 'the lengthened shadow of a man is history',[2] Abdülhak Hâmid,[3] referred to during the second half of his life as 'the great poet',[4] could well be chosen to represent a thread of cultural continuity running through the labyrinthine and cataclysmic decades that led to the extinction of the Ottoman Empire. Abdülhak Hâmid has rightly been regarded by most eminent contemporary as well as subsequent Turkish writers and critics as a dramatic poet of genius.[5] Sensitive, proud, honest, capricious, conscious of his many failings, Abdülhak Hâmid spent most of his working life as a diplomat, away from the Ottoman capital that he loved. Hâmid stayed in London for more than 25 years.

Abdülhak Hâmid is credited with being the founder of modern Turkish dramatic poetry. Innovative in style and content though it is, the Turkish of Abdülhak Hâmid has much of the ponderous majesty and luxuriant flowering of eloquence that characterize the Ottoman poetry of his time. Rare Arabic and Persian words and expressions, lost in the treasure chests of Ottoman tomes over the centuries, emerge like precious stones and are set by Abdülhak Hâmid in otherwise flowing verse and dialogue. It is an incredibly rich diet and not for weak palates.

Another aspect of Abdülhak Hâmid that has attracted attention over the years has been his personal life, coloured as it was by impulsive and romantic involvement with many women. Several times married, Abdülhak Hâmid candidly writes that wherever he lived, he got along better with the women than with the men.[6] To return to the theme of the present article, Abdülhak Hâmid adds two strange items to the long line of his mentors and inspirers. He mentions that a tomb[7] was responsible for the production of Makber [The Sepulchre], one of his masterpieces,[8] and that a little clay doll dressed like an Indian dancing girl[9] provided the inspiration for him not only to read about Indian history and write his play Duhter-i Hindu[10] but also to accept the post of Ottoman Chief Consul in Bombay[11] many years later, in 1884.

Hâmid's Indian sojourn covers some 20 pages of his memoirs, but the material can be fleshed out because several letters written by him from India are also available.[12] The Bombay appointment came at a low point in Hâmid's life. He was a junior consular official, tired of the backwater that Golos[13] was, and had put in through his sources in the palace administration for Bombay or Odessa. He was the father of two children and had been married for 12 years to Fatma Hanım,[14] who was in poor health. Hâmid was allotted a travelling allowance of 60 Ottoman liras, which was not sufficient as he wished to take his family along with him to Bombay.[15] It was only by obtaining an advance on his future salary that he was able to manage, even though he was worried that this would inevitably lead him to suffer financially in Bombay. In December 1883 Hâmid took the plunge and sailed via Egypt[16] for India with his wife and children. His wife's illness, diagnosed as bronchitis which later turned into consumption, appeared to be on the mend, but he had mentally prepared himself to leave her in Egypt if it became necessary, because the senior Ottoman representative in Cairo (who also loaned him 50 pounds sterling) was a family friend and former employee of Hâmid's late father.

The ten-day voyage from Suez to Bombay in a French vessel was smooth and pleasant. There were 33 passengers in the first class, none in the second class, and Hâmid's cook Mehmed Ali was the only passenger travelling third class. It was the autumn of 1883, with 'clement weather, calm seas and beautifully sad sunsets'. Hâmid and family took rooms in one of the Bombay hotels for a few days while searching for suitable accommodation, but one of the wealthy local Muslim traders, Muhammad Ali Nakhuda,[17] insisted on placing one of his bungalows (in Mahim) at their disposal for this period. Hâmid later took lodgings on Malabar Hill, a well-known location in Bombay.[18]

First impressions may be unfair, but on arrival in India Hâmid did not find the world of magic and exotic women conjured up by the little clay doll. In one of his private letters, he caustically comments that the monkeys that roam the forests of Matheran[19] are more intelligent than some of the men and better looking than some of the women. He also states that in Bombay he found that the Parsis were fire-worshippers, the Hindus idol-worshippers, and the Muslims, unfortunately, were worshippers of superstition. He excepts Muhammad Ali Nakhuda, who was a man of the world and a friend. He mentions that the Indians were all hospitable, and comments on their love of pomp and show. The British, he says, are well aware of this weakness, which is why any Englishman who might find nothing better than a walking stick to lean upon when in London metamorphoses himself into a royal knight with all the trappings of glory in India. The governor of Bombay, Sir James Fergusson,[20] who drove around Bombay in a carriage with four horses preceded and followed by an escort of Indian cavalry, acted like the proud ruler of a kingdom when he received Hâmid at Government House.[21] It might be added that Hâmid's own life in Bombay, apart from worrying about funds, was easy enough. He spent only a few hours a day in his office.[22] He made friends with the prosperous Muslim businessmen of Bombay, and was surrounded by servants. There was plenty of leisure, with drives in carriages on the sea front either alone or with his wife and children, dinner invitations, games of chess and even time for composing poetry.[23]

At a later stage, impressed by the enthusiasm shown by the Indian Muslims for the Ottomans, Hâmid suggested to the grand vizier Said Pasha[24] that some political capital might be made out of this attachment, and penned an official memorandum on the subject. The Pasha told him: 'Look, let us become powerful enough to control the province of Aydın,[25] and think of India later.'

Hâmid's first letter from Bombay is dated 6 January 1884 and states:[26]

> For the time being we are in Bombay. This is a pleasant and even pretty place. But our expenses are far too great. Had my friend and retainer Ahmed Ağa[27] deigned to accompany us to Bombay, he would have slammed the doors on my life of luxury. Pleasantries apart, there is no luxury. Everything is far too costly. There is the necessity of keeping horses and carriages and about 20 servants. My office is in the commercial part of town, my house in the suburbs. Dinners and return dinners have to be given and the 15-room mansion has to be kept lit at night. One has to show that the consulate of the Caliph is great and glorious. All this is unavoidable.

Hâmid also made friends with Maulvi Hidayatullah,[28] a local scholar, who was both learned and graceful. On their walks together they often discussed aspects of beauty such as female attraction and the charm of pretty faces – an important topic, says Hâmid, for lovers of poetry. On a picnic when confronted with an exquisitely beautiful young Englishwoman, Hâmid said: 'Now what do you say to this, Maulvi Sahib?' and received the reply: 'Fine, but what is the use, she lacks colour'. Hâmid says that Hidayatullah would have preferred a copper-toned beauty. The concept of beauty – be it physical or spiritual – varied, no doubt, from place to place.

Well before the arrival of the impending monsoon, Hâmid and his family joined government officials as well as the foreign representatives for the move to Matheran in April. In a letter to Recaizade Ekrem,[29] Hâmid gives his address as 'the country of the birds' and continues:

For the last month and a half, I have shifted my own nest to the country of the birds ... Matheran is a complex of 20 or 25 mountains that form a range leaping into the sky. Forests surround us on all sides. There are 80 or 90 residences here, not counting those of the birds. They are the real denizens of this place, and we humans the transient visitors ... I am not joking when I say that the birds here have a tongue of their own, they howl, they neigh, they scream, they erupt into peals of laughter...[30]

Hâmid stayed in Matheran for two months. It was pleasant enough, says Hâmid, but there was no life at night and there were more monkeys than people, though some of the birds were 'as pretty as flowers'.[31] His friend Muhammad Ali Nakhuda was also in Matheran with his family, and they went out horse-riding daily. He also got acquainted with a rich Indian who kept a young English mistress – an invitation at their place was like an evening reading Othello, says Hâmid.[32] After two months, therefore, Hâmid was content to move on to Poona[33] with the rest of officialdom. He mentions that the train journey to Poona took eight hours, but he found the Poona climate far less damp and much more to his liking. He recalls a trip on an elephant to see a massive Hindu temple located on a hilltop outside Poona.

Hâmid's joy in his leisurely pursuits and light duties did not last long.[34] His wife's illness recurred. He secured the services of a well-known specialist, a Doctor Cock who, after an examination of the patient, suggested that Fatma Hanım suffered from pleurisy. Cock was, of course, unaware of any previous diagnosis, and Fatma Hanım's illness continued. The family doctor asked Hâmid if any other illness had been diagnosed, and Hâmid prevaricated. However, Fatma Hanım improved in health and this crisis was over. It was while at Poona that Hâmid learned of the arrival of Ahmed Ağa at Bombay and, later, of the arrival of Hüsnü Bey[35] as consular official. As expected, Ahmed Ağa took matters in hand and terminated the services of both the Iranian Hacı Ali[36] and the cook, Mehmed Ali, in an economy effort. The season over, Hâmid returned to Bombay with his family and took up residence on Malabar Hill in a bungalow with a verandah.[37]

It was during Hâmid's time in Bombay that the former British Ambassador to the Sublime Porte, Lord Dufferin,[38] was appointed Viceroy of India and landed at Bombay en route to the capital, Calcutta, to take up office.[39] During Lord Dufferin's three-day stay in Bombay, there was an official reception in his honour by the Governor of Bombay at which all foreign diplomatic representatives were invited; however, the two Muslim representatives (of Iran and the Ottoman Empire) were overlooked, ostensibly on the grounds that their ladies did not appear unveiled in public.

Hâmid made a representation through his staff to the office of the Governor against this high-handedness and an invitation was issued; he went to the reception in formal dress and was the object of much polite attention by Lord and Lady Dufferin. Lord Dufferin was full of praise for the sultan Abdülhamid and mentioned that the speech he had delivered at the Bombay Muslim Society that day would give the sultan much pleasure. Lady Dufferin was wearing the decoration the sultan had presented to her, and told Hâmid that it was a most precious souvenir. Hâmid later searched out reports of Lord Dufferin's speech in the local newspapers and says that Lord Dufferin could not have spoken more positively about Turkey had he been in fact chosen and sent to India by the Sublime Porte. In summary, Lord Dufferin stressed the importance of preserving excellent relations with Turkey because Great Britain itself had to look after many millions of Muslim subjects. He himself was a friend of the Muslims and had been chosen for the post of Viceroy partly because of his experience in Istanbul. Hâmid translated the speech into Turkish and sent it at once to the Ottoman Foreign Ministry.[40]

On a Sunday in February 1885 Fatma Hanım collapsed at the dining table at her home before a meal. Medical experts and laymen were all agreed that this indicated the final stages of consumption. It was hastily decided to take the patient to Beirut where Hâmid's elder brother Nasuhi[41] was posted as Mutasarrıf.[42] The necessary permissions from the Ottoman Foreign Ministry were obtained. However, there were commitments to visit the Nizam of Hyderabad and the Nawab of Rampur, and to look in on Delhi and Agra. Taking along Hüsnü Bey, Maulvi Hidayatullah and a secretary, Hâmid left behind both his office and his family in the care of Stepan Efendi,[43] who had been instructed to wire twice a day about Fatma Hanım's health.

As an envoy of the Sultan-Caliph, Hâmid first visited the Maharani of Baroda through the court minister Muhammad Khan, who was one of his Bombay acquaintances. There was a tussle for power between the Maharani and her son the Gaekwar,[44] the latter being supported by the British Resident. Hâmid diplomatically solved the crisis by meeting the son during the day and staying at the Maharani's palace for the night. Hâmid and his party next broke journey at Jaipur, the rose-coloured city, where the Maharaja was reputed to have 900 concubines. Hâmid points out that in India the Christian rulers often criticize the Muslim sanction of polygyny, although not only is it subject to stringent regulation in theory but also more or less extinct in practice. However, they turn a blind eye to Hindu polygyny.

Arriving at Allahabad, Hâmid observed multitudes of people garbed in white. He felt that Allahabad was a city of serious and religious people, and regretted that no Ottoman consulate had been established there.[45] Moving on to Delhi and Agra, centres of Muslim rule over India, Hâmid noted that impressive palaces and garrisons were the hallmarks of such sovereignty. Hâmid found the Red Fort at Delhi and the Taj Mahal at Agra to be architectural masterpieces. Hâmid and his companions moved on to Rampur, but the Nawab was unable to receive them formally and so Hâmid did not enter the boundaries of the state. However, he sent the Nawab some of his own books and received a couple of booklets of the Nawab's Persian verse in return. There being no railway link between Rampur in the north and Hyderabad in the south, Hâmid had perforce to return to Bombay to make the connection.

But it was not to be. His wife had once again become gravely ill, and the Hyderabad plans were dropped. Instead, calculations were made for the journey to Beirut, and Hâmid found himself deeply in debt. Money for the carriage and horses was owing to their former owner Qamar Sultan Sahib, and a further two hundred pounds was also needed for the sea voyage to Beirut. When Qamar Sultan learnt from Hâmid's munshi[46] that Hâmid might well have to resort to the local moneylenders for a loan of 200 pounds, he was most upset and at once rode back with the munshi to the Ottoman consulate and pleaded with Hâmid to allow him to lend the required sum as 'an application for a loan from the Consul-General of the Caliph of Islam to idol-worshipping people would hardly reflect with strength and credit upon the Muslims'. Hâmid was, as might be expected, most relieved and grateful.[47]

In the 20 days of the sea journey, says Hâmid, Fatma Hanım was at her very best, contriving even to look both cheerful and beautiful in the face of death. She played with the children, joked with the wife of the Austrian consul who was a fellow passenger, and amused not only Hâmid but also the redoubtable Ahmed Ağa. The ship's doctor warned Hâmid that there was no real hope and, in the event of her death, she would have to be buried at sea. Hâmid's misery had extracted a promise by the doctor to reconsider his decision should the catastrophe occur. Fatma Hanım herself is quoted by Hâmid:

> She said: I would be ill at ease
> If left behind in Indian seas.[48]

At Port Said, there was a change of ship, and the new doctor felt it unsuitable to allow Fatma Hanım on board, but he too was persuaded. As the distance to Beirut grew less, Fatma Hanım became afflicted with shortness of breath. They reached Beirut and were taken to the mansion of Hâmid's elder brother Nasuhi, where they were received by his wife Feride Hanım, because Nasuhi was due to return from an official inspection tour the next morning. Fatma Hanım said: 'If this breathlessness does not abate, I do not think I shall survive for another 24 hours' and, later, she added: 'Tomorrow you will be rid of me and become a lucky man again.' As a sign of celebration that the family was once again together, champagne was served, and Fatma Hanım said: 'Shall one tread tipsily into the Divine Presence ?'

Thus passed what Hâmid describes as the darkest night of his life. The only consolation was that Nasuhi returned the next morning and, respectful to the last, Fatma Hanım kissed the hand of the head of the family, saying: 'In you I salute all those left in Istanbul.' Fatma Hanım was buried in Beirut. Hâmid, in desolation, visited her grave every day and by the time he left for Istanbul had also left behind a monument in verse to his wife.

NOTES

I wish to express my gratitude to Professors Polat Gülkan, Tuğrul Tankut and S. Munir Wasti for their assistance and encouragement.

1. İ. Enginün [Editor], *Abdülhak Hâmid'in Hatıratı* (Istanbul, 1994). Abdülhak Hâmid points out that his memoirs are being written primarily from memory, and the reader should therefore not expect to find a chronological record. In the event, the only important date mentioned in the autobiography is 1852 for the year of birth of Hâmid, and this too happens to be disputed by other biographers. See Note 3, below.
2. The phrase is from Ralph Waldo Emerson.
3. Abdülhak Hâmid was born in Istanbul on 5 February 1851 into a well-established Istanbul family. At the age of ten he accompanied his elder brother Nasuhi Bey to Paris for a year and a half. He studied Arabic and Persian privately and at the young age of 13 joined the Chamber of Translators at the Sublime Porte. Hâmid's father, Hayrullah Efendi, served in important posts in the Ministry of Education and was appointed Ambassador at the court of the Shah in Tehran in 1864 and died there while on duty in 1866. Abdülhak Hâmid was also attached to the Ottoman Embassy in Teheran at the same time as a junior officer. He returned to Istanbul after the death and burial (in Tehran) of his father and took up various posts in the government Secretariat. In 1871, in Edirne, he married Fatma Hanım of the Pirizâde (also known as Pirioğlu) family. Hâmid's elder sister was married to Sahib Bey of this family, as a result of which warm relations existed between the two houses. Hâmid's talent for literature resulted in the publication in 1873 of *Macera-yı Aşk* [The Adventure of Love], followed by *Sabr-ü Sebat* [Patience and Perseverance], *İçli Kız* [The Sensitive Girl] and *Duhter-i Hindu* [The Daughter of the Hindu, or the Indian girl]. Subsequently, he was inducted into the Ottoman Consular service by being offered a post in Berlin. He made many excuses because he did not wish to go to Germany. He was next sent to Paris as Second Secretary in 1876, and stayed there two and a half years, while his wife and children were in Istanbul. Because of the suspicion aroused by the manuscript of his work entitled Nesteren, Hâmid was recalled to Istanbul and remained without any official appointment for some years. Subsequently, in 1881 he was appointed Consul in Poti in Georgia and transferred to Golos (Volos, a port in Thessaly) in 1882. In 1883 he was appointed to the post of Chief Consul in Bombay, where he served for a total of about 15 months. He had to cut short his stay and return because his wife Fatma Hanım's illness took a turn for the worse. On the journey to Istanbul they had to disembark at Beirut, where she died. Hâmid was next appointed to the Ottoman Embassy in London in 1886, where (although accredited to the Dutch court for some years) he remained

until sent to Brussels as Ambassador in 1908. He maintained his residence in London for the most part. With the installation of the government of Ahmed Muhtar Pasha in Istanbul in 1912, Hâmid's services were dispensed with, and he spent some time in Vienna. Eventually returning to Turkey, he was appointed to the Ottoman Senate, and remained a member till its dissolution. Subsequently, he was awarded a pension, and the Istanbul Municipality allotted him a place of residence. Abdülhak Hâmid was elected to Parliament in 1928. He took the surname Tarhan when the law relating to the acquisition of surnames was passed in 1934. Hâmid died in Istanbul on 12 April 1937.

4. 'Şair-i Azam' in Turkish; no other claimants to this title are known. The title for celebrated prose writer is 'Şeyhülmuharririn'.

5. Among such are Cenap Şahabeddin, Süleyman Nazif, Mehmet Akif, Mithat Cemal Kuntay, Orhan Seyfi Orhon, Ahmet Haşim and others. However, Hâmid has also attracted less friendly criticism from other well-known writers.

6. Such evidence as is available suggests that Hâmid was by no means flippant or callous, but genuinely attached to the women in his life, many of whom are commemorated by name or anonymously in his works. A detailed examination of this aspect of Hâmid's personal life may well be left to the labours of professional analysts and psychologists.

7. This was the grave in Beirut of Abdülhak Hâmid's first wife, Fatma Hanım, mother of his son and daughter. See Notes 3 and 8.

8. A long and moving elegy, written over the period of the 40 days of formal mourning during which the distraught Hâmid visited his wife's grave every day in the company of Ahmed Ağa. An English rendering of the first stanza is given below: Alas! For me no place or face is left, Full of sighs and tears, my heart is bereft. Here she was now and suddenly she went From past to future eternity sent.I had to leave, she under earth remains, In a forlorn corner, in disarray, remains. From her, who was my heart's desire, alas, A grave in Beirut is all that remains. Another verse by Hâmid, though not in the above elegy, was set to music by Mehmet Baha Pars and became famous in a rendering by Hamiyet Yüceses: Darkness everywhere, but effulgent is that spot ! Is it a fiery sunset, Lord, or that burial plot ? Flowers have turned her grave into a sepulchre now,Into a bridal chamber it is transformed somehow.

9. Hâmid writes: 'I purchased this little clay doll at the stall of the Indian Hasan Efendi in Bayezid during the month of Ramadan. So attached was I to it that it accompanied me to Paris.' In view of this statement, it may be surmised that Hâmid must have been ten years old when he bought the doll.

10. *Duhter-i Hindu* literally means 'the daughter of the Hindu' and, more poetically, 'the Indian girl'. Published in 1876, the play is set in India and treats the unacceptable face of colonialism. It introduces the Indian heroine Suruciyi (or Surucoyi) who aligns herself with the British officer Thompson only to be jilted later without compassion. Much later, Hâmid was to point out that he used the foreign format of the play to be able to write freely about Turkey, in disguise, as it were. The play was a great success, and he says that the little clay doll that inspired him was thus responsible for introducing him to his own countrymen. When a re-staging of the play many years later was being considered, Hâmid wrote in one of his letters that the name of one of the main characters, the Governor-General Sir Bortel, be corrected to Sir John Bortel to conform to the proper usage which was not known to him when he wrote the play as a young man in Turkey.

11. Bombay, part of the dowry of Catherine of Braganza, is today also known as Mumbai. The Ottoman Consulate was established in 1849, and the post was occupied by many notable and qualified Ottomans including Hüseyin Hasib Efendi and, many years later, in 1912, by Hâmid's friend Halil Halid.

12. As part of İ. Enginün [Editor], *Abdülhak Hâmid'in Mektupları* [The Letters of Abdülhak Hâmid] (Istanbul, 1995), 2 volumes, which contain most of Hâmid's extant letters. The letters of Hâmid from India comprise a dozen items, addressed mainly to Recaizâde Ekrem, Namık Kemal, Osman and Bahaeddin.

13. Volos in Greek, a seaport in Thessaly.

14. Fatma Hanım (1859–1885) was Abdülhak Hâmid's first wife and the mother of his two children. She was the daughter of Ahmed Bey, who was the cousin of Sahib Bey, Hâmid's

brother-in-law. A posthumous child whose mother died in giving birth to her, Fatma had been brought up in the household of Sahib Bey. When Hâmid's arranged engagement to a young lady in Istanbul was announced, he overheard Fatma lamenting: 'From now on I shall wear only black.' This little sentence affected Hâmid so deeply that he cancelled the engagement and got married to Fatma.

15. His wife, Fatma Hanım, his son Abdülhak Hüseyin and his daughter Hâmide. A relative of his wife, Ferahnüma Hanım, was also to accompany them, as was a cook, Mehmed Ali. Hâmid's son joined the Ottoman Foreign Service, married an English girl by whom he had two daughters and died at a young age while posted in the United States of America. In one of his letters lamenting his son's early death, Hâmid also mentions that it is a strange twist of fortune that he, a lord of the Turkish language, should have grandchildren who do not speak a word of it.

16. The boat from Istanbul docked for several hours in Midilli (Mytilene), an island in the Aegean, where Hâmid spent time discussing poetry and politics with the famous poet and freedom-fighter Namık Kemal, one of his mentors, who had been posted there as Governor.

17. Referred to in Hâmid's memoirs as Mehmed Ali Röge Nâhüda Sahib. A rich bon viveur, Nakhuda [literally captain/helmsman of a boat] became one of Hâmid's Muslim friends and also visited him later in London.

18. Hâmid, writing about Malabar Hill, which is the highest point in Bombay, refers to the Parsi 'tower of silence' situated there and describes the funerals at the place.

19. Then, as now, a popular hill-station in the Western Ghats which is about 30 miles from Bombay at an altitude of 2,500 feet.

20. Hâmid's relations with this important British functionary remained somewhat frosty while Hâmid was in India; it was not the custom of the representatives of the Crown to return visits by Ottoman Chief Consuls. Later, when Hâmid was posted to London, he came to acquire a regard for Sir James Fergusson, and writes that, years later, he was genuinely grieved on hearing of Sir James's death in an earthquake. In 1880 a College in Poona was named after Sir James Fergusson.

21. Hâmid writes: 'Three days after our arrival in Bombay, while we were still in the hotel, the *maidan* in front of the hotel was flooded with a crowd of men and women and an ocean of coloured costumes. The reason for the huge commotion was that the Duke of Connaught, son of Queen Victoria, was due to arrive to take up command of the British forces in India. It was a salute of the weak to the powerful. The imperial son and his wife passed by in a carriage with four horses, proud and disdainful, with a large escort. We observed the pomp and majesty of England paraded, but they did not notice the Caliph's consul standing on the hotel balcony.'

22. The Consulate office was located in Breach Candy, at the northern foot of Malabar Hill. Breaches and creeks in Bombay were filled up in reclamation schemes over the centuries. One of Hâmid's 'Indian' poems is, appropriately enough, entitled 'Biriç Kendi' [Breach Candy]. Hâmid's work covered trade and commercial interests apart from sending reports to the Sublime Porte on political matters, especially relating to the position of the Muslims in India.

23. Hâmid was deeply impressed by the tropical verdure of Bombay and the surrounding areas. Later writers have expressed the opinion that Hâmid's emotional descriptions of Nature owe much to his Indian stay. In one of his poetical collections, published shortly after the death of Fatma Hanım, entitled *Bunlar O'dur* [These are She] there are poems entitled Malabar Hill, Mahim, Kambala Hill and others such as Hindistan'daki Odam [My room in India] and Bağı Rani [The Rani's garden].

24. Mehmed Said Pasha (1838–1914), also known as Küçük [little] Said Pasha because of his diminutive stature, was several times Grand Vizier of the Ottoman Empire.

25. A prosperous and developed Ottoman province in the Aegean region of the empire. Said Pasha's reference was presumably to the large Greek population in the province at the time.

26. This letter is addressed to Yusuf Bahaeddin (1850–1916), the son of Ziver Pasha and the son-in-law of Celâl Bey, the elder brother of Hâmid's great friend Recaizâde Ekrem.

27. Ahmed Ağa of Çemişkezek was a faithful family retainer from Hâmid's bachelor days who travelled with him to Poti. He also went to India and returned with Hâmid and his family. He

stayed on in the family, serving Hâmid's brother until his own death on 7 June 1904 at about 75 years of age. Hâmid recalls him with great affection.

28. Hâmid had the habit of giving characters in his works the names of people he knew and met, as a memento of past friendship. Thus, in his play *Zeynep* one of the characters is named Mevlevi Hidayetullah. *Zeynep* also features another character by the name Hacı Ali, who was an Iranian employee of Hâmid's in Bombay. Hâmid writes that in a bizarre misunderstanding, a high ranking official in the Ottoman Ministry of Education some years later suggested to the Palace Secretariat that this name represented Hacı Ali Bey, one of the favourite secretaries of the sultan Abdülhamid, resulting in the temporary termination of Hâmid's services.

29. Recaizade Mahmud Ekrem (1846–1913), was a civil servant and a prolific writer. His mentor was the poet Namık Kemal, and he himself was a great friend of Hâmid.

30. The Indian subcontinent is extremely rich in bird life. See Salim Ali, *Handbook of the birds of India and Pakistan; together with those of Bangladesh, Nepal, Bhutan and Sri Lanka* (Delhi, 1983), Compact Edition. The original work by Ali is in 10 volumes. More recently, T. J. Roberts has issued *The Birds of Pakistan* (Oxford, 1992) in two massive volumes.

31. The Hindus revere monkeys, and erect temples to the monkey-god, Hanuman.

32. From Hâmid's letters we learn that this episode, as well as Nakhuda's adventures with women in London were partly the background for Hâmid's work *Finten*, a complicated tragedy involving a rich Canadian adventuress (called Lady Finten or Lady Finton in Turkish) and her Hindu servant and lover, Davalaciro. For a description of the first presentation of the dramatic version on the Turkish stage in 1908, refer to Halidé Edib, *Inside India* (London, 1937), pp.15–16.

33. Now called Pune, this city of two million inhabitants at an altitude of 1,500 feet is a place where Hâmid says that the meadows and hills, the trees and streams, the houses, paths, birds and flowers are all green and even the rains appear green. Poona is 115 miles from Bombay in the Western Ghats.

34. Perhaps Hâmid looked for meaning in omens, because he mentions, as a prelude to his wife's relapse, the sudden arrival of a parliament of owls and their colonization of a tree in their garden. Next, a gazelle owned by his wife was torn to pieces by wild dogs.

35. Hüsnü Pirizade was the brother of Hâmid's wife, Fatma Hanım, and had known Hâmid since childhood. He stayed on in India, died in 1902 and was buried in Bombay.

36. A cultured but impecunious Iranian living in Bombay. Hâmid employed him as a walking companion and says that Hacı Ali had literally inveigled himself into this employment.

37. Hâmid employs both 'bungalow' and 'verandah'; the first is an Indian word for large villa used in both Urdu and Hindi, and the second is a modification of the Persian 'bar amadah' literally meaning 'came out on'. Hâmid is full of praise for this beautiful bungalow and its view as a result of which 'every thought that occurred to one there was poetic'.

38. Frederick Blackwood, Lord Dufferin (1826–1902), an Irish peer with the full title of Marquis of Dufferin and Ava. He served as Governor-General of Canada (1872–78), Ambassador at St. Petersburg (1979 – 1881), Ambassador at Istanbul (1881– 84) and Viceroy of India (1884– 88). Subsequently he was appointed as Ambassador at Rome (1888– 91) and Paris (1892–96). His wife, Harriot, Lady Dufferin, was also active in social work in India. Few men have held such a succession of top jobs as Lord Dufferin.

39. Lord Dufferin kept a journal, and describes his arrival at Bombay. See excerpts in Sir Alfred Lyall, *The Life of the Marquis of Dufferin and Ava* (London, 1905), Ch.XI.

40. In parentheses, Hâmid adds, partly in criticism and partly self-deprecatingly that, coming from him, maybe they thought it was poetry and probably did not bother to read it.

41. Abdülhalik Nasuhi (1836–1912), a sorely-tried elder brother of Abdülhak Hâmid part of whose job appears to have been to remove his younger brother from scrapes and to solve his problems. Nasuhi was for some time a military officer and then became a high-ranking civil servant.

42. The title of *Mutasarrıf* was used for the governor of a special small administrative division called a sancak. Jerusalem and Beirut, partly because of their importance, were each designated as a sancak.

43. A junior consular official who had arrived in Bombay along with Hüsnü Bey.

44. The Gaekwar [literally cowherd] is the title of the (male) rulers of Baroda.
45. Consulates tended to be located in sea ports for commercial purposes, and cultural relations were not overplayed.
46. *Munshi* is an Urdu word still in use, for Secretary.
47. Hâmid, in his autobiography, takes care to mention that he repaid all personal loans in the many countries in which he lived and worked.
48. In the elegy *Makber* (see Note 8).

Collective Action and the Turkish Revolution: Towards a Framework for the Social History of the Atatürk Era, 1923–38

GAVIN D. BROCKETT

Historians of the modern Middle East will be familiar with the monochromatic historiography of inter-war Turkey, limited to explicating political developments especially those related to the ideas and person of Mustafa Kemal Atatürk. The prevalence of Mustafa Kemal in representations of early Republican history or the Turkish Revolution, as the years of his presidency (1923–38) are known, is evident in two rather divergent historiographic trends. The one concentrates on the Atatürk era exclusively and is rooted in the scholarship of Turks concerned to demonstrate that this period symbolized a distinct break with the past and thus marked the birth of an entirely new Turkish nation-state.[1] The other situates the Atatürk era in a much broader chronology, spanning at least two centuries, and is characteristic of the work of foreign historians who emphasize the continuity between modern Turkey and its predecessor, the Ottoman Empire.[2] Despite the potential inherent to these contradictory interpretations for very different and therefore fruitful analysis of the Atatürk era, however, the two approaches yield remarkably similar images each depicting a political process dominated by Mustafa Kemal.

The narrow focus of this historiography is due primarily to the particular sources exploited by historians to date: these include the many recorded speeches of Mustafa Kemal and his loyal political cadre, their published memoirs, and the records of Turkey's Grand National Assembly. Although these sources provide sufficient grounds for documenting the dynamics of Turkish politics as well as the corpus of reform legislation that constituted the Turkish 'Revolution', their focus is restricted almost exclusively to the activities of the political elite. On those occasions when this elite actually looked beyond the political intrigue unfolding in Ankara and recorded their observations concerning popular Turkish experiences of and responses to a revolution by legislation, their thoughts reflected the positivist rational tenets of Kemalist ideology. Implicit in this ideology was the conviction that the Kemalist elite was distinct from the Anatolian 'masses' in terms of rational intelligence and adaptability, and was therefore responsible for leading Anatolian townsmen and peasants out of darkness and into light. The Kemalist conception of progress derided institutions and cultural accretions – especially religious beliefs and practices – associated with the Ottoman-Islamic past; it reflected not only the elite's limited understanding of but also its hostility towards the very beliefs and rituals crucial to the definition of Anatolian Muslim identities.

'Histories' of the Turkish Revolution, therefore, must be treated with considerable circumspection not simply because their sources are explicitly biased in favour of a Kemalist interpretation of political developments, but also because the same sources present an extremely distorted impression of popular Turkish experience. Furthermore, the litany of reform legislation around which historians typically structure their minimal assessments of the social history of the Turkish Revolution, must be recognized for its normative idealization of Kemalist doctrine, proclamation of the hoped-for future, and assertion that what the Kemalist elite believed should happen was indeed taking place.

The discrepancy between reported fact and probable reality with regards to the political history of the Atatürk era has recently inspired historians to reappraise the same sources and challenge previous orthodox Kemalist interpretations.[3] Revisionist historiography, however, has focused almost exclusively on Turkish politics. Despite tacit recognition that to cast Turkish social relationships in terms of an antagonistic elite–mass dichotomy is misleading and that the equation of complete cultural transformation with reform legislation is naïve, historians have not seriously examined just how the Turkish populace experienced the profound changes posited in political historical accounts. This hesitancy is attributable, in part, to scholarly awareness that not only must socio-historical analysis of the Turkish Revolution be predicated on a re-evaluation of Kemalist rhetoric, but also that it can only be undertaken within the confines of a limited corpus of source material.

Nevertheless, the task of delineating the extent to which Kemalist reforms affected Anatolian society is eased significantly by the current availability of socio-anthropological studies that document shifting social relations and practices in specific locales subsequent to the Second World War.[4] The authors of these studies are generally careful to situate their observations in broader historical contexts, sensitive to the varying degrees to which identifiable social groups participated in the modernization programme promoted by Mustafa Kemal. The details contained in these studies may be of questionable reliability given the time-lapse between the Atatürk era and when scholars conducted their research, as well as the potential unreliability of their oral informants; however, they do constitute an embryo that, if nurtured in the context of our current understanding of late Ottoman Anatolian society as well as insights derived from new sources, may mature into a foundation for future socio-historical analysis of inter-war Turkey.

This essay is intended to contribute to the establishment of such a foundation; derived from a more thorough study of the available information concerning the social history of the Atatürk era, it examines incidents of collective action – specifically those claiming Islamic legitimation – that occurred between 1923 and 1938.[5] The following reconstruction of these events is based upon a variety of sources with which historians are already familiar, but which have not previously been used in harmony for this specific purpose. Although historical analysis of the Atatürk era is indeed limited by the inaccessibility of state archives, newspapers, population censuses and British consular documents all constitute important sources for social history. Newspapers, existing at both the national and local level, may have been mostly organs of the Kemalist elite, but they did publish detailed investigations of incidents of collective action and it is from these reports that our initial understanding must stem.[6] Population censuses carried out in 1927 and 1935 provide valuable insights into the context of the movements and permit analysis of a local population's ethnic and linguistic make-up as well as of regional trends in rural–urban migration and even economic change.[7] British consular reports constitute a particularly revealing source all too often discounted on the grounds that they were written by observers unfamiliar with and unsympathetic to the society they described. Nevertheless, given the paucity of other written records, these documents cannot be ignored; indeed, written by officials stationed in major Anatolian cities and responsible for travelling throughout the country, they present astute observations of Anatolian society in this important period, and frequently provide details and perspectives concerning collective action found nowhere else.[8]

It is on the basis of these sources that I narrate the occurrences of collective action themselves and situate them in their appropriate contexts. In so doing the purpose is twofold: first, to clarify movements of 'Islamic reaction' [irtica] that historians have not previously treated comprehensively and which are therefore mired in myth and misunderstanding; and second, to study collective action – of particular incidents in not just political but specific social and cultural contexts – in order to arrive at a more complete understanding of Turkish society as a whole and to challenges the crystallized elite–mass dichotomy typically portrayed in historical studies of the Atatürk era.[9] The absence of detailed descriptions of these events, written by either participants or eyewitnesses, severely limits the degree to which it is possible to understand the motivations and actions of individual participants. Nevertheless, the available information is sufficient for considering what the actions of a relatively small number of 'reactionaries' reveal about the experiences of the entire Anatolian populace exposed to the Kemalist programme of secularization and Turkification. Moreover, the same information offers an insight into why collective action was in fact a rare occurrence during the Atatürk era, and as such it illuminates the experiences of the 'silent masses' all too often neglected by an elite-oriented historiography.

Collective association outside the narrow limits established by the state, to say nothing of collective *action*, presented a potential challenge both to the dominance of the Kemalist elite within Turkish politics as well as to its vision of a Turkish nation-state that would unite a culturally and socially diverse Anatolian populace according to secular, Turkish ideals. Loath to permit any form of collective association that he himself could not control, Mustafa Kemal deemed political affiliation with either the Ottoman Committee of Union and Progress or communist organizations as threatening as personal allegiance to Muslim associations – primarily dervish *tarikats* – not within the purview of the state's Ministry of Religious Affairs. The earliest years of Republican history, therefore, witnessed the concentrated efforts of the Kemalist elite to consolidate its power by purging the Turkish political and socio-religious elite of possible opponents as well as the public and private forms of collective association – political parties, cultural institutions (such as the Turkish Hearths), and *tarikats* – upon which it might depend in order to mobilize a popular challenge to the Kemalist state. Contrary to assumptions implicit in historical accounts of the Atatürk era, however, these efforts were not wholly successful: Mustafa Kemal did regulate formal political participation effectively, but the local, ethnic and religious bonds that engendered less visible but extremely strong forms of collective association – and therefore identity – remained largely beyond the reach of Kemalist legislation. Any social history of the Atatürk era must necessarily consider the perpetuation of these shared identities, particularly those of a religious nature that became conspicuous when mere collective association translated into collective action as Anatolian inhabitants rallied around a shared 'Islamic' symbol – forms of headgear or the call to prayer, for instance – and responded to calls to action issued by local members of the ulema or dervish *şeyhs*.

Such a transformation occurred on a number of occasions between 1923 and 1938. Unfortunately, only those movements located in Kayseri, Maraş, Erzurum, Rize (1925), in Menemen (1930), in Bursa (1933), and in various locales in 1935 and 1936 are sufficiently documented to permit investigation into the circumstances in which a shared identity provided a foundation for collective action.[10] Historical accounts of the Atatürk era do not treat these incidents comparatively; rather, they typically refer to them only cursorily and in so doing they perpetuate a number of false images. Indeed, these accounts invariably defer to interpretations first promoted by Mustafa Kemal, who instinctively feared collective action invoking Islamic legitimation because he himself had previously met with considerable success at mobilizing popular support as the *gazi* fighting to defend the Ottoman Sultan-Caliph during the Turkish War of Independence.[11] Consequently, the incidents examined here emerge in Turkish historiography as skirmishes in a perpetual, uniquely Turkish conflict [*bitmeyen savaş*] over control of public life between conservative Islamists and secular Kemalists: allegedly organized by *Nakşibendi şeyhs*, these events are portrayed as 'rebellions' and labelled with the pejorative epithet *irtica* on the assumption that collective action resulted not from conscious decisions reached by thoughtful people but from the adroit manipulation of symbols – those common to a 'naïve' population still fettered by Ottoman-Islamic traditions – by devious Islamists, crazed fanatics (*yobazlar*) and even disaffected immigrants.[12]

This Kemalist paradigm not only supposes a degree of continuity between incidents of collective action and a shared objective amongst participants where neither existed, but it also has the important consequence of denying Turks a rational and credible role in their own history. As a remedy to such a misinterpretation, therefore, this study classifies these events according to prominent characteristics which permits their classification into three distinct groups: collective public protests in which participants did not resort to force; in only three instances, violent insurrections against the state; and, active participation in Muslim *tarikats* and brotherhoods. Analysis along these lines is sensitive not only to different forms of expression but also to the different issues at stake as well as the ethnic and social background of participants. It suggests that so long as the social history of the Turkish Revolution remains unexplored, scholars are free to interpret collective action from a Kemalist perspective rather than to investigate actual circumstances. Similarly, if these events continue to be dismissed as 'Islamic reaction' rather than be subjected to careful analysis, then the pervasive historical interpretation of the Turkish Revolution as a period of rapid legislated modernization stands unchallenged.

The few instances in which a crowd gathered peacefully under the leadership of a respected local *şeyh* or *hoca* were indisputably associated with Mustafa Kemal's efforts to secularize Anatolian culture. The close succession of three protests in the cities of Kayseri, Erzurum and Maraş between 22 and 26 November 1925 sets them apart chronologically from a fourth which transpired in Bursa on 1 February 1933. In substance, however, all four protests had much in common for they represented the efforts of Turks living in and around provincial centres to express their consternation over the public debate of two issues that arguably affected the Anatolian populace more than any other aspects of Kemalist reform. Occurrences of collective action in November 1925, although evidently not linked in the form of a conspiracy as the Kemalist elite feared, were each related to the final passage of legislation replacing the fez and other headgear worn by Turks – the ulema excluded – with the hat [şapka] following many months of intense political and social debate. Similarly, the Bursa protest was a result of popular discontent with Kemalist efforts to Turkify ritual worship by requiring local officials to proclaim the call to prayer [ezan] and deliver entire sermons [hutbe] in Turkish. The eight years separating these reforms reveal the lengthy nature of the programme intended to secularize and Turkify Anatolian culture: each was undertaken in very different political circumstances, the hat law at a time when the legitimacy of the Kemalist elite was still a matter of debate, the Turkification of rituals following the consolidation of Kemalist political power. Although public protests following these laws were remarkably similar, the Kemalist response was noticeably different.[13]

Demonstrations in Kayseri (22 November) and Maraş (26 November)[14] included the explicit denunciation of the hat, by crowds, at the instigation of respected Islamist leaders. In Kayseri, a crowd of at least 45 men[15] sporting turbans peacefully protested against having to wear the hat; the chief protagonist was an alleged Nakşibendi şeyh, Mekkeli Ahmet Hamdi, who incited the crowd with the rumours that the government also intended to force women to unveil as well as to outlaw possession of the Qur'an. In Maraş, the protest was provoked by the discovery on a mosque door of a treatise condemning the change in headgear; upon the conclusion of a time of prayer [namaz], a crowd bearing the green mosque flag marched through the streets of Maraş shouting 'We don't want hats.' In response, local officials ordered soldiers to surround the mosque and arrest some 39 protestors.[16]

Whereas Mekkeli Ahmet Hamdi and four collaborators from Kayseri were eventually sentenced to death by the Eastern Independence Tribunal [Şark İstiklâl Mahkemesi],[17] it is not clear how many protestors from Maraş were executed, for some were tried by a local military tribunal and others were dispatched to Ankara for trial by the Ankara Independence Tribunal [Ankara İstiklâl Mahkemesi]. The latter condemned five men to death and sentenced another fifteen to prison terms of between three and ten years; a British consular document implies that the military tribunal executed as many as twenty 'reactionaries.'[18] Those tried by the Ankara Independence Tribunal were apparently not just protestors, but included local notables whose very existence posed a challenge to the authority of the Governor [*Vali*] of Maraş.[19]

Events in Erzurum on 24 November[20] were similar to those in Kayseri and Maraş, but on a much larger scale. After morning prayers at a mosque, one *şeyh* Osman *Hoca* and a group of approximately 20 to 30 supporters proceeded to government buildings where they petitioned the Governor of Erzurum to allow them to continue to wear the local *ağniye* or *kabalak*, a traditional form of headgear better suited than the *şapka* to the cold winters of eastern Anatolia. Upon the Governor's dismissal of the request and order that the spokesmen be arrested, members of the crowd – which had reportedly grown to include some 3,000 men and women, many of the former wearing fezes and turbans – expressed their disapproval by encouraging those present to defy the hat law, and by shouting 'We do not want a heretical official' ['bir gâvur memur istemeyiz'].[21] For reasons that remain unclear, local gendarmes then opened fire upon the crowd, killing as many as 23 protestors before the rest dispersed.[22]

Surprised and disturbed by this popular protest, the government of İsmet İnönü declared martial law around Erzurum for one month. During this period, a local military tribunal tried more than 100 protestors; because officials of the Ankara Independence Tribunal decided not to interfere in the affairs of the military tribunal, details of the trials are not available, and there is no way to confirm the assertion that between twenty and thirty alleged reactionaries, including Şeyh Osman *Hoca*, were executed.[23] In the course of the investigation, Kemalist officials determined not only that members of the local elite loyal to the Ottoman Caliphate and belonging to the pre-Republican Society for the Protection of Religion [Muhafaza-i Mukaddesat Cemiyeti] had figured prominently in the protest, but that Şeyh Osman *Hoca* had contrived the Erzurum protest as one part of a larger movement evidenced by contemporaneous unrest in Rize and the questionable activities of Islamists in Giresun. It was on the basis of this conviction that the Ankara Independence Tribunal undertook an intensive investigation in subsequent months, eventually sentencing to death a prominent opponent of the hat, İskilipli Atıf Hoca.[24]

No doubt it was partly due to the harsh response of the government to these instances of collective action that only one other similar protest apparently occurred during the Atatürk era, and that eight years later. The Bursa protest occurred as a result of ambiguous directives from Mustafa Kemal concerning whether Turkish alone, or also Arabic, was permissible for the proclamation of the call to prayer and the delivery of an entire sermon, including passages from the Qur'an and Hadith.[25] Although no directive had been issued on a nation-wide level, officials in Bursa were under instructions to ensure the use of Turkish during Ramazan (December 1932–January 1933). They evidently failed to enforce this order strictly, and on 1 February, a *muezzin*, Topal Halil, proclaimed the call to prayer in Arabic from the Ulu mosque; later, prior to the actual prayers, one Tatar İbrahim also proclaimed the call to prayer [*kamet*] in Arabic according to custom. On this particular occasion a local police officer happened to be present and subsequently declared his intention to report the 'offenders' to his superiors. In response, one of those present addressed the congregation and expressed his dissatisfaction with the fact that Muslims remained subject to state regulation, while Christians and Jews were free to practise as they wished. Acting in unison, the congregation then decided to seek to have this injustice redressed and proceeded first to the offices of the Ministry of Religious Endowments [*Evkaf*], and then to *vilâyet* offices in the city centre.[26] Some protestors situated themselves inside the government buildings, but most remained outside and volubly demanded that Arabic be permitted in accordance with tradition, and that at least Bursa should be subject to the same regulations as other cities, such as Istanbul, where Arabic continued in use. The only response on the part of officials was to order the arrest of the most prominent protestors.

Mustafa Kemal, coincidentally, had passed through Bursa only a few days previously, and upon learning of the demonstration he and other members of the government immediately returned to the city to oversee the investigation and ensure that no further unrest would occur. Such prompt action only added fuel to the rumours that the punishments meted out to Bursa protestors would mirror those given previous 'reactionary' opponents of the state. On the contrary, this proved to be the first occasion when the Kemalist elite, feeling sufficiently confident of their grip on power, responded to a popular Islamic protest by genuinely investigating the circumstances. As a consequence, at least 30 protestors – a number of whom were immigrants[27] – were ordered to stand trial, but three local officials were also called to explain their failure to enforce the law and effectively represent the government. By contrast with the outcome of similar trials in the recent past, the most severe sentence awarded participants in the Bursa protest was two and a half years imprisonment with hard labour,[28] while the Mufti of Bursa, a judge, and a public prosecutor were all dismissed from office on the grounds of malfeasance. Although the government remained uncomfortable with the public expression of discontent by Muslim Turks, its response to the Bursa protest signalled the advent of a more moderate approach to collective action, even that invoking Islamic legitimation.

The manipulation of common Islamic symbols by malcontents committed to mobilizing a local populace for the purposes of mounting an armed insurrection against the Kemalist state was the phenomenon most intensely feared by the Kemalist elite, for they themselves had employed precisely this method to mobilize the same Anatolian population during the War of Independence. Events in the Atatürk era, however, demonstrate that Islamic legitimation alone provided insufficient justification for violent rebellion; success along these lines depended on the simultaneous appeal to non-religious ethnic or 'national' identities. The *Şeyh* Sait Kurdish rebellion of February–April, 1925, the only significant internal threat to the security of the Turkish state in the Atatürk era, is by far the best example of the possibilities inherent in a communal identity defined in religious as well as ethnic terms. Kurdish leaders publicly may have emphasized their opposition to secular reform, but their success at mobilizing a viable Kurdish force depended equally on a shared ethnic identity from which emerged a shared sense of grievance at Kemalist efforts at Turkification. At the same time, analysis of participation in the revolt reveals the vulnerable alliances upon which large-scale collective action depended, the defeat of the *Şeyh* Sait rebellion owing as much to the failure of the Kurdish-Islamic appeal to knit together the tribal, religious and class fissures characteristic of eastern Anatolian society, as to the superior strength of the Turkish military. This insurrection is not discussed in any greater detail here because it has already been the subject of considerable study.[29] The two occurrences of non-Kurdish violent insurrection during the Turkish Revolution, however, substantiate the above observations: on the one hand rebels failed to mobilize the population of Menemen in 1930 despite their many claims to Islamic legitimacy, while on the other hand rebellion in the province of Rize (1925) likely stemmed from shared religious and ethnic grievances but probably failed in part because of conflicting loyalties.

Scholars typically classify as just another protest against the hat a violent insurrection in the Potemya district of the city of Rize on approximately 25 November 1925.[30] It was in fact very different from the crowd protests that occurred in Kayseri, Erzurum and Maraş. In this instance, popular concerns about the implementation of Kemalist secularism evidently dovetailed with other deep-seated causes of resentment, enabling local leaders to mobilize the populace to take violent action on the basis of an appeal to religious identity. Ergün Aybars, the accepted authority on events dealt with by the Independence Tribunals, does not emphasize the violent side of this collective action: a crowd of as many as 1,000 'unsuspecting' peasants gathered in front of a Potemya mosque and were harangued by a local village headman [*muhtar*] and *imam* into launching an effort to capture Rize. Accompanied by armed bandits from nearby mountains, and believing that Mustafa Kemal and İsmet İnönü were either dead or injured and that Ankara was in the hands of Islamists loyal to the *şeriat*, the peasants proceeded to capture the local gendarme post, symbolic of a government that was rumoured to be intent upon unveiling women and outlawing possession of the Qur'an. It is at this point that Aybars' unsatisfactory account of the event stops abruptly, with the rampaging peasants 'coming to their senses', realizing the consequences of their actions, and releasing their hostages.

Other sources, on the contrary, suggest the far-reaching and violent nature of this insurrection which lasted for as many as ten days, possibly spreading into neighbouring Of district. So serious was the unrest that the government dispatched a warship to the Rize coast to bombard the affected villages, and one British consular document even reports that government troops suffered some 100 casualties in their efforts to quell the movement.[31] Although the government made every effort not to portray the event as unique, and the Ankara Independence Tribunal concluded that it was one part of the larger conspiracy organized by Şeyh Osman Hoca of Erzurum and other prominent opponents of the hat, this explanation is severely deficient. The primary reason to doubt that extensive violence in Rize was simply the outcome of a conspiracy that inspired only peaceful protest elsewhere, lies in the fact that the Rize region was home to a large population of non-Turks – most frequently referred to as Laz, although such a definition is deceptively simple – quite conscious of an identity and heritage distinct from that of Anatolian Turks. The population census of 1927 did not distinguish between Laz and Turks – 99.95 per cent of the province's population was registered as speaking Turkish as a mother tongue – but anthropological and historical studies of the region suggest that despite Ottoman efforts to subjugate prominent local leaders [*derebeys*] in the nineteenth century, their descendants continued to lead inhabitants in opposition to the state. This heritage of independence from and conflict with central authorities was only augmented by the impact of conflicting claims to Rize and Trabzon among Greeks, Armenians and Russians prior to the establishment of the Turkish Republic.[32]

The Kemalist government does not appear ever to have publicly acknowledged that the Rize insurrection was related to efforts by the local populace to secure autonomy or even independence. Nevertheless, British officials evidently understood the insurrection in these terms and even asserted that the government, in fact, had been acutely aware of the potential of a Laz insurrection during the *Şeyh* Sait rebellion earlier in 1925.[33] While on very different scales, these two movements were indeed similar in that both gave expression to grievances, rooted in common ethnic and religious identities, but fuelled by Kemalist efforts to impose both political and cultural control. Currently available information is too scant to permit the examination of the Rize insurrection in any further detail, but it seems justifiable to suggest that if a shared identity accounted for the reported scale of unrest, then other local commitments and loyalties likely spawned social fissures that forestalled an even greater degree of popular participation and hence the achievement of the ambiguous purposes harbored by respected local leaders. As it stands, the 'official' version, that subsequent to the revolt eight participants were condemned to death merely on account of encouraging opposition to the hat, clearly does not reflect the whole truth.

Equally ambiguous in terms of verifiable details, but of a very different nature from the Rize insurrection, is the infamous Menemen *Olayı* ['event']. It has been appropriately labelled for it most definitely did not constitute a violent rebellion and arguably not even a popular protest. Limited to just a few hours on the morning of 23 December 1930, the Menemen *Olayı* proved such a shock to an insecure Kemalist elite that a total of 36 alleged participants were later sentenced to death for 'opposing the state'. Ever since 1930, the event has been the subject of a highly emotional debate: Kemalists have perpetually cited it as evidence of the potential threat posed by radical Islamists,[34] while Islamists themselves have pointed to the unjust punishments as proof that the Menemen *Olayı* was in fact orchestrated by Kemalists intent on finding a pretext to eliminate potentially popular political opponents, namely respected members of the *Nakşibendi tarikat*.[35] Neither conspiracy theory, however, is based upon incontrovertible evidence.

The event derives its name not because it originated with the inhabitants of Menemen but because the chief protagonists – six men who hatched their plot in the nearby city of Manisa – unveiled their cause in Menemen.[36] *En route* there, the six had passed a number of weeks in the isolated village of Bozalan where they allegedly indulged in narcotics and practised various *Nakşibendi* rituals. Proceeding to Menemen, the six entered a mosque and, armed with a gun, insisted that locals arriving for early morning prayers recognize their leader, *Giritli* [Cretan] Mehmet, as the long-awaited *Mehdi*. Having forced these locals to join their revolt against the 'heathen' Kemalist state, the rebels then seized the mosque flag and herded their followers through the city streets, loudly proclaiming the *tekbir* and announcing that they were but the vanguard of an army 70,000 strong and committed to the restoration of the *şeriat*. Although passers-by were forced to join the procession, the rebels were unable to enlist the support of a highly respected local leader, Hoca Saffet Efendi; the crowd then proceeded to the city centre where it gathered under the mosque flag and the leaders continued their vitriolic rhetoric against the state.

In the midst of this spectacle – the rebels wore symbolic turbans and robes, and were accompanied by a dog prophetically named 'Kıtmir' – three separate officials confronted the rebels and demanded an explanation. The first two apparently departed confused but determined to seek assistance, while the third, a young reserve officer known as Kubilay and in charge of a small regiment, grabbed *Giritli* Mehmet and challenged him publicly. In response to this provocation, one of the rebels shot Kubilay who, while staggering away, witnessed his regiment scatter in confusion. It was at this point that the most sensational act occurred: not satisfied with the maiming of Kubilay, *Giritli* Mehmet pursued him and then, in front of the crowd, proceeded to decapitate him with a small saw. Having thrashed the head against a stone, he had it ceremoniously mounted on the top of the flag pole. Before long, the rebels were again confronted by state authorities, first by two local guards – both of whom were killed – but later by a military unit in armoured vehicles. When ordered to surrender, the rebels boldly declared that bullets could not harm them. They were wrong, for within minutes three rebels, including *Giritli* Mehmet, had been shot dead and one severely wounded. The two remaining protagonists managed to escape but were later captured in Manisa and brought to trial in Menemen, along with hundreds of alleged reactionaries.

Following so closely on the heels of the political and social turmoil that had characterized the short life span of the Free Party [Serbest Cumhuriyet Fırkası] in late 1930, the Menemen *Olayı* was a rude shock to Mustafa Kemal. Menemen had been one of the few locales to choose a Free Party candidate in municipal elections, and its inhabitants had suffered considerably from economic depression and heavy flooding in the previous year.[37] Concurrently, the city's population included a significant proportion of immigrants (28 per cent), many of whom had no doubt been subjected to Kemalist efforts to 'Turkify' all Anatolian inhabitants. Given this context, it is perhaps understandable why Mustafa Kemal became convinced that the Menemen *Olayı* was a spectre of that which he feared most of all: the manipulation of shared Islamic symbols, by popular local leaders, to mobilize a populace already harbouring grievances and therefore willing to oppose actively the 'legitimate' government.

Nevertheless, despite the credibility of Mustafa Kemal's fears and the all-too-common image of the Menemen *Olayı* as a popular revolt, the available evidence contradicts these, rendering its inclusion within the category of popular protests – such as those of 1925 and 1933 – all but unjustifiable. The protagonists (who were not local leaders) did not actually succeed in mobilizing the local populace to do anything other than gather as a crowd, and that under the threat of retribution for their lack of co-operation. Accounts concerning the response of the crowd to Kubilay's execution illustrate the difficulty of actually ascertaining the crowd's mood: according to one authority, the crowd actually dissolved and spectators fled in horror, while another suggests that they applauded and actively encouraged *Giritli* Mehmet.[38] A report carried in *Cumhuriyet* neatly portrayed half the crowd watching with indifference, while the other half expressed its approval.[39] Excitement is one thing, vocal condemnation of the state and its policies another; the actions of the crowd were apparently limited to the former. At the same time it is worth noting that many likely watched in sanguine fascination, for it was an unusually fascinating spectacle and the rebels' diatribes against the government undoubtedly struck a chord in the minds of the spectators. Significantly, however, neither this potentially powerful motivating force, nor the Islamic rhetoric employed by the rebels proved sufficient to mobilize the populace of Menemen to actively take up arms against the state. The outcome of the Menemen *Olayı* alone would also seem to cast doubt on the veracity of the extensive '*Nakşibendi* plot' allegedly uncovered by state prosecutors in the course of the subsequent trials. Not only does it seem unlikely that Menemen would have been chosen as the place to unveil a plot, given its proximity to the military centre of Izmir, but an extensive *Nakşibendi* network of *şeyh-murid* relationships would surely have provided the basis for a more popular, if no more successful, challenge to the government.

There is tragic irony in the fact that the Kemalist elite took the Menemen *Olayı* far more seriously than did the inhabitants of Menemen themselves. The rigorous prosecution of alleged participants resulted in the execution of 28 people from Menemen, Manisa and nearby villages, each 'guilty' of abetting the rebels in some way. The Menemen *Olayı* remains an enigma in modern Turkish history, but it is very clear that it was not a mass movement and that the punishment of local Turks was more an attempt by the government to deter future genuine unrest than a legitimate punishment of the guilty.[40] That a public collective protest occurred only three years later in Bursa suggests that when Turks did feel the need to express opposition to state policies, public action was not necessarily deterred by Kemalist efforts to effect co-operation via intimidation.

Active participation by Muslim Turks in *tarikat*[41] and brotherhood[42] networks driven underground by Mustafa Kemal's efforts to outlaw them in 1925 represents a very different form of collective action from those previously discussed. Nevertheless, to the Kemalist elite, Muslim social networks were potentially threatening forms of collective association and Kemalists were unable to conceive that in fact these movements might function as politically benign but socially beneficial organizations for a

Muslim population floating unanchored in a sea of secular legislation. Precisely because Muslim networks were forced underground it is very difficult to assess their influence during the Atatürk era, but the very occurrence of the incidents examined here refutes the assumption common to most historical accounts of modern Turkey that *tarikat* networks simply disappeared with the passage of the 1925 law outlawing them.

Information concerning the networks uncovered by Kemalist officials in 1935 and 1936 is frustratingly scant, although it is apparent that, contrary to Kemalist suspicions, participants were hardly engaging in treasonous activities. The brotherhood exposed in May 1935 proved to comprise an extensive network of Turks from all over western Anatolia who looked to the Kurdish mystic, Said Nursi, for spiritual guidance at a time when their practices and beliefs – and thus their identities – were under attack by an unsympathetic political elite.[43] Şerif Mardin's analysis of Nursi and his followers suggests that this particular form of collective action was actually of benefit to the Turkish state, for rather than secretly undermine its stability Nursi evidently encouraged *both* Muslim faith and loyalty to the established political order. The Kemalist elite evidently failed to grasp this nuance and, loath to encourage secret religious association, the courts eventually sentenced Nursi and 15 of his followers to short prison terms.[44] The second movement – frequently referred to as the İskilip 'uprising' – was very similar to that associated with Said Nursi. Although it was directly linked to the *Nakşibendi tarikat*, it does not deserve the importance ascribed it by Tarık Tunaya.[45] According to newspaper reports, it was limited to an effort to 'revive' the *Nakşibendi* order in a number of centres, including Ankara of all places.[46] Those arrested included a watchmaker, a *bakkal*, a judge and an *imam*, all of whom allegedly corresponded by letter but engaged in little more than this.

This *Nakşibendi* movement is not to be confused with newspaper reports concerning the other alleged *tarikat* members arrested at the same time (January 1936),[47] but subsequently released when it was determined that they had not been actively pursuing illicit association. Indeed these cases are only the most prominent of many similar instances in which Kemalist officials detained Muslim Turks on the suspicion that they were active participants in *tarikat* networks.[48] It is impossible to know just how many of those accused were 'guilty' of such activities, but given the evidence for this sort of collective action in 1935 and 1936 there seems sufficient justification to conclude that these two movements were in fact symptomatic of much more widespread brotherhood and *tarikat* activities throughout the Atatürk era. Consideration of the substance of the legislation outlawing *tarikats* (1925) also lends credibility to this conclusion:[49] *tarikat* association was indeed forbidden, but *şeyhs* were permitted to maintain their residence in buildings once used as *tekkes*, and they might even continue to receive revenue from properties originally set aside for the support of their particular *tarikat*. The 1925 law, therefore, was not designed either instantly to create a destitute class of unemployed *şeyhs* or to purge them from Anatolian society. Many likely found employment as state religious functionaries.[50] It seems that Kemalists, confident of the superiority of rational nationalism, evidently believed that given a chance Turks would desert these 'reactionary' institutions and allow them to die a quiet death. These cases of collective action reveal this to have been a false assumption; they also suggest that Kemalist legislation fell far short of effecting the desired transformation of Anatolian culture along national Turkish and secular lines.

Important though it is to recognize the particular characteristics of these different incidents of collective action during the Atatürk era as well as to reject the deceptive Kemalist interpretation of them as links in a chain of Islamist efforts to overthrow the state, it is also necessary to acknowledge that they were not absolutely discrete. Indeed, with the exception of the *Şeyh* Sait rebellion, they each occurred in the common context of Anatolian provincial centres, and even more significantly, the participants in each legitimated their actions by appealing to shared Islamic symbols at a time when Kemalist secularism [*lâiklik*] was at its zenith. Anatolian society during the inter-war period, however, was anything but homogenous and there existed not a single identifiable Muslim identity but a diverse array of Muslim identities defined by ethnic, regional, and sectarian loyalties;[51] in this regard, Ottoman ulema and dervish *şeyhs* had been crucial to providing a degree of cohesion to pre-Republican Anatolia.

Consequently, Kemalist secularism was necessarily double-faceted. On the one hand it was intended to sever Anatolian society from its Islamic moorings, thereby negating the influence and even relevance of a Muslim elite that posed a challenge to secular Kemalists. On the other hand, in conjunction with the principles of nationalism and populism, secularism was supposed to effect the unification of the diverse Anatolian populace as a modern, *Turkish* nation. Initially, Kemalist secularism was particularly destructive, as evidenced by the passage of laws aimed at the dissolution of the Caliphate (1924), the closure of *medreses* and *şeriat* courts (1924), and the outlawing of dervish *tarikats* (1925). Combined with various measures intended to render Muslim leaders no more than state civil servants, these laws had a noticeably detrimental impact upon the public influence wielded by former local Ottoman ulema and *şeyhs*.[52] This process initiated, Mustafa Kemal then launched an ambitious programme to inculcate a new Turkish identity by transforming those symbols and habitual practices that had been crucial to previous Anatolian-Muslim identities.[53] Aware that Anatolian-Islamic traditions could not be eradicated completely, the Kemalist elite resorted to manipulating them, and 'Kemalist Islam' became an important tool in the effort to craft a cohesive, civilized nation.[54] It was aspects of this process of 'secularization' that provided the kernels around which collective action publicly opposing the state coalesced.

Collective action in public opposition to the Turkish state occurred within this context of secularization, but it was also necessarily predicated upon pre-existing and sufficiently strong ties of communal association from which a shared identity and also a shared sense of grievance might emerge when participants mobilized around a respected leader and/or valued symbol. The incidents examined here suggest those social networks in which common identities were rooted. Tribal and ethnic loyalties[55] were clearly important to violent insurrection in Rize and the much larger Şeyh Sait rebellion; heightened ethnic identity in the face of Turkification perhaps also contributed to the actions of those rebels in the Menemen *Olayı*[56] and those protestors in Bursa who had recently emigrated to Anatolia from lands once claimed by the Ottoman Empire. *Tarikat* affiliation was another dimension crucial to the mobilization of Kurds in the Şeyh Sait rebellion, and it is also a very real possibility that *tarikat* and brotherhood networks provided a foundation for the Rize revolt and the public protests of 1925 and 1933. Nevertheless, as Hamid Algar has argued, there currently exists little evidence to substantiate allegations – such as those made by Tarık Tunaya – that each event was carefully orchestrated by Nakşibendi şeyhs.[57] There can be little doubt, however, that life in provincial urban centres provided an important foundation on which peaceful collective action was constructed, for social cohesion can be attributed to a shared identity among Muslim residents of the same quarter and to social networks derived from the legacy of Ottoman guilds. It was also in provincial cities that Kemalist reforms were applied most assiduously, with conservative town-dwellers acutely conscious of the gulf that separated them from the zealous nascent Kemalist elite eager to implement new legislation.

The preceding analysis of violent insurrection alluded to both the necessary elements – religious as well as ethnic – necessary to this form of collective action, but also to the reality of the complex loyalties that limited the success of such popular mobilization. It is understandable that violent rebellions were rare. The limited occurrence of peaceful public protest, however, requires further explanation, for collective action in 1925 and 1933 was clearly linked to secularization. Given that historical accounts of the period – founded upon Kemalist visions of the Turkish Revolution – emphasize both the conservative nature of the Anatolian populace and the unity of the Turkish experience, as well as perpetuate the illusion of tremendous legislated change, it must be asked why so few protests actually materialized. The answer lies in two observations concerning the social history of this period, both of which revise commonly held assumptions.

The first observation pertains to the significance of the various pieces of secular legislation around which histories of the period are structured despite scholars' limited understanding of their actual impact. The result of this approach is an extremely deceptive account of the Atatürk era. It is crucial to recognize that the litany of legislation passed in Ankara did not necessarily define the lives of the Anatolian populace and that each law deserves individual consideration. Various laws, such as those instituting either the use of the Gregorian calendar (1926), or the observation of Sunday as a day of rest (1935), may have been secular in implication but were of little practical importance to most Turks. The actual text of others, such as that outlawing *tarikats* (1925), reveals that 'abolition' of previous institutions and/or practices was sometimes qualified by clauses designed to soften the immediate impact. At times, legislation was sometimes no more than a confirmation of existing practices – as was likely the case with the outlawing of polygamy in the Civil Code of 1926 – and in those cases where it did establish new standards the desired result was hardly effected immediately. Instead, compliance tended to be gradual and even with high-profile issues such as the hat and the call to prayer, it is evident that in remote regions these laws were either ignored or submission was to the letter rather than the spirit of the law.[58] Perhaps most important of all, it appears that the impact of legislation was also minimized by far greater variation in the standards of implementation than Kemalists would have cared to admit. Insufficient institutional bases throughout the vast region of Anatolia rendered communication and enforcement particularly difficult: and even the Kemalist governor of Konya, a province undoubtedly within the purview of Ankara, admitted to a British official that it was preferable to permit the application of local legal customs by town councils and village elders rather than insist upon strict adherence to new regulations included in the Civil Code of 1926.[59] Clearly, the proclamation of each new piece of secular legislation, although significant from a political perspective, did not necessarily mark a profound challenge to the practices and beliefs crucial to Anatolian-Muslim identities.

The perpetuation of these identities can largely be attributed to the continuing significance of Muslim *tarikats* and brotherhoods throughout the Atatürk era, and herein lies the second observation. Social networks of this sort had already endured a century of Ottoman centralization and even secularization; rather than fade away when denied formal institutional legitimacy by Mustafa Kemal they appear to have adapted to the circumstances of the Turkish Revolution and made an important social and cultural contribution. Perhaps less intent upon fostering mystical beliefs and rituals, *tarikats* and brotherhoods were instead committed to the preservation of the 'truth' so long as it was besieged by the state. In effect they assumed full responsibility – one once shared with Ottoman-sponsored Islamic institutions – for addressing the spiritual needs of a Muslim society experiencing considerable change. Rather than spawn automatic rejection of change, they provided Turks with sufficient stability and security to assess the circumstances, and to accommodate, adapt, or reject those secular policies that they did encounter. In doing so they also preserved the roots of Anatolian-Muslim identities which persisted, indeed even remained dominant, alongside the nascent Turkish identity actively promoted by Mustafa Kemal. The outcome of these parallel cultural developments was arguably a hybrid identity, a Turkish-Muslim synthesis which has been a significant theme in Turkish history to the present day.

The tendency among scholars simply to assume that the conjunction of an Anatolian Islamic heritage and secular legislation directed towards modernization quite naturally resulted in conservative 'reactions' against the Kemalist state reveals the limited nature of research into the experiences of the Turkish populace during the Atatürk era. Despite the conservative attitudes of the Anatolian populace, the severe material deprivation experienced following more than a decade of war, and the ostensibly radical nature of Kemalist reforms, collective action was by no means inevitable, the incidents examined here being the only ones for which sufficient evidence exists as to their popular nature. Collective action claiming Islamic legitimation was not the predictable outcome of Kemalist efforts to close the cultural gap separating an 'enlightened' elite from a 'backward' populace. In fact, just as Kemalists reacted to collective action according to specific criteria that reflected their own need for security, so too Anatolian Turks possessed a repertoire of responses to varying circumstances. More often than not they abstained from publicly opposing the state, and it is these conscious decisions as to the most appropriate manner to articulate their personal experiences that illuminate the social history of the Turkish Revolution.

NOTES

I am indebted to Professors William Cleveland (Simon Fraser University), Reşat Kasaba (University of Washington) and Hasan Kayalı (University of California at Sandiego) for their encouragement and advice in preparing this manuscript for publication.

1. For example Suna Kili, *Türk Devrim Tarihi* (Istanbul: Tekin Yayınevi, 1982); and Mahmut Gologlu, *Devrimler ve Tepkileri (1924–1930)* (Ankara: Başnur Matbaası, 1972) and *Tek Partili Cumhuriyet (1931–1938)* (Ankara: Kalite Matbaası, 1974).

2. The two best examples being Roderic Davison, *Turkey: A Short History* (Walkington: The Eothen Press, 1981); and Bernard Lewis, *The Emergence of Modern Turkey*, Second Edition (Oxford: Oxford University Press, 1968). Two recent works conceptualize Ottoman/Turkish history in new ways but present little new information on the Atatürk era: Feroz Ahmad, *The Making of Modern Turkey* (New York: Routledge, 1993); and Eric Zürcher, *Turkey: A Modern History* (London: I.B. Tauris & Co., 1993).

3. See Eric Zürcher, *The Unionist Factor: The Role of the Committee of Union and Progress in the Turkish National Movement, 1905–1906* (Leiden: E.J. Brill, 1984) and *Political Opposition in the Early Turkish Republic: The Progressive Republican Party 1924–1925* (Leiden: E.J. Brill, 1991); and Mete Tunçay, *Türkiye Cumhuriyeti'nde Tek Parti Yönetiminin Kurulması (1923–1931)* (Ankara: Yurt Yayınları, 1981).

4. These include one study undertaken during the Atatürk era: J. Morrison, *Alışar: A Unit of Land Occupance in the Kanak Su Basin of Central Anatolia* (Chicago: University of Chicago Libraries, 1939); a comprehensive overview of Turkish society in this period by Richard Robinson, *The First Turkish Republic: A Case Study in National Development* (Cambridge: Harvard University Press, 1963); and numerous specific studies conducted since the Second World War, many of which are discussed in Haim Gerber, *The Social Origins of the Modern Middle East* (London: Mansell, Ltd., 1987).

5. See my unpublished MA thesis, 'Islamic "Reaction" to the Turkish Revolution: A Framework for the Social History of the Atatürk Era (1923–1938)', Simon Fraser University, 1995).

6. Newspapers are used sparingly by various historians of modern Turkey and await a thorough analysis. Those consulted for this study were *Cumhuriyet* (Istanbul), *Son Posta* (Istanbul), *Akşam* (Istanbul), *Ulus* (Ankara), and *Anadolu* (İzmir). Clearly local newspapers – where they are still available – have the potential to be very useful to social historians.

7. The population censuses, despite questions concerning their reliability, are also a largely unexploited source; careful analysis of their data will reveal a great deal about the Atatürk era. *Umumi Nüfus Tarihi, 1927* (Ankara: İstatistik Umum Müdürlüğü, 1929), and *Genel Nüfus Sayımı, 1935* (Ankara: Başbakanlık İstatistik Genel Directörlüğü, 1937).

8. British consulates existed in Istanbul, İzmir, Edirne, Trabzon, and Mersin during this period. British officials admittedly relied heavily on Turkish newspapers for much of their information, but they also had access to government officials and other informants.

9. My methodology derives from essays in the following works: Edmund Burke III, and Ira Lapidus (eds.), *Islam, Politics, and Social Movements* (Los Angeles: University of California Press, 1988); Natalie Zemon Davis, *Society and Culture in Early Modern France* (Stanford: Stanford University Press, 1965); Lynn Hunt (ed.), *The New Cultural History* (Los Angeles: The University of California Press, 1989); and, Hisham Sharabi (ed.), *Theory and Politics and the Arab World: Critical Responses* (New York: Routledge, 1990).

10. The incidents about which we know very little appear to have involved very few people or to have constituted abortive efforts by individuals to incite public action. The exception to this was unspecified unrest in Gaziantep-Urfa (south-eastern Anatolia) following the abolition of the Caliphate in March, 1924. The other incidents included the activities of *hocas* following the abolition of the Caliphate, and efforts to oppose the hat law in late 1925 made by individuals in Malatya, Bursa, Milas, Zonguldak, Bandırma, Uşak, Sivas, Çerkeş, Tokat and Giresun. A movement about which frustratingly little is known allegedly was uncovered in December 1928: some 100 members of the 'Revolutionary Committee for the Protection of the Moslem Religion' were arrested in Bursa, state officials denying British reports that cells existed in Konya and Sivas. It is not clear how many, if any, were actually executed as a result. Özek puts the number at 9, but a PRO report states that the four sentenced to death later had their sentences commuted to prison terms. See FO 371/13824/E906 Turkey Annual Report, 1928; FO 371/14578/E729 Turkey Annual Report, 1929; Çetin Özek, *Türkiye'de Gerici Akımlar* (Istanbul: Gerçek Yayınevi, 1968), p.158.

11. This is well summarized in Paul Dumont, 'Hojas for the Revolution: The Religious Strategy of Mustafa Kemal Atatürk', *American Institute for the Study of Middle Eastern Civilization Journal*, Vol.1, Nos.3–4 (Autumn–Winter, 1980–1981), p.17–32.

12. See Tarık Tunaya, *Islamcılık Akımı* (Istanbul: Simavi Yayınları, 1991); Binnaz Toprak, *Islam*

and Political Development in Turkey (Leiden: E.J. Brill, 1981) and 'The Religious Right', in Irvin Schick and E.A. Tonak (eds.), *Turkey in Transition: New Perspectives* (Oxford: Oxford University Press, 1987), p.218–35.; and Çetin Özek, *Türkiye'de Lâiklik Gelişim ve Koruyucu Ceza Hükümleri* (Istanbul: Baha Matbaası, 1962), and *Türkiye'de Gerici Akımlar*. Tunaya's Kemalist interpretation in *Islamcılık Akımı* has been extremely influential: both Toprak and Özek depend on his sketchy details for their own analyses. Tunaya rarely reveals his sources (probably newspapers) and does not justify his assertions on the frequent role of *Nakşibendi şeyhs*. See *Islamcılık Akımı*, pp.167–76. Özek's representation of events is arguably more balanced and yet he too oversimplifies them in his effort to emphasize their common characteristics. He also uses highly connotative but unjustified terminology. See *Türkiye'de Lâiklik Gelişim ve Koruyucu Ceza Hükümleri*, pp.95–8. Citing Tunaya, Toprak also overemphasizes the role of the *Nakşibendi*, while superimposing her interpretation of the *Şeyh Sait* revolt onto all of these events regardless of their unique circumstances. See *Islam and Political Development*, pp.66–70. It should be noted that Mete Tunçay does make an effort to reconsider the various dimensions of the protests of 1925 and the Menemen *Olayı* of 1930. See *Türkiye Cumhuriyeti'nde Tek Parti Yönetiminin Kurulması*, pp.149–61; and 293–5.

13. The fez was worn primarily by Turks in towns and cities; the *şapka* was officially introduced by Mustafa Kemal in August, 1925, and then made mandatory for *memurs* and members of the armed forces. Mustafa Kemal himself spearheaded public debate on the issue. Information regarding the process by which the hat law was introduced is found in Gotthard Jaschke, *Yeni Türkiye'de Islâmlık*, trans., Hayrullah Örs (Ankara: Bilgi Yayınevi, 1972), pp.28–9; Hasan Hüseyin Ceylan, *Din-Devlet İlişkileri*, 2 vols. (Istanbul: Risale Yayınları, 1991), 2:37–57; FO 371/10870/p.213 Foreign Office Minutes, 12 December, 1925; FO 371/10863/pp.146–55 Lindsay (Constantinople) to FO, 31 March, 1925. Concerning the experiences of Turks see the cases in Ahmed Nedim, Hzn., *Ankara İstiklâl Mahkemesi Zabıtları 1926* (Istanbul: İşaret Yayınları, 1993). The debate concerning the language of the *ezan* and *hutbe* became prominent in early 1932 when Mustafa Kemal had Turkish used for *Kadir Gecesi*; Bursa was evidently one locale in which the debate was particularly strong. For details see Ceylan, *Din-Devlet İlişkileri*, 2, pp.63–4; Jaschke, *Yeni Türkiye'de Islamlık*, pp.39-52. And, FO 371/16092/E702 Clerk (Angora) to FO, 5 February, 1932; FO 371/16092/E969 Bramwell (Constantinople) to Clerk, 6 February, 1932; and, FO 371/16984/E534 Clerk (Angora) to FO, 21 January, 1933; and, Charles Sherrill, *A Year's Embassy to Mustafa Kemal* (New York: Scribner's Sons, 1934), pp.199-201.

14. Different accounts give different dates for events in 1925 and I have generally followed those given by Ergün Aybars whose investigation into the *İstiklâl Mahkemeleri 1925-1927* (Ankara: Kültür ve Turizm Bakanlığı, 1982) has long been accepted as the most authoritative account of these protests. Aybars, however, presents only limited details and from a Kemalist perspective – his conclusions, therefore, must not be accepted uncritically.

15. Ceylan puts the number at 300 – see Hasan Hüseyin Ceylan, *Cumhuriyet Dönemi Din-Devlet İlişkileri*, 2, p.32. On the Kayseri protest see also Ergün Aybars, *İstiklâl Mahkemeleri 1925-1927*, pp.304–5; and, Ahmed Nedim, Hzn. *Ankara İstiklâl Mahkemesi 1926*, p.348.

16. Accounts of the Maraş protest are ambiguous: Tunaya (*İslamcılık Akımı*: 167) and a British consular document (FO 371/10863/E7512 Lindsay (Constantinople) to Chamberlain, 1 December, 1925) emphasize the march through the streets, while dramatic accounts mentioning the surrounding and 'storming' of the mosque are found in newspaper excerpts in Ceylan, *Din-Devlet İlişkileri*, 2, pp.33–4; and Mete Tunçay, *Türkiye'de Cumhuriyeti'nde Tek Parti Yönetiminin Kurulması (1923–1931)*, p.153. Aybars (*İstiklâl Mahkemeleri*, pp.312–17) asserts that the leaders of the protest planned to free prisoners from the local jail.

17. Kayseri protesters were tried by this tribunal because of alleged connections between Mekkeli Ahmet Hamdi and the *Nakşibendi şeyhs* involved in the *Şeyh Sait* revolt.

18. See FO 371/11528/E1899 Chamberlain to FO, 17 March, 1926. See also figures in Ceylan, *Din-Devlet İlişkileri*, 2, pp.33–34. Those tried by the *Ankara İstiklâl Mahkemesi* claimed that they were not opposing the state but returning hats which were of poor quality. See Aybars, *İstiklâl Mahkemeleri*, p.317.

19. See *Ankara İstiklâl Mahkemesi Zabıtları*, pp.350–51.

20. Tunaya gives the *wrong* date (January 1925) for this event: *İslamcılık Akımı*, p.167.

64   TURKEY BEFORE AND AFTER ATATÜRK

21. The best account of this protest is in *Ankara İstiklâl Mahkemesi Zabıtları*, p.349. See also Aybars, *İstiklâl Mahkemeleri*, p.305–310; Tunçay, *Türkiye Cumhuriyeti'nde*, p.114; Ceylan, *Din-Devlet İlişkileri*, 2, pp.30–31.
22. Estimates vary between 3 and 23 killed. At least one gendarme was injured.
23. Various figures are mentioned in *Ankara İstiklâl Mahkemesi Zabıtları*, p.349; Ceylan, *Din-Devlet İlişkileri*, 2, p.30–31; FO 371/10863/E7512 Lindsay (Constantinople) to Chamberlain, 1 December, 1925; and, FO 371/11528/E59 Knight (Trebizond) to Lindsay, 20 December, 1925.
24. Aybars, *İstiklâl Mahkemeleri*, pp.309–10. For details of these investigations, and transcripts of the trials of those alleged conspirators from Erzurum see *Ankara İstiklâl Mahkemesi Zabıtları*. It must be recognized that these inquisitorial trials did not allow for the complete facts to surface, and instead were intended to corroborate conclusions already reached by the Kemalist elite. The transcripts from the trial fall far short of presenting incontrovertible evidence that such a conspiracy existed. For a counter argument see Necip Fazıl Kısakürek, *Son Devrin Din Mazlumları* (Istanbul: Toker Yayınları, 1970), pp.37–77.
25. Mustafa Kemal first introduced Turkish to ritual worship one year previously for Ramazan (January) 1932; although Turkish became common as a result, no nation-wide legislation was adopted and Mustafa Kemal himself appears to have been convinced in late 1932 to allow Arabic to be used again.
26. The crowd reportedly numbered between 30 and 80 protestors, but grew larger once it reached the city centre. Detailed accounts are found editions of *Cumhuriyet* for February and March, 1933; and in FO 371/17959/E596 Turkey Annual Report, 1933; FO 371/16984/R771 Newspaper Excerpts, 6–8 February, 1933; FO 371/16984/E1056 Clerk (Angora) to FO, 17 February, 1933; and, FO 371/16984/E1274 Clerk (Angora) to FO, 23 February, 1933.
27. At least six immigrants from the Crimea, Georgia, and Albania were arrested. By 1935, 28% of the population of Bursa had been born outside of Turkey.
28. If in fact this had been the *Nakşibendi* plot alleged by Tunaya, surely the sentences would have been far more severe; see *İslamcılık Akımı*, p.174. Details of the sentences are contained in FO 371/16984/E2604 Clerk (Angora) to FO, 10 May, 1933.
29. It should be noted that this rebellion opened a wound that continued to fester throughout the Atatürk era, there being many smaller instances of rebellion and suppression by the state. Sources include: Robert Olson, *The Emergence of Kurdish Nationalism and the Sheikh Sait Rebellion 1880–1925* (Austin: University of Texas Press, 1989); Martin Van Bruinessen, *Agha, Shaikh and State: The Social and Political Structures of Kurdistan* (London: Zed Books, 1992); and Faik Bulut, *Devletin Gözüyle Türkiye'de Kürt İsyanları* (Istanbul: Yön Yayıncılık, 1991).
30. It is unclear just when the event began and ended: however it did coincide with the other hat protests. 25 November is the date cited by Aybars in *İstiklâl Mahkemeleri*, pp.310–311.
31. For these details see FO 371/10863/E7512 Lindsay (Constantinople) to Chamberlain, 1 December, 1925; FO 371/10863/E7918 Lindsay (Constantinople) to Chamberlain, 15 December, 1925; Tunaya, *İslamcılık Akımı*, p.167; Ceylan, *Din-Devlet İlişkileri*, 2, pp.34–5; and, Tunçay, *Türkiye Cumhuriyeti'nde*, p.154.
32. On the Laz population see: Anthony Bryer, 'The Last Laz Risings and the Downfall of the Pontic Derebeys, 1812–1840', *Bedi Kartlisa*, 26 (1969), pp.191–210; and Peter A. Andrews (ed.), *Ethnic Groups in the Republic of Turkey* (Weisbaden: Dr. Ludwig Reichert Verlag, 1989), pp.176–8; 429–33; 497–502.
33. FO371/10867/p.133 Lindsay to FO, 3 March, 1925; FO 371/10863/p.182 Lindsay to FO, 23 September, 1925; FO 371/11556/E4798 Turkey Annual Report, 1925.
34. An impressive monument, dedicated to Kubilay and the two guards killed in the event, stands on a military base outside Menemen, and every year on 23 December a commemorative ceremony is held in Menemen and a documentary broadcast on television. Kemalist literature dealing with the event includes Mustafa Baydar, *Kubilay* (Istanbul: Üstünel Yayınevi, 1954); Neyzar Karahan, *Şehit Edilişinin 50 Yılında Kubilay* (Ankara: Spor Toto'nun Kültür Hizmeti, 1981); Celal Kırhan, *Öğretmen Kubilay ve Uydurma Mehdi* (Istanbul: Sıralar Matbaası, 1963).
35. Mustafa Kemal certainly took advantage of the event for this purpose, as alleged

reactionaries were subsequently arrested throughout the country. The prominent *Nakşibendi*, *Erbili Şeyh* Esat, was accused of master-minding the event but died in prison; his supporters allege that he was in fact murdered. The best example of the Islamist interpretation is Kısakürek, *Son Devrin Din Mazlumları*, pp.167–208; see also the thought-provoking account in *Yakın Tarih Ansiklopedisi*, Vol.10 (Istanbul: Yeni Asya Gazetesi, 1990). There is, however, insufficient evidence to justify the Islamist claim that the Menemen *Olayı* was concocted by Kemalists.

36. The most detailed published account of the Menemen *Olayı* is Kemal Üstün's *Menemen Olayı ve Kubilay* (Istanbul: Çağdaş Yayınları, 1977) that includes the text of a journalist's investigation into the related court documents. Üstün's account is evidently Kemalist in perspective and must therefore be treated with some circumspection – his emphasis on the innocence of Menemen inhabitants, while convincing, is perhaps overdone. As no credible contradictory accounts exist, however, his remains largely unchallenged.

37. See editions of *Cumhuriyet* for October 1930; and Walter Weiker, *Political Tutelage and Democracy in Turkey: The Free Party and Its Aftermath* (Leiden: E.J. Brill, 1973), pp.91 and 115.

38. See Üstün, *Menemen Olayı*, p.69; and, Kısakürek, *Son Devrin Din Mazlumları*, p.189.

39. *Cumhuriyet*, 8 Kânunusani (January), 1931.

40. Those executed included men and women who had provided assistance (food and lodging) to the rebels in the weeks prior to the event, and also a Jew – convicted of assisting the rebels – who went to the gallows proclaiming 'Long live the Republic!' Not all those sentenced to death were executed: a few had their sentences commuted to prison terms by virtue of age. The sentences are dealt with in Üstün, *Menemen Olayı*.

41. Tarık Tunaya (*İslamcılık Akımı*, p.175) describes the activities of one *Şeyh* Halit of the *Nakşibendi* order as constituting a violent reactionary movement in December 1935. According to Tunaya, *Şeyh* Halit proclaimed himself the *mehdi* and sent his disciples to find followers in Beşiri *kaza* (Siirt): local villagers did not respond positively and violence ensued, thus necessitating the involvement of gendarmes. Although *Şeyh* Halit was captured, his son took to the mountains and continued the movement, later escaping to Syria. This movement is not improbable, but in the course of a careful examination of newspapers – *Cumhuriyet, Son Posta, Ulus, Akşam, and Anadolu* – published between November 1935 and February 1936, I have been unable to find any report of this event. British consular documents do not mention it either. It seems likely that, because Siirt was an isolated *vilâyet*, news of such events did not travel quickly; also, Siirt was overwhelmingly Kurdish and the press may have discounted such a movement as typical of the unrest associated with the Kurdish-populated region.

42. I intentionally distinguish between these forms of social organization not because their functions were necessarily all that different but because of debate concerning the definition of Said Nursi's movement. Nursi denied founding a *tarikat* and the state subsequently passed a law (1937) outlawing sectarian association so as to deprive Nursi of a defence.

43. Those arrested came from Milas, İsparta, Bursa, Yalova, Dınar, Aydın and Eğridir. For details see FO 371/19040/E3369 Loraine to FO, 24 May 1935; and editions of *Cumhuriyet, Akşam* and *Son Posta* for May 1935.

44. Şerif Mardin, *Religion and Social Change in Modern Turkey: The Case of Bediüzzaman Said Nursi* (New York: State University of New York, 1989), pp.17, 96–7, 156–8, and 191–3.

45. Tunaya suggests that it was second in importance to the Menemen *Olayı*, but the available evidence in no way justifies this or the use of the term 'uprising' to describe it. *İslamcılık Akımı*, p.175.

46. The chief protagonist was based in İskilip and had contact with others in Kırıkkale, Keskin and Tokat. Scant details are to be found in editions of *Cumhuriyet, Akşam* and *Son Posta* published in late January 1936.

47. These included members of the *Nakşibendi* and *Rufai tarikats* and they were eventually released after it was determined that they had not in fact been actively pursuing *tarikat* activities.

48. These include, but are not limited to: *Bektaşis* in Istanbul (1930); *Bektaşis* in Manisa (1932); dervishes in Amasya and Sivas (1933); women in Kırşehir (1935); and *Nakşibendis* in

Mersin (1936). See also Hasan Hüseyin Ceylan, *Cumhuriyet Dönemi Din-Devlet İlişkileri* (Ankara: Rehber Yayıncılık, 1992), Volume 3 for some details of underground *tarikat* activities.

49. An English translation of the law is contained in FO 371/10870/p.208 Translation of Telegram, 3 September 1925. See also Jaschke, *Yeni Türkiye'de İslamlık*, pp.33–7.

50. See for example, Mustafa Kara, *Bursa'da Tarikatlar ve Tekkeler*, 1 (Bursa: Uludağ Yayınları, 1990), p.139.

51. This diversity, because it contradicted the Kemalist emphasis upon cultural homogeneity, has not been given enough emphasis in histories of the period. A primary division was between Alevi and Sunni, but even these differed according to urban and rural communities. Similarly, the various *tarikats* created social divisions. The Anatolian populace was also ethnically extremely diverse as a result of immigration and artificially imposed international boundaries that included non-Turkish ethnic groups in geographic Turkey. This diversity no doubt meant that reform legislation had a varying impact, and it also rendered efforts to mobilize popular movements difficult, as Mustafa Kemal himself discovered during the War of Independence.

52. Reduced to the status of civil servants, *hocas* and *şeyhs* were subject to laws regarding dress and the titles they used, and also to government decisions to 'lay off' religious officials at various times. Nevertheless, being literate they must also have been able to find new forms of employment given the low rate of literacy in this period.

53. These included the *şapka* law (1925), the abolition of the tithe (1925), the introduction of the Gregorian calendar (1926), the adoption of the 'Turkish' alphabet (1928), the Turkification of the call to prayer (1933), the adoption of Turkish surnames (1934–1936), the declaration of Sunday as the day of rest (1935), and various efforts to transform the role of women in Turkish society.

54. The most common form of manipulation was government-sponsored sermons that local officials were required to deliver as a part of the *hutbe*; also Kemalists were quick to use the education system to disseminate their ideas, and 'Kemalist Islam' was propagated through many textbooks and the efforts of Kemalist teachers.

55. While tribal networks were concentrated in eastern Anatolia and their numbers are hard to estimate, ethnic communities were found in concentration all over Anatolia. In the second half of the nineteenth century some 5 million Muslim refugees and immigrants settle in Anatolia constituting almost one third of the pre-war population. The 1935 census recorded 962,000 people as having been born outside Turkey. *Genel Nüfus Sayımı, 1935*; and Kemal Karpat, *Ottoman Population 1830–1914: Demographic and Social Characteristics* (Madison: The University of Wisconsin Press, 1985).

56. Of the protagonists at Menemen, two were clearly immigrants – one from Crete, the other from Damascus.

57. Hamid Algar, 'Political Aspects of Naqshbandi History', in Marc Gaborieau *et al.* (eds.), *Naqshbandis: Historical Developments and Present Situation of a Muslim Mystical Order* (Istanbul: Editions Isis, 1990), pp.123–52.

58. Even the *şapka* and *ezan* laws were arguably ineffective. The latter was one of the first dealt with – reversed – by the new Democratic Party government in June 1950; and observations made by non-Turks suggest that often the hat law was not obeyed, and that when it was, the '*şapka*' was of such interesting forms that while the letter of the law was complied with, the spirit was not: what was under the hat did not change.

59. FO 371/13094/E2871 Chaffy (Mersina) to Clerk, 14 May 1928.

The People's Houses and the Cult of the Peasant in Turkey

M. ASIM KARAÖMERLİOĞLU

'Only one peasant stronghold remained in or around the neighbourhood of Europe and the Middle East –Turkey,' wrote historian Eric Hobsbawm, 'where the peasantry declined, but in the mid-1980s, still remained an absolute majority.'[1] One can argue that Hobsbawm made a mistake or exaggerated a little. Statistics, however, confirm the historian's point.[2] Indeed, until recently Turkey remained a 'peasant country', and the consequences of this fact, usually unnoticed, have had great impact on the social and intellectual life of the country.

The structural reasons behind the predominance of a peasant economy and society in Turkey have been investigated to a great extent, owing largely to the extensive development of the fields of economic history and political economy. However, the subjective factors such as ideas and culture that helped shape and reproduce this phenomenon have not been studied adequately. The role and impact of ideas are essential, for they are the factors which affect the *specific* ways of historical development, especially when they inspire political movements or become institutionalized as part of a state policy. This paper argues that, as far as the intellectual level is concerned, the lack of a consistent, well-devised, serious and prolonged urban and industrial policy and the predominance of a peasantist outlook among the ruling circles of the single-party regime contributed to the persistence of a predominantly peasant society for much of the twentieth century in Turkey. In other words, the ambiguities and eclecticism of the ruling circles, hesitantly pretending to embrace an urban and industrial outlook on the one hand, and embracing a peasantist one on the other, most probably helped sustain a huge peasant mass. In order to substantiate this argument, we shall analyse the peasantist ideology, whose significance in Turkish intellectual history is underestimated, although it gained widespread currency among the intelligentsia of the 1930s. We shall focus on the People's Houses since this institution was directly founded for the purpose of disseminating the propaganda of the governing People's Republican Party (RPP) and mobilized in its activities the prominent intellectuals and officials of the time. In this respect, we examine first the establishment of the People's Houses and then its peasantist activities and ideology.

In 1932 the Republican People's Party established the People's Houses as adult education centres to conduct cultural, sporting and educative activities.[3] In general, the Houses were expected to propagate the principles of the ruling RPP. Among the extraordinary indigenous developments that foreshadowed the founding of the People's Houses was the surprising success of the new opposition party, the Free Party [Serbest Fırka], in 1930 which unexpectedly appealed to a significant number of people.[4] This multi-party experience strengthened the culture of fear, a deeply rooted mentality in the late Ottoman Empire and the early Republic, that times were volatile and that the enemies of the Kemalist regime were consolidating their power for their 'separatist' goals.[5] This attitude of the ruling circles shaped the mood of the Third Republican People's Party Congress of 1931, in which a series of new politico-ideological measures were taken, among them the founding of People's Houses. These measures mostly involved redefining the relationship between the Party and the state. For instance, governors of cities also became Party leaders of the cities. The Party-state control of any non-state institution allowed to continue in existence was strengthened. The rhetoric was 'unifying the forces' and it increasingly shaped the attitudes of the ruling elite for the coming two decades. For the sake of 'unifying the forces', many institutions which were outside absolute governmental control were forced to 'join' the state-controlled institutions such as the People's Houses.[6]

In the light of this mentality that the activities of the People's Houses can be better understood. The People's Houses embodied the project of replacing any autonomous pre-existing intellectual and political associations. One of the most important of these organizations at the time was the Turkish Hearths [*Türk Ocakları*], founded in 1912 to spread Turkish nationalism.[7] This institution, like the Free Party, was perceived to be a political threat, or at least an alternative to the Kemalist leadership. That the People's Houses even used all the former buildings of Turkish Hearths, which were forced to shut down, reveals the extent of the replacement.[8] Hamdullah S. Tanrıöver, the director of the Hearths, later accused the RPP of resorting to totalitarian tactics in closing his institution. He claimed that the purpose of the People's Houses resembled the totalitarian practices prevailing in Germany and Soviet Russia.[9]

The mass support given to the Free Party alarmed the Republican People's Party, for it indicated that the Kemalist Revolution had not reached the hearts and minds of the people.[10] Consequently, the RPP established the People's Houses as propaganda institutions in order to spread the principles of Kemalism,[11] which were barely supported by the average people. This was especially true as far as the rural population, which made up almost 80 per cent of Turkey's population, was concerned.[12] It is within this context that the People's Houses increasingly resorted to utilizing a peasantist ideology.

This is also the context within which we can understand why the People's Houses were perceived as adult education centres. Not only in Turkey, but also in many European countries of the 1930s, adult education centres flourished. The German and Central European experiences especially exemplified the success of adult education centres and influenced the Turkish intelligentsia.[13] As a matter of fact, in the early 1930s the state sent several intellectuals and officials to Europe in order to examine institutions of adult education in Europe.[14] The result was that in many of the writings of the ruling elite of the early 1930s we see an emphasis on the necessity of adult education. In the speech with which he opened the People's Houses in 1932, Kemal Atatürk pointed out that an education system not supported and complemented by adult education could never achieve nationalist goals.[15] According to the RPP elite, the People's Houses were supposed to create a mass society which in turn would serve to create the true nation.[16]

To motivate and transform ordinary people were not the only goals of the People's Houses. Also important was to mobilize the intelligentsia, who could in turn be used for educating ordinary people. The problem was not that Turkey lacked intellectuals who could spread the ideology of the new regime, but that the Turkish intelligentsia, according to many contemporaries, was unwilling to take on the task of serving the principles of the revolution.[17] The contemporaries pointed out the loss of enthusiasm among the Turkish intelligentsia and the upper classes for the Kemalist reforms. The complaints of two prominent Kemalist writers in this regard demonstrate the apathy among the intelligentsia of the early 1930s. Writing in 1933, Falih Rıfkı Atay claimed that nothing since 1914 had occupied the attention of ruling circles so much as beauty contests. According to him, the word 'revolution' had recently become tiresome to the people. 'The words of revolution and regime,' continued Atay, 'were met by the question "still?" by the journalists.'[18] Likewise, in 1934 Y. Kadri Karaosmanoğlu noted that he had seen the most enthusiastic gathering of the previous ten years in the famous Ankara Palas Hotel, where a French fashion exhibition was taking place.[19] As these examples show, by the early 1930s the state desperately needed to extend its influence among the intelligentsia. Many official speeches made it clear that intellectuals should join the people in the cause of totally transforming the country.[20] Intellectuals should communicate with the people in ways that ordinary people could understand.[21] In this respect, the People's Houses were regarded as places where intellectuals and ordinary people should meet and bridge the gap that had widened between them, and between the urban and rural population.[22] The peasantist ideology and activities in the People's Houses were perceived as the key to bridge these gaps.

The People's Houses gave a special role and significance to its Peasantist Divisions [Köycülük Kolları] which was one of the nine divisions necessary to establish a People's House.[23] The basic duty of the Peasantist Divisions was 'the development of social, medical and aesthetic aspects of villages while establishing mutual respect and solidarity with the city dwellers'. In order to do so, the members of the Peasantist Divisions should go to the villages, give theatrical performances there and do anything that could 'enlighten' the peasants. Some villages were chosen as models for the nearby villages. The overall aim of all these, it was claimed, was to create prosperous and educated Turkish peasants.[24]

The cultural advancement of peasants remained an outstanding concern for the Peasantist Divisions of the People's Houses. Such an attitude is reminiscent of the habit of many intellectuals in developing countries to emphasize culture in general and ideology in particular. They believe that the right ideology will solve their country's problems. Similarly, the People's Houses, more than anything else, focused on raising the cultural level of the people. For this reason, the aim of defining the intellectual basis of the peasantist ideology was given priority.[25] Owing to the need to establish an ethos, in its first issue *Ülkü*, the official organ of the Ankara People's House, announced what kind of articles it aimed to publish as far as the peasants were concerned. The articles had to focus on 'interpreting the significance of the peasantist ideas for the sake of the future of the country', 'showing youth the honour of working for the villages', 'improving the cultural and material life of peasants', and 'reforming village life on the basis of local conditions.'[26]

The Peasantist Divisions of the People's Houses were the most active. In their inaugural year, the divisions had 2,908 members nationwide, and by 1940 there were 154,000. In the same year, their members visited over two thousand villages all over the country.[27] Visiting villages was the most important activity of the Peasantist Divisions. *Ülkü* depicted a typical village visit as follows:

> First the flag is hoisted while the people are singing the national anthem. After this ceremony, the high officials and members of the People's Houses mix with the people. They donate books and journals to the peasants and doctors take care of the diseased peasants. Then, everybody listens to authentic music sung by local youth, and watches

sporting activities. Usually some members of the Dramatics Divisions of the People's Houses perform a theatrical show and at the end of the day the visitors return to the cities.[28]

One of the most important aims of these village visits was to bridge the gap between the city intellectuals and the people. The visits were intended to allow both the intellectuals and the peasants to become better acquainted, as previously they had been separated culturally and geographically.[29] The village visits also offered both parties practical guidance. Experts in several fields gave advice to the peasants on topics such as how to increase agricultural productivity, how to market products, how to establish producer co-operatives and the like. The members of the People's Houses led the commemoration of national festivals including the newly inaugurated 'Land Festival'. Medical care of the peasants was always a significant task of the visits. The Divisions not only worked in the villages, but also organized groups to help peasants visiting cities. Especially when peasants had any demands from or problems with the officials, the members of the divisions supported them in their dealings with officialdom. Furthermore, the collection of authentic, folkloric data from different regions became an important task, and this constituted one of the most important and lasting effects of these village visits.[30] The national culture was enhanced by the anthropological, linguistic and musical information which was gathered. For instance, the famous Hungarian composer Bela Bartok was invited by the People's Houses to help collect Anatolian folk songs in villages.

In addition to the People's Houses, the government established the People's Rooms [Halkodaları] in 1939. These small versions of the People's Houses established in the villages so enabled the members of the Peasantist Divisions to visit irrespective of the weather conditions and the lack of transportation facilities. The project of the People's Rooms then aimed to extend the activities of the People's Houses to the entire year and control the villages from within.[31] The People's Rooms were also expected to resolve local difficulties and prevent cases being brought before the city courts, thereby saving time and energy for both the courts and the peasants.[32] Needless to say, as in the People's Houses, only RPP members or state officials could be directors of the Rooms; and their activities, like those of the People's Houses, were strictly controlled by the RPP.[33]

Neither the Peasantist Divisions nor the People's Rooms succeeded in transforming the Turkish countryside. In the first place, the structure of villages in Anatolia made such an attempt incredibly difficult. The size of an average village in Turkey was small, and villages were so widely dispersed throughout the country that it was quite impossible to reach all of them. In other words, there were material impediments to reaching the diversely settled Anatolian peasants. More importantly, however, the mentality that prevailed in the People's Houses became an obstacle in achieving the goal of allowing intellectuals to mix with the peasants. First, the bureaucratic nature of these activities impeded progress towards transforming the countryside. For example, the villages to be visited were notified officially beforehand so that the peasants could make the necessary preparations. The state and Party were so concerned to control any autonomous and creative activity that local initiative was stifled by bureaucratic pressure. It should have been obvious from the outset that such an approach would hardly win the hearts and minds of the peasants.[34] Moreover, the members of the People's Houses looked on the peasants as objects of social engineering. This attitude, however, only increased the rural population's distrust of the intellectuals and city-dwellers, which, in the eyes of the peasants, was deep rooted.[35]

The village visits of the People's Houses ended in a fiasco. Fay Kirby characterizes the people who participated in these village visits as 'foreign tourists or travelers who try to discover the dark corners of Africa'.[36] Similarly, as Cavit Tütengil contends, the village visits did not go beyond the 'picnics' of intellectuals in summertime. Even the goals that the Peasantist Divisions set for themselves were not realized, except for a few collections of anthropological and cultural information about the countryside of Turkey.[37] Even if they had been able to achieve their goals, the nature and extent of their aims were such that the real problems of the peasants would not have been solved. The focus of peasantist activities of the People's Houses was mostly limited to the cultural sphere. It was argued that raising the consciousness of Turkey's peasants would solve all their problems. While a change in social and economic relations was required, the People's Houses were content merely with changing the peasants' outlook. It was obvious that these endeavours were doomed to fail from the outset.

Life in rural Turkey remained largely unchanged by the People's Houses because they failed to transform the rural structure. This fact should not lead us to downplay the significance of peasantist ideas. Ironically, the impact of these ideas was more on the intellectuals than on the peasants. For this reason, we must examine in detail the cultivation of the peasantist ideology among the intelligentsia.

Before focusing on the 1930s, we should note the existence of peasantist activities in the late Ottoman Empire. During this period, the emergence of peasantist leanings went hand in hand with the emergence of Turkish nationalism. The concern for the peasants started during the Second Constitutional Period (1908–18),[38] especially in the pages of the influential journal *Türk Yurdu*. In this journal, Yusuf Akçura and particularly Helpfand-

Parvus,[39] time and again emphasized the significance of the peasant support for the nationalist ideology and movement.[40] We see the first peasantist movement after the First World War. After the War, 15 medical doctors established the Peasantist Association [Köycüler Cemiyeti] and decided to go 'to the people' in order to educate the peasants in their struggle against the hardships of the village environment and offered them medical assistance. They also helped organize an anti-resistance movement in this region until 1920, when the growing foreign invasion of the Empire made it impossible for them to continue their activities.[41] Among them was Dr Reşit Galip, the later Minister of Education in the early 1930s, who assumed the leadership of this organization. Although these young and idealistic doctors worked among the peasants in Western Anatolia like religious missionaries, nothing significant remained from their experience. After the foundation of the Republic in 1923 until the early 1930s intellectual and practical concerns of the new regime about the peasants did not go beyond simple words such as the peasant as 'the real master of the nation'.[42]

It was in the 1930s that the peasantist ideas began spreading among the Turkish intelligentsia, especially among those who wrote in *Ülkü*. A study of peasantist thought in this period should focus on *Ülkü* for it represented the dominant views among the ruling and intellectual circles. The names of the *Ülkü* contributors reveal the significance of the journal since many leading RPP and state officials, famous intellectuals and academics, wrote in this semi-official journal.[43] However, *Ülkü* was not an ideologically strict and theoretically monolithic journal. This was partly due to the fact that Kemalism as an ideology neither intended to be monolithic, nor was it so in reality. In other words, the ambiguity of Kemalism was reflected in the pages of this journal as well.[44]

Around 1932 the interest in developing the villages gained momentum in Turkey. As a matter of fact, this was a world-wide phenomenon between the two world wars, in part due to the Great Depression, which was seen as a result of urbanization and industrialization, and in part because of the catastrophic drought of the early 1930s which made the problem of agricultural production extremely crucial. Historian Ö. Lütfi Barkan reveals the changing ideological orientation of the times in 1935:

> Today even the most leading industrialized countries take all kinds of precautions by jealously preserving peasant life against the proletariat, which shows the internationalist and revolutionary trends, and against the political currents which desire to pull the peasants into the cities and evacuate the countryside. In order to do so, they consider villages and village life the abundant and clear resource of national life and the instrument for social stability.[45]

Turkey surely was not an exception. Much evidence can be cited for the interest in villages and villagers during this time. Official speeches, including Kemal Atatürk's, started paying more attention to the development of the countryside arguing that Turkey's most crucial task lay in developing the villages; the members of the People's Houses considered the peasantist activities as supremely important and attempted to mobilize their forces about this issue; students and teachers were encouraged to go to villages in the summer; and, last but not least, the Ministry of Education started devising projects on improving education in villages.[46]

Although the peasantist ideology became quite influential in the early Republican Turkey, the characteristics of this ideology still await an in-depth analysis. This essay will endeavour to highlight the main characteristics of this ideology: its anti-urbanist and anti-industrialist bias, the exaltation of villages and peasants, its attitude toward Westernization, and finally its perception of education as the motor of rural transformation. These characteristics can be seen in peasantists such as N. Köymen, who had formed peasantist principles and who presented this ideology in detail. Although this peasantist worldview differed somewhat from the official perceptions of the peasantry, it is important to note that their similarities exceeded their differences, so this discussion of the characteristics of peasantist ideology transcends the pure, full-fledged peasantists and helps us to understand the ideological orientation of many of the ruling elites of the time.

One of the most distinctive characteristics of the peasantist ideology in Turkey was its denunciation of urbanization. Other peasantist ideologies, such as that under the Third Reich in Germany, also had anti-urban biases, but in this and other examples the consequences of industrialization and the fear of the growing working class consciousness and activities occupied a more central role. In Turkey the crucial question was not being for or against industry, notwithstanding the fact that many of the peasantists had critical attitudes towards it. They all agreed on the necessity for a national industry but their concern was the formation of an industry which would favour the peasants. Interestingly enough, they were for *industry* but against *industrialization*, a term they used to refer to the historical experience of Western Europe. These intellectuals envisaged an industrial development which would not dislocate the bulk of the population in the countryside and would not dissolve the traditional relations of production while improving the technological structure.[47]

It was the cities, especially the big cities, the Turkish peasantists claimed, which symbolized the worst of all possible worlds. Cities embodied cosmopolitanism, class struggle, unemployment, economic depressions, workers' strikes, insecurities of all kinds, less social control and degeneration of all sorts[48] According to Köymen, for example, it was urbanization, not industrialization, which was the root cause of all social problems since urbanization preceded industrialization. Although he accepts that social problems related to urbanization rose to unprecedented levels with the rise of industrialization, their origins still lay in the formation of cities, not in industrialization *per se*. In the cities, even before industrialization, Köymen argued, one saw social problems such as class struggles, which should be avoided by all means.[49]

According to the peasantist ideology, one of the most important concerns was to prevent migration to the cities. This was, of course, a corollary of the anti-urban bias of peasantist ideology. For this reason, attaching the peasants to the countryside became a major concern of the peasantists. They accordingly argued that it was essential to develop the villages in order to bond the peasants to them; otherwise the peasant might attempt to seek in the city the rights and comfort he lacked in the village.[50]

It should be noted that the peasantists were also against small and dispersed villages, as much as they opposed big cities. There were two reasons: on the one hand, small villages scattered randomly throughout the nation were quite difficult to incorporate into national life because of economic infeasibility. In other words, such a village structure could not benefit from economies of scale. Secondly, it was difficult to establish state authority in these smaller villages.[51]

The critical attitude of the peasantists towards urbanization went hand in hand with their resentment of the city dwellers. Many articles written from a peasantist outlook and many surveys and reports from villages identified the peasants' deep hostility towards the urban population.[52] It should be noted, however, that the target of this hostility was not distinct social groups, but the abstract city dweller. So an imagined contradiction was presented between the city and rural population.

The peasantists resented the uneven development of the city and the countryside. They claimed that cities and villages should benefit from the same rights and privileges but in reality the situation was quite to the disadvantage of villages. In a sense, the peasantists argued that what was needed was an equalization between the living and learning conditions of the villages and cities. They believed that the peasants were discriminated against. For example, the taxes taken from the peasants, they contended, were spent for public works in cities. For these reasons, what was necessary was bending the stick to the other side, since for centuries cities had been thriving at the expense of villages. Although village life was superior to city life, so they argued, owing to the power of the cities the villages had been exploited by the cities.[53] According to Köymen, the 'unproductive' cities had the economic, cultural, administrative and civilizational power which made it possible for the city dwellers to exploit the 'productive' peasants even though the wealth and power of the cities depended on the sacrifices of the villagers.[54] A similar mentality in the West, the argument went, led to one of the most important mistakes of human history by creating the division of labour unfavourable to villages.[55]

The dominance of cities and city people over the countryside, according to the peasantists, led to the misconception that villages were simple extensions and complements of cities. In other words, the mistake that many intellectuals made was to regard villages as small entities dependent on cities. In reality, they argued, cities were the ones which were dependent on the villages and it was a great mistake to relate the development of villages to urban development. Cities, in fact, were just the complements of villages, which offered them market places for agricultural products and functioned as centres of public works for villages, but not centres in themselves. In this respect, many argued, a city was nothing more than a big village.[56]

The peasantists' strong hostility towards urbanization coexisted with the glorification of village life and peasants. The peasantists portrayed a utopian and unrealistic village life and economy to foster their cause. Peasants were the pure, unspoiled, noble, intelligent, flexibly thinking people who made up the roots of the Turkish nation and the motor of national development.[57] In this respect, they always harshly criticized the Ottoman Empire for favouring cities at the expense of villages. According to them, this attitude was the consequence of the anti-nationalist and anti-peasantist character of the Ottoman Empire. They saw a correlation between urbanism and anti-nationalism. During the Ottoman Empire, their argument went, the national identity and national culture were lost (as if they had really existed!) since Ottoman intellectuals were individualistic and did not have the sense of community consciousness, and were perceived to be antithetical to the peasantist ideology. According to them, the Ottoman intellectuals achieved no more than ornamental writings about the peasants.[58]

Although numerous factors were cited for the superiority of village life, such as the fact that villages had good weather for child rearing and were less vulnerable than cities for national defence,[59] three areas of purported superiority of village life and people enable a better understanding of peasantist ideology: finding the 'true' Turkish culture and race in villages, the eminence of the peasant economy, and the conservatism of the peasants.

In the 1930s many peasantists emphasized that villages were the places where the 'pure' culture of the nation was preserved intact.[60] As a matter of fact, although the peasantist extensively used the notion of superiority, the perception that villages contained the origins of national culture cannot be attributed exclusively to peasantist ideology. The idea of 'pure cultural traits preserved in the countryside' had a long history in nationalist rhetoric all over the world, including the Turkish one. The outstanding Young Turk ideologue, Ziya Gökalp, for one, stressed such a notion of pure cultural traits that could be found among the villagers as early as the 1900s.[61] Many nationalist movements, regardless of whether they had a peasantist orientation or not, believed in finding the roots of national culture and identity in villages. This is understandable from a nationalist perspective since cities embodied cosmopolitanism with their ethnically, culturally and economically mixed nature.

Another presumably superior feature of villages was their preservation of the Turkish race. It is beyond the aims of this paper to discuss whether the peasantists, in particular the People's Houses, engaged in racist activities and endorsed a racist outlook, or to what extent its activities and publications evinced racism.[62] There were certainly racist elements, such as biological and anthropological research in search of the Turkish race, the use of the concept ırk with reference to blood,[63] discussions on how the Turkish language and race are superior to others and the like. Apparently, the peasantist ideologues frequently used a racist rhetoric to make their cases.[64] Nevertheless, their perception of race also included respecting other races and cultures.[65] The peasantist rhetoric on this issue was much less aggressive and exclusive than the German Blut und Boden ideology in the same peasantist context.[66]

The second merit of villages and peasants, according to the peasantists, stemmed from the supposed superiority of the agricultural economy over the urban and industrial economies. They worshipped the petty production characteristics of the agrarian economy, for this made it possible to use the household as the basic unit of production. The household economy of rural life enabled the peasants to stay away from the harsh alienation in the workplace, a negative phenomenon characteristic of industrial production.[67] Since the producers owned their own land, they were more motivated and interested, economically and psychologically, in their work. This in turn enabled the survival of a more harmonious society due to the fact that household production did not necessitate wage labour, a category perceived to corrupt not only the workplace but also the society as a whole.[68] In other words, the peasantists glorified the countryside for the absence of a working class.[69]

It was small agrarian production, Köymen argued, which fed the world throughout the ages. Yet, it was not 'money' but 'joy' that was at the centre of this production, unlike the industrial commercialized economies. The agrarian economies relied on 'honesty' and 'trust', unlike the corrupt economic transactions in the cities, which once more indicated the superior feature of rural to urban production.[70] Furthermore, there was a more important characteristic of small agrarian production: its tendency to self-sufficiency. According to the peasantist rhetoric, self-sufficiency was a crucial feature of the Turkish agrarian economy. Indeed, did not the Great Depression once more vindicate the extraordinary necessity and advantage of self-sufficiency?[71]

The third merit of the peasants was that they did not make up a restless and an internationalist class like the urban working class; rather they were characterized by conservatism. According to Köymen, this conservatism was the 'social insurance' against the moral deterioration of the cities.[72] For one thing, most peasants had at least a small amount of property, which made them in some sense entrepreneurs and prevented their turning into a 'proletariat'.[73] On the other hand, industrialization in the cities, according to Köymen, created a division of labour in which humans were reduced to mere extensions of machines.[74] Like many peasantists around the world, the Turkish advocates of this ideology thought that workers were subject to lose their personal character due to the harsh division of labour brought about by industrialization.[75]

Given the hostility toward urbanization and industrialization together with the glorification of the village life and people, it is no surprise that the peasantists developed a hostile rhetoric toward Westernization. This is because Western Europe historically embodied many characteristics that were antithetical to the peasantist ideology. The peasantists advocated the predominance of agriculture in the economy and argued that the path Turkey should take had to be determined by its own historical conditions.[76] Besides, peasantists such as Köymen held a critical theoretical position towards Westernization since the discrepancy between cities and villages, first and foremost, was a phenomenon of the West. Furthermore, Köymen insisted repeatedly that the Great Depression was the product of the urban and industrial Western civilization, which was going through a deep crisis.[77] What the peasantists inferred from this historical experience was that the West should not be an example for the future development of Turkey. As a matter of fact, peasantist ideology and its principles were apparently at odds with the two major historical developments that took place in the West, namely urbanization and industrialization. We should, of course, note that the world of the 1930s was one of the best periods for such critiques of Westernization to flourish. After all, the Great Depression, perceived to be an inherently Western and urban phenomenon with its horrible consequences, made it quite difficult to be an ardent supporter of Westernization.

The hostile rhetoric of the peasantists towards Westernization also reflects their assumptions about the world-wide division of labour. They developed a theory of exploitation of the rural world by the industrialized West. The latter developed its wealth at the expense of the former. In this way, the Turkish peasantists carried the logic of the urban versus rural dichotomy inside Turkey to the world scale. They developed a theory of division of labour in the world between the urban/industrial and rural/agricultural countries. Since the West exemplified the first, it is no surprise that they developed a critical attitude toward Westernization.[78]

We should note, in passing, that it was not only the peasantists, but other small groups as well who had a similar attitude toward Westernization in the 1930s. One group consisted of the intellectuals grouped around the famous journal *Kadro*. This journal, like the peasantists, championed a different developmental path for Turkey, although one remarkably different from that endorsed by the peasantists. The *Kadro* writers offered a 'third' way different from both liberalism and socialism, but their vision was mostly an urban and industrial one. They harshly condemned the West for its imperialism, liberalism, democracy and individualism. They were particularly critical of the French Revolution and its individualistic and liberal principles. According to the *Kadro* contributors, it was justifiable to adopt Western methods and techniques since they belonged to the entire humanity. The fact that at the time these methods and techniques were found only in the West, those intellectuals thought, stemmed from Western exploitation of the world. In other words, the non-Western countries also had a share in the formation of Western methods and techniques. They also saw no problem in adopting Western social theories insofar as they were useful for their own goals. *Kadro* frequently criticized pro-Western journals and newspapers and condemned the inferiority complex towards the West which prevailed among many Turkish intellectuals.[79]

How should one explain the juxtaposition of a critical attitude toward Westernization seen above and the rampant Westernization of the times in social life, as many academics have so long pointed out?[80] It is probably owing to the fact that there was a great discrepancy between the rhetoric and the reality. For instance, although no endorsement of full-fledged Westernization appears in the pages of *Ülkü*, if one carefully reads the accounts of the activities of the People's Houses, even among the peasantists, it is possible to locate quite a significant number of cases in which ambitious Westernization was pursued. Just to give an example, the only sport performed in Adana People's House was tennis, which even today is regarded as an elite sport in this region.[81] Furthermore, Anıl Çeçen, who wrote a book on the People's Houses and who was extremely sympathetic to them, could not help but confess that the People's Houses ended up contributing to the formation of a 'bourgeois' (read Western) life and cultural style in Turkey.[82] Despite this evidence, barely did anyone use the term Westernization. The preferred term to describe these phenomena was 'progress towards the level of contemporary civilization'['muasır medeniyetler seviyesine yükselmek'],[83] but obviously this meant Westernization since, even according to many peasantists, the West still embodied contemporary high civilization. On the whole, it is fair to say that the peasantist rhetoric on the issue of Westernization also contributed to the ambiguous and contradictory nature of the single-party regime.

So far three basic characteristics of peasantist ideology have been discussed. It is now important to see the way and manner in which the peasantists wanted to accomplish their goals. To highlight this, we need to take into account their emphasis on education and human will.

The peasantists saw education as the most important factor in transforming Turkey's countryside. This was because, for most peasantists, the root cause of economic and social backwardness in villages rested on the lack of education rather than on social structure and relations. They ignored the eminence of social relations and struggle, and instead focused on the struggle against the hardships of nature and the ignorance of the peasants. For this reason, they believed in educating the peasants to achieve their goals.

Their belief in education for social transformation notwithstanding, they rejected mainstream education and advocated a distinct style for educating the peasantry from the city dwellers. In the first place, peasants had to be educated in villages, not in cities. The educational system for villages should be based on the necessities of rural life. In this respect, they opposed the system of general education as had been applied in cities. The peasantists demanded a village education system completely different from that of the cities, one based on vocational training.[84]

The most crucial role in the achievement of a successful educational reform should rest with a new and different generation of village teachers. The peasantists, together with many others, agreed on the vital role expected of village teachers.[85] These teachers should be recruited from the peasant population since, their argument continued, teachers of city origin tended to return to cities at the first opportunity. Those teachers were unwilling to bear the difficulties of village life.[86] For this reason, not only should teachers be educated in such a way that they would not leave the villages, but also granted some economic privileges in the villages.[87] These ideas about village education became the core values for the Village Institute experiment that started in 1937.

We should note that expecting a social transformation from education was related to another significant characteristic of the peasantist ideology, namely its emphasis on voluntarism. Peasantists expected too much from subjective factors such as education. As the first director of the People's Houses pointed out, there was nothing that the power of human agency could not achieve.[88] A peasantist, S. Aydoslu, who contributed articles on economics to *Ülkü*, denied all existence of historical necessity, and argued that human voluntarism was enough to accomplish any social change.[89] Likewise in his article regarding voluntarism, Köymen noted that it was with an anti-urbanist and peasantist perspective that people should intervene in their own lives and should not allow their lives to be determined by the course of events and history.[90] The peasantists rightly anticipated that even if they could not divert the historical development of Turkey toward urbanization and industrialization, by using state power these processes could somehow be controlled. After all, as Köymen pointed out, was the Turkish Revolution not a direct product of idealism and voluntarism?[91]

After 1936 these general characteristics of peasantist ideology gave way to a different interpretation advocated by senior state officials. While the ruling circles were extensively using and adopting some of the tenets of this ideology, the ideology itself was reinterpreted according to the pragmatic necessities of governmental policies. In order to understand the further development of peasantist ideology, one must examine the changes that took place in the mid-1930s.

Starting in late 1935, some self-criticisms appeared in *Ülkü*. A realistic and sound one by S. Kandemir in his article entitled 'Our Peasantist Ideology' [Köycülüğümüz] signalled the coming of other critiques. According to Kandemir, the development of villages and peasants could only be possible with the full-fledged assistance of the state. Institutions such as the People's Houses and personal initiatives were not enough to handle this enormous task. The People's Houses could be helpful only insofar as they conducted activities complementary to those of the state. In other words, the expectations of the People's Houses were too immense and unrealistic.[92] Moreover, Kandemir pointed out that the theoretical search for peasantist ideology failed to go beyond presenting the problem itself. What had to be done was to create theoretical projects that could be applicable to practical situations. He admitted that the peasantists ideas in Turkey were still passing through its 'romantic' phase.[93]

Early 1936, however, constituted a turning point for discussions on peasantist ideology. The Prime Minister of the time, Celal Bayar, wrote an influential article in *Ülkü* discussing some of the repercussions of peasantist ideology. In addition, in the same year some peasantists such as Köymen questioned the viability of their project in the pages of *Ülkü*. Both of these developments marked a change in the way in which the peasant question had been discussed. Shortly after this incident, the number of articles in *Ülkü* advocating a peasantist agenda decreased dramatically. This does not mean, however, that discussion of and interest in the question of the peasantry slowed down in Turkey; as a matter of fact, the concern with village issues, especially on the part of the official elites, continued and even increased.

Celal Bayar, in his *Ülkü* article of March 1936, discussed whether Turkey should be predominantly an industrial or an agrarian country. He strongly criticized the idea that agriculture ought to take priority in the development of Turkey. According to him, to be successful and prosperous even at the level of agricultural production, the country needed a sound industrial base.[94] This does not mean that he favoured a full-fledged industrialization, but he made it clear that industrial concerns should have priority among state concerns. In the next issue of *Ülkü*, Köymen replied to Bayar's views on industry and agriculture. Instead of an industry-versus-agriculture duality, Köymen devised the term *köycü endüstri* [peasantist industry], meaning that Turkey should be industrialized, provided that the peasants, first and foremost, benefit from this development and the horrible consequences of industrialization be avoided. In this sense, his priority apparently lay with the interests of the rural classes.

Köymen's concept of *köycü endüstri* has quite interesting peculiarities. Industries should be established in the countryside only, which would make it possible for workers to be able to retain their own land. Citing the example of German factories' granting land to their workers, Köymen argued that this was a significant way of preventing the formation of a 'proletariat'.[95] Constructing industries outside of the cities,[96] he believed, would have prevented many of the ills that cities had created, such as class struggle, shanty towns, the existence of two different realms of life in the cities and the villages, social corruption and the like.[97]

Compared to urban industries, Köymen's *köycü endüstri* would:

> benefit from the low prices of land, wages and raw materials; be more resistant against negative effects such as strikes, fire, theft, and disasters in the countryside; be better protected from air bombardment; be less costly in times of temporary closure; employ fewer permanent workers who will be easier to replace when demand was high; benefit from the availability of a direct consumption market which has no intermediaries; be part of the culture of the region, which will foster the interest of the workers in their jobs and make them culturally more sophisticated; can survive even in times of depression since the workers can easily switch to working on their lands.[98]

Köymen's *köycü endüstri* would consist of small-scale factories. He criticized the fetish of establishing large factories,[99] which would benefit from economies of scale on the basis of their declining productivity. He was probably scared that workers in large factories would organize and achieve class consciousness. He argued that large-scale factories carried the risk of being idle from time to time and of accumulating excess inventory. Even in the stronghold of big factories, the United States, Köymen pointed out, recalling the 'flexible specialization' discussions in the world political economy of the 1980s, large-scale had started giving way to flexible, small-scale factories.[100]

To what extent this elaborate theory, presented as the peasantist answer to Bayar, was realistic is difficult to judge. It is possible to find in the history of Republican Turkey some evidence to support such a theory. For instance, we know that most governmental policies discouraged the separation of workers from their villages,[101] and that the state-owned enterprises in Turkey were situated in such a way that workers would be 'largely isolated in widely separated state plants'.[102]

This endeavour to redress peasantist ideology while retaining its core ideas was followed by another interesting and fanciful *Ülkü* article by Köymen which contained significant self-criticism. He first confessed that the peasantists did not really know the peasants. Any reform, he argued, if not coming from below of necessity, could never be understood and supported by the peasants. Yet the peasants were unaware of their real interests because of their low intellectual capacity. For this reason, his argument went, the reforms that had begun in villages could not be successfully finished.[103] He declared that the peasantists had to give up working in villages since not much could be gained from these activities. Not only was the peasant insensitive to any reform, but the dispersed nature of Turkish villages also made it virtually impossible to accomplish any nationwide success.[104] He came up with the 'only way' to solve the peasant question without ever going to the villages: Peasant lodges [*Köylü Hanı*]. By establishing peasant lodges and recruiting clever peasants when they came to cities, things could be done for the peasants in the cities. This, however, was a very paradoxical theory, since it was on the cities, which the peasantists in theory were against, that the fortune and prosperity of villages depended once again.

After 1936 one can scarcely find in *Ülkü* a peasantist rhetoric as pure as it was, the characteristics of which have been presented above. But, ironically, the state's involvement in village and peasant issues gained momentum around the same time.[105] Especially after 1937, the state-sponsored peasantist rhetoric using many of the themes and viewpoints of the ideology (even if it were not as pure as depicted above) reached its apogee with the launching of the idea of land reform, and the Village Institutes, a rural educational programme aiming to transform the Turkish countryside, both of which aroused immense controversies in Turkish history and politics.[106]

The peasantist activities of the People's Houses can hardly be considered a success. This perhaps stemmed from the mentality of 'for the people, despite the people'. According to this mentality which has been quite strong among Ottoman/Turkish politicians and intellectuals, the elites had the right to think and decide instead of the people themselves and implement policies regardless of whether the people would approve or like them. The ordinary people of the cities and peasants of the countryside never became actively involved in the activities of the People's Houses. The members of these institutions were usually officials of the central government, intellectuals, landlords and 'prominent citizens' of the region.[107] Dr İlhan Başgöz, who himself worked in the Ankara People's House between 1941 and 1946, for instance, points out that he never saw any person of working-class origin in Ankara People's House.[108] These facts are certainly at odds with the original intentions of the People's Houses. As Kemal Karpat rightly argues, 'the gap between government and people, something which the Houses were originally intended to eliminate', deepened. 'The rigorous power of the bureaucracy and its arbitrary use of the Houses, especially in small towns, coupled with *their disdain of the common people*', writes Karpat, 'gradually turned the latter away from these institutions and left them without support'.[109] The success of the People's Houses would have necessitated allowing the ordinary people greater initiative, but the People's Houses failed to go beyond functioning like an official institution. The state and the Party were exempt from criticism. When criticisms were raised once in a while, they found harsh responses from the Party and state officials.[110]

Though the peasantist activities of the People's Houses did not transform the rural people and their environment, the peasantist ideology certainly influenced the intelligentsia and the official ruling circles. Many intellectuals who later worked in the Village Institutes, for instance, subscribed to the peasantist ideology. Although this ideology had a considerable impact on the world-views of the governing elite, they often contradicted them with a purely peasantist outlook. For instance, whereas most ardent supporters of this ideology conceptualized the nation as equivalent to the peasants, most leading bureaucrats such as Recep Peker opposed this idea. According to him, the nation meant the people, an abstract concept defined on a legal basis that included everybody who enjoyed equality before the law. Peker carefully and insistently differentiated his concept of *Halkçılık* from the concept of Populism.[111] It seems that government policies represented ambiguities and eclecticism that encompassed many different viewpoints. This situation can be seen clearly in the existence of different complaints and expectations from the governmental policies. For instance, peasantists such as Köymen always hoped to see more peasantists policies,[112] while intellectuals of opposite viewpoints, such as contributors to *Kadro*, accused the state of not paying enough attention to *étatist* industrialization.[113]

Mainstream Turkish historiography has so long presented the history of Republican intellectual life as an unfolding of an 'industrialist idea' and vision. The dominance of approaches focusing on 'modernization' and 'industrialization' have obscured divergences from those ideals, as well as the ambiguities of the time and the eclectic nature of the ruling elite's ideology. The extent of the Turkish elite's hostile peasantist attitude towards industrialization and urbanization has usually been underestimated. In fact, the peasantist rhetoric of the single-party era should be seen as contributing to the creation of very ambiguous and eclectic state policies for issues vital to Turkey, especially with regard to plotting a consistent path for the country's development. This can be seen in many cases: As late as 1936, Prime Minister Celal Bayar could talk about the lack of consensus as to whether Turkey should be a predominantly agricultural or an industrial country.[114] Given all these facts, it should by now be no surprise that industrialization did not constitute a significant part of the programmes of the 14 governments formed during the 1920s.[115] Nor is it just a coincidence that two of the prominent senior officials, Dr Reşit Galip and Mehmet Saffet (Arıkan), both of whom had several important official posts including that of Minister of Education in the 1930s, were known for their peasantist leanings. Likewise, even in the heyday of 'democracy' in the early 1940s, M. Esendal, who became the general-secretary of the RPP, a post dealing mainly with indoctrination, was known as the 'enemy of industry and industrialized civilization'.[116] More examples can be cited, but suffice it to say that it is now impossible to accept the claim that industrialization was one of the main tenets of ruling ideology.[117]

Even when favourable conditions to industrialize emerged in the 1930s, and even the intention to industrialize gained strength among the intelligentsia and the officials, their conservative, peasantist outlook and their great fear of the social and political consequences of industrialization and urbanization restricted the depth and scope of all their attempts. They feared the formation of a dynamic, organized society, and the growth of working-class political activity, all of which could threaten the ruling elite's monopoly of political power. There was virtual consensus on preventing the dissolution of the rural social structure. Even the attempts at land reform that began around 1934 and gained momentum after 1937 aimed, first and foremost, to return to the idealized Ottoman land tenure system rather than to transform rural social relations. The corollary of this was that the state was unable to provide any well-thought-out or consistent policies toward either industrialization or rural transformation. The ruling circles wanted to see industries flourishing, yet at the same time feared the consequences. They were anxious to transform the rural structure without destroying the traditional fabric of the countryside. All of these concerns, in fact, prevented the application of any kind of radical policy, which would have paved the way for Turkey to be urbanized and industrialized much earlier. In addition to the structural limitations of early Republican Turkey, the ambiguities and eclecticism of state ideology contributed to the peasantry's preponderance in Turkey even into the 1980s.

NOTES

1. E. Hobsbawm, *The Age of Extremes: A History of the World, 1914–1991* (New York, 1994), p.291.
2. See, for instance, The World Bank, *Workers in an Integrating World, World Development Report 1995* (New York, 1995), pp.222–3 and pp.147–148, a database compiled by the World Bank for the post-Second World War period.
3. Throughout the 1930s, 379 People's Houses were established in most of the major cities and towns of Turkey, and this number increased to 455 by 1946 in addition to 4,066 People's Rooms (village version of the Houses). İlhan Başgöz, *Türkiye'nin Eğitim Çıkmazı ve Atatürk* (Ankara, 1995), p.198.
4. Şevket Süreyya Aydemir, *İkinci Adam* Vol.I (Istanbul, 1968), p.403.
5. Aydemir, *İkinci Adam* Vol. I, p.403.
6. The rhetoric of 'unifying the forces' can be seen all through the official publications of the 1930s such as *Ülkü*. See for example, Necip Ali. 'İsmet Paşa ve Halkevleri', *Ülkü*, Vol.3, No.18 (1934), p.403. Istanbul Teacher's Union 'terminated' its existence by criticizing itself for its particularistic activities and decided to join the People's Houses. See a news item that appeared in *Ülkü*, Vol.6, No.36 (1936), pp.462–3. In the same vein, the Women's Association was closed. The reason for closing this association was that because the state had officially granted women the right to votes, there was no need for such an organization to exist! Ç. Yetkin, *Türkiye'de Tek Parti Yönetimi* (Istanbul, 1983), p.86.
7. More information on *Türk Ocakları* can be found in Y. Akçuraoğlu, *Türkçülük* (Istanbul, 1990), pp.176–81; M. Arai, *Turkish Nationalism in the Young Turk Era* (Leiden, 1992), pp.71–5; İ. Karaer, *Türk Ocakları: 1912–1931* (Ankara, 1992); and F. Üstel, *İmparatorluktan Ulus-Devlete Türk Milliyetçiliği: Türk Ocakları, 1912–1931* (Istanbul, 1997).
8. D. E. Webster, *The Turkey of Atatürk; Social Process in the Turkish Reformation* (Philadelphia, 1939), p.186; K. H. Karpat, 'The People's Houses in Turkey, Establishment and Growth', *Middle East Journal*, Vol.17 (1963), p.59.
9. Hamdullah Suphi Tanrıöver quoted in S. Aydın, 'Türk Tarih Tezi ve Halkevleri', *Kebikeç*, Vol.2, No.3 (1996), p.109.
10. For a very good story of the mood among the ruling circles of the time see A. H. Başar's *Atatürk'le Üç Ay ve 1930'dan Sonra Türkiye* (Ankara, 1981).
11. For the propagandistic expectations from the People's Houses see A. A. Kolesnikov, *Narodnye Doma v Obshchestvenno-politicheskoi i Kulturnoi Zhizni Turetskoi Respubliki* (Moscow, 1984), pp. 76–9; and Webster, *The Turkey of Atatürk*, pp.186–96.
12. The official statements regarding the primary role of the People's Houses in reaching the hearts and minds of people can be found in many articles in *Ülkü*. See, for instance, İsmet İnönü, 'Halkevleri Yıl Dönümünde', *Ülkü*, Vol.1, No.2 (1933), p.100; Atatürk quoted in Nafi Kansu, 'Halkevlerimiz', *Ülkü*, Vol.12, No.68 (1938), p.213; B. K. Çağlar, 'Halkevlerinde Göze Çarpan Çalışmalar ve Beliren Değerler', *Ülkü*, Vol.10, No.60 (1938), p.550; A. Çeçen, *Halkevleri* (Ankara, 1990), p.107 for clear examples of the intention to spread the ideology of the regime to the masses. As Tütengil and many intellectuals who wrote in the publications of the People's Houses pointed out the peasantist activities of the People's Houses was an attempt to reach the people. C. O. Tütengil, *Kırsal Türkiye'nin Yapısı ve Sorunları* (Istanbul, 1983), p.87.

13. Çeçen, *Halkevleri*, p.91; Aydın, 'Türk Tarih Tezi...', pp.108–9.
14. Selim Sırrı Tarcan was sent to Sweden and Vildan Savaşır to Central Europe to examine adult education. Çeçen, *Halkevleri*, p.95. According to Başgöz and Howard 'it was alleged that the formation of *Halkevleri* program was strongly influenced by both the Soviet and Fascist (Italian) practices.' İ. Başgöz and H. E. Wilson, *Educational Problems in Turkey, 1920–1940* (Bloomington, 1968), p.152.
15. Tütengil, *Kırsal Türkiye'nin* ..., p.87. The emphasis on the necessity of adult education continued all through the 1930s. See N. A. Kansu. 'Halk Terbiyesi ve Halkevleri', *Ülkü*, Vol.17, No.97 (1941), p.3; N. Köymen, 'Halk Seferberliğine Doğru', *Ülkü*, Vol.1, No.5 (1933), p.358; N. Köymen, *Halkçılık ve Köycülük* (Ankara, 1934), p.18.
16. See, for example, Recep Peker, the general secretary of the RPP in the first issue of *Ülkü*. R. Peker, 'Halkevleri Açılma Nutku (Parçalar)', *Ülkü*, Vol.1, No.1 (1933), p.6.
17. Peker, 'Halkevleri Açılma Nutku', p.7.
18. Atay quoted in K. Alemdar, 'Basında Kadro Dergisi ve Kadro Hareketi ile İlgili Bazı Görüşler', published in the reprint of *Kadro*, Vol.1 (1932), p.26.
19. Yakup Kadri (Karaosmanoğlu), 'Moda ve Sakarya', *Kadro*, No.28 (1934), p.103.
20. B. K. Çağlar, 'Halkevlerinde Göze Çarpan Çalışmalar ve Beliren Değerler', *Ülkü*, Vol.10, No.57 (1937), p.282; B. K. Çağlar, 'Halkevlerinde Göze Çarpan Çalışmalar ve Beliren Değerler', *Ülkü*, Vol.11, No.65 (1938), p.469.
21. Hâmit Zübeyir, 'Halk Terbiyesi Vasıtaları', *Ülkü*, Vol.1, No.2 (1933), p.159.
22. Çeçen, *Halkevleri*, p.123.
23. In order to found a People's House in a city or town, at least three of the nine divisions had to exist. These included 1) Language, Literature, and History, 2) Fine Arts, 3) Dramatics, 4) Sports, 5) Social Assistance, 6) Folk Schools and Courses, 7) Library and Publishing, 8) Peasantism, and 9) Museums and Exhibits. K. Ünal, 'Halkodaları', *Ülkü*, Vol.14, No.79 (1939), p.13.
24. Çeçen, *Halkevleri*, p.127.
25. 'Köycüler Bölümü', No author given, *Ülkü*, Vol.2, No.7 (1933), p.63.
26. 'Ülkü'nün Yazı Bölümleri', No author given, *Ülkü*, Vol.1, No.1 (1933), p.93.
27. N. Ali, 'Halkevleri Yıldönümünde', *Ülkü*, Vol.1, No.2 (1933), p.113; '1940 Yılı Halkevleri ve Halkodaları Çalışmaları', No author given, *Ülkü*, Vol.17, No.97 (1941), p.71 and Çeçen, *Halkevleri*, p.195.
28. B. K. Çağlar. 'Halkevlerinde Göze Çarpan Çalışmalar ve Beliren Değerler', *Ülkü*, Vol.11, No.66 (1938), p.558.
29. Çeçen, *Halkevleri*, p.123 and p.162.
30. C. O. Tütengil, *Türkiye'de Köy Sorunu* (Istanbul, 1969), pp.11–12.
31. Kolesnikov, *Narodnye Doma v Obshchestvenno-politicheskoi* .., pp.124–8.
32. Ünal, 'Halkodaları', p.15; Çeçen, *Halkevleri*, p.179.
33. Ünal, 'Halkodaları', pp.13–15; 'Halkevleri Postası', No author given, *Ülkü*, Vol.14, No.79 (1939), p.78.
34. Başgöz recalls that many of the projects initiated during the village visits were consciously ignored by the peasants after the visitors left the village. Interview with Dr İlhan Başgöz, Bloomington, Indiana, 4 May 1997.
35. 'I have found it impossible to form any impression regarding this division's work... If there is a question as to the value of these efforts to the village people, there is no doubt that it is good for city and town dwellers who serve in the Village Welfare Division. They cannot make excursions into the country without learning a few things of value to their social and political thinking ... Whenever I talked with Party and *Halkevi* officials I asked about the success of this element of the program: always the replies were anything but informing.' Webster, *The Turkey of Atatürk*, p.191.
36. Fay Kirby. *Türkiye'de Köy Enstitüleri* (Ankara, 1962), p.60.
37. Tütengil, *Türkiye'de Köy Sorunu*, p.93.
38. See H. R. Buxton, *Turkey in Revolution* (London, 1909), p.36, p.56 for the interest of Committee of Union and Progress in peasants.
39. Parvus or Alexander Helphand actively participated as one of the leaders in the activities of both the Russian and German Social Democratic Party. He lived in Istanbul from 1910

through 1915 and wrote in several Young Turk journals and newspapers on the peasantry, imperialism, and the fiscal problems of the Ottoman state. For more information on Parvus see Z.A.B. Zeman and S.B. Winfried, *The Merchant of Revolution; the Life of Alexander Israel Helphand (Parvus) 1867–1924* (New York, 1965) and O. F. Solov'ev, 'Parvus: Politicheskii Portret', *Novaia i Noveishaia Istoriia*, No.1 (1991), pp.162–85.

40. See the following articles related to the Ottoman peasantry by Parvus: 'Köylüler ve Devlet,' *Türk Yurdu*, Vol.1, No.9 (1912), pp.264–5; 'Köylü ve Devlet,' *Türk Yurdu*, Vol.4, No.10 (1913), pp.1158–62; 'İş İşten Geçmeden Gözünüzü Açınız', *Türk Yurdu*, Vol.3, No.12 (1913), pp.363–4; 'Devlet ve Millet', *Türk Yurdu*, Vol.3, No.3 (1913), p.85; 'Esaret–i Maliyeden Kurtulmanın Yolu', *Türk Yurdu*, II, no 7, 1328, p.587 (all in Ottoman Turkish).

41. See Ş. Elman, *Dr. Reşit Galip* (Ankara, 1953), pages 12–15, 19, 21, 28, 37–38, 48–50, 109, 133, 187–8 for Galip's life, career and peasantst activities. See also Halide Edip Adıvar, *Türkün Ateşle İmtihanı* (Istanbul, 1973), p.15; and U. İğdemir, *Yılların İçinden* (Ankara, 1976), pp.292–3 for the Peasantist Association.

42. Ömer Lütfi Barkan's assessment of the issue regarding the early Republican era is interesting: 'In our country, leave aside the practical side of the matter, even theoretically as an idea or problem, land issues had not occupied significant a place as they deserved among intellectuals and academics.' Ö. Lütfi Barkan, 'Balkan Memleketlerinin Ziraî Reform Tecrübeleri,' in Ö.L. Barkan (ed.), *Türkiye'de Toprak Meselesi, Toplu Eserler I* (Istanbul, 1980), p.377.

43. Just to give an idea of the writers, the leading statesmen included K. Atatürk, İ. İnönü, Ş. Kaya, R. Peker, C. Bayar, A. Çetinkaya, academics included F. Köprülü, N. Berkes, İ. Uzunçarşılı, Ö. L. Barkan, P. Boratav, Ş. Kansu, N. Kansu, P. Wittek, V. V. Bartold. Needless to say, the prominent peasatists N. Köymen, İ. H. Tonguç, M. Saffet, S. Aydoslu and the like contributed to the journal.

44. In an article in *Kadro* evaluating *Ülkü*, the *Kadro* contributors argued that what *Ülkü* was lacking was the ideological consistency and the authority of 'Ziya Gökalp.' By this, they meant the lack of homogeneity of the journal. See 'Mecmualarımız', no author given, *Kadro*, No.26 (1934), p.47. Unlike *Ülkü*, the famous periodical *Kadro* which was published at around the same time with *Ülkü* but forced to terminate itself in late 1934 had a strictly homogeneous theoretical and ideological position.

45. Barkan, *Türkiye'de Toprak Meselesi*, p.26.

46. For the emerging interest in villages of the time see Köymen, 'Halk Seferberliğine Doğru', p.361; N. Köymen, 'Bir Köycülük Projesi', *Ülkü*, Vol.2, No.8 (1933), p.57; N. Köymen, 'Köylü Hanı', *Ülkü*, Vol.3, No.16 (1934), p.319; N. Köymen, *Köycülük Esasları* (Ankara, 1934), p.6 and p.19.

47. Aydoslu Sait, 'Köycülük Esasları', *Ülkü*, Vol.4, No.22 (1934), p.300.

48. Köymen, *Köycülük Esasları*, pp.19–20.

49. N. Köymen, 'Sanayide Yayıcılık', *Ülkü*, Vol.7, No.39 (1936), p.175.

50. A. Ziya, 'Köy Mimarisi', *Ülkü*, Vol.2, No.7 (1933), p.38. One of the characteristics that *Ülkü* announced as a criteria for publication was that they had to show the damages of immigration into the cities. 'Ülkü'nün Yazı Bölümleri', no author given, *Ülkü*, Vol.3, No.13 (1934), p.79.

51. S. Aydoslu, 'Ökonomik Devridaim III', *Ülkü*, Vol.4, No.23 (1935), p.356.

52. B. R. Dülger, 'Köyün Gücü', *Ülkü*, Vol.7, No.37 (1936), p.53; A. S. İşgör, 'Giresun Zihar Köyü', *Ülkü*, Vol.8, No.48 (1937), p.451.

53. For an example supporting the existence of such a discriminatory exploitation of the rural people, see F. Madaralı, *Tonguç Işığı*, No further information, p.107.

54. Köymen, *Köycülük Esasları*, p.13.

55. Köymen, 'Halk Seferberliğine Doğru', p.355.

56. Köymen, *Köycülük Esasları*, p.23; Dr M. Celâl Duru, 'Halkevleri ve Halkodaları Çalışmaları', *Ülkü*, Vol.17, No.102 (1941), pp.541–543.

57. H. A. Malik, 'Kışla ve Köy Terbiyesi', *Ülkü*, Vol.1, No.3 (1933), p.237; M. Saffet, 'Köycülük Nedir?', *Ülkü*, Vol.1, No.6 (1933), p.424; Elman, *Dr. Reşit Galip*, p.15; M. C. Duru, *Sağlık Bakımından Köy ve Köycülük* (Ankara, 1940), p.7; Duru, 'Halkevleri ve

Halkodaları Çalışmaları', p.541.

58. Ali, 'Halkevleri Yıldönümünde', *Ülkü*, Vol.1, No.2 (1933), pp.108–9; Kadri Kemal, 'Anadolu'nun Doğusunda Dil Meselesi', *Ülkü*, Vol.1, No.5 (1933), p.406; Ziya, 'Köy Mimarisi', p.37; 'İnkilap Kürsüsünde İsmet Paşanın Dersi', *Ülkü*, Vol.3, No.14 (1934), p.83; Tütengil, *Kırsal Türkiye'nin ...*, p.78.

59. H. Raşit, 'Köy Muhiti ve Çoçuk Terbiyesi', *Ülkü*, Vol.4, No.20 (1934), p.154; and Aydoslu, 'Ökonomik Devridaim III', p.358.

60. M. Saffet, 'Kültür İnkilabımız', *Ülkü*, Vol.1, No.5 (1933), p.352; H.R. Öymen, 'Köy İçin Yüksek Halk Okulları', *Ülkü*, Vol.5, No.25 (1935), p.18.

61. Georgeon, Francios, *Türk Milliyetçiliğinin Kökenleri, Yusuf Akçura, 1876–1935* (Ankara, 1986), p.193. Although this romantic perception of the countryside as the reserve of the national flavor permeated in the contemporary writings of the intelligentsia, those same people also viewed the peasants as the least 'nationalized' group of the people. This, in fact, was very much the real case since the national project was more of an urban phenomenon. Given the necessity to spread the nationalist ideology to the countryside, the same Köymen writes: 'There are some villages in which a foreign language is spoken although they are often racially Turkish and have been living in this country for centuries; and there are even some villages in which people speak Turkish but do not adhere to Turkism sufficiently.' N. Köymen, *Köycülük Programına Giriş* (Ankara, 1935), p.20.

62. A discussion of racism in the People's Houses can be found in Aydın, 'Türk Tarih Tezi ve Halkevleri', pp.107–30.

63. See for instance Prime Minister İsmet İnönü's speech for the argument that the noble Turkish blood could be found only in villages. Ali, 'İsmet Paşa ...', p.403.

64. F. Kerim, 'Milli Nüfus Siyasetinde (Eugenique) Meselesinin Mahiyeti', *Ülkü*, Vol.3, No.15 (1934), pp.206–212; and Duru, *Sağlık Bakımından Köy*, pp.7–8.

65. Necip Ali, 'Halkevleri Yıldönümü Nutku', *Ülkü*, Vol.3, No.13 (1934), p.8.

66. According to the Nazis, the peasants represented freedom, loyalty, hard work, pure race, healthy upbringing and the like. According to them, for the peasant, 'land is more than a means with which to earn a living; it has all the sentimental overtones of *Heimat*, to which the peasant feels himself far more closely connected than the white collar worker with his office or the industrial worker with his shop.' Likewise, the famous Agricultural Minister Darré saw 'a causal relationship between German 'peasantness' and Germany's national survival and creative capacity.' Were it not for the contact with the urban and mercantile lifestyles, German peasants could be much better off. According to him, the peasants were the only people to supply the 'best blood' which had been declining due to warfare and lower-birth rates. For these views see Anna Bramwell, *Blood and Soil: Walter Darré and Hitler's Green Party* (Buckinghamshire, 1985), p.8, p.62, p.68 and p.203; Barrington Moore, Jr, *Social Origins of Dictatorship and Democracy, Lord and Peasant in the Making of the Modern World* (Boston, 1967), pp.449–50.

67. According to Aydoslu, there was nothing inherently superior in industrial production. He argued that productivity of an industrial worker was not more than that of an artisan. Aydoslu, 'Ökonomik Devridaim III', p.357.

68. S. Aydoslu, 'Köylü ve Köylü Ekonomisi', *Ülkü*, Vol.5, No.27 (1935), p.176.

69. Köymen, *Köycülük Esasları*, p.25.

70. K. Aydıner, 'Yurdumuzun Agaçlandırılması ve Zirai Hapishaneler', *Ülkü*, Vol.10, No.57 (1937), p.267.

71. Köymen, *Köycülük Esasları*, p.23.

72. Ibid., p.30. This is reminiscent of Nazi rhetoric. See the striking similarity of even the phrasing: Hitler in *Mein Kampf* saw the rural population as the 'best defence against the social diseases that afflict us'. See Gustavo Corni, *Hitler and the Peasants: Agrarian Policy of the Third Reich, 1930–1939*, translated by David Kerr (New York, 1990), p.19. For the official Nazi attitude toward the peasantry and a similar rhetoric see R. W. Darré, *Das Bauerntum als Lebensquell der Nordischen Rasse* (Munich, 1929); A. Hitler, 'Parteiamtliche Kundgebung über die Stellung der NSDAP zum Landvolk und zur Landwirtschaft', *Völkischer Beobachter*, 6 Mar. 1930, and R.W. Darré, 'Landstand und Staat,' *Völkischer Beobachter*, 19–21 April 1931.

90 TURKEY BEFORE AND AFTER ATATÜRK

73. N. Köymen, 'Sanayileşmemiz Üzerinde Düşünceler', *Ülkü*, Vol.7, No.37 (1936), p.22.
74. S. Hüsnü, T. Tola and İ. Hakkı, *Köycülüğümüzün Temelleri* (Istanbul, 1935), p.6. Ö. Lütfi Barkan also called attention to the double effects of industrialization in 1935. On the one hand, it created a world polarized within metropolises and colonies and on the other hand, it led to unfavorable working conditions for the growing number of working classes. See Barkan, *Türkiye'de Toprak Meselesi*, p.27.
75. Köymen, *Halkçılık ve Köycülük*, p.18.
76. Ö. Lütfi Barkan pointed out similar views regarding the difference in understanding agrarian societies and industrial societies. Barkan, *Türkiye'de Toprak Meselesi*, p.24.
77. Köymen, 'Halk Seferberliğine Doğru', p.355.
78. For an interesting example in this regard, see Hüsnü, *Köycülüğümüzün Temelleri*, p.8.
79. With regard to Westernization the following articles should be cited from *Kadro*: Şevket Süreyya, 'Biz Avrupanın Hayranı Değil, Mirascısıyız!', *Kadro*, No.29 (1934), pp.43–6; Yakup Kadri, 'Eskiler Almayalım!', *Kadro*, No.4 (1932), pp.44–5; Yakup Kadri, 'Samimiyete Davet', *Kadro*, No.16 (1933), pp.29–30; 'Mecmualarımız,' No author given, *Kadro*, No.27 (1934), pp.52–3; Vedat Nedim, 'Devletin Yapıcılık ve İdarecilik Kudretine İnanmak Gerektir', *Kadro*, No.15 (1933), pp.13–14.
80. See for instance Şerif Mardin, 'Religion and Secularism in Turkey,' in A. Kazancıgil and E. Özbudun (eds.), *Atatürk: Founder of a Modern State* (London, 1981).
81. 'Halkevleri Postası', no author given, *Ülkü*, Vol.14, No.79 (1939), p.77.
82. Çeçen, *Halkevleri* (Ankara, 1990), p.387.
83. See, for example, Saffet, 'Kültür İnkilabımız', p.352.
84. Öymen, 'Köy İçin Yüksek Halk Okulları', p.19; İ. H. Tonguç, 'Köy Eğitimi Meselesi', *Ülkü*, Vol.11, No.65 (1938), p.442; T. Hayrettin, 'İnkilap ve Köy', *Ülkü*, Vol.4, No.20 (1933), p.33; Köymen, *Köycülük Programına Giriş*, pp.42–3.
85. Saffet, 'Köycülük Nedir?', p.428; Elman, *Dr. Reşit Galip*, p.49.
86. H. R. Öymen, 'Tek Dersaneli Okullar', *Ülkü*, Vol.7, No.41 (1936), p.353; Tütengil, *Kırsal Türkiye'nin ...*, p.87.
87. C.H.P İzmir Halkevi Köycülük Kolu Neşriyatı: 7. *Umumî Mecliste 937 Yılı Toplantısında Kabul Edilen İzmir İli Köylerinin Kültür Bakımından Beşyıllık Kalkınma Programı* (İzmir, 1937), p.2 and pp.12–13; 'Köy Öğretmen ve Eğitmeni Yetiştirme İşi', No author given, *Ülkü*, Vol.8, No.46 (1936), pp.262–3.
88. Ali, 'Halkevleri Yıldönümünde', p.106.
89. Sait, 'Köycülük Esasları', p.298.
90. N. Kemal, 'İradecilik ve Köycülük', *Ülkü*, Vol.4, No.21 (1934), p.236. See Köymen, *Köycülük Programına Giriş*, p.10 for Köymen's critique of historical materialism.
91. N. Kemal, 'İnkilap İdeolojisinde Halkçılık', *Ülkü*, Vol.3, No.13 (1934), p.44
92. S. Kandemir, 'Köycülüğümüz', *Ülkü*, Vol.6, No.31 (1935), pp.32, 34.
93. Ibid., p.33.
94. C. Bayar, 'C. Bayar'ın Endüstri Planımız Üzerinde Söylevi', *Ülkü*, Vol.7, No.37 (1936), pp.9–11.
95. Köymen, 'Sanayileşmemiz Üzerinde Düşünceler', p.22.
96. Another Köymen article emphasizing the diffusion of industries in different places rather than concentrating on certain regions see N. Köymen, 'Parti Programında Köycülük', *Ülkü*, Vol.5, No. 29 (1935), p.396.
97. Köymen, 'Sanayileşmemiz Üzerinde Düşünceler', p.21.
98. Ibid., p.22.
99. 'Gigantomania' at the time was a fetish especially in the former USSR and, to a lesser extent, in the USA.
100. N. Köymen, 'Sanayileşmemiz Üzerinde Düşünceler', p.21.
101. Ahmet İnsel and Cengiz Aktar, '"Devletin Bekası" İçin Yürütülen Çağdaşlaşma Sürecinin Toplumsal Sorunları', *Toplum ve Bilim*, No.31/39 (Fall 1985–Spring 1987), p.40.
102. Max W. Thornburg, *Turkey, An Economic Appraisal* (New York, 1949), p.130.
103. N. Köymen, 'Köy Çalışmalarında Tek Müsbet Yol: Köylü Hanı', *Ülkü*, Vol.7, No.40 (1936), pp.299–300.
104. For a discussion of why villages in Anatolia was historically so dispersed see Barkan, *Türkiye'de Toprak Meselesi*, pp.483–4.

105. Ş. S. Aydemir, *İkinci Adam* Vol.II (Istanbul, 1968), p.326.
106. For a comprehensive analysis of the Village Institutes in Turkey see M. Asım Karaömerlioğlu, 'The Village Institues Experience in Turkey', *British Journal of Middle East Studies*, Vol.25, No.1 (1998), pp.47–73.
107. Karpat, 'The People's Houses in Turkey...', p.65.
108. Başgöz, *Educational Problems in Turkey*, p.157.
109. Karpat, 'The People's Houses in Turkey...', p.66 [Italics mine]. Karpat also thinks that 'the differences in mentality stemming from the new secularist-modernist indoctrination of the cities and industrialization through the exploitation of agriculture pushed the village further into its traditional isolation and poverty.' See p.61.
110. An interesting case in point is an article that appeared in May 1934 issue of *Ülkü* complaining about the ways officials behaved toward the people. The complaints included bad treatment of peasants in city hospitals, unfair credit practice in the *Ziraat Bankası* (Bank of Agriculture), and the ignorance of the village teacher. In November of the same year, the governor of Bursa rigorously denied the complaints. See Refik and Ziya, 'Bursa'nın Keleş Köyü, Köy Anketi', *Ülkü*, Vol.3, No.15 (1934), pp.234–40; and for the reply see 'Keleş Köyüne Dair Bursa Valiliğinin Bir Tavzihi', *Ülkü*, Vol.4, No.21 (1934), pp.238–40.
111. Recep Peker, 'Partinin Yeni Programı için Kurultayda R. Pekerin Söylevi', *Ülkü*, Vol.5, No.28 (1935), p.249.
112. Köymen, 'Büyük Kurultaydan ...', p.226.
113. Vedat Nedim, 'Niçin ve Nasıl Sanayileşmemiz Lazım', *Kadro*, No.6 (1932), p.16, p.18; Aydemir, *İkinci Adam* Vol.I, p.411, p.424.
114. Bayar, 'C. Bayar'ın Endüstri Planımız Üzerinde Söylevi', p.9. For some leading officials, the ambiguities and eclecticism meant flexibility in the principles of the Party. N. Ali Küçüka, 'Parti Kurultayı', *Ülkü*, Vol.5, No.27 (1935), p.164.
115. Orhan Kurmuş, 'Cumhuriyetin İlk Yıllarında Sanayiin Korunması Sorunu ve Ticaret Sermayesinin Tavrı', in TMMOB *Tarihsel Gelişimi İçinde Türkiye Sanayii* (Ankara, 1977), p.13.
116. Ş. S. Aydemir, *Suyu Arayan Adam* (Istanbul, 1995), p.464.
117. 'But at that time the word industrialization, though every so often pronounced, was a disbelieved and dubious term. The phrase 'the use of domestic goods' became a matter of ridicule.' Ibid., Aydemir, *Suyu Arayan Adam*, p.453.

The Ideology of the *Kadro* [Cadre] Movement: A Patriotic Leftist Movement in Turkey

MUSTAFA TÜRKEŞ

As the *Kadro* movement is one of the deep-rooted influential intellectual movements in Turkey and as almost all studies concerning Turkey refer to the movement and its imprints, it is worth attempting to examine its ideology. The *Kadro* movement takes its name from the monthly *Kadro* journal, published between January 1932 and November–December 1934. Its founders were Şevket Süreyya Aydemir, the ideologue of the *Kadro* movement, Yakup Kadri Karaosmanoğlu, the legal licensee (franchise holder), Vedat Nedim Tör, editor, and Ismail Hüsrev Tökin and Burhan Asaf Belge, regular contributors. *Kadro* appeared as the leadership of the newly established republican regime allowed it, and was forced to cease publication when its franchise holder, Karaosmanoğlu, took up a diplomatic appointment. Indeed, this study is the second of a series of articles on the *Kadro* movement which I have written. The first, 'A Critique of Studies of the *Kadro* (Cadre) Movement', introduced the subject and largely reviewed existing studies, indicating the contributions and weaknesses of the previous studies on the *Kadro* movement. It also clearly suggests that previous studies provide no clear or comprehensive picture of the ideology of the *Kadro* movement, though each study touched on one or more of its aspects. The present study attempts to identify and examine in detail *Kadro*'s five possible sources of inspiration and to give an outline of *Kadro*'s critiques of capitalism, socialism and Fascism, as well as of its interpretation of international system, historical materialism, national liberation movements, nationalism in general, social nationalism in particular and the 'cadre'. The essay concludes with an assessment of the ideology of the *Kadro* movement as a whole.

The first of *Kadro*'s possible sources of inspiration to be examined here is two Turkish nationalist authors who had come to prominence in the Unionist era, Yusuf Akçura and Ziya Gökalp. Their views exerted some influence on the

Kemalist regime, and it might therefore be thought that Akçura and Gökalp would also have exerted some intellectual influence on *Kadro*.

In fact, the *Kadro* writers made almost no reference to Yusuf Akçura,[1] though their interpretation of the collapse of the Ottoman Empire was remarkably similar to that propounded by Akçura. Like Akçura, the *Kadro* writers emphasized the negative effects of the industrial revolution on Ottoman artisan production, the influence of the notions of the French Revolution in stimulating Balkan separatist movements, and the military and economic ascendancy of the Western Powers, as factors which had led to the dismemberment of the Ottoman Empire.[2] This similarity does not necessarily prove influence for the reason that this line of argument was common. However, it would be idle to dismiss imprints of the nationalist atmosphere, dominated by the Unionist writers, during which the future *Kadro* writers were in their childhood.

As to Gökalp, when in 1932 Ali Nüzhet Bey [Göksel] published his study *Ziya Gökalp'in Hayatı ve Malta Mektupları* [Life of Ziya Gökalp and his Malta Letters], Aydemir wrote an article in *Kadro*, 'Ziya Gökalp', reviewing Gökalp's views.[3] Here Aydemir made a few significant points, which were subsequently echoed in separate articles by Tör and Karaosmanoğlu.[4] Aydemir said that Gökalp deserved a great deal of respect for his intellectual endeavour, but he was highly critical of Gökalp's views, particularly on Gökalp's book, *Türkçülüğün Esasları* [The Principles of Turkism], published in 1923.[5] Firstly, Aydemir argued that Gökalp's views were fragmented. Secondly, Aydemir noted that Gökalp had neither created a new school of thought, nor applied the method of any particular school to analyze the new modern Turkey. Aydemir added that Gökalp's solidarism was simply translated from Durkheim, though Aydemir himself did not comment on Durkheim, saying that it was not for him to defend Durkheim against Gökalp or vice versa. Thirdly, in a more severe tone, Aydemir criticized Gökalp for misunderstanding historical materialism and distorting Marxism. Aydemir concluded his article by noting that as an intellectual, Gökalp belonged to the pre-First World War generation of Turkish intellectuals, whose demands for such social reforms as the unification of religious and non-religious education, women's participation in economic life and secularization, had been implemented by the Turkish revolution. It followed that the Turkish revolution had superseded Gökalp's views.[6]

Evidently, Aydemir was anxious to draw a line between the intellectuals of the Unionist era and those of the republican period, and on another occasion, Aydemir asserted that the intellectuals of the Unionist period had lacked any consistent principles.[7] As Tekeli and Şaylan have suggested, the intellectual currents of the last years of the Ottoman Empire did not exert much influence on the world-view of *Kadro*, and, as Sadıq has noted, while intellectuals of the Unionist period put much emphasis on history, culture and ethnicity, *Kadro* regarded economic development as its ideological substance, and 'any similarity between the nationalist trends of the Young Turks era and *Kadro* is more fortuitous than deliberate'.[8]

In the second place, Aydemir did not make it clear whether he, and the other *Kadro* writers, would adopt solidarism, though it is possible to speculate that Aydemir, and in general *Kadro*, preferred a historical materialist approach to solidarist, since from the start Aydemir made it clear that *Kadro* was to follow historical materialism as its method,[9] and dismissed other world-views as idealism.[10] In 1933 Tökin took up the issue of corporatism, arguing that corporatism was a Fascist means to neutralize class conflict in the interest of the bourgeoisie, thus *Kadro* categorically rejected corporatism.[11] However, in no case did *Kadro* explicitly reject or accept Durkheim's solidarism, nor did it state whether it regarded Durkheim's solidarism as 'idealism' or not. Nor did they comment on the solidarism of the Republican Peoples' Party (RPP). It appears that *Kadro* refrained from commenting on Durkheim and solidarism; possibly for fear of conflict with the RPP, which had adopted solidarism into its programme. As a matter of fact, throughout its existence *Kadro* had to face the tension between its own ideal and existing official reality: *Kadro* may well have aspired to achieve a classless society, but the existence of social classes and the RPP's adoption of solidarism were facts.

The second possible source of ideological inspiration of the *Kadro* movement, to which previous studies have not referred, was Leninism. As in the early 1920s Aydemir had been attracted by the anti-imperialist implications of the socialist revolution in Russia, carried out under the leadership of Lenin. More important, Aydemir had lived in Baku, and then, together with Tökin, in Moscow, during the first years of the Bolshevik revolution.[12] During their studies in Moscow, Aydemir and Tökin were introduced to Marxist views and, more important, to Lenin's works, in particular his *Imperialism, The Highest Stage of Capitalism* and *Theses on the National and Colonial Question*.[13] Putting together the Baku Congress's anti-imperialism and these works of Lenin's, it may be suggested, Aydemir drew two conclusions: first, all colonies would gain national political independence; second, this would lead to the destruction of the capitalist-imperialist status quo. These two points were Lenin's points,[14] and were adopted by *Kadro* as the essence of its own argument, though their source was never openly acknowledged. *Kadro*, however, did not adopt Lenin's argument fully, for while Lenin argued that his two points pointed to the dictatorship of the proletariat and socialism, and his support for national liberation movements was conditional and temporary, based on the argument that national differences would disappear as the international proletariats united, *Kadro* suggested that national political independence would be followed by the achievement of national economic independence.[15] As defined in issues of *Kadro*, *Kadro*'s definition of 'revolution' had two stages: *ihtilal* and *inkilap* [revolution and reform]. It appears that *Kadro* regarded Turkey's War of Liberation as the first stage – the gaining of political independence; and the second stage would be the achievement of economic independence. This argument was fundamental to *Kadro*'s outlook.

A third possible source of inspiration was the Tatar Bolshevik Sultan Galiyev. As noted in the article, 'A Critique of Studies of the *Kadro* Movement', Merdan Yanardağ and to a limited degree Ayşe Trak and Eyüp Özveren argue that the Galiyevist discussions in the 1920s must have had an impact on *Kadro*, and in particular, on Aydemir, by emphasizing the dichotomy between the metropole and its colonies.[16] This is plausible, but caution is needed. Although there is no direct reference to Sultan Galiyev in the issues of *Kadro*, nor in any of the autobiographies by *Kadro* writers, and although in 1991 Tökin said that he did not meet Sultan Galiyev when he was in Moscow, adding that he did not think that Aydemir had any contact with Galiyev,[17] there are prima facie reasons for assuming that Aydemir and Tökin were aware of Galiyev's views: firstly, they had studied in the KUTV, where Galiyev was a lecturer;[18] secondly, they had influential Tatar friends, such as Abid Alim,[19] and must have known what was going on among the Tatar intellectuals; thirdly, Aydemir noted that when he was in Moscow he followed the journal *Novyy Vostok* [the New East] (1922–30),[20] and presumably he was familiar with the journal *Zhizn' Natsional'nostey* [Life of Nationalities]. In both journals 'Muslim socialists' expressed their views, and *Zhizn' Natsional'nostey* was edited by Galiyev.[21] It seems likely that Aydemir and Tökin had some familiarity with Galiyevist views.

To judge how far Galiyevist arguments may have had an impact on the *Kadro* writers, and on Aydemir in particular, it is necessary to examine the key characteristics of 'Galiyevism'. From 1917 to 1923, Sultan Galiyev argued that there was a strong reason to work for the cause of the Bolshevik revolution, since the Bolshevik Revolution offered an opportunity to overthrow Western as well as Russian domination in the Muslim-populated regions of the Russian Empire.[22] During that period Galiyev and other 'Muslim socialists' argued that their main objective was to secure national liberation from foreign tutelage, whether Western or Russian: they gave priority to national liberation movements, rather than to the class struggle. In justifying this reasoning, Galiyev argued in 1918 that Muslim society was not yet divided into warring classes, and was a single entity, a 'downtrodden society'. In 1923 the Galiyevists argued that the common front of the 'downtrodden' embraced all classes in Muslim society, with the sole exception of the upper bourgeoisie and the feudal chieftains.[23] With regard to proletarian dictatorship, in 1918 Galiyev did not believe that Western workers would, in their relations with the colonies, behave in any more moral a manner than had their bourgeois oppressors. He suggested that the Muslim masses should unite in a Communist movement that would be their own and autonomous. In 1923 Galiyev came to think that the real dichotomy was not between capitalists and the working class, but between industrialized and non-industrialized nations. By 1928, he rejected any possibility of collaboration with the Russian Bolsheviks.[24]

Evidently, there were some similarities between the arguments of Galiyev and *Kadro*. However, there were some dissimilarities too. For example, while Galiyev was in favour of creating a united front, which embraced large parts of society, *Kadro* was opposed to such a united front, and argued that a small minority of intellectuals, 'the cadre', should take up a leading role in Turkey. While priority for the Galiyevist was to be free from the Russian tutelage, for *Kadro* it was the Western imperialism. As to their ultimate objectives, while the Galiyevists looked for autonomy within the Soviet Union, *Kadro* argued for both political and economic independence. All in all, it may be suggested that although there were similarities between the two views, in the final analysis they should be placed in different contexts.[25] Besides, there is no need to underestimate the ability of Aydemir to develop independently arguments similar to those of Galiyev. Rather than speculate about influences, it may be suggested that Galiyev and Aydemir developed similar lines of reasoning, and that *Kadro* followed Aydemir's arguments, not necessarily those of Galiyev.

The fourth possible source of *Kadro*'s inspiration, which was indicated by some of the previous studies in a sarcastic manner, was the Soviet experience, particularly in the economic field, during the successive phases of the 'New Economic Policy' (NEP) and the planned economy. When the NEP (1921–28) was introduced in the Soviet Union, Aydemir and Tökin were studying in Moscow. When, from 1928 onwards, the NEP gave way to a planned economy in the Soviet Union, Aydemir, certainly, and Tökin, presumably, were employed in translating Soviet planning documents into Turkish for official use.[26] This, naturally, suggests that the NEP and planned economy experiences of the Soviet Union may have influenced *Kadro*.

The NEP had two aspects, one concerning foreign policy, and the other, domestic affairs.[27] With respect to foreign policy, the October 1917 Bolshevik Revolution, and the Bolsheviks' victory in the subsequent civil war (1918–20) had left the Soviet Union politically and economically isolated, since the establishment of an anti-capitalist regime which proclaimed its intention to destroy the established capitalist system was opposed by the Western Powers. Initially the Bolshevik leaders had hoped that their isolation would be terminated by a world socialist revolution, but contrary to this expectation, in 1919 Bela Kun was defeated in Hungary, in October 1920 the Red Army was defeated in Poland, and the expected German revolution failed to occur. As a result, the Soviet leaders started to pursue a policy of normalizing the Soviet Union's relations with immediately neighbouring states, as well as with the Western Powers, in particular Great Britain. The Polish-Soviet Agreement of November 1920 was followed by the Soviet-Persian Treaty of Friendship on 26 February 1921, a Soviet-Afghan Treaty of Friendship two days later, and a Soviet-Turkish Treaty of Friendship on 16 March 1921.

The process of pragmatic normalization of Soviet foreign policy reached a peak when, on 16 March 1921, the Anglo-Soviet trade agreement was signed,[28] confirming that the Soviet leaders, including Lenin, had come to a firm decision to establish trade relations with the Western Powers, against whom they had thus far agitated in the expectation of a world socialist revolution. In conformity with this decision, in return for trade relations with Britain, the Soviet Union agreed to stop propaganda against the British presence in India and Afghanistan.[29] This confirmed that the Soviet leaders had lost their faith in an imminent world socialist revolution, and were ready to establish their relations with capitalist states on a pragmatic basis. From the mid-1920s the Soviet leadership came to pursue a policy of building socialism in a single country – Soviet Russia.[30]

More or less simultaneously, the Kemalist government at Ankara had also embarked on a policy of normalization of its foreign relations on a pragmatic basis, even while its War of Liberation was still raging. The Treaty of Gümrü of 1920 normalized the Ankara government's relations with Armenia, and more important, secured the Eastern front while fighting continued on the Western front during the War of Liberation, and the Turkish-Soviet agreement of March 1921 ensured Soviet assistance with arms supplies. Following the Treaty of Lausanne of 1923, the Kemalist government concluded a series of friendship agreements with neighbouring states, and in particular with Greece, culminating in the Balkan Pact of 1934, concluded with Greece, Romania and Yugoslavia.

Soviet and Turkish foreign policies thus moved in parallel from a revolutionary to a pragmatic orientation, though admittedly from different starting points: the Bolsheviks, from a policy based on hopes of a world socialist revolution, the Kemalists, from a policy directed towards the narrower goal of Turkey's liberation from foreign domination and occupation.

It is worth asking whether this common shift from a revolutionary to a pragmatic, rationalized foreign policy had any impact on the future *Kadro* writers. Although there is no concrete evidence upon which to base a judgement, it is possible to speculate. In the first place, Aydemir, Tör and Belge started to oppose the decisions of Comintern in 1924, precipitating a split within the TWPSP. In addition to this, the policy of building up socialism in a single country, Soviet Russia, may have influenced the future *Kadro* writers, and, in particular, Aydemir, to consider developing an idea of an independent foreign policy based on national interests. This is the impression given in the autobiographies written by *Kadro* writers, though nothing was mentioned on this subject in *Kadro*. *Kadro*, in fact did not comment on issues of foreign policy, except for condemning Mussolini's policies in the Balkans and Austria.[31] In the second place, the turn to pragmatism in Soviet and Turkish foreign policies may have encouraged the future *Kadro* writers, and, in particular, Aydemir, to adopt a similarly pragmatic conception of foreign economic relations. Aydemir's first book, *Cihan İktisadiyatında Türkiye* [Turkey in the World Economy] (1931) reveals that he was not ideologically opposed to Turkey's entering into trade relations with western capitalist states, though he had been attracted to the anti-imperialist characteristics of the socialist arguments advanced at the Baku Congress. He also now argued that Turkey had to compete with capitalist states.[32] On the issue of foreign capital, in 1931 Aydemir did not state whether he was ideologically against foreign capital investment in Turkey, but he noted that in any case there had been a sharp change in the direction of foreign capital flows in general, and that France, Britain and Belgium, which had been major foreign investors in Turkey before the First World War, had shifted their capital investment away from Turkey to Australia, New Zealand and South America. He predicted that there would be no major foreign capital influx into Turkey.[33] This basic analysis was repeated in the following years in the pages of *Kadro*, though in a somewhat radicalized form: *Kadro* gave the impression that it was against foreign capital in principle, arguing that all foreign capital was self-seeking.[34]

The domestic aspect of the NEP had a more explicit impact on *Kadro*. In its domestic aspect, the NEP was in part a political measure, aimed to prevent peasant resistance to the Soviet regime, which had been provoked by forcible seizure of grain during the civil war. In addition, the NEP was an economic measure, which aimed to accelerate grain production by eliminating certain restrictions on the use of land, private trade and small scale industrial production.[35]

It seems possible that the *Kadro* writers, especially Tökin and Aydemir, who had been in Moscow when the NEP was introduced, were influenced by the domestic aspects of the NEP too. Politically, *Kadro* sought to ensure that peasants in Turkey would side with the state by proposing a substantial land reform, which would dismantle the existing rural structure. However, while the NEP in Soviet Russia had provided only private usage of land which belonged to the state, *Kadro* favoured private land ownership. Economically, too, *Kadro* shared the NEP assumption that peasants would accelerate grain production provided they were given some lands.

In 1928, however, the Soviet government abandoned the NEP policy of providing private use of land to peasants in favour of collectivization: initially 15 per cent of farms were to be collectivized, but in December 1929 it was decided that all lands be collectivized under Kolkhoz administrations. *Kadro* urged the Turkish government to carry out a substantial land reform, but never suggested anything like collectivization.

However, *Kadro* did express considerable interest in the Soviet Union's post-NEP policy of centralized economic planning. In 1928 the Soviet Union started to implement its First-Five Year Industrialization Plan, and like agricultural policy, in 1929 the Soviet government changed the initial plan in favour of a radicalized plan, which embraced light and heavy industries, and in particular electrification, to be developed exclusively by the State.[36]

As early as 1931 the Turkish government had started to contemplate an industrialization plan, and in the following years, it invited Soviet planning experts to Turkey. During this period, thanks to their links to government circles through the 'National Economy and Thrift Society', the future *Kadro* writers obtained information concerning Soviet planning experience, and as noted earlier, Aydemir and, presumably, Tökin, who both knew Russian, helped in translating the Russian planning experts' studies into Turkish for official use. As a result, the *Kadro* writers were probably better equipped than many in Turkey to draw conclusions from the Soviet experience of planning.

Two points are worth making concerning the impact of the Soviet planning experience on *Kadro*. First, *Kadro* urged the government to prepare a comprehensive industrialization plan similar to the Soviet one, to provide for heavy industry and electrification, which the Turkish government's First Five-Year Industrialization Plan did not include. Second, while the Soviet industrialization plan was conducted and implemented exclusively by the state, the Turkish government's plan gave a role to the private sector. *Kadro*, willingly or unwillingly, admitted that some limited parts of industry, which were not vitally important in terms of scale and political implications, could be left to the private sector. It seems probable that *Kadro* would have preferred to see the First Five-Year Industrialization Plan implemented exclusively by the state. In the final analysis, it accepted the reality that some activities like the coal, copper, sugar and glass industries were left to the private sector, and specifically, to the Business Bank [İş Bank].

In addition to studying the Soviet planning experience, the *Kadro* writers also followed planning discussions in western literature, particularly those in German. It appears that the *Kadro* writers scanned literature in other languages, and in 1932 Aydemir noted that in France discussions of the planned economy had started to gain ground;[37] however, no particular French writer or journal was ever referred to by *Kadro*.

This brings us to the fifth of the possible sources of inspiration: the German economists, Friedrich List, Adolf Wagner, and in particular, Werner Sombart. The views of List had exerted a powerful influence on intellectuals of the Unionist period, and the *Kadro* writers were familiar with List's advocacy of protective tariffs as an indispensable element in industrialization. However, by the 1930s protectionism and interventionism had become widespread, and on one occasion Aydemir argued that List's teaching had been superseded by other works and by actual events.[38] It may be suggested that although List's views were known to the *Kadro* writers, they were of no particular importance in the formation of *Kadro*'s arguments. As to Adolf Wagner, Tökin paid attention to his views, in particular, on state socialism, though he was critical of it. Wagner, a leading representative of the theory of state socialism, had argued that the state should own and manage certain sectors of the economy and intervene in the economic process through protective tariffs, taxes and social policies. Tökin argued that the basic idea behind Wagner's theory of state socialism was interventionism, but added that Wagner accepted the primary role of private property, and included the private sector in decision making. Wagner's state intervention in the economy was largely restricted to protective tariffs, income distribution and social insurance, and to a certain degree these had been put into practice by Bismarck, upon whom Wagner, Tökin argued, had exercised some influence.[39] Although Wagner's views exerted some influence on the Turkish intellectuals in general,[40] including the *Kadro* writers, *Kadro*'s arguments do not necessarily accord with that of Wagner's theory of state socialism. First, while Wagner included the private sector into decision-making, *Kadro* argued for the exclusion of the private sector from decision-making. Second, while Wagner did not oppose the private sector's involvement on a large scale in industrial investment, *Kadro* argued that the larger part of industrial investment should be undertaken by the state, leaving only small fields to the private sector. Third, while Wagner supported an alliance between the large landowners, the state bureaucracy, and the working classes, in opposition to the rising industrial, commercial and financial interests, *Kadro* opposed such an alliance. Although *Kadro* did not adopt Wagner's state socialism, it was clearly sympathetic to Wagner's anti-free trade arguments.

Since all the *Kadro* writers, with the exception of Karaosmanoğlu, referred to Werner Sombart, Sombart's views deserve closer examination. Sombart,[41] a younger member of the German historical school, taught economics at the University of Berlin, and some Turkish students, who attended his classes, were attracted by his views in the 1920s and early 1930s.[42] It appears that Sombart's writings in particular were the 'best' available sources for the *Kadro* writers. As Aydemir noted, Sombart was regarded by both Marxists and non-Marxists as a non-Marxist, but well-respected critic of Marx,[43] and the *Kadro* writers must have felt a strong need to distance themselves from Marxist views, since *Kadro* was potentially vulnerable to the charge of being Communist. As early as May 1932, in the fifth issue of *Kadro*, Tör introduced Sombart's views on planning, in an article, 'A study confirming *Kadro*'s view: Die Zukunft des Kapitalismus by Werner Sombart.' In February 1932 Sombart had delivered a talk in Berlin about the future of capitalism, which then appeared as a pamphlet under the title of 'Die Zukunft des Kapitalismus' [The Future of Capitalism]. By extracting from this pamphlet, Tör outlined Sombart's views on planning. Sombart, Tör reported, had said that a plan should have three essential features: it should be comprehensive, embracing every aspect of the economy; it should be prepared and supervised by a central organ, the state; and it should be in conformity with each national economy.[44]

The view of Sombart as simply a non-Marxist critic of Marx did not last long: soon after Hitler came to power in 1933, Sombart changed his views on a number of issues, such as the role of Jews in economic history. In his pre-First World War book *The Jews and Modern Capitalism*[45] he had viewed Jews as a positive factor in economic history; however, in his book *A New Social Philosophy* (July 1934),[46] he clearly saw Jews as an enemy, and this book was regarded by many as an apology for Hitler, though official Nazis never accepted him as their ideologue or interpreter.[47] Indeed, as Jürgen Kuczynski puts it, 'Sombart had no "school", just as he himself had never, for any length of time, belonged to any "school".'[48]

How far *Kadro* was aware of Sombart's change of views is not clear, but in 1934, when Aydemir reviewed Tökin's book *Türkiye Köy İktisadiyatı* [Turkey's Rural Economy], Aydemir noted that Tökin's approach was similar to that of Sombart in respect of their application of statistics and method in general.[49] This may suggest that the *Kadro* writers were not aware that Sombart had changed his views, for otherwise *Kadro* would either have distanced itself from Sombart, because *Kadro* opposed the Nazis' racism and imperialism, or it would have simply stopped mentioning Sombart. In any case, some five months after the publication of Sombart's book, *A New Social Philosophy* (July 1934), *Kadro* was forced to cease publication as the franchise holder, Karaosmanoğlu, was appointed ambassador abroad. As a result, there is no evidence by which to judge *Kadro*'s reaction to Sombart's later writings.

Despite the enthusiastic reception which *Kadro* accorded to Sombart's

pamphlet 'Die Zukunft des Kapitalismus', it seems doubtful whether
Sombart influenced the *Kadro* writers' views on planning to any significant
degree. Sombart himself wrote relatively little on the topic,[50] and as noted
above, the *Kadro* writers had an alternative source of information and ideas
in the Soviet experience of planning. Rather, it appears that Sombart's major
influence on *Kadro* came through his critical view of free trade and on the
chronology of the development of capitalism. As pointed by Nussbaum,
Sombart was highly critical of laissez-faire.[51] Sombart's critical views on
free trade policy and his exposition of economic history were repeatedly
mentioned in the pages of *Kadro*, though not always properly
acknowledged. Sombart had divided the development of capitalism into
three stages: early capitalism, from about the fifteenth to the middle of the
eighteenth century; high capitalism, from 1760 to 1914; and late capitalism,
beginning with the First World War. According to Sombart, the driving
forces during the first period of capitalism were noblemen, adventurers,
merchants, artisans and the Jews.[52] During the period of high capitalism,
Sombart argued, capitalist entrepreneurs were the driving force; the
necessary men with the spirit of enterprise had developed, and acquired the
capital necessary to introduce the new modes of industrial organizations; the
necessary market had developed, especially in the great military
organizations and the luxury-demanding town population; and industrial
productions had developed into the factories, with its own labour force; the
supply of necessary materials and means of production, and outlets to
markets were assured by the development of transportation and of
commercial organization, and the state granted many capitalists a privileged
position, especially in industry. All these factors transformed handicraft
production system into modern capitalist production.[53] The termination of
the period of high capitalism, Sombart asserted, was 1914. As pointed by
Nussbaum, Sombart discussed late capitalism only briefly.[54]

    Kadro followed Sombart's chronology of the development of capitalism,
and repeated some of Sombart's points, though in a different context: the
development of colonies. With respect to imperialism, unlike Sombart,
Kadro argued that the late capitalism was characterized by economic and
political rivalries between imperialist powers, a clear, though
unacknowledged, reflection of the Leninist view. It may be suggested that
Kadro borrowed some ideas from Sombart but not as a whole, rather it
referred to Sombart to distance itself from Marxism, thereby bypassing the
accusation of being a Communist publication.

    Having reviewed the putative sources of *Kadro*'s ideological inspiration, it
would be appropriate to examine *Kadro*'s own views on capitalism,
socialism and Fascism. *Kadro* argued that capitalism had historically

developed in Europe: from the fifteenth century onwards, European powers had looted the natives in America, and transferred raw materials and slaves from Asia and Africa to Europe. This was, *Kadro* suggested, initial capitalist accumulation, which had taken place at the expense of the colonies.[55] Aydemir noted that Marx defined capitalism in terms of the relations between a class of free wage labourers and a class of capitalists,[56] but this, according to Aydemir, was only part of the problem of the unequal distribution of income, where the share of the capitalist class became larger and larger. The origins and rapid development of capitalism in Europe, Aydemir and other *Kadro* writers noted, might be explained by the exploitation of colonies.[57] On this matter Aydemir unjustifiably attacked Marxism, arguing that Marx had neglected the fact that capitalism needed subordinate hinterland-colonies.[58] Up to the industrial revolution, the *Kadro* writers suggested, capitalism's external relations were mediated through merchant capital, and once the industrial revolution gained momentum in the eighteenth century, giving rise to technological progress as well as to increasing specialization and intensity of production on a large scale, the European Powers started to produce large amounts of industrial goods, which they exported to colonies and semi-colonies in Asia and Africa, killing off indigenous small artisan production.[59] To use more recent terminology, *Kadro* held that underdevelopment in colonies and semi-colonies was caused primarily by the development of capitalism in Europe.

Aydemir noted that capitalism in Europe had given rise to two important developments, the first of which was growing antagonism between the bourgeoisie and the proletariat. This was, Aydemir maintained, a European phenomenon, and not yet an Asian problem. He argued that one could not talk of an Asian working class in a proletarian sense, because although the Pariahs (Indian poor) and Coolies (Chinese worker) were poor, they could not be properly regarded as a proletariat because they were not organized in any way.[60] Secondly, Aydemir noted that the development of capitalism in Europe gave rise to two opposing groups of countries: industrialized metropolitan, and non-industrialized colonial and semi-colonial countries.[61]

Before pursuing this last point it would be appropriate to examine *Kadro*'s critiques of socialism and Fascism. It was the capitalist system, Aydemir noted, that created the class struggle, and both socialism and Fascism derived from capitalism. However, Aydemir argued that Marx's division between an exploited working class and an exploiting bourgeoisie was a concept which belonged to nineteenth-century Europe. Marxism, Aydemir noted, was unable to explain the qualitative differences between Western industrialized and Asian non-industrialized countries, and in the twentieth century the dominant and primary dichotomy was between the industrialized and non-industrialized countries.[62]

The argument that Turkey, and Asian countries in general, had not yet industrialized, and that Turkish and Asian working classes were consequently still in their infancies, Aydemir explained, was one of the reasons for *Kadro*'s rejection of socialism.[63] More important, Aydemir argued, although socialism asserted equality among working classes and strove to unify the working classes of world, socialist thinkers overlooked the fact that the working classes of industrialized Europe and those of Asia were different in character. Aydemir argued that even if there had been a world socialist revolution, socialism would have been unable to overcome the qualitative differences between working classes in industrialized Europe and non-industrialized Asia and Africa; for even the only socialist example, the Soviet Union, did not ensure equality for its own working classes. In the final analysis, Aydemir asserted, the working classes of Europe would not give up the surplus income which industrialized Europe received from Asia and Africa. *Kadro* concluded that socialism would not resolve the qualitative differences between industrialized Europe and non-industrialized Asia and Africa.[64]

As to Fascism, in 1932 Belge suggested that it was a movement peculiar to a semi-capitalist structure, and that Fascism in Italy was a movement to save semi-capitalist Italy from capitalism's class conflict by means of corporations.[65] In 1933 this line of analysis shifted, and Aydemir and Tökin argued that Fascism in Italy, and Nazism in Germany, both strove to consolidate the interests of the industrial bourgeoisie. Tör and Belge then followed this line of analysis.[66] No matter that Mussolini in Italy and Hitler in Germany appealed to and received support from the man in the street, Aydemir claimed, they were the representatives of the industrial bourgeoisie. In 1933 and 1934 *Kadro* repeatedly stressed that Fascism was a movement to ease the problem of the class struggle and internal anarchy by means of corporations at the expense of the working classes.[67] In addition, Aydemir and Tökin warned that Fascism meant imperialism, since the Italian Fascists sought to gain colonies in order to gain an outlet for Italy's surplus population, while Nazism in Germany was racist and asserted that the white races, and in particular, the Germanic race, were superior to other races.[68] From 1933 onwards, all *Kadro* writers consistently rejected Fascism and Nazism.

This condemnation of Fascism might be viewed as a reflection of the Turkish government's suspicion of Mussolini's ambitions in Anatolia and in the Balkans, ambitions which also drew critical comment from *Kadro*.[69] In so far as Italian Fascism is concerned, this view may be correct, but it cannot explain *Kadro*'s hostility to Nazi Germany. In mid-1933 the Turkish government had concluded an important bilateral clearing agreement with Germany, which was then supplemented by a compensation agreement, and

in 1933 and 1934 Germany, under the leadership of Hitler, did not constitute
any particular threat to Turkey. However, in 1933 and 1934 *Kadro* opposed
the Nazis in Germany with the same vigour with which it opposed Italian
Fascism. It appears that in 1933 Aydemir and Tökin examined Italian
Fascist labour law, and Hitler's speeches of 1933, and then redefined
Kadro's line on Fascism.[70]

In developing its arguments on the subject of socialism and Fascism,
Kadro touched on such important points as the qualitative differences
between the working classes of industrialized and non-industrialized
countries, and the class character of Fascism and Nazism. However, in
analysing Fascism and socialism, *Kadro*'s primary aim, it appears, was to
distinguish itself from Fascism and socialism, for *Kadro* was already being
accused of being 'social Fascist', or 'Communist'.[71] Although *Kadro* did not
reveal who made such accusations it may be speculated that the illegal
'Communist Party', ex-friends of the *Kadro* writers, might have accused
Kadro of being 'social Fascist'. As to the charge of 'Communism', it may
be suggested that 'liberals', and, in particular, Mahmut Soydan, an MP and
Director General of the İş Bank, were responsible. Writing in the daily
newspaper *Milliyet* in 1933, Soydan accused *Kadro* of being a pro-
Comintern publication.[72]

Leaving such rhetoric aside, *Kadro* was eclectic in its sources of
inspiration, and it would be wrong to claim dogmatically that *Kadro* was
uninfluenced by socialism and Fascism. The *Kadro* writers were familiar
with Marxism, and Aydemir and Tökin in particular were influenced by
Lenin's views and the experiences of Soviet Union's NEP and planned
economy. As to the question of Fascist influence, it is true that *Kadro*
opposed Fascism's imperialism, racism, and presumed links with the
industrial bourgeoisie. Nevertheless, *Kadro* and Fascism shared a common
authoritarianism and striving for the creation of an organically unified
nation. It is true that authoritarianism was widespread in the 1930s.
However, *Kadro* adopted authoritarianism as a principle, dismissing
parliamentary democracy as internal anarchy, and advocating single-party
government.[73] As to the common goal of an organically unified nation, it is
true that Aydemir drew a distinction between *Kadro* and Fascism, arguing
that one of the aims of Fascism was to unite populations in the cause of
creating an organic united society, and that while this was also *Kadro*'s aim,
Fascism aimed to create a unified society in the interests of bourgeoisie,
while *Kadro*'s aim was to create a unified society embracing the whole
nation, and based on the interests of the nation. The difference, Aydemir and
Tökin noted, was that while Fascism wanted to achieve the organic united
society at the expense of the working class, *Kadro* did not prefer one class
over another, and *Kadro*'s striving for the creation of an organic unified

society aimed to prevent the emergence of any dominant class. This was what *Kadro* called the originality of *Kadro*.[74] Nevertheless, the call for greater unity in society was common to almost all Fascist parties in the 1930s,[75] as the *Kadro* writers were themselves aware: in addition to scanning the Italian Fascist labour law and the German Nazis' speeches, Belge examined the British Fascist movement, the British Union of Fascists (the BUF), led by Mosley.[76] Interestingly, in each case, the *Kadro* writers identified the Fascist parties as movements desiring greater unity in society, though *Kadro* also emphasized the imperialism and class character of these parties, seeing in these latter characteristics the essential difference between Fascism and *Kadro*'s own vision of an organically unified society.

All in all, it may be suggested that *Kadro* was influenced by the current ideologies at the time, such as socialism and Fascism. However, this does not mean that *Kadro* advocated Fascism. The *Kadro* movement cannot possibly be classified as a Fascist movement; it not only rejected Fascism for being imperialistic and racist, but also for a reason that the arguments of Fascism and *Kadro* were different except for the fact that both were authoritarian.[77] As to the argument for the creation of an organically unified nation, which might have been viewed as a reference to Fascism, *Kadro* meant mobilization of people for political independence and an appeal for economic development, rather than a reference to the Fascist arguments that class antagonism must be harmonized, in the case of Italian Fascism, and rejection of class antagonism in the case of German Nazism. Thus, it may be suggested that the connotation of an organically unified nation in *Kadro* and in Fascism may be put in different contexts.

Fundamental to *Kadro*'s view of the international system was the dichotomy between industrialized and non-industrialized countries. *Kadro* acknowledged that exploitation of the European working classes had contributed to capital accumulation in Europe, but explicitly claimed that the exploitation of colonies had contributed more. *Kadro* assumed that the European Powers would want to keep their colonies, without which they could not survive as Imperialist Powers.[78]

Clearly, *Kadro* was concerned to dismantle the existing international status quo, and believed that the means to this end lay in 'national liberation movements'. *Kadro* was confident that such movements would eventually drive the imperialists out of their colonies, and thereby, cut off the imperialists' raw material sources, as well as their colonial markets.[79] This was politically forthright, but failed to answer the economic problem posed by the fact that colonies needed western industrial products, whether intermediate or capital goods, in order to establish their industries. This is one of the weakest points of the *Kadro* movement.

Kadro's argument was patriotic rather than socialist in character. Although

Aydemir had been attracted by the anti-imperialist features of socialist arguments since the Baku Congress of 1920, *Kadro* did not emphasize any form of solidarity between those countries which had experienced or were likely to experience wars of liberation. *Kadro* simply assumed that the period following the First World War was the age of national liberation movements, and rather than assert anti-imperialist solidarity it placed its faith in the inherent rivalries between capitalist countries.[80] Another weak point of *Kadro* was on this issue; *Kadro* never considered that imperialist powers could rationalize their rivalries. The *Kadro* writers noted that the relations between the imperialists (the terms imperialist, metropolitan, capitalist and industrialized countries were applied interchangeably) were not smooth: the increasing large-scale intensity of production, and the formation of huge blocs of capital, organized in a hierarchical way by financial groups, had resulted in competition among imperialist powers, and political rivalry between financial groups would result in military confrontation. The First World War, in *Kadro*'s view, had broken out as a result of competition between Britain and France on the one hand, and the growing industrial power of Germany on the other; the First World War was the zenith of inherent competition between the imperialist powers. However, *Kadro* warned that the First World War had not solved the problem: pre-War problems of competition between Imperialist Powers continued. Giving Italy as an example, *Kadro* argued that the Italian government felt cheated, because Italy had not obtained what she had been promised in return for entering the War on the side of the Allied powers. In similar fashion, *Kadro* noted that Germany had been deprived of its industrial raw materials as a result of the French occupation of the Ruhr region, and that Germany lacked colonies, the main reason why she had entered the First World War.[81]

Kadro insisted that conflicts between capitalist states were ineradicable, dismissing the League of Nations, for example, as no more than an instrument of the French and British governments.[82] In a similar fashion, *Kadro* predicted that the attempt to construct a 'European Directory', through the 'Four Power Pact', signed in June 1933 between Britain, Italy, Germany and France, was bound to fail, because the French government would not ratify it, a further manifestation of the inherent rivalry between the European Powers. *Kadro* drew an optimistic conclusion: imperialism was bound to fall a victim to those conflicts because it contained within itself the germs of conflicts of interest.[83] In this respect, evidently, *Kadro* was essentialist and determinist.

It is necessary to examine *Kadro*'s interpretation of historical materialism, which from start to finish *Kadro* adopted as its 'method'. In explaining the economic and social development of humanity, *Kadro*, and in particular Aydemir and Tökin, followed the Marxist sequence of stages from a primitive communal society, where there was no state, followed by a feudal society in which the State emerged, landowners being dominant. But, when it came to the capitalist stage, the *Kadro* writers drew a distinction between Europe and Asia. Aydemir noted that in Europe feudal society had been followed by the capitalist stage, but that in Asia and Africa capitalism had not yet been developed. To explain the sequence of stages, Aydemir referred to the 'fundamental laws of social development' of historical materialism: relationships between the forces of production and the relations of production. There were, Aydemir noted, two principal factors which determined social development. One was the development of the forces of production, which arose from man's striving to master nature, and was the root cause of all social development. The second was the relations of production; that was, relations between people.[84]

Aydemir tried to distinguish historical materialism from dialectical materialism. Aydemir noted that the dialectical materialism of Marx could be divided into five principal points.

1. Everything is in a state of continuous movement and change.

2. The Law of the transformation of quantitative into qualitative changes.

3. Qualitative changes happen with relative suddenness- by a leap.

4. Development takes place through the unity and struggle of opposites.

5. Everything is connected to, dependent on and determined by everything else. Hence nothing can be understood taken by itself, in isolation, but must always be understood in its inseparable connection with other things, and as conditioned by them. ... Conflict is the mother of all happenings. Historical necessity and class struggle in Marxist theory flow from this dialectical understanding.[85]

Aydemir noted that Marx had applied dialectical materialism to explain capitalist development in Europe, and he did not disagree with this.[86] However, Aydemir distinguished historical materialism from dialectical materialism, suggesting that origins of the former might go as far back as the fifteenth and sixteenth centuries, and might be related to Machiavelli's views. To Aydemir, the essence of historical materialism was the view that change and development of the productive forces led to change in men's socio-economic relations. Aydemir added that historical materialism was not an absolute abstract philosophical system, but a method, which could guide one in understanding things so as to change them.[87]

Clearly, some distancing from Marx's views was essential if the *Kadro* writers were to justify their primary dichotomy between the metropole and the colonies, and their assertion that the development paths of European and Afro-Asian countries had diverged at the capitalist stage. The point is illustrated by Aydemir's attempt to apply historical materialism to Turkey. Historical materialism, he asserted, necessarily led one to embrace the ideological standpoint of the 'Turkish National Liberation Movement', but in commenting on the Kemalist regime he side-stepped the point that historical materialism saw a necessarily causal relationship between the forces of production and the relations of production. Instead, he noted that the forces of production were still primitive in Turkey, but could be developed through technological innovation.[88] Evidently, Aydemir sensed that strict adherence to the historical materialist doctrine that the forces of production determined the relations of production might oblige him to confront the issue of the class character of the Kemalist regime. As Gülalp and Sadıq indicate in general terms,[89] Aydemir was selective in applying historical materialism to the Turkish revolution. Like Tökin, Aydemir drew a tacit distinction between the class structure of Turkey as a whole, and the class character of the Kemalist regime. The latter issue was simply avoided, but the former was not. Aydemir never regarded Turkey as a classless society, though he refrained from detailed discussion of Turkey's class structure, preferring to shift his emphasis from class analysis to the international dichotomy between industrialized and non-industrialized countries,[90] stressing that capitalism had developed in Europe, and that Asia and Africa were subordinate to Europe.[91]

Unlike Aydemir, Tökin did comment on Turkey's class structure, and did not distinguish historical materialism from dialectical materialism. He claimed that he followed dialectical materialism and, insofar as Europe was concerned, he endorsed the Marxist argument that capitalism would lead to socialism. With respect to Turkey, however, he did not endorse socialism as an option, possibly because he believed the proletariat was too small: he noted that according to the 1927 census there were only 55,000 workers in Turkey, and half of them were seasonal workers. Like Aydemir, Tökin did not comment on the class character of the Kemalist regime, but he clearly identified social classes in Turkey. He divided them into two categories: urban and rural. He divided the urban classes into medium and small shopkeepers, who employed their own family members, and merchants. The rural class structure he detailed as follows:

1. Big landowners [Beyler ve toprak ağaları],

2. Rural entrepreneurs [Köylü müteşebbisler],

3. Small landowning farmers [Küçük mülkiyet sahibi müstahsiller],

4. Share-croppers [Ortakçılar ve marabacılar],

5. Farm workers [Köy amelesi].

6. Landless peasants and slaves [Topraksız köylüler ve toprak köleleri].[92]

Such an analysis bore obvious signs of Marxist influence, and might appear to contradict *Kadro*'s commitment to a classless society. As Tökin himself admitted:

> Are we not contradicting ourselves in arguing, on the one hand, that the Turkish nation is not divided into conflicting classes and on the other hand, identifying social classes in Turkey? ... Is the Turkish society sui generis? ... [Turkey] cannot possibly be regarded as a classless nation. Such an understanding contradicts the reality, because in every corner of the country groups of people, who are differentiated according to their participation in, and their incomes from, the economy, can be identified.[93]

In the final analysis, however, Tökin's arguments did not contradict the general view of *Kadro*: Tökin, like Aydemir, argued that a pre-capitalist structure was prevalent in Turkey. His concern, shared by other *Kadro* writers, was precisely how to avoid the establishment of a capitalist class structure, which *Kadro* repeatedly characterized as not good for Turkey.[94]

As to the other regular writers, Karaosmanoğlu did not comment much about ideological matters, though he wrote approvingly of the need for disciplined youth and intellectuals, and showed a bent towards authoritarianism. Similarly, it appears that Tör and Belge were not deeply concerned about the class structure of Turkey, though Tör made some bold claims, such as that history had falsified Marx, and that Turkey would achieve a classless society without experiencing a capitalist stage or a proletarian dictatorship.[95]

From start to finish, the *Kadro* writers urged that a new set of economic policies, which they variously called 'étatism', 'the étatism of the liberation movement' or 'Turkish étatism', were needed. The details of such policies are very long to summarize here, but for present purposes, it suffices to note that the *Kadro* writers, relying upon their own peculiar interpretation of historical materialism, believed that these policies would necessarily produce new relations of production, and that during this process, the State could play a leading role in preventing the emergence of capitalist socio-economic relations.

As for nationalism, *Kadro* never examined it as an ideology, except on two occasions; first, when he criticized Gökalp's definition of nationalism, Aydemir argued:

Ziya Gökalp went some way insofar as he included in his definition of nation social phenomena, such as race, geography, religion, will and common culture, and thus his definition makes sense in comparison with many others, which take into account only one of these elements. But, Gökalp's definition of the nation falls short of explaining to-day's nations. ... to-day's nations are products of technical development, and the utmost national unity can only be found among technologically developed countries. ... to-day's nations are determined by participation in the economy.[96]

Aydemir apparently regarded economic integration as one of fundamental factors in defining a nation. Second, when Aydemir attacked Marxism he argued that Marxist attitudes towards the nation and nationalism were wrong. Marxism not only overlooked the reality of nationhood, Aydemir argued, but also rejected nationalism for being a camouflaged bourgeois class characteristic. Against this, Aydemir asserted that the nation was a reality, and that national liberation movements were the only thing which could stand up against imperialism.[97] It is reasonable to assume that the *Kadro* writers were aware that nationalism was not a monolithic ideology, but it appears that *Kadro*, by rejecting racism and imperialism, was able to reconcile itself to a form of nationalism, or, in a more suitable term, patriotism. Here again, *Kadro* borrowed something from nationalism but did not adopt it totally.

Throughout its publication, *Kadro* labelled itself as an advocate of 'national liberation movements', and of the 'Turkish national liberation movement'. In the journal's second year, in addition to these terms, the *Kadro* writers spoke of 'Turkish nationalism',[98] and in its third year, and only in the last issue of *Kadro*, Aydemir asserted that the ideology of *Kadro* was 'social nationalism'.[99] By employing the term 'national liberation movements', *Kadro* appeared to put emphasis on the international aspect of wars of liberation, arguing that colonies and semi-colonies, on a world scale, had entered an era when they would obtain their independence. By the terms 'Turkish national liberation movement' and 'Turkish nationalism', *Kadro* referred to the Turkish War of Liberation and subsequent political and social reforms. *Kadro* regarded the Turkish national liberation movement as the first of its kind, and a precedent for other national liberation movements.

The term 'social nationalism', which Aydemir introduced only in the last issue of *Kadro*, deserves closer examination. To explain the term, Aydemir proposed the following equation: the establishment of a classless and privilegeless nation=social nationalism [İmtiyazsız, sınıfsız bir millet kuruluşu=sosyal milliyetçilik].[100] Though the term 'social nationalism' appears to resemble 'national socialism', it is clear that *Kadro* meant something else. In his article, entitled 'The Victory of Social Nationalism', Aydemir explained the term in some detail:

> If there had not been readily applied translated concepts, the Turkish intellectuals would have been braver in their attempt and their horizons would have been wider to understand the meaning of social nationalism. But, to-day there are some readily applied words, which are frustrating the Turkish intellectuals and revolutionaries in their endeavours. For instance, for some people, discipline in the establishment of the national economy and the plan simply means something which belongs only to socialism. Many suppose that if a regime is national there has to be class struggle. In a similar fashion, some think a national regime could only occur in a democracy, and according to them democracy could only be found in France and Belgium. If these words had not penetrated into their mind, they would have been freer to develop their own judgement.
>
> Words like socialism, communism and fascism, which are thought to have been disconnected by huge walls, are the major obstacles for any endeavour to develop an ideology. In fact, each regime can borrow something from the others without changing its own substance. For instance, a republic is common to socialism and liberal democracy. While there can be no comparison between a planned economy and a liberal economy, socialism and the national liberation movement can be put in the same category insofar as planning is concerned. But this does not necessarily mean changing their substances. For example, socialism and communism refer to class dictatorship, the dictatorship of the proletariat, and by the same token, liberal democracy is a class dictatorship. However, both liberal class dictatorship and proletarian dictatorship are rejected in the national liberation movement; that is what the difference is, and therefore the national liberation movement differs from the others. In other words, in the national liberation movement, the national economic interests are the interest of whole nation and that is what social nationalism is about.
>
> As a national liberation movement, what is the Turkish revolution? Is it a socialism? Is it a liberal democracy?
>
> Doubtless, in the past there has been national liberation in the forms of liberal democracy and socialism. For instance, after the war of liberation in America, after 1830 in Greece, after 1917 in Poland

and Czechoslovakia, national liberation movements resulted in the establishment of liberal bourgeois capitalism. Likewise, after 1917 in the Ukraine, Georgia, and some parts of China, national liberation movements turned to the establishment of socialist regimes. In India and the other parts of China, national liberation movements, it may be said, turned towards the establishment of liberal capitalism.

But, the reasons and conditions for the establishment of liberal capitalism and socialist regimes in the above-noted countries were different from the reasons which led to the establishment of the Turkish liberation movement.

Firstly, the American and Greek liberation movements occurred during the early period of capitalism. In the cases of Poland and Czechoslovakia, national regimes were led by the liberal bourgeoisie, who had already established liberal capitalism when they had been colonized. In the Ukraine and Georgia, the character of regimes was shaped and determined by geography and political conditions. In India and China, national liberation has not achieved political victory, and in fact, those liberal capital accumulations are made with the help of foreigners and in the form of semi-colonies. If India and China achieve their political and military victory in the future, it is highly probable that they may pursue an étatist development strategy similar to the Turkish one.

Consequently, we have to interpret the Turkish national liberation movement in its historic conditions.

The ideological components of social nationalism are developing:

The contents of the Turkish constitution, which had been written under the influence of the principles of French revolution, have been reinterpreted in accordance with the speeches of the leaders [şefler] of the revolution and the research of the party [the RPP]. In addition to the constitution, there has appeared a large amount of literature concerning social reforms and ideological matters. In this large amount of literature, it can be seen that our national regime is totally different from the French revolution; the differences are, for instance, economic and cultural étatism, rejection of parliamentary democracy, and anti-colonialism etc. This is what the Turkish revolution is about and thereby it is an original movement...

Here, let us mention the economic achievements of the Turkish revolution:

The State took control of national credits. ... Today we have got a national credit network. ... The State controls credit facilities, and railways, ports, mining, industry, import and export are being developed by national credits and the majority of the credits for these investments, which used to belong to foreigners during the Ottoman Empire, belong to the State. ... Today étatism is the policy of Turkey and advanced technology is introduced by the State. ... The State prepared and put into practice the First Five Year Industrialization Plan, ... and this plan embraced industries such as cotton, iron, coal, copper, paper, porcelain, chemicals, glass and etc. ... The State is the owner and undertaker of these industries, except for glass and coal, which were left to the private sector. ..... If this industrialization plan is followed by a second Five Year Industrialization plan, the capacity for industrial production will increase and many problems will be solved....

The perspective of social nationalism: although much has been achieved, it is necessary to say that land reform and rural transformation have not yet been achieved, and now the achievement of these are the perspective of social nationalism. ... Everything is for the revolution.[101]

Evidently, by the term social nationalism, Aydemir meant the rejection of class dictatorship, both bourgeoisie and proletariat. He also expressed his desire for the continuation and deepening of socio-economic reforms. Needless to say that although the term social nationalism may seem to reflect national socialism or Fascism, here the term as applied by Aydemir, it must be stressed, is different and has nothing to do with Fascism. By the term social nationalism, it may be suggested, he referred to an integrated national economy.

Finally, it is appropriate to examine *Kadro*'s interpretation of the cadre. As noted on the first page of its first issue, *Kadro* had spoken of a 'conscious minority', the cadre, which would ensure the implementation of *Kadro*'s proposals. It must be stressed that *Kadro* always conceded that the general principles of reform had been defined by the leader [*şef*], to whom *Kadro* remained loyal, and although *Kadro* did not state the name of the leader, there can be no question that it referred to Mustafa Kemal Atatürk.

The cadre, *Kadro* argued, was under a moral obligation to evaluate the principles of the reform defined by the leader (Atatürk), to identify the economic and social problems of the nation, and to find solutions for them. As noted in *Kadro* journal, this was the duty as well as the ideal of the cadre:

The ideal can be achieved under the guidance, as well as the administration of, the devoted, disciplined cadre, which is indifferent to class or individual interests. Such a cadre, which has discerned the principles of the reform and adopted them as moral values, and a reform generation, are needed for the sake of the success of the reform.[102]

But who were the members of this cadre? *Kadro* appears to have had in mind a group of bureaucrat-intellectuals, though *Kadro* never specified who they were. Did *Kadro* refer to certain quarters in the RPP? *Kadro* never expressed itself clearly on this matter, but it gave the impression that *Kadro* saw itself among the cadre. After all, it had appointed itself to develop a framework in which to interpret the Turkish revolution, as well as expressing its views on economic development. Beyond this, however, there is no evidence to show exactly whom *Kadro* saw as the cadre.

It is conceivable that the *Kadro* writers, and Aydemir in particular, may have had in mind the creation of a party or a league, composed of like-minded bureaucrat-intellectuals. But it must be stressed that there is no hard evidence to prove it. It is possible that in 1931 Aydemir may have hoped that Atatürk might repeat the experiment, already tried in the case of the Free Republican Party, of setting up another political party, but this time one more radical than the Republican Peoples' Party under İnönü. If this was Aydemir's calculation, then he may have seen a role for himself and for *Kadro* in the new party. But even if Aydemir had contemplated such a thing, by late 1933 he must have realized that such a change of policy by Atatürk was no longer an option, since Atatürk had shown a clear tilt towards the Business Bank group by appointing Celal Bayar as the Minister for the Economy who had been Director General of the Business Bank. In sum, the question of the *Kadro* writers' personal political ambitions, if any, remains entirely obscure.

The key characteristics of the ideology of *Kadro* were: first, *Kadro* held that the twentieth century was the age of national liberation movements, in which all colonies and semi-colonies would inevitably achieve their political independence, destroying the capitalist-imperialist status quo. However, this would not necessarily liquidate the dichotomy between industrialized and non-industrialized countries, and thus, *Kadro* emphasized, political independence must be followed by economic independence. Second, *Kadro* rejected capitalism, socialism and Fascism, on the grounds that capitalism caused the underdevelopment in colonies and semi-colonies, in the interests of the development of capitalism in Europe as well as creating class-based society; that socialism implied a dictatorship of the proletariat; and that Fascism was a dictatorship of the bourgeoisie. It may be stated that *Kadro* was eclectic in its sources of ideological inspiration, and that while it borrowed ideas extensively, it did not take over any ideology or world-view in its entirety. *Kadro* borrowed socialism's anti-imperialist analyses, Fascism's authoritarianism, and Marxism's historical materialism. Third, *Kadro* attempted to formulate an ideological framework

116   TURKEY BEFORE AND AFTER ATATÜRK

in which to interpret the Turkish revolution in a historical context. *Kadro*
specifically attributed a responsibility to the cadre, bureaucrat-intellectuals
in formulation of ideological framework. *Kadro* proposed that the state, led
by the cadre, should be given both political and economic powers as
opposed to social classes and interests groups, who were self-seeking.
All in all, ideologically, the *Kadro* movement may well be defined as an
example of an influential patriotic leftist movement in Turkey and in world
history, since it was against extension of the influences of the bourgeoisie
and of the interest groups to the state, and advocated establishment of an
autonomous state above social classes. Indeed, this was one of the most
important weaknesses of *Kadro*'s assumption. Even if the state was run by
a revolutionary leadership under the influence and leadership of the cadre,
this would not necessarily mean that the state would be free of influences of
classes, since the cadre might have turned into a self-seeking bureaucratic
class. For a matter of fact, the Soviet Union and many East-Central
European states had such experiences in recent history.

NOTES

1. Except that Aydemir knew Akçura in person and mentions that he paid several visits to
   Akçura in Ankara. Şevket Süreyya Aydemir, *Suyu Arayan Adam*, 8.Baskı (İstanbul, 1987),
   passim. However, Aydemir does not mention when this occurred and what they talked
   about.
2. For Akçura's view, see Yusuf Akçura, 'Türk Milliyetçiliğinin İktisadi Menşelerine Dair' in
   Siyaset ve İktisat Hakkında Bir Kaç Hitabe ve Makale (İstanbul, 1340/1924), pp.141–68),
   for *Kadro*'s view on the issue see *Kadro*, Vol.1, No.1 (1932), pp.21–27; *Kadro*, Vol.1, No.5
   (1932), pp.19–24.
3. *Kadro*, Vol.1, No.2 (1932), pp.29–40.
4. *Kadro*, Vol.2, No.15 (1933), pp.13–19; *Kadro*, Vol.2, No.21 (1933), p.19; *Kadro*, Vol.2,
   No.15 (1933), pp.25–27.
5. Ziya Gökalp, *Türkçülüğün Esasları* (Ankara, 1923). It has been translated into English:
   Ziya Gökalp, *The Principles of Turkism*, translated from the Turkish and annotated by
   Robert Devereux (Leiden: E. J. Brill, 1968).
6. *Kadro*, Vol.1, No.2 (1932), pp.29–40.
7. Ibid., pp.5–8.
8. İlhan Tekeli and Gencay Şaylan, 'Türkiye'de Halkçılık İdeolojisinin Evrimi', *Toplum ve
   Bilim*, Yaz-Güz 1978, 6–7, pp.44–110; Mohammad Sadıq, 'The *Kadro* Movement in
   Turkey', *International Studies*, Vol.2, No.4 (1986), pp.329–30.
9. *Kadro*, Vol.1, No.4 (1932), pp.3–4; *Kadro*, Vol.2, No.19 (1933), p.10. Aydemir did not
   mention in *Kadro* from where he learned dialectical materialism and historical materialism.
   However, he noted in his book *Suyu Arayan Adam*, p.338 that he studied historical
   materialism when he was a student at the KUTV.
10. In particular Henri Bergson's world-view, which was advocated by 'liberals' such as
    Hüseyin Cahit Yalçın, was regarded as idealism. See, *Kadro*, Vol.1, No.11 (1932), pp.43–7;
    Kadro, Vol.2, No.13, 1933 pp.42–3; *Kadro*, Vol.3, No.29 (1934), s. 45.
11. *Kadro*, Vol.3, No.26 (1934), p.24.
12. For a detailed study on the education of the *Kadro* writers, see Türkeş, op.cit., chapter 3.
13. In a footnote Aydemir mentions Lenin's work *Theses on the National and Colonial*

THE IDEOLOGY OF THE *KADRO* MOVEMENT 117

Question and Karl Kautsky's, Nationalism and Internationalism. See *Kadro*, Vol.2, No.21 (1933), pp.8–10.

14. V. I. Lenin, *Imperialism, The Highest Stage of Capitalism*, Fifth Printing (Peking, 1975).
15. *Kadro*, Vol..2, No.19 (1933), p.12.
16. Merdan Yanardağ, *Türk Siyasal Yaşamında Kadro Hareketi* (İstanbul, 1988), pp.168–185; Ayşe Trak, 'Development Literature and Writers from Underdeveloped Countries: The Case of Turkey', *Current Anthropology*, Vol.26, No.1 (February, 1985), p.94; Gülalp used a general term 'discussions in the Third International', Haldun Gülalp, 'Nationalism, Statism and the Turkish Revolution: An Early 'Dependency' Theory', *Review of Middle Eastern Studies*, Vol.4 (1985), p.81; Eyüp Özveren, 'The Intellectual Legacy of the Kadro Movement in Retrospect', *METU Development Studies*, Vol.23, No.4 (1996), p.571.
17. See Ertan's interview with Tökin, F. Temuçin Ertan, *Kadrocular ve Kadro Hareketi*, Doktora Tezi (Hacettepe Üniversitesi, Atatürk İlkeleri ve İnkilap Tarihi Enstitüsü, 1992), Ekler, pp.1–13.
18. See A. Bennigsen and C.L. Quelquejay, *Islam in the Soviet Union*, Translated by E. Wheeler and Hubert Evans (London, 1967), pp.57, 110.
19. Aydemir, *Suyu Arayan Adam*, p.216.
20. Şevket Süreyya Aydemir, *Makedonya'dan Ortaasya'ya Enver Paşa*, 3 (İstanbul, 1972), p.571.
21. Bennigsen and Quelquejay, op.cit., p.110.
22. A. Bennigsen and M. Broxup, *The Islamic Threat to the Soviet State* (London, 1983), p.81.
23. Bennigsen and Quelquejay, op.cit., p.112.
24. Ibid., p.114.
25. In addition to Galiyevism it is possible that the *Kadro* writers, in particular Tör and Belge, who had studied in Berlin, might have been familiar with the Spartakist movement, as well as with the 1903–4 discussions concerning the national question between Rosa Luxemburg and Lenin. But, we have so far no evidence to prove this. For the Spartakist movement and the discussions between Lenin and Luxemburg see Nigel Harris, *National Liberation* (London and New York, 1990); Anthony Brewer, *Marxist Theories of Imperialism: A Critical Survey*, Second Edition (London and New York, 1990).
26. Şevket Süreyya Aydemir, *İkinci Adam*, 1 (İstanbul, 1966), p.404, footnote 1.
27. E. H. Carr, *The Bolshevik Revolution 1917–1923*, 3 (London, 1953), pp.271–304.
28. Indeed, as early as October 1920 a Soviet trading company, Arcos (All-Russian Co-operative Society) had been set up to trade in London, Carr, *The Bolshevik Revolution*, 3, pp.280–90.
29. Ibid., 3, p.288.
30. Carr, *Socialism in One Country 1924–1926*, 1 (London, 1958), p.54.
31. *Kadro*, Vol.1, No.6 (1932), p.40; *Kadro*, Vol.1, No.6 (1932), pp.21–9; *Kadro*, Vol.2, No.16 (1933), pp.31–38; *Kadro*, Vol.3, No.32 (1934), pp.33–6.
32. Şevket Süreyya [Aydemir], *Cihan İktisadiyatında Türkiye* (Ankara, 1931), passim.
33. Ibid., p.119.
34. See Mustafa Türkeş, 'Ideological Tendencies in the Republic of Turkey: the Case of Kadro(1932–1935)', unpublished Ph.D. Thesis (University of Manchester, 1993), chapter 5.
35. *Russia in the Era of NEP*, Edited by Sheila Fitzpatrick, Alexander Rabinowitch, and Richard Stites (Bloomington and Indianapolis, 1991).
36. E.H. Carr and R.W. Davies, *A History of Soviet Russia: Foundations of A Planned Economy 1926–1929*, 2 (London, 1969), pp.787–898.
37. See *Kadro*, Vol.1, No.5 (1932), p.5, footnote 2.
38. *Kadro*, Vol.2, No.23 (1933), p.8.
39. *Kadro*, Vol.2, No.19 (1933), p.25.
40. It may be suggested that Ahmet Cevat Emre, the editor of the magazine *Muhit*, advocated state socialism in the sense in which Wagner had formulated it, see Emre's articles 'Sınıflar Arasında Ahenk, Kemalizmin Büyük Prensiplerinden Biri Sınıflar Arasında Ahenk Temin Etmektir' *Muhit*, 32, 33 (Haziran, Temmuz 1931), pp.1–3, pp.1–2. Mahmut Esat Bozkurt, the Minister of the Economy (1923) and the Minister of Justice (1924–1930), was also an

advocate of state socialism, see Hakkı Uyar, 'Türk İhtilali'nin Düsturları ve Mahmut Esat Bozkurt I', *Tarih ve Toplum*, 99 (Mart, 1992), pp.18.

41. For Sombart (1863–1941), see Jürgen Kuczynski, 'Werner Sombart', *International Encyclopaedia of the Social Sciences*, 15 (London, 1968), pp.57–9; Philip Siegelman's Introduction to Werner Sombart, *Luxury and Capitalism*, translated by W. R. Dittmar (Michigan, 1967), pp.v–xxix; Frederick L. Nussbaum, *A History of the Economic Institutions of Modern Europe: An Introduction to Der Moderne Kapitalismus of Werner Sombart* (New York, 1968).

42. In the first half of the 1930s in Turkey, Sombart's writings were regularly cited, for instance, Ö. C. Sarc, who had studied in Berlin University in the 1920s, and said subsequently he had studied under Sombart's supervision, wrote in 1934 *Ziraat ve Sanayi Siyaseti* [Agricultural and Industrial Policy] (İstanbul, 1934). This book was almost a translation of Sombart's main writings. When Sombart died in 1941, Sarc wrote an obituary, see Ö. C. Sarc, 'Werner Sombart' in *İstanbul Üniversitesi İktisat Fakültesi Mecmuası*, Vol.3, No.1–2 (1941–1942), pp.60–3.

43. *Kadro*, Vol.1, No.5 (1932), p.8.

44. *Kadro*, Vol.1, No.5 (1932), pp.37–8

45. It was first published in 1913 and in the same year M. Epstein translated it into English, see second edition, Werner Sombart, *The Jews and Modern Capitalism*, translated by M. Epstein (New York, 1951).

46. Werner Sombart, *A New Social Philosophy*, translated by Karl F. Geiser (New York, 1937). First published as *Deutscher Sozialismus* (German Socialism) (July 1934).

47. Kuczynski, op.cit., p.59.

48. Ibid., pp.57–59.

49. *Kadro*, Vol.3, No.34 (1934), pp.34–9.

50. Sombart's pre-First World War writings sought to criticize and disprove Marx. Three of his major writings came out before the First World War and did not include anything particularly about planning: *Socialism and the Social Movement*, translated by M. Epstein (London, New York, 1909), and *The Quintessence of Capitalism*, translated by M. Epstein (London, 1915), *Der Moderne Kapitalismus*, 3 vols., first edition in 1902 and second in 1924–1927, for the latter, see Frederick L. Nussbaum, *A History of the Economic Institutions of Modern Europe: An Introduction to Der Moderne Kapitalismus of Werner Sombart* (New York, 1968).

51. Nussbaum, op.cit., pp.274–5.

52. While Weber puts emphasis on the spirit of Protestantism, Sombart puts emphasis on the spirit of Judaism, Siegelman, op.cit., pp.v–xxix

53. Nussbaum, op.cit., p.228.

54. Ibid., pp.259–80; see also Kuczynski, op.cit., pp.57–9; see Philip Siegelman's introduction to Werner Sombart, *Luxury and Capitalism*, translated by W. R. Dittmar (Michigan, 1967), pp.v–xxix.

55. *Kadro*, Vol.2, No.16 (1933), p.5–10; *Kadro*, Vol.3, No.27, (1934), p.38; *Kadro*, Vol.2, No.16 (1933), pp.31–8; *Kadro*, Vol.3, No.32 (1934), p.17.

56. As his source on Marxism, Aydemir cited mainly the 'Communist Manifesto' and on one occasion referred to A. Paperni, an author whom it has not been possible to trace *Kadro*, Vol.2, No.19 (1933), p.12.

57. *Kadro*, Vol.2, No.16 (1933), pp.5–10; *Kadro*, Vol.3, No.32 (1934), p.17. It is not clear whether the *Kadro* writers were familiar with Rosa Luxemburg's point that as capitalism developed it conquered rural regions within the metropole as well as the colonies. However, when taken as a whole, *Kadro*'s argument does not accord with Luxemburg's. For a summary of Luxemburg's views, see Nigel Harris, *National Liberation* (London and New York, 1990) and Anthony Brewer, *Marxist Theories of Imperialism: A Critical Survey*, Second Edition (London and New York, 1990).

58. *Kadro*, Vol.2, No.19 (1933), p.10. However, some Marxists argue that it is possible to trace elements of this argument in Marx. For a summary of Marxist debate, see Brewer, op.cit.

59. *Kadro*, Vol.2, No.19 (1933), p.10; *Kadro*, Vol.2, No.16 (1933), pp.31–8; *Kadro*, Vol.3, No.32 (1934), p.17

60. *Kadro*, Vol.2, No.19 (1933), p.15.
61. *Kadro*, Vol.2, No.16 (1933), pp.5–10, 32–37; *Kadro*, Vol.3, No.27 (1934), p.38; *Kadro*, Vol.3, No.32 (1934), pp.16–17.
62. *Kadro*, Vol.2, No.19 (1933), pp.13–15; *Kadro*, Vol.2, No.18 (1933), pp.18–24.
63. *Kadro*, Vol.2, No.19 (1933), pp.6–16; *Kadro*, Vol.2, No.21 (1933), p.12.
64. *Kadro*, Vol.2, No.19 (1933), p.15.
65. *Kadro*, Vol.1, No.8 (1932), pp.36–39.
66. *Kadro* 2, No.18 (1933), pp.8–12; *Kadro*, Vol.2, No.24 (1933), pp.17–21; *Kadro*, Vol.3, No.25 (1934), pp.24–30; *Kadro*, Vol.3, No.26 (1934), pp.20–26.
67. *Kadro*, Vol.2, No.18 (1933), pp.5–14; *Kadro*, Vol.3, No.25 (1934), pp.24–25.
68. *Kadro*, Vol.2, No.18 (1933), pp.13–15; *Kadro*, Vol.3, No.26 (1934), pp.20–6.
69. *Kadro*, Vol.1, No.6 (1932), p.21–9, 40; *Kadro*, Vol.3, No.32 (1934), pp.33–6.
70. *Kadro*, Vol.2, No.18 (1933), pp.13–15; *Kadro*, Vol.2, No.19 (1933), p.15; *Kadro*, Vol.2, No.21 (1933), pp.8–10; *Kadro*, Vol.3, No.26 (1934), pp.20–26, 30–36
71. Aydemir noted that *Kadro* was accused of being Communist, nationalist Communist, national socialist, social Fascist, neo-Hitlerist, anarchist and nihilist, *Kadro*, Vol.2, No.18 (1933), pp.5–6.
72. *Milliyet*, 5 Kasım 1933.
73. *Kadro*, Vol.1, No.12 (1932), pp.38–43; *Kadro*, Vol.2, No.14 (1933), pp.5–11.
74. *Kadro*, Vol.2, No.18 (1933), p.10; *Kadro*, Vol.3, No.26 (1934), pp.20–6.
75. D. S. Lewis, *Illusions of Grandeur, Mosley, Fascism and British Society, 1931–1981* (Manchester, 1987); Ernst Nolte, *Three Faces of Fascism, Action Française, Italian Fascism, National Socialism*, Translated by Leila Vennewitz (London, 1965).
76. *Kadro*, Vol.3, No.26 (1934), pp.30–6.
77. By the same token, any comparison between Fascism and the Kemalist regime is dubious: the Kemalist regime did not employ industrial or youth corporations to control society, and nor did it use trade unions, which, by 1926, had disappeared in Turkey. It can be said that the Kemalist regime was authoritarian, but not Fascist.
78. *Kadro*, Vol.3, No.32 (1934), pp.17–21; *Kadro*, Vol.2, No.16 (1933), pp.31–8.
79. *Kadro*, Vol.2, No.16 (1933), pp.5–10; *Kadro*, Vol.3, No.32 (1934), pp.17–21.
80. According to *Kadro*, China was the country whose loss would most damage imperialists' access to raw material sources and markets. *Kadro*, Vol.1, No.1,1932,pp.45–47; *Kadro*, Vol.1, No.3 (1932), pp.11–16; *Kadro*, Vol.1, No.8, 1932), pp.6–12.
81. *Kadro*, Vol.2, No.16 (1933), pp.5–10, 31–38; *Kadro*, Vol.3, No.32 (1934), p.17.
82. *Kadro*, Vol.1, No.6,1932), pp.21–9, 40
83. *Kadro*, Vol.2, No.16 (1933), pp.5–10; *Kadro*, Vol.3, No.32 (1934), p.17, 33–36
84. *Kadro*, Vol.1, No.4 (1932), p.3–4; *Kadro*, Vol.2, No.19 (1933), p.10.
85. *Kadro*, Vol.2, No.19 (1933), p.10.
86. *Kadro*, Vol.2, No.19 (1933), pp.6–16.
87. *Kadro*, Vol.2, No.19, 1933), pp.6–16; *Kadro*, Vol.3, No.29 (1934), p.45.
88. *Kadro*, Vol.2, No.13 (1933), pp.42–43; *Kadro*, Vol.2, No.19,1933), pp.6–16.
89. Gülalp, op.cit., pp.69–85; Sadıq, op.cit., p.330.
90. *Kadro*, Vol.1, No.4 (1932), p.3–4; *Kadro*, Vol.2, No.19 (1933), p.10.
91. *Kadro*, Vol.1, No.4 (1932), p.3–4; *Kadro*, Vol.1, No.11 (1932), pp.43–47; *Kadro*, Vol.2, No.13 (1933) pp.42–43; *Kadro*, Vol.2, No.19, 1933), p.11; *Kadro*, Vol.3, No.29 (1934), s. 45.
92. *Kadro*, Vol.3, No.25 (1934), pp.34–7; *Kadro*, Vol.3, No.26 (1934), pp.20–6.
93. *Kadro*, Vol.3, No.25 (1934), p.34, 21.
94. *Kadro*, Vol.3, No.25 (1934), pp.34–8; *Kadro*, Vol.3, No.26 (1934), pp.20–6.
95. *Kadro*, Vol.2, No.18 (1933), pp.24.
96. *Kadro*, Vol.1, No.2 (1932), p.40.
97. *Kadro*, Vol.2, No.19 (1933), p.10.
98. *Kadro*, Vol.2, No.20 (1933), pp.4–11; *Kadro*, Vol.2, No.21 (1933), pp.5–14.
99. *Kadro*, Vol.3, No.35–6 (1934), pp.5–22
100. *Kadro*, Vol.3, No.35–6 (1934), pp.5–7.
101. Ibid., pp.8–22.
102. *Kadro*, Vol.1, No.8 (1932), p.11.

The Programme of the Nationalist Action Party: An Iron Hand in a Velvet Glove?

E. BURAK ARIKAN

The death of Alparslan Türkeş (1917–1997) brought to the surface rivalries within the Ülkücü Camia (Idealist Community)[1] which in the early 1990s had led to the division of the party into two separate political bodies.[2] Today, the competition between the more Islamist and grass-root Idealists is expected to intensify, since Milliyetçi Hareket Partisi (MHP) faces a leadership crisis following the death of their *Basbuğ*.[3] In their first party congress without the presence of their supreme leader, on 18–19 May 1997, the rivalries within the party surfaced and eight candidates, including the son of Türkeş, ran for the leadership of the party. Following the first round of the elections, six candidates decided to support Devlet Bahçeli, who had been trailing Tuğrul Türkeş. This decision was a turning point in the congress. At around 4.00 a.m. Türkeş, realizing that his chances of victory were minimal, organized a *putsch* and with the support of militant Idealists seized the congress administration chair. The scenes that followed resembled a gangster film. Fights broke out in the congress hall and even gunshots were heard. Consequently, the congress was suspended by the party administration. The scene seriously damaged the functioning of democracy in Turkey, and MHP lost its chance to present itself to the electorate as a respectable and democratic force. Before the congress, many commentators had been expecting the leadership election to enable MHP to reappraise itself and to find a legitimate place in Turkish politics by accepting democratic procedures, as some extreme right-wing parties have done elsewhere in Europe. However, the high hopes raised before the congress disappeared in the dark corridors of militant terrorism.

The anti-democratic incidents that dominated the congress did not surprise many academics, politicians and press members. MHP's name in Turkish politics has long been associated with the pre-1980 political turbulence, during which nearly 5,000 people were killed and around 20,000 wounded. Before the 1980 coup, the Idealists openly declared war against the Communists, and with their strong pro-state and anti-Communist stance believed that for the great cause (the preservation and continuity of the Turkish Republic) even armed struggle was legitimate.[4] The basis of MHP's programme is Turkish nationalism, that is, in its narrowest definition: 'The love of Turkish nation, and loyalty and service to the Turkish state.'[5] However, the limits of this service were rather obscurely interpreted by the Idealist cadres and as one recent development has shown, many MHP supporters were manipulated by the state in pursuing criminal activities. The latest scandal, which surfaced after a traffic accident, proved the illegal links between the state and the Idealists.[6] A member of Parliament, Sedat Bucak, a police chief, Hüseyin Kocadağ and an Idealist, Abdullah Çatlı (or at least he himself claimed to be one),[7] on Interpol's wanted list for international drug trafficking, were in a car involved in an accident in Susurluk province. The accident raised doubts in the minds of citizens as to whether the country was run by the state or by gangs. It was then that people better understood the words of one Idealist writer. In his book *Ülkücüye Mektuplar* [Letters to the Idealists] Adnan Büyükbas examines the psychology of the Idealist, claiming that Idealists are always ready to be shot for their native country, which nurtured them.[8]

TABLE 1

THE RESULTS OF MHP PARTICIPATION IN TURKISH ELECTIONS

	Elections	Votes cast in %	Number of MPs
CKMP	1965	2.2	11
MHP	1969	3.3	1
MHP	1973	3.4	3
MHP	1977	6.4	16
MÇP[9]	1987	2.9	–
MÇP	1989*	4.1	–
MÇP-RP[10]	1991	16.9	19 (RP 43)
MHP	1994*	8	–
MHP	1995	8.6	–

* Local elections

As this latest incident has shown, for the Idealists and the MHP it is the preservation of the native country that takes priority over all other issues. Any tactic, legal or illegal, is legitimate for achieving this sacred mission.

MHP ideology is predicated on a defensive reflex based on the existence of an enemy, fictitious or real, which has to be challenged and destroyed.[11] During the 1960s the enemy was the Demokrat Parti (Democrat Party, DP) government,[12] in the 1970s it was Communism, in the 1980s it was the

Partia Karkaren Kürdistan (Kurdistan Worker's Party, PKK), and today it is the pro-Islamist Refah Partisi (Welfare Party, RP).[13] By creating an enemy, the party on the one hand aims to unite elements of the extreme right in Turkey, and on the other seeks to find itself a legitimate place in the Turkish political spectrum. Accordingly, the most broadly held view of the MHP programme is that it is a single-issue party, the product of a defensive obsession with the preservation of the Turkish state. However, this fails to explain the presence of the MHP in Turkish politics for more than four decades, and the fact that it enjoys the support of ten per cent of the electorate.

The party programme is broadly influenced by the writings of a right-wing think-tank, known as Aydınlar Ocağı (Hearth of Intellectuals, AO), similar to the Nouvelle Droite in France. The programme in essence points towards a Fascist ideology which is subsumed by Turkish nationalism. Considering Fascism's narrowest definition, the MHP is anti-egalitarian, extreme nationalist, opposed to both liberalism and Communism, accepts the use of violence (although this is not in its programme, it is a historical fact that even party officials do not deny), and defends discrimination. The party claims to be supporting parliamentary democracy but the latest congress shows how it can easily push aside democratic means. On economic matters the party favours a protectionist model, based on import substitution. It advocates a mixed economic structure in which the state would control the strategic economic enterprises.[14] Industry would be encouraged to use only Turkish resources.[15] It is obvious that in the post-GATT world (which enforces free trade measures in the world) the economic programme of the party fails to offer any alternatives that would integrate the Turkish economy into the world markets.

The purpose of this essay is to clarify the programme of the MHP and to see whether the party is disguising a Fascist doctrine as a nationalist conservative programme based on the acceptance of the primary principles of the Turkish Republic. Firstly, the development of the MHP programme will be emphasized, paying special attention to the Aydınlar Ocağı, given its influence on right-wing politics in Turkey in general and on extreme right-wing ideas in particular. The efforts of Aydınlar Ocağı, to present a legitimate façade for extreme nationalist and racist ideas are extremely important if the MHP is to establish its own version of Turkish nationalism. The ideas that are covered in the programme will be explored in the next section with reference to three main areas: Turkish nationalism, the economy, and the family. The MHP programme is a good example of how such movements can prepare a democratic programme while in fact combining Fascist elements with militant terrorism.

The early foundations of the MHP programme date back to the late 1940s. In 1948, the first extreme right-wing party, Cumhuriyetçi Köylü Millet Partisi (Republican Farmers Nation Party, CKMP), was founded by the coalition of small proto-Fascist parties and movements. It was led by Marshal Fevzi Çakmak, who at the time was the symbol of extreme nationalistic ideas in Turkey. During the 1950s, under the leadership of Osman Bölükbaşı, the party acquired a populist, conservative and nationalist stance, primarily supported by peasants and middle classes. In 1965, Alparslan Türkeş and his friends were elected to the party chair. The first party programme, valid until the 1960s contained a corporatist, developmental-modernist ideology primarily underlined by a Kemalist restoration agenda. Between 1965–69, Turkist and virulent anti-Communist features started to acquire importance in party rhetoric. During the period the party was in close contact with Fascist organizations, such as Türkiye Milliyetçiler Birliği (Turkish Nationalists Union),[16] Aydınlar Klübü (Intellectuals Club), and Vatansever Türk Teşkilatı (Native-Country Lovers Turkish Organization). These organizations, together with Komünizmle Mücadele Dernekleri ('Struggle Against Communism' Clubs) served an important role in the re-organization of the party and its ideology. In the 1967 congress of the party, a new programme was accepted, the main principle being 'communitarian nationalism' represented by the Dokuz Işık Doktrini (Nine Lights Doctrine, DID). Türkeş was declared *Basbuğ*, and he made his famous declaration: 'whoever joins the cause and becomes a traitor, kill him'.

Until the end of the 1960s the MHP supported the secular forces in the country. However, during the 1970s Türkeş and the MHP speakers defined Islam as an indispensable part of Turkish culture. Türkeş formulated this new combination as follows: 'We are as Turk as the Tengri mountain [it is in Central Asia where MHP believes Turk's ancestors migrated from] as Muslim as the Hira mountain [which is located in the holylands for Muslims in Saudi Arabia]. Both philosophies are our principles.'[17] This change in the party programme in fact was tactical and instrumental. It was instrumental since Islam was interpreted as an ideology that strengthened and endorsed Turkish identity. It was also tactical because the party aimed to channel the support of the Muslim masses towards itself, and their level of anti-Communist mobilization rose as a result.

The party congress in Adana in February 1969 marked the end of the transformation period for the party, and its name was changed from CKMP to MHP. The congress instituted a hierarchical structure within the party, primarily expanding the powers of Türkeş. The grass-root Turkists of the MHP opposed the Islamisation of the party's rhetoric, and as a result were expelled from the party. The party's strong anti-capitalist and anti-masonic stance was also reduced, a tribute to the workings of the forces of the system, which increasingly considered the MHP as a legitimate force because of its stringent anti-Communism. Between 1969 and 1974 the MHP was not an important actor in Turkish parliamentary politics. The party's share of the vote in the elections of 1969 and 1974 were 3 per cent and 3.4 per cent respectively.

The MHP started to build up its support during the government of the Cumhuriyet Halk Partisi (Republican People's Party) in 1974 and was given a great opportunity when the party was invited to join the new Milli Cephe (National Front) government in 1975, with the centre right Adalet Partisi (Justice Party, AP) and the Milliyetçi Selamet Partisi (Nationalist Salvation Party, MSP).[18] The MHP was invited to join the coalition government on the one hand for its strong anti-Communist position, which was regaining support from the right of the political spectrum parallel to the rise of revolutionary movements. Secondly, the centre right was aware of the need for a coalition of the right-wing forces against the rising CHP that was gaining support from the outcome of the military intervention in Cyprus, conducted under Bülent Ecevit's premiership.[19]

Between 1974 and 1977 the MHP became the party for marginalized middle classes who faced difficulties in adapting to the rise of entrepreneurial capitalism and inflation. Although the MHP almost doubled its support in the 1977 elections, the coalition experience was not as beneficial as its leaders had expected. It had been hoped that this experience would integrate the party into the system as a legitimate actor and widen its basis of support. The party failed to redefine its strategy, and its tactics remained the mobilization of the masses around a primitively defined anti-Communist ideology. The party employed an inflexible attitude towards change, which damaged its electoral prospects. The curtain fell on the MHP in 1980 when the party was closed down and its leaders were banned from indulging in political activity.

If it was the Nouvelle Droite that has become the primary source of French extreme right-wing ideology in France, it is the Aydınlar Ocağı in Turkey that has armed the right in general and the extreme right in particular with a powerful doctrine. The AO was founded in 1970 by a number of respected professors from various disciplines, including economics, engineering and medical science. Its purpose was to unite the 'right' in Turkey, which at the time was disintegrating. This process resulted in the foundation of three different parties, all coming from the DP tradition. As a result the centre right was represented by the AP, the Islamist right by the MSP and the nationalist right by the MHP. The founders of the organization worried that this fragmentation only benefited the left. The primary aim of the AO was to bring the right under one ideological umbrella, and strengthen it in its fight against the increasing Communist threat. According to Abdurrahman Dilipak, a well-known Islamist writer, the founders of the think-tank 'were under the influence of neither masonic groups as was the AP, nor Islamist groups as was the MSP, nor nationalist groups as was the MHP, but were close to these groupings without, however, representing any of them'.[20] But, according to Tanıl Bora and Kemal Can, given the Turkist-nationalist past of the first chairman, İbrahim Kafesoğlu, and the think-tank ideologue Muharrem Ergin, and the strong anti-Communist element during the foundation of the organization, the AO set itself the task of establishing a bridge between the AP and the MHP.[21] The politicization of Islam by the MSP was not supported by the organization, but it rather maintained a secular-conservative stance in line with the Turkish centre right's traditions.

It was this position that has increased the communication between Kemalist military-civilian bureaucracy and the Aydınlar Ocağı, and helped legitimize the organization's ideas. Actually, the rhetoric of the AO has always has always been informed by Kemalist ideology. According to Tanil Bora and Kemal Can, this relationship, as frequently stressed by the left, cannot be dismissed as a purely tactical manoeuvre, intended to hide a different ideology behind Kemalism.[22] The early republican period under the leadership of Atatürk is interpreted as the glorification of Turkish nationalism. In this respect, Atatürk is considered to be the greatest of all Turkish nationalists. The first phase of the republic deserves utmost respect, because it takes 'national culture' as its basis.

Like the Nouvelle Droite in France, Aydınlar Ocağı is careful to define Turkish nationalism in terms of 'national culture' rather than race.[23] Political authority could only be legitimate if it is derived from this national culture. Here one can trace the marks of authoritarianism in the AO's ideology. Hence, it may be argued that an authoritarian regime based on Turkish national culture is a legitimate form of government. Following the 1980 coup, the AO's glorification of the Turkish state and national culture gave the organization a special position in its relations with the military junta. This privileged posture went as far as the active participation of the AO in preparing the 1982 constitution, from which other civilian organizations were normally banned.

In their proposed Milli Mutabakatlar (National Consensus) programme, the organization created a new doctrine, Türk-İslam sentezi (Turkish-Islamic synthesis), which was well tailored to fit the aims of the military junta to create a harmonious society. Turkish-Islamic synthesis successfully combined republicanism with conservatism (which is shaped by moderate Islamic motives). This strategy had twofold advantages for the AO. On the one hand, through its support for the Kemalist reforms and republicanism, the organization was respected at the state level. On the other hand, its new doctrine coincided with that of the military junta, which was trying to cement the nation with Islam.

Turkish-Islamic synthesis was first mentioned and named by Professor Ibrahim Kafesoğlu, the first chairman of the Aydınlar Ocağı, in the 1970s. In the 1970s Kafesoğlu, not departing remarkably from his earlier writings which were underpinned by grass-root Turkist ideas and a version of romantic Turkish nationalism, started to view Islam as an important part of Turkish culture. However, Islam is interpreted only as a part of Turkey's glorious history, and it serves the highest ideal: to achieve Turkish domination over the world. Hence Islam is one of the components of Turkish culture among many others, and does not have any superiority over the other constituents. The thesis that the Turks always had a monotheistic belief is strongly emphasized and Islam is seen as the last stage in the historical evolution of the Turks in achieving their goal to rule the world. It is for this reason that many Turks willingly accepted Islam as their religion. It is also argued that it was the Turks who saved Islam from defeat through accepting its principles and who reunited the Islamic peoples of the world. The Turks have also revised Islam realistically and rationally and through their secular ethos, deeply rooted in their history, introduced the separation of state and religion, the first and only Islamic society to do so. Hence it was the secular tradition and the national culture of the Turks that glorified Islam and established a civilization that was comparable to the earlier civilizations of the followers of the prophet Mohammed. Rather than Turks adapting to the principles of Islam, it was Islam that was tailored to the national culture of the Turks.

The synthesis manifested by Aydınlar Ocağı not only combines Turkish and Islamic values but also incorporates western elements into its ideology. Advancement in science, technology and economics, and support for the military and political doctrines of the West are all parts of the synthesis. For Abdurrahman Dilipak, the Turkish-Islamic synthesis would be better described as 'Kemalist-Islamic'.[24] It is for this reason that the MHP easily internalized the ideology of the AO. The three elements of MHP ideology are ranked, in descending order, as Turkish, Islamic and western. The critical significance of the AO's amalgamation, however, does not derive from its capacity to combine these three elements successfully, but lies in the authoritarian framework which it proposes. The Aydınlar Ocağı fostered the authoritarian elements in the MHP programme, and through its good relations with the civilian-military bureaucracy gave the MHP a legitimate and sometimes respected place in the state apparatus. The MHP did after all use its status as a party to advance the Turkish nationalist ideal, and so it deserved a priviliged position *vis-à-vis* other right-wing parties.[25]

In economic matters, the think-tank favoured the preservation of the status quo, strongly advocated private entrepreneurship and always claimed to support private property. Given its intermediary role between the centre right and the MHP, it never voiced anti-capitalist sentiments, and was in fact closely linked with big capital. The MHP, primarily supported by deprived peasants, small entrepreneurs and small craftsmen could not adopt the economic programme of the AO. The party, rather, stuck to an old-fashioned extreme right-wing economic programme, essentially corporatist. In France, after internalizing the respectable economic programme of the Nouvelle Droite, the FN nearly doubled its support at the polls. This might explain why the MHP could not achieve a similar electoral turnout to that of the FN in France.

The influence of the Aydınlar Ocağı on Turkish politics was thus extensive, despite its being a small organization with only around 130 members. The organization always kept its elite nature and successfully established a reputation for taking in the entire right of the political spectrum, without associating itself with any of the parties. For this reason, the contribution of the organization to the MHP programme was limited. However, in the final analysis it was the MHP which most benefited from the 'nationalization of politics' in Turkey, the outcome of the endless efforts on the part of the AO.

The attempt by the MHP leaders to mobilize the masses through violent anti-Communist ideas has caused some writers to make a fundamental error in interpreting the position of the party in Turkish politics. The MHP was said to be only a reactionary single-issue movement, its electoral prospects heavily related to its ability to exploit the issue of anti-Communist sentiments among the population.[26] However, following the collapse of the Communist bloc in 1989, the continuing appearance of the party at the polls has proven that while the Communist ideology was in decline in the world and while its fortresses were falling apart one after the other, the MHP was still a dynamic and a promising force in Turkish politics. Between the years 1989 and 1995 the party nearly doubled its electoral turnout and became a political force ready to pass the ten per cent national threshold for parliamentary representation. As Wolfreys has shown for the FN in France, the MHP in Turkey 'Motivated by the pragmatic demands of satisfying a heterogeneous membership and the opportunist desire to benefit from events … proved itself capable of adapting its message to a given situation.'[27]

Since the early 1990s it has exploited the Kurdistan Worker's Party[28] (PKK) issue, claiming that there is a conspiracy of foreign enemies to use the PKK to destroy the unity of the Turkish state. During a period in which the funerals of soldiers who were killed in clashes with terrorists often turned into political rallies against the PKK and separatism, the message of the party was readily accepted by an increasing proportion of the electorate. The party in fact, through mobilizing anti-PKK sentiments among the population, was not deviating from its original path, to declare war against a fictitious or a real enemy. Therefore, switching from an anti-Communist stance to an anti-PKK one only shows that the party as an institution is capable of adapting to changing conditions.

Since the 1967 congress, the centrepiece of the party programme has been based on the Dokuz Işık Doktrini (DID), 'the path of development and glorification' written by Alparslan Türkeş.[29] In the 1993 party programme, the DID is introduced to the reader as a doctrine that eliminates all liberal-capitalism, Communism, westernism, and imitationism as systems that are against the history and traditions of the Turks. Therefore, it is absolutely essential to draw a purely national path that would glorify the history, traditions and the roots of the Turkish nation. Against possible criticisms that would label the DID Fascist, Türkeş underlines the differences between national-socialism and his principles: 'National-socialism is based on capitalism, (anthropological) racism, created in laboratories, and anti-democratic ideas. However, the followers of the DID believe in Turkish communitarianism, a social-pyschologically defined (moral) respect for ancestoral traditions (lineageism), and a true democratic system.'[30] The MHP believes that this doctrine is the exclusive guide for a people loyal to Turkish nationalism. The DID's nine principles are: nationalism, idealism, moralism, communitarianism, positivism, ruralism, libertarianism and character-building, modernization and populism, and industrialism.

The first four principles show the corporatist nature of the programme. It is clearly stated that the MHP movement is a reaction to individualism, competition and a society based on the political economic struggles between the classes. Turkish society is viewed as an organic whole and the programme aims to abolish class conflict and to create a harmonious society. As with corporatism, Turkish society is seen as a body and the individuals as the cells composing it. The criticisms of both egalitarianism and capitalist economic ideas, and the extreme glorification of a paternalist state idea, strengthen the corporatist character of the MHP programme.

The party views democracy as a virtuous regime and believes it to be superior to Communism, Fascism and Nazism. Turkish nationalists claim to be democrats who have adopted democratic rules and principles. However, the latest developments in the congress (explored in detail above), and the corporatist and Fascistic elements in the party programme raise doubts as to the position of the MHP vis-à-vis democracy. The MHP, like many West European extreme right-wing parties, has successfully clothed a Fascist ideology in conservative language. Therefore, it is not a mistake to call the

MHP programme 'an iron hand in a velvet glove'.[31]

Departing from neo-liberal extreme right-wing parties in Europe, the MHP does not accept economic liberalism, but continues to favour traditional corporatist policies.[32] For instance, the FN in France considers capitalism as 'the highest form of democracy, making individuals responsible for the setting up and running of businesses and then subjecting their decisions to the will of the people, via the market'.[33] However, the MHP discards capitalism on the grounds that it is individualist, fosters cosmopolitanism and because it strongly rejects interventionism. The rejection of capitalism is based on the phrase 'big fish eat small fish', and the small fish is Turkey while the big industrialists and western capital are the big fish. It is capitalism, under the mask of democracy, that is responsible for the poverty and backwardness of Turkish society.[34] Marxism on the other hand is rejected because of its class-based materialistic ideology.

The economic programme of the MHP is based on import substitution, which of course conflicts with the direction of world trade after the GATT agreement. The party favours import substitution in fundamental industrial sectors, while it also encourages an export-oriented strategy in the sectors which have a potential for competition in the world markets. With the application of this policy, the national resources of Turkey will not, it is claimed, be wasted anymore. The MHP puts itself forward as defender of the farmers. The agricultural sector will be modernized, living conditions and educational opportunities for farmers' families will be improved, and a state subsidy will continue, though kept at a reasonable level. The party aims to build 'agriculture cities' which would be surrounded by light industrial plants.[35] This would also help to solve the increasing unemployment problem in Turkey.

The MHP sees unemployment as the most important problem facing Turkey. The party, unlike its counterparts, is not against birth control,[36] and argues that unemployment can only be defeated through investment, and the creation of jobs to match the increase in the population.[37] A change in the national education priorities to widen technical and professional education would also result in reducing unemployment rates. Apart from highly qualified students, who would attend universities, the rest would be channelled into vocational education. Hence, in a short period of time, the active population between the ages of 15 and 16 would be employed in various fields of the economy.

The MHP favours tax reductions for the lower and lower-middle classes. For instance, the minimum wage is to be allowed against tax. Taxes will be collected according to the capacity of citizens and the citizens will be educated so that tax paying becomes a national duty and a matter of social responsibility. Unemployment insurance will be introduced in Turkey, as it is in many advanced and prosperous societies in the West. Trade unions are to be accepted as legitimate actors in politics and free trade unionism is advocated. In every sector, strong trade unions will be encouraged and the rights of the workers will be guaranteed *vis-à-vis* the employers. Two major reservations remain on the trade unions: Firstly, the trade unions must not become centres for class struggle,[38] and secondly, the trade unions' power must not be abused by its leaders for other ends.

It is clear that during the period of an expanding universal market, the MHP's traditionally defined right-wing nationalism and authoritarianism does not offer much to the average Turkish citizen, whose economic ideas are shaped increasingly by the globalization of world trade. The MHP's manifest desire, for example, to institute state intervention in the economy, contrasts with the ideas of many Turks, who favour large-scale privatization and the minimization of state intervention. Rejecting full membership of the EU, based on cultural aspects and an anti-imperialist ideology, the MHP also disregards the opinion of nearly two-thirds of the Turkish population, which believes that membership of the EU would be to the benefit of Turkey. The greatest contradiction of the MHP programme lies in its recognition of individual and democratic freedoms. This contradiction is especially apparent in the party's attitude towards gender-related issues.

The family is seen as the core social unit of Turkish society. The MHP considers a strong family structure as guaranteeing the preservation of Turkish culture. Mothers, as devoted housewives, will be educated in order to create traditional close-knit families. Feminism, considered a threat to the family and its social functions, is firmly rejected. However, the party claims to support women's rights. The protection of women is necessary; they will be respected equally with men. Abortion is strictly rejected on the grounds that it is the result of ineffective family planning schemes. Therefore, diverging from many European extreme right-wing parties, the MHP in Turkey is not against contraception. The MHP, opposing artificial insemination, openly states how it regards individual freedoms:

> It is not enough if husband and wife decide to have babies through artificial insemination. The family is a member of society and it cannot be excluded from it. Against the common morality of the society and its traditions we reject unlimited individual freedoms.[39]

Hence, the party is in contradiction with its own principles stated under the 'The Protection of Basic Rights and Freedoms' section of the programme.[40]

The MHP today is trapped in a deadlock in redefining its ideology as a consequence of the rise of political Islam in Turkey. A part of the Idealist cadres following the 1980 military intervention were influenced by the winds of political Islam and consequently founded their splinter party, the Büyük Birlik Partisi (Grand Unity Party, BBP).[41] The splinter party's place in Turkish politics could be defined as falling somewhere between the Islamist RP and the nationalist MHP. The rivalries between the Islamists and the Turkists are in fact part of MHP history. The difficult combination of nationalism (the idea of belonging to a nation) and Islam as a world religion (belonging to a larger Muslim family) has always been problematic for the party. The MHP as a body embraced a wide spectrum of ideas, very often in contradiction with each other, such as paganism, Kemalism and strong Islamic beliefs. However, the party was able to keep its unity for nearly four decades and has always been a significant actor in Turkish politics, through legal or illegal means. The MHP's success is underpinned by two factors. On the one hand, the MHP accepts all of Turkey's past. All pre-Islamic, Ottoman and Republican periods are considered to be parts of Turkey's glorious heritage.[42] On the other hand, the leadership principle, supported by a hierarchical structure, has kept different factions within the party together.

To the small merchant, small artisan, farmer and unemployed worker who have suffered from an inflationary economy for decades, the MHP offers an identity, a past to be proud of and a place in the hierarchy, granting the weak the safety of authority while satisfying their need to dominate. The observations of one MHP sympathizer, Osman Ateş, during Türkeş's visit to their town are as follows: '[Türkeş] is a very serious man. He is disciplined and authoritarian, therefore, I liked him ... he also talks about our history and traditions, underlines the importance of morality...I have decided to support such a man under any circumstances.'[43] As a result of his observations the sympathizer accepts an active role in the setting up of the MHP party organization in Gümüşhane. Hence it is the traditional men in an identity crisis, intensified as a result of the modernization process in Turkey, the secularization of lifestyles and decline in traditional values, who support the party and in it find themselves a new identity. Mustafa Çalık's words, who has been a member of the Idealist community in the past, shows us what the MHP offers to the ordinary man challenged by modernization:

> I am not no longer given either the false security or the untrustworthy power of an organized society [the Idealists]. For this reason, I do not carry with me the tribal responsibility derived from 'belonging', that is restrictive, unreasonable and vain.[44]

It is, therefore, the offer of security by the MHP, that has attracted many people to vote for the party. With reference to the idea of a state that protects its citizens as a father protects children, tax reductions for lower and middle income groups, exploitation of the fear of Communism that is common for the ordinary man in small provinces, and a strong emphasis on conservative moral and family values, the MHP's ideas were all tailored to fit the ideas of the marginalized blue-collar workers, small shopkeepers and artisans, unemployed and small farmers.[45] However, today the challenge of the RP and the BBP threatens the traditional electoral basis of the MHP. The Aydınlar Ocağı is no longer an active organization that may help the MHP to redefine its ideology and become a centre for attraction for the deprived citizens. The MHP today fights a war on two fronts; one against the centre parties, which are increasingly incorporating nationalist rhetoric into their ideology, and the other against the Islamists represented by the RP and the BBP.

Today, Turkey is going through a period of vehement political chaos. The so-called 'Refahyol' coalition government between the RP and the Doğru Yol Partisi (True Path Party, DYP), has intensified the polarization between the secular republicans and the advocates of shariah rule. The polarization of the system has not yet reached the level of civil war; however, the unrest of the military gives the early signals of an anti-democratic take-over; a military coup. What is more worrying for Turkish democracy is the attitude of some sections of the media which advocate (reading between the lines) military intervention and anti-democratic measures in order to preserve the secular republic. During such a chaotic period it is probable that the Fascist and authoritarian ideas of the MHP may find fertile ground. However, the MHP, like the centre right Anavatan Partisi[46] (Motherland Party, ANAP), seems to be trapped between Islamist and pro-republican ideas, and hence may split into a number of parties. The most popular slogan of MHP supporters in the 1990s shows this dilemma. Although claiming to give priority to Turkist ideas over Islamic ones, the slogan of the party has an Islamic undertone rather than a Turkist one. The supporters shout in MHP meetings: 'Ya Allah, Bismillah, Allahü Ekber' [Oh God, in the name of God the compassionate the merciful, God is the greatest].

The future prospects of the party are directly linked to the developments that will take place during the suspension of congress. If MHP successfully transforms its ideology towards a more centre-oriented one, as the Movimento Italiano Sociale-Destra Nazionale (Italian Social Movement-National Right, MSI-DN)[47] in Italy has done, the party will have the chance to gain a more respectable and significant place in Turkish politics. Otherwise, it is most likely that the heritage of the MHP will be divided among a number of parties, including the Islamist RP and the BBP as well as the centre-right parties. Today, the MHP no longer has a monopoly of Fascistic elements and authoritarianism.

NOTES

1. According to Alparslan Türkeş, the ideal is to construct a Turkish nation that is the most advanced, civilized, and powerful entity of the world. People who follow this ideal, are the idealists. Idealists must be ready to sacrifice themselves in serving the state and the nation. See, Türkeş, Alparslan, *Milliyetçilik* (Istanbul: Hamle Basın-Yayın, 1996), p.16.
2. The splinter party is Büyük Birlik Partisi (Grand Unity Party, BBP) led by Muhsin Yazıcıoğlu a former NAP member. The party emphasizes the Islamic roots of Turkish culture and advocates a Turkist-Islamist programme. For Yazıcıoğlu and his friends Islam occupies a central role in Turkish nationalism, while for the NAP followers Islam is only one of the ingredients of Turkish nationalism among others.
3. Turkish word for 'Führer'.
4. For the pre-1980 MHP atrocities see the confessions of two Idealists, Omer Tanlak and Ali Yurtaslan. Tanlak, Omer, *Itiraf: Eski Ülkücü MHP'yi Anlatıyor* (Istanbul: Kaynak Yayınları, Second Edition, 1996). Yurtaslan, Ali, *Itiraflar: MHP Merkezindeki Adam Abdullah Catlı'yı Anlatıyor* (Istanbul: Kaynak Yayınları, Second Edition, 1997).
5. Türkeş, Alparslan, *Milliyetçilik*, p.16.
6. The MHP administration denied such an illegal link and argued that such a person could not be a member of their community. However, his funeral was dominated by the Idealists, and he was claimed as a martyr who fought for the cause of Turkish nationalism.
7. The relationship between Abdullah Çatli and the MHP is explained in the confessions of Ali Yurtaslan. See, Yurtaslan, Ali, *Itiraflar: MHP Merkezindeki Adam Abdullah Çatlı'yi Anlatıyor.*
8. Büyükbaş, Adnan, *Ülkücüye Mektuplar* (Istanbul: Hamle Basin-Yayin, 1995). I have rephrased the words of Adnan Buyukbaş, since a direct translation from Turkish to English turns out to be meaningless.
9. At the time the party used a different name, Milliyetçi Çalışma Partisi (Nationalist Work Party, MÇP), for the previous one was still banned from politics.
10. In order to pass the national threshold of ten per cent, an electoral pact between RP, MHP and a minor third party was formed before the 1991 general elections. Therefore, the results represents neither the electoral strength of the RP nor the MHP alone.
11. Coşkun, Bekir, *Hürriye*t, 8 April 1997, p.3.
12. DP government was ended by the 1960 military intervention and three ministers, including the prime minister, Adnan Menderes, were executed by the military junta. Alparslan Türkeş, as a colonel, was active during the early phases of the *coup d'état.*
13. The last one, RP, is at least considered to be an enemy by the top administration of the party. In his last interview before his death, to which the media gave extensive coverage, Alparslan Türkeş pointed at the threat of Islamic Fundamentalism represented by the RP.
14. Alparslan Türkeş , *Milliyetçilik*, p.17.
15. Milliyetçi Hareket Partisi Programı (Ankara, 24 Ocak 1993), pp.37–8.
16. This organization was the continuation of Türkçüler Derneği (Turkists Club), which was founded in 1963 by grassroot racists, such as Nihal Atsız and İsmet Tümtürk.
17. Tanıl Bora and Kemal Can, *Devlet, Ocak, Dergah: 12 Eylül'den 1990'lara Ülkücü Hareket* (Istanbul: İletişim Yayınları, Third Edition, 1994), p.54.
18. Today's Islamist RP is the continuation of the MSP.
19. Bülent Ecevit at the time was the leader of CHP.
20. Dilipak, Abdurrahman, *Türkiye Nereye Gidiyor?* (Istanbul: Risale Yayınları, 1988).
21. Bora, Tanıl and Kemal Can, *Devlet, Ocak, Dergah*, pp.152–3.
22. Ibid., pp.155.
23. For a summary of Nouvelle Droite's ideas on the matter, see Jim Wolfreys, 'The Programme of the National Front: An Iron Hand in a Velvet Glove', *Parliamentary Affairs*, Vol. 46, No. 3 (July 1993).
24. Dilipak, Abdurrahman, *Türkiye Nereye Gidiyor?*
25. Turkish-Islamic synthesis section is primarily adapted from, Tanıl Bora and Kemal Can, *Devlet, Ocak, Dergah*, pp.160–77.
26. Ömer Laçiner, 'Foreword', Tanıl Bora and Kemal Can, *Devlet, Ocak, Dergah*, p.10. The

interviews conducted with 870 MHP voters as to how they had become supporters of the movement in the late 1970s reveals that only 30 per cent of them voted for the party with pure anti-Communist motives. Here one needs to stress that during this period anti-Communist sentiments were at their peak in Turkey. For the results of the interviews see Mustafa Çalık, *MHP Hareketi, -kaynakları ve gelişimi-, 1965–1980* (Ankara: Cedit Neşriyat, 1995), pp.149–61.

27. Jim Wolfreys, 'The Programme of the National Front: An Iron Hand in a Velvet Glove'.
28. An outlawed Kurdish terrorist organization which fights for a free Kurdistan, including lands from Turkey, Iraq, Iran and Syria.
29. Milliyetçi Hareket Partisi Programı (Ankara, 24 Ocak 1993), pp.16–8.
30. Alparslan Türkeş, *Milliyetçilik*, p.19.
31. The FN programme is referred to as 'an iron hand in a velvet glove' by the organization itself. See E. Plenel and A. Rollat, *La République Menacée* (Paris, 1992), p.248 cited in Wolfreys, 'The Programme of the National Front'.
32. For instance, both the FN in France, and the Freiheitliche Partei Österreich (Freedom Party of Austria, FPO), have adopted economic liberalism in their programmes. For the FN, see Wolfreys, 'The Programme of the National Front'. For the FPO, see FPO, Programm für Wien 1991(Vienna: Landesgruppe Wien, 1991).
33. Wolfreys, 'The Programme of the National Front'.
34. *Bizim Ocak*, May 1990, p.3, cited in Bora and Can, *Devlet, Ocak, Dergah*, p.349.
35. For a more detailed analysis of the 'agriculture cities', see Tahsin, Yahyaoğlu, *Tarim Kentleri-Milliyetçi Toplumcu Düzen (Dokuz Işık Üzerine Incelemeler)* (Istanbul: Milli Ülkü Yayınevi, 1975).
36. See below on family and moral values.
37. The average increase in the population in Turkey is 2.4 per cent per year.
38. The MHP is against Marxist or Socialist trade unions.
39. Milliyetçi Hareket Partisi Programı (Ankara, 24 Ocak 1993), p.8.
40. Ibid., pp.12–13.
41. For a detailed analysis of how the 1980 military coup affected the Idealist cadres see, Bora and Can, *Devlet, Ocak, Dergah*, pp.101–47.
42. For a detailed analysis of the MHP's interpretation of Turkish history, see Türkeş, *Milliyetçilik*, pp.29–40.
43. Mustafa Çalık, *MHP Hareketi, -kaynakları ve gelişimi-, 1965–1980* (Ankara: Cedit Neşriyat, 1995), pp.133–4.
44. Ibid., backcover.
45. Türkiye Sosyal Ekonomik Siyasal Araştırmalar Vakfı (TÜSES), *Türkiye'de Siyasi Partilerin Seçmenleri ve Sosyal Demokrasinin Toplumsal Tabanı* (Ankara: Cem Yayınevi, 1995), pp.47–8.
46. For instance, when women's associations marched against sharia rule, the leader of ANAP, Mesut Yılmaz, stated that they do not support a march against sharia rule, because it can be interpreted as a march against religion.
47. The party changed its name to Alleanza Nazionale (National Alliance, AN).

Ottoman Policy during the Bulgarian Independence Crisis, 1908–9: Ottoman Empire and Bulgaria at the Outset of the Young Turk Revolution

HASAN ÜNAL

There have been some studies about the dealings of the Young Turks, while in power 1908–18, with the Europeans Great Powers, but very little has been written about their policies towards the Balkan states during the period in question. A possible explanation for this dearth of scholarly research on the Young Turks' Balkan policies is that many experts appear to think that the Balkan states, small in size and dependent on Great Power Patrons were of negligible importance in Ottoman strategic planning and, therefore, played second fiddle, at best, in the Porte's policy formulation to the Great Powers which had the determining influence on the Empire's external policies. However, archival documents suggest that the Balkan states did have an important, if not decisive, impact on the Ottoman Empire's foreign policy-making process. An attempt will be made in this essay to prove that the Balkan states were in a position to deal a serious, if not mortal, blow to the Ottoman Empire in the early twentieth century. This will be done by analysing the strategic thinking of the Ottoman military and the civilian administration, and by pointing to Ottoman concerns *vis-à-vis* Bulgaria during the Bulgarian independence crisis. However, before embarking upon an analysis of Ottoman policy formulation during that crisis, it is best to glance at the Empire's policies towards the Balkans during the last decades of the nineteenth and early years of the twentieth centuries.

Towards the end of the nineteenth and early twentieth centuries, in particular, it was becoming hard for the Ottoman Empire to play off the Powers against each other, a game quite successfully played by Abdülhamid II during his long reign.[1] The obvious reason for that was that the Powers, which had long been at each other's throats either due to their colonial disputes or because of mutual suspicions about their intentions on the Continent, were edging towards each other. The division of the Powers into two camps was taking shape. This was in turn narrowing the room for manœuvre for the Ottoman Empire, making the Empire's relations with the Powers increasingly problematic though there was not yet an immediate threat to the Empire's political existence. But the outlook in the Balkans was quite disturbing. The potential for hostility between the Balkan states and the Ottoman Empire was self-evident. Greece, Serbia, Montenegro and Bulgaria were trying to eat up the Empire. All of these states and Romania owed their existence to national revolts against Ottoman rule, and Romania excepted, all harboured well-advertised, though conflicting, designs upon the Ottoman Empire's remaining Balkan territories. Even so, for most of the nineteenth century these designs had not ranked as the principal threat to Ottoman security: the small Balkan states remained politically and militarily weak, and were easily dominated by the Great Powers.[2] From the late 1890s onwards, however, this picture began to change. The Balkan states were growing in wealth and population,[3] and emancipating themselves from the diplomatic tutelage of Great Power patrons. Above all, they were emerging as significant military powers in their own right, capable of posing independent threats to the Ottoman Empire: the Bulgarians in particular were building up an impressive modern army, while the Greeks were laying the foundations of a modern navy. By 1900 the balance of power in the Balkans was fast turning against the Ottoman Empire.[4]

The consequences of these adverse international shifts were revealed in the Macedonian question. Macedonia, the core of the Ottoman Balkans, was a mixture of Turkish, Bulgarian, Albanian, Greek, Serbian, Vlach and Jewish populations. Greece, Bulgaria, Serbia and even Romania had long-standing ambitions in the region, and for decades these states had striven to build up their own rival parties among the Christian population through peaceful propaganda.[5] To this, Abdülhamid's regime responded with a policy of 'divide and rule', seeking to retain the loyalty of the Muslim Turks and Albanians, while also playing off the rival Christian nationalities against one another.[6] In the late 1890s, however, the Bulgarian element in Macedonia turned to violent methods: under the leadership of a political group conventionally referred to as the Internal Macedonian Revolutionary Organization (IMRO),[7] it embarked upon a campaign of agitation and terrorism against the Ottoman authorities, with the professed aim of securing a system of autonomous administration for Macedonia. Nonetheless, it was widely believed that the real objective of IMRO and its adherents was the eventual absorption of Macedonia into the neighbouring Principality of Bulgaria. In 1903 IMRO launched the unsuccessful Ilinden uprising against Ottoman rule;[8] the outcome was a low level civil war in Macedonia which lasted until the Young Turk revolution of 1908. Bulgarian armed bands harassed the Ottoman administration and army; Turks and

Albanians organized counter-bands; with the more or less open toleration of the Ottoman authorities, the local Greeks, Serbs and Vlachs also organized armed bands to fight the Bulgarians.[9]

In a broader sense, Ottoman-Bulgarian relations were quite tense on the eve of the Young Turk revolution. Nevertheless, the Sultan was bold enough to appeal to the Bulgarian government during the difficult days of the Young Turk revolution. It seems that when he ran out of options in crushing the armed rebellion which erupted in various parts of Ottoman Macedonia, he contemplated provoking a frontier crisis with Bulgaria as a means of diverting attention and restoring the solidarity of the army, large parts of which had by then turned against him.[10] The crisis, it should be added, was to have been created in connivance with the Bulgarian government.

According to Bulgarian sources, the Sultan's right-hand man, Kâmil Bey, the Ottoman Imperial Commissioner at Sofia, approached the Bulgarian Foreign Minister, Paprikov, with the following offer: Bulgaria should move troops towards the frontier to divert the forces of the Young Turks and thereby indirectly assist Abdülhamid in his attempt to crush the rebellion. It appears that even after the proclamation of the constitution, Kâmil Bey continued to press Paprikov to send troops to the border or to take other military measures to divert attention at home.[11] It also appears that other diplomatic missions got wind of these *démarches* by Kâmil Bey. For instance, Sir George Buchanan, the British representative at Sofia, reported to London on 1 August that the Ottoman Commissioner had approached Paprikov with such an offer.[12] According to French documents, Russia's diplomatic mission at Sofia was aware of Kâmil Bey's proposal, and the Russians even tried to exchange information with the French about that.[13] The First Grand Vizier who took office after the restoration of the 1876 Constitution, Said Pasha, confirmed all these rumours in an interview to the Chief British Dragoman, G.H. Fitzmaurice, that the Sultan 'rather than consent to the revival of the Constitution, had thought of creating complications with Bulgaria and even other Powers'.[14]

When Abdülhamid finally threw in the towel on 23 July by agreeing to the proclamation of the constitution, and after the appointment of Kâmil Pasha to the Grand Vizirate on 6th August, the involvement of the Committee of Union and Progress (hereafter CUP) in foreign policy-making became the order of the day. From the start, there existed scope for disagreement between Kâmil Pasha and the CUP over foreign affairs. And all this seems to have affected the Ottoman government's handling of Bulgaria during the crisis which erupted when Bulgaria declared full independence from the Empire in October 1908, coupled with the corresponding announcement by Austria-Hungary of the an nnexation of Bosnia and Herzegovina left under Austro-Hungarian occupation since 1878.

The Young Turks, widely known as the CUP in Turkish historiography, had been indulging in foreign policy analysis since 1902. A cursory look at their publications and the CUP secret communications while in opposition reveal that those Young Turks who later became influential in Ottoman politics following the proclamation of the Constitution of 1908 embraced some sort of a nationalism from 1906 onwards. But their nationalism was laced with a strong dose of 'Turkishness' as opposed to the Ottomanism of the previous decades. From the perusal of their assessments of foreign affairs, two principal observations may be made. First, the CUP exhibited a marked hostility and suspicion towards all the Powers, great and small, including Bulgaria and all other Balkan states, and a strong resentment of their interference in Ottoman internal affairs. Manifesting no special sympathy towards any Power, the CUP made no bones about its deep-rooted suspicion with regard to Bulgaria in particular, and other Balkan states in general. Second, the CUP was always at pains to disguise its Turkish nationalist, and by implication, anti-Christian leanings especially in its Ottoman-Turkish publications.[15]

At the outset of the Young Turk revolution, there remained a fundamental question: whether and how these nationalist leanings could be made use of in moulding foreign policy. The Bulgarian independence crisis which erupted soon after the Young Turk revolution of 1908 appears to have been taken by the CUP leadership as an opportunity for exercises in foreign policy-making for about six months. During this period prominent members of the CUP played an important role in Ottoman foreign policy-making though the Grand Vizier Kamil Pasha did not always see eye to eye with them.[16] And these fundamental differences between the Grand Vizier and the CUP in policy assessments as well as in practical approaches during the crisis were to cause muddling in Ottoman policy-making.

The Grand Vizier had clear views on the subject of the Empire's relations with the Balkan states. During the 1880s and early 1890s he had been known as something of a Bulgarophile, tolerating Bulgaria's absorption of Eastern Rumelia in 1885 and arguing that the Empire's security was best assured by close relations with Sofia.[17] With the emergence of a serious Macedonian problem after 1903, however, his attitude changed: he then began to speak of Bulgaria as a fundamentally hostile state, whose national ambitions posed a major security threat to Ottoman territorial integrity. In 1905, for instance, he urged Abdülhamid to conclude an alliance with Greece and Romania as the best means of containing the territorial ambitions of Bulgaria, and of its fellow-Slav states, Serbia and Montenegro. He made plain his fear that Bulgaria was preparing for a war with the Empire, perhaps to be launched in conjunction with an armed uprising in Macedonia, and that it might seek to gain the alliance of the other Balkan states by proposing a mutual partition of the Ottoman Empire's Balkan territories. He even argued that an alliance between the Empire, Greece and Romania would be the best means of deterring Bulgaria from war: it might also enable the Empire to drive a wedge between Bulgaria, on the one hand, and Serbia and Montenegro, on the other.[18] Over the following years, Kâmil Pasha continued to express considerable pessimism about the course of Ottoman-Bulgarian relations; indeed, shortly before the Young Turk revolution, he suggested to Abdülhamid that a war between the Empire and Bulgaria was likely sooner or later.[19]

As to the CUP, in the immediate aftermath of the Young Turk Revolution, its underlying anti-Europeanism and lack of any firm diplomatic preferences were expressed in vague professions of friendship for every power, big and small. While a number of CUP emissaries, mostly members of the CUP's inner circle, tried to cultivate relations with representatives of the Great Powers,[20] other prominent members were pursuing independent diplomatic contacts with the Balkan states, though here too the contacts were vague in content, and gave no convincing indication of diplomatic preference. The CUP leadership endeavoured to make use of its contacts, which it had established prior to the revolution, with various revolutionary groups in Macedonia, Bulgarian, Greek or other, to further its relations with the Balkan states to which these communities in Macedonia looked for advice and support. The Bulgarian groups, which had been on the point of exhaustion by the outbreak of the Young Turk revolution, were assisted by the CUP in various places, where the Greek armed bands were told to desist from further attacks on the Bulgarian community.[21] Fallen Bulgarian bandit leaders were exalted as 'heroes' by the CUP in various parts of Macedonia.[22] The CUP's pro-Bulgarian demonstrations soon reached a point where some representatives of the Powers at Constantinople thought that an alliance between Constantinople and Sofia was imminent.[23] In this, however, they proved mistaken. The CUP was anxious not to antagonize the Greek element in Macedonia. It continued the intimate relations which it had built up over the years with the Greek revolutionary groups,[24] and although certain Greeks do not seem to have been enthusiastic about collaborating with the CUP, the CUP's relations with the Greeks remained satisfactory right up to the Bulgarian independence crisis.[25]

The crisis which broke out at the beginning of October 1908 offered a serious and sustained test of the foreign policy of the new Ottoman regime and of its two principal components: the anti-Hamidian statesmen of the old regime who predominated in Kâmil's cabinet, and the CUP which had assumed the role of guardian of the revolution. For the European Powers, it was the issues arising out of Austria-Hungary's annexation of Bosnia-Herzegovina which loomed largest: not surprisingly, many historians refer to the international crisis of October 1908–April 1909 as the 'annexation crisis'.[26] For the Ottoman Empire, however, it was the issue of Bulgarian independence which took precedence, for pressing political and strategic reasons.

For decades, following the establishment of a fully autonomous Bulgaria under the suzerainty of the Ottoman Empire at the Berlin Congress, the objective of formal independence was a secondary priority in Sofia's policy-making because consecutive Bulgarian governments had been 'busy' in Ottoman provinces, first Eastern Rumelia and then Macedonia. Following the absorption of the former, Sofia governments resorted to aggressive policies in Ottoman Macedonia in the late 1890s through to 1908.[27] But the Young Turk revolution put Bulgaria on the spot, taking Sofia's government completely by surprise and utterly unawares: indeed, Prince Ferdinand was abroad, and Malinov's Democratic Party cabinet maintained an absolute public reserve: only after some three weeks, under pressure from the opposition, did the semi-official newspaper *Pryaporets* announce that it was abstaining from approval or disapproval until the shape of the future Ottoman administration was definitively established.[28] This official reserve seems to have reflected genuine uncertainty as to the import of the revolution in the Ottoman Empire, and as to its likely impact upon Bulgaria's interests, above all, in Macedonia. In the long term, as viewed from Sofia, the revolution might conceivably herald the Empire's descent into anarchy and final dissolution, but it might also presage the Empire's revival. The short-term outlook was equally obscure. Optimists believed that the new constitutional regime would facilitate Bulgaria's programme of Macedonian autonomy: they were encouraged by the CUP's friendly overtures to the Bulgarian element in Macedonia,[29] and saw the revolution as a blow to Greek and Serb aspirations in the region. Reporting to Prince Ferdinand on 25 July, two days after the restoration of the constitution Paprikov declared:

> In a few days Macedonia has become unrecognizable ... In a word something inexplicable and improbable has happened. The frontier is open and entry into Macedonia is most free, the fallen Bulgarian chetniks are exalted even by the Turks as popular heroes.[30] All this is improbable, but it is true; that which the revolution has given to the Macedonians in ten days, the reforms could not have given in as many years. Now in Macedonia, the Serbian element no longer exists, that which Serbia has built up over long years has collapsed in a week. The Greeks have lost a great deal. However things may turn out hereafter, the position of the Bulgarian element is affirmed...[31]

On the other hand, pessimists were quick to point to the Young Turks' underlying nationalism, to their ambitions to revive the Ottoman Empire as a unitary state, and to rumours that the CUP had plans to undermine the established cultural and communal privileges of the Empire's non-Muslim populations, including its Bulgarians. Above all, the Powers' willingness to abandon their various reform projects in Macedonia caused serious concern, by closing off one route to Macedonian autonomy. When the British Foreign Office announced that it had suspended all representations to the Porte for the creation of a mobile force in Macedonia, and would also withdraw its gendarmerie officers from the region, the Bulgarian Agent at London retorted that the Young Turk revolution was totally 'illusory', and that nothing useful was to be hoped for from it.[32]

While Bulgarian authorities were weighing the pros and cons of the Young Turk revolution, the first practical proposal as to what to do came from Ivan Geshov, the Bulgarian agent at Constantinople. He suggested as early as 1 August that Bulgaria should respond to the revolution with a declaration of independence:

> ... the Young Turk revolution is not something good for Bulgaria ... because it is clear that the revolution pushed away from Bulgaria at a still greater distance the solution of the Macedonian question as we have understood it and as we have yearned for it... My conclusion is that in the final analysis, we, as a state, lose from the revolution because it has displaced the Macedonian question and our position in it has been significantly weakened ... As we lose by the Young Turk coup, we are obliged to seek some revenge. At today's time, this cannot be other than the full independence of Bulgaria ...[33]

It appears that Geshov's stance was soon adopted by Paprikov, and that by mid-September, following discussions between Malinov and Prince Ferdinand in Hungary, it had been decided to take early steps to procure Bulgaria's full and formal independence from the Ottoman Empire. This was a decision in principle only. The question of timing was left open, as was the question of means: indeed, there are indications that at this stage the Bulgarian government had hopes of achieving independence by agreement through direct negotiations with the Porte and the CUP.[34]

As it turned out, however, Bulgaria's path to independence was anything but harmonious. From mid-September onwards, relations between Constantinople and Sofia deteriorated markedly, with the result that Bulgaria's declaration of independence, when it came, took the form of an act of open hostility towards the Ottoman Empire. The first stage in this deterioration of Ottoman-Bulgarian relations arose with the 'Geshov Incident' of September 1908. This incident was triggered off by the

Ottoman government's failure to invite Geshov, in his capacity as Bulgaria's agent in Constantinople, to a banquet for the Diplomatic Corps held in honour of the Sultan's birthday on 12 September. It is not clear what had prompted the Porte to withhold the invitation,[35] or indeed, whether its decision was deliberate. On the one hand, as the Porte was subsequently to argue, Geshov was the representative of a vassal state, and as such, not an accredited member of the Diplomatic Corps: the question of an invitation did not arise. On the other, there was some speculation that the new Ottoman regime was determined to re-emphasize its rights as Bulgaria's formal suzerain,[36] and that its action in not inviting Geshov was a calculated 'snub' or provocation.[37] There is even some doubt as to what passed between Kâmil Pasha and Geshov when the latter first came to the Porte to complain. According to what Geshov told an Ottoman journalist, the Grand Vizier had said that 'you will not be invited because Bulgaria is a Principality under Turkey, whereas the banquet has been arranged for foreign representatives'.[38] But, according to Kâmil Pasha's subsequent account, Geshov had failed to inform him of his displeasure; had he done so, Kâmil added, the incident could easily have been avoided, as the Porte would have invited Geshov in company with some other senior officials, thus giving the banquet a less exclusively diplomatic character.[39]

Be that as it may, it soon became clear that neither side was willing to concede, and the attempts of Marschall and Pallavicini, respectively ambassadors of Germany and Austria-Hungary, to mediate proved fruitless.[40] The Bulgarian government instructed Geshov to leave Constantinople should the Porte not give way, and Geshov duly withdrew to Sofia on 13 September, the day after the banquet.[41] At this stage, neither side seemed prepared to force a more serious breach. The Bulgarians appear to have sensed that the Geshov Incident could not of itself justify a declaration of independence,[42] while the Ottoman government professed itself anxious to smooth matters over.

The Ottoman Imperial Deputy-Commissioner at Sofia, Refik Bey, was quick to express his surprise to Paprikov at Geshov's sudden arrival in Sofia, 'at a time when good relations between the two countries needed to be strengthened'. He asked Paprikov to send Geshov back at once, before the whole matter became known to journalists. Paprikov, for his part, expressed concern at the straining of relations, but he made it clear to Refik Bey that the Bulgarian government could not stomach the 'treatment' to which their agent had been subjected, and warned that his return to Constantinople was out of the question until and unless the Ottoman government apologized profusely for its behaviour, reassuring Bulgaria that its agents at Constantinople would never be treated similarly again. Paprikov went so far as to threaten that 'if the official diplomatic title of their agent to the Porte was not to be recognised as it had been in the past, the Bulgarian government would, in his personal opinion, feel the need to reduce the title of the Ottoman Imperial Commissioner to that of Commissioner for Religious Foundations' (Vakıf Komiseri).[43]

At this stage, the dispute still centred upon the technical issue of the invitation to the banquet. According to Refik Bey, the Bulgarians argued that their agents at Constantinople had been invited to ceremonial occasions in the Palace together with foreign representatives on previous occasions, most recently when Geshov and other accredited diplomats had offered their congratulations to the Sultan on his proclamation of the constitution.[44] The Porte replied with a denial that Bulgarian agents had previously attended all official receptions, and added that none of the occasions when they had been received could be regarded as official, or exclusively reserved for diplomatic 'Chefs des Missions'. As to Geshov's presence at the Palace on the occasion of the proclamation of the constitution, the Porte added, this was the responsibility of the Acting Doyen of the Diplomatic Corps, not of the Sublime Porte.[45] Even so, Refik Bey seemed optimistic that the episode could be smoothed over: he reported that the attitude of the Bulgarian press was 'moderate and prudent'.[46]

However, on 16 September, Refik Bey struck a less optimistic note, reporting rumours that Geshov's recall from Constantinople had been designed behind the back of the government by the Bulgarian diplomatic agents at Paris and St Petersburg, with a view to ousting the Bulgarian foreign minister in the ensuing diplomatic squabble. There were apparently those who believed that as Prince Ferdinand had, with the advent of the Young Turk Revolution, despaired of becoming 'King of Macedonia', he now thought that by 'insulting' Geshov the Turks were intending to inflict another blow to his domestic standing.[47] Before any progress could be made towards a satisfactory resolution of the Geshov Incident, Ottoman-Bulgarian relations took a further turn for the worse when, on 20 September, Bulgarian troops seized the section of the Oriental Railway passing through Eastern Roumelia.[48]

What apparently prompted the seizure of the railways was what the Bulgarians regarded as yet another humiliating example of the Ottoman Empire's determination to re-emphasize Bulgaria's vassal status. Following the Young Turk revolution, strikes among workers, hitherto prohibited, had broken out all over the Empire, particularly in urban centres. This wave of strikes had eventually affected the Oriental Railway Company's Constantinople depot. The Porte, it appears, was anxious that this particular strike should not spread to the company's workers in Eastern Rumelia in Bulgaria, for otherwise, coming on the heels of the Geshov Incident, it might offer Sofia further ground for complaint and protest. In order to forestall this contingency, the Ottoman government immediately dispatched a group of military officers to Eastern Rumelia in a specially prepared train, with instructions to talk the workers out of going on strike. To the Bulgarian government, however, this direct intervention by the Porte in Eastern Rumelia was quite unacceptable.[49] Troops on the frontier point were ordered not to allow in the Ottoman officers; meanwhile the Oriental Railway Company's workers came out on strike.

Faced with the outbreak of the strike, the Company felt that it had no choice but to ask the Bulgarian railway authorities to take over the lines and run them until the strike was over, and on 20 September the lines were duly occupied. It was soon apparent that this occupation was intended to be permanent. The Bulgarians had long resented the Oriental Railway Company's presence in Eastern Rumelia, seeing it as a reminder of their vassal status, and even though the strike was over within one or two days in certain sections, the Bulgarian railway authorities categorically refused to allow the Company's officials to resume normal work.[50] On 22 September, Colonel Mehmed Şükrü Bey reported from the Ottoman Imperial Commission at Sofia that the Bulgarian authorities were explaining their refusal to return the lines as a temporary measure, whose purpose was to force the Company to compensate Bulgaria for losses of trade suffered during the strike; he suggested, however, that the Bulgarian government's real intention was to nationalise the lines, and reported rumours that the financial aspects of nationalization were already under discussion.[51]

Meanwhile the Oriental Railway Company itself asked the Porte to take steps to secure the return of the lines.[52] However, on 24 September the Bulgarian government warned the Porte off. In a *note-verbale* delivered to the Ottoman Commission in Sofia, it explained that:

> la prise de l'exploitation des chemins de fer de la Compagnie Orientale par l'administration des Chemins de fer bulgares a eu lieu par suite de la grève et sur une entente avec le représentant de la Compagnie des Chemins de fer. Toutefois, la remise de l'exploitation de cette ligne ferrée à la susdite Compagnie est une question qui sera réglée entre le gouvernement Princier et la Compagnie des Chemins de fer Orientaux.[53]

In a separate memorandum to the Powers, the Bulgarian government alleged that the strike had been engineered by the Porte with a view to paralysing vital railway lines in Bulgaria, and that it could not consider the strike terminated.[54]

Coming hard on the heels of the Geshov Incident, and being accompanied by the first rumours of a Bulgarian mobilization, the railway dispute cast an ominous light on Bulgaria's intentions, and the Grand Vizier was quick to sense that a declaration of independence might follow: he instructed the Foreign Minister, Tevfik Pasha, to approach the governments of Greece, Serbia and Romania, and ascertain their likely reactions to such a move. At the same time, however, he sought to appease Sofia, instructing Refik Bey on 26 September to remind the Bulgarian government of the benevolent role he had played during the Eastern Rumelian crisis of 1885, and to express his anxiety to close the Geshov Incident.[55] Three days later Refik Bey replied that Malinov had expressed his and Prince Ferdinand's regret that the Geshov Incident should have occurred, though without abandoning their insistence that the Bulgarian side had been in the right throughout; as to the railway dispute, however, Malinov had given no clear-cut answer, except to mention the possibility of offering the Ottoman government some compensation for Bulgaria's take-over of the lines.[56]

By now, the Bulgarian government had made up its mind to press ahead to formal independence. It still had hopes of doing so with the Porte's agreement, and apparently instructed its Commercial Attaché in Salonica, Shopov, to make a confidential approach to the CUP. According to Shopov's reports, his CUP contacts expressed their desire to be on the best possible terms with Bulgaria, and stated that the question of independence for Bulgaria could, at an appropriate moment, easily be settled between two friendly countries. Paprikov in turn empowered Shopov to suggest to the CUP that it should oblige the Ottoman government and the Sultan to recognise Bulgaria as an independent state; in return, 'we are not far from the idea that we should enter into an alliance which will be useful for both sides'. On 25 September, however, Shopov replied that the CUP was of the opinion that it could not possibly take the initiative in getting Bulgaria recognised, but that it would be quite a different matter should it be placed before a 'fait accompli'. According to Shopov, the CUP believed that a sincere agreement between Constantinople and Sofia would strengthen their regime, whereas a serious rupture of relations between the two countries would undermine their authority and create favourable terrain for a resurgence of reaction within the Empire. Therefore, in their conversations with Shopov, they stressed that they desired an agreement and an alliance with Bulgaria, emphasizing that 'the question of independence for Bulgaria is nothing in comparison with the important and great idea of serious and lasting agreement between Turkey and Bulgaria'.[57]

Shopov was not Bulgaria's only channel. It appears that the Bulgarian government also sent Konstantin Hadzi Kalchov, an old acquaintance of Kâmil Pasha, to Constantinople for talks with the Grand Vizier, as well as with Ahmed Rıza and other CUP representatives.[58] Little is known about this mission, though it appears that Hadzi Kalchov subsequently claimed that his mission was remarkably successful: he persuaded the CUP to agree to the transfer of the Eastern Rumelian railways to Bulgarian control, though without mentioning the question of ultimate ownership, and he also persuaded the CUP to agree in principle to the recognition of Bulgarian independence. According to the plan, worked out between Hadzi Kalchov and the CUP and the Grand Vizier, Kâmil Pasha, was to have paid an official visit to Sofia during which Bulgaria was to have been proclaimed an independent kingdom with the approval of the Sultan.[59] Whatever the truth of these claims, it is clear that the Grand Vizier remained anxious to avoid an open breach with Sofia, and at the beginning of October he asked the Bulgarian government to send Grigor Nachovich, a Bulgarian statesman of pronounced pro-Ottoman leanings,[60] to Constantinople for talks. However, Sofia refused this request.[61]

At this stage, the Powers began to sense the seriousness of the situation: almost all pointed out that the Ottoman side had been legally in the right. But they expressed a wish to see the whole matter closed. They even warned Sofia of the consequences of a declaration of independence. The British in particular made the strongest representations at Sofia. But by the beginning of October it was clear to London that these warnings had failed to produce the desired effect: rumours of an impending declaration of independence by Bulgaria were growing. The British chose to take the diplomatic lead, and on 2 October they issued a circular calling on the Powers to urge restraint upon Sofia. Austria-Hungary in particular was asked to bring pressure on Prince Ferdinand, who was then in Budapest. France and Germany at once accepted the British proposal.[62] So did the Russians, who even expressed readiness to join in representations with the other Powers, but they independently reminded the Bulgarian government of the dangers with which a declaration of independence would be beset. As a last resort, the Russian Minister at Sofia, on instructions from his government, suggested that the declaration of independence be postponed until March 1909, by which time the issue might be resolved by means of negotiations. It is interesting to note that the only Power which did not join in the representations, and which professed disbelief that a Bulgarian action was imminent, was Austria-Hungary.[63]

However, none of these warnings on the part of the Powers made any impression upon the Bulgarian government.[64] Though the Bulgarian government was well aware of the dangers a declaration of independence would involve, the rumour that Austria-Hungary was about to announce the annexation of Bosnia and Herzegovina was sufficient encouragement for Sofia to press ahead. Having personally obtained Prince Ferdinand's blessing in Austria-Hungary, Malinov returned to Sofia, where on 29 September the cabinet formally agreed to proceed to a unilateral declaration of independence. It was decided that the declaration should be made at

Veliko Tarnovo on 5 October, as soon as Prince Ferdinand returned to Bulgaria.[65]

The Bulgarian declaration of independence took place against a background of speculation that the Sofia government might be preparing to launch an invasion of the Ottoman Empire, and for much of October fear of a Bulgarian attack was the single most important factor in the Porte's strategic planning. From late September onwards, in fact, the Ottoman government received a stream of reports from the military officers attached to its Commission at Sofia, all suggesting that the Bulgarian army was conducting a major mobilization under the cover of its annual autumn manœuvres. The first reports were confused, and led the Ottoman War Ministry and the General Staff to ask for clarification: the Commission replied that it had no funds to support an extensive espionage service, and added for good measure that its own officers' salaries were some four months in arrears.[66] Nevertheless, the picture soon grew clearer and more disquieting. The War Ministry received information that the reservists summoned to the Bulgarian army's manœuvres might not be discharged, or that if they were, their places would be taken by other reservists.[67] It also learned that the Bulgarian army's contingency plans for war with the Ottoman Empire envisaged the delivery of an early knock-out blow, taking advantage of the Bulgarians' superior mobilization speed, and that there was a belief in Sofia that the Young Turk revolution and its attendant domestic confusion offered Bulgaria an opportunity for a successful offensive campaign.[68] The Commission also reported the alarming news that the Bulgarian government was preparing to instigate trouble in Macedonia: it had allegedly distributed 50 million francs to its 'agents-provocateurs' in the region, had equipped them with a printing-press, and was granting generous 'severance payments' to Bulgarian officials who would go to Macedonia.[69]

By the time the declaration of independence took place, the situation on the Empire's frontier with Bulgaria looked ominous. The Bulgarian army had mobilised between 100,000 and 115,000 men,[70] and there were suggestions that this number might shortly be increased to 215,000.[71] True, the message in which Prince Ferdinand announced the declaration of independence to the Sultan was couched in conciliatory terms.[72] But, it was followed by further alarming news of Bulgarian military preparations: the Sofia government had allegedly ordered 200,000 kilograms of rations for its troops, for delivery by the end of October;[73] troops were being moved towards the frontier,[74] and the mobilization of reservists accelerated; arms were being distributed to the population in districts bordering on the Empire.[75]

Measures of counter-mobilization were set in train by the Ottoman military authorities, but it was obvious that the Bulgarians had a considerable head start: the Ottoman army was in no position to launch an offensive campaign against Bulgaria.[76] This effectively ruled out any military response to the declaration of independence, and when the Ottoman cabinet met on 7 October, the War Minister stated the position bluntly: 'We don't even have rawhide shoes for our soldiery to put on, let alone fight.' Kâmil Pasha threw the blame onto the ex-War Minister Rıza Pasha, maintaining that he had done nothing but accumulate personal wealth during his long term of office. The Porte decided that it must find a way out through diplomacy, and postponed a reply to Ferdinand's message until it had consulted the Powers; it also decided to ask the Powers to restrain Bulgaria from further mobilization.[77]

The Powers' responses were generally favourable. Britain, France, Italy, Germany and Russia all deprecated Prince Ferdinand's violation of the Treaty of Berlin, and indicated that they would abstain from recognizing Bulgaria's independence. In addition, all these Powers promised to instruct their representatives at Sofia to press the Bulgarian government from further measures of mobilization, or any steps that might endanger the peace. Only Austria-Hungary refused to follow suit on the grounds that it had no information suggesting that the Bulgarians were preparing for war.[78]

Having been reassured that a majority of the Powers would not recognize Bulgaria's independence, the Porte was finally able to send a reply to Prince Ferdinand on 13 October, reminding him that the international status of Bulgaria had been defined by international treaties signed by the Powers and the Ottoman Empire, and could not be altered by a unilateral act by Sofia. To rub the point in, the reply was sent in the name of the Grand Vizier and not of the Sultan, as a formal reminder of Bulgaria's vassal status.[79] The result was a further increase in Ottoman-Bulgarian tension: Prince Ferdinand complained that the reply was 'insolent', and threatened to order a general mobilization.[80]

Thereafter the tension gradually eased. On 15 October Refik Bey reported from Sofia that the Bulgarian cabinet, which had been in secret session for some days,[81] had finally ruled out a military solution in favour of a settlement through negotiations.[82] Two days later an Ottoman journalist arrived in Sofia, conveying a message from the Grand Vizier to the Bulgarian government: this indicated that the Porte was ready for direct bilateral negotiations, and would not necessarily prefer to leave matters to a conference of the Powers.[83] On 19 October the Bulgarian government despatched Dimitrov, the Secretary-General of the Foreign Ministry, and Stoyanovich, the Director of the Posts and Telegraphs, to hold talks with the Grand Vizier at Constantinople. The details of the discussions between these two emissaries and Kâmil Pasha have not been traced, though it appears that the Grand Vizier at first took a tough line, insisting that Sofia must pay substantial financial compensation for its independence, and even hinting that Bulgaria should abandon Eastern Rumelia.[84] Evidently this was not his final word, for the outcome of the discussions was neither a rupture nor a revival of tension; instead, as will be seen, the Bulgarian government sent a higher-level mission to Constantinople for further talks at the end of the month.[85]

In the meantime the CUP had also taken steps to calm the situation. It despatched two emissaries to Sofia, Lieutenant-Colonel Faik Bey and Major Fethi Bey, hoping not only to contact the Bulgarian government but also to influence Bulgarian public opinion, where partisans of good relations with the Ottoman Empire had already responded to the Young Turk revolution by forming an 'Allied Committee for Political, Economic and Cultural Rapprochement between Bulgaria and Turkey'.[86] Addressing a gathering of this association, Faik Bey and Fethi Bey stressed that it was, after all, the Bulgarians in Macedonia and Bulgaria who had taken up the most sympathetic attitude towards the Young Turk revolution, and that a war between the two countries would ruin them both.[87] The Bulgarian association, for its part, responded warmly to the CUP emissaries' call to prevent war. The upshot was a joint declaration to the effect that 'the populations of both countries are against an armed conflict, for which there exist no motives, and expect both governments not to decide to disturb the peace against the will of their peoples'. The two committees also vowed to do all in their power to influence their respective governments towards a *rapprochement* between Bulgaria and the Ottoman Empire.[88]

There are some indications that the Bulgarian government, too, was anxious to deal directly with the CUP. On 19 October the British Consul-General in Salonica reported that he had been approached by his Bulgarian colleague Shopov, who had requested the use of the consulate's telegraph facilities. Shopov had explained that he was about to enter into negotiations with the CUP, with a view to the conclusion of an alliance between Bulgaria and the Ottoman Empire.[89] Evidently, this amounted to a reprise of the discussions which Shopov had held with the CUP immediately prior to the declaration of independence. It is possible that the CUP was tempted: Kâmil Pasha told Lowther that the CUP appeared to favour a Bulgarian alliance, but added that for his own part he was reluctant to enter into any discussion of this issue until all questions arising out of the declaration of independence had been resolved.[90]

There remained the question of Bulgaria's demobilization. As early as 17 October, Paprikov had told the British Minister at Sofia that Bulgaria would stand down her forces if the Porte would do likewise, and the Russians soon indicated that they would prefer any demobilization to be mutual.[91] The Porte remained cautious: from London, Rifat Pasha, Ottoman

Ambassador there, counselled against placing faith in Bulgarian guarantees.[92] Equally important, the Porte's belated counter-mobilization was now in full swing, with large numbers of reservists being transferred to the Bulgarian frontier from Ottoman Asia, and the military balance was beginning to shift in the Empire's favour.[93] The British proved reluctant to press the Porte too hard on this issue, despite Russian promptings: Lowther pointed to the danger of 'reactionary' outbreaks against the new regime, particularly in the capital, and suggested that the Porte's military precautions were justified on these grounds alone.[94] Not until the beginning of November, after the Bulgarians had demobilised some 50,000 troops, did Britain advise the Porte to respond in kind. This advice was promptly taken.[95]

In the meantime the Grand Vizier had initiated steps to enhance the Ottoman Empire's military security against Bulgaria through understandings with the other Balkan states. It appears that as early as 2 October, before Prince Ferdinand's declaration of independence, the Porte had approached the governments of Romania, Serbia and Greece with offers of military alliances. As early as 7 October, Kâmil Pasha was able to report to the cabinet that Serbia's response had been welcoming, that the reaction of Greece had been non-committal, but that Romania, a long-standing ally of Austria-Hungary, had returned a clear refusal.[96] Evidently, the Grand Vizier's immediate concern was to enhance the Empire's security against the threat of an early Bulgarian attack, but there is also evidence that he entertained longer-term conceptions. In a letter to Gabriel Noradonghian, the Minister of Public Works, Kâmil Pasha reiterated his view, already expressed before the revolution, that a war between the Ottoman Empire and Bulgaria was sooner or later inevitable, and indicated that he would regard an alliance with Romania, Serbia and Greece as having offensive as well as defensive implications. He envisaged that the alliance should run for a period of three years, during which time it would serve to insure the Empire against Bulgarian aggression. At the end of three years, however, the Empire should be strong enough to launch an offensive war against Bulgaria, if need be, unilaterally, with two war aims in view: firstly, to destroy at source Bulgaria's capacity to threaten the Empire in Macedonia, and secondly once more to detach Eastern Rumelia from Bulgaria.[97]

The Grand Vizier's proposal to separate Eastern Rumelia from Bulgaria was particularly striking, and appears to have been seriously meant: as will be seen, both the Porte and the CUP were to raise the idea of such a separation in their discussions with the Powers, and to suggest that it might be achieved by diplomatic means. There can be little doubt that their fundamental concern was to enhance the Empire's military security by transforming Eastern Rumelia into a demilitarised buffer-state: as Kâmil

Pasha subsequently explained to Lowther, as long as Bulgaria remained in possession of Eastern Rumelia, the Empire would face the heavy burden of maintaining large forces on its frontier.[98]

The Porte promptly drew up draft conventions for discussion with Serbia, Romania and Greece. The draft convention with Serbia had a number of peculiarities, and is discussed below. The conventions with Greece and Romania, however, were almost identical: the sole difference was that the convention with Greece was to run for five years, and that with Romania for three.[99] The available documentation does not explain the reasons for this difference. These conventions with Greece and Romania each stipulated that the contracting parties should engage to make common cause in every war, offensive or defensive, which any of them would find necessary to wage, but added that no party to either convention could open hostilities without having previous consultation. The draft conventions also stipulated that, should an attack upon one of the contracting parties be feared, the contracting parties should act in perfect accord in all military matters, and that each party should make military preparations in accordance with the spirit of the agreement. As the conventions had an offensive character, too, it was stipulated that each party should profit equally from all advantages and territorial gains resulting from a successful war. Finally it was stipulated that absolute secrecy should be observed with regard to the conventions.[100]

In practice, however, the Grand Vizier's project for a grand anti-Bulgarian alliance embracing all the other Balkan states ran out of steam rather rapidly. As noted, the Romanians had rebuffed his initial approach, and it remains unclear whether serious negotiations with Bucharest were ever begun. With Greece, on the other hand, relations were quickly overshadowed by a local crisis in Crete, an autonomous province of the Empire which had long since ceased to be under the Porte's effective control: on 7 October, taking its cue from the annexation of Bosnia-Herzegovina and the Bulgarian declaration of independence, the Cretan provincial assembly proclaimed the island's union with Greece.[101] However, both countries were at pains to minimize the affair. The Greek Minister to the Porte reported home that the CUP and the Turkish press were ignoring the Cretan issue, and had taken up a very friendly attitude. The Greek side apparently responded in kind.[102] Indeed, on 11 October the CUP confidentially informed the Greek Consul at Salonica that, war with Bulgaria now seeming unavoidable, the CUP had decided to arm the population, but that, as there were not enough rifles to go round, they would be grateful if the Greek government would supply them with some.[103]

Also on 11 October, the Ottoman Minister to Athens was instructed ask Greece to associate herself with the Ottoman protest against the violation by

Bulgaria and Austria-Hungary of the Treaty of Berlin. When the Greek Foreign Minister remarked that such a move by Athens would be the first step in the direction of hostility towards Bulgaria, and asked whether he should take this request as an open invitation to an alliance, the Porte's representative admitted that he himself regarded the matter in that light.[104] The official Greek reply to the Porte's overture emphasized that any association with the Ottoman protest would be tantamount to open hostility to Bulgaria, and the beginning of an effective common action with the Porte. The Greek government added that, despite all that, they were 'désireux, non seulement d'entretenir les meilleures relations amicales avec l'Empire voisin, mais de voir aussi s'établir entre les deux pays le rapprochement le plus étroit', and asked to know on what basis such a common action might be founded.[105]

It is possible that this Greek reply opened the way to further exchanges, perhaps involving some discussion of the Porte's projected military convention, but the available sources furnish no details. Before long, however, there were signs that the Ottoman side was drawing back. When the Greek Minister at Constantinople approached the Grand Vizier on 11 November to propose steps towards a closer understanding, he was fobbed off by Kâmil Pasha with the remark that the Greeks had better wait until the Cretan question got out of the way.[106] Probably, the British Minister to Athens was correct in his assessment that conditions had changed since the idea of an alliance was first mooted, as the danger of war between the Ottoman Empire and Bulgaria was now over. The Greek Prime Minister himself conceded that the grounds for an alliance had now been diminished, although the necessity for closer co-operation and a better understanding was as urgent as ever.[107] At all events, it seems clear that no Ottoman-Greek treaty was finalized or signed.

There remained the possibility of an alliance with Serbia and Montenegro. As already noted, the Serbs had returned a clearly positive response to Kâmil Pasha's overtures at the beginning of October, and the Ottoman Legation in Belgrade had been the object of several popular demonstrations of support.[108] This was scarcely surprising, for Serbia and Montenegro both had long-standing territorial aspirations in Bosnia and Herzegovina, whose population was in good part ethnically Serb, and both viewed the Austro-Hungarian annexation as a direct blow to their national interests. In any case, relations between Serbia and Austria-Hungary were poor: since 1906 the two states had been engaged in a customs war.[109] However, the opening of alliance negotiations between Constantinople and Belgrade was delayed, since Serbia wished first of all to reach a formal agreement with Montenegro. A Serb-Montenegrin military convention was signed on 24 October:[110] though its terms were secret, the Serbs went out of their way to assure the Porte that it was in no way directed against the Ottoman Empire, and indeed, the Ottoman Minister to Serbia, Azarian Efendi, was the only foreign representative invited to the banquet given by the Serbian King on the occasion of the convention's signature.[111]

The signature of the Serb-Montenegrin convention opened the way to alliance negotiations between these two Balkan states and the Ottoman Empire in November. Given that the Porte had failed to win over Romania, and that it was soon to lose interest in the possibility of an understanding with Greece, it is worth asking why it should have continued to pursue an alliance with Serbia and Montenegro. The answer would appear to lie partly in the hope of bringing pressure to bear upon Austria-Hungary, but partly, too, in the Porte's fear, already expressed to the British, that Serbia and Montenegro might be tempted to demand compensation for the annexation of Bosnia and Herzegovina at Ottoman expense. No doubt this fear was further stimulated by the knowledge that Serbia and Montenegro enjoyed close relations with Russia. This points to an undeclared consideration behind the Grand Vizier's policy of *rapprochement* with the Balkan states: namely, a concern to keep the Balkan states in play, and to dissuade them from entering into commitments or combinations which might threaten Ottoman interests.

At the beginning of November, the Serbian government despatched a special envoy, Novaković, to Constantinople to negotiate an alliance with the Porte;[112] Novaković was followed by a Montenegrin delegate, Vuković.[113] Kâmil Pasha promptly showed Novaković the draft of an 'alliance défensive'. This stated that Serbia and the Ottoman Empire, animated by the desire to safeguard their respective territorial possessions against all eventual aggressions, had decided to conclude 'une convention spéciale défensive'.[114] According to the original text, the Ottoman Empire would be expected to use its good offices with the Great Powers, as well as with Austria-Hungary, in the case that an attack by the Dual Monarchy upon Serbia were threatened, in order to prevent a final 'rupture' between these two states. Should the Porte's efforts fail to stop the war, and should a Great Power (by implication, Russia) indicate its desire to make common cause against the Dual Monarchy, the Ottoman government would not hesitate to offer Serbia military assistance. However, it was made clear that Serbia was under no circumstances to declare war upon Austria-Hungary without having previously informed the Porte and obtained its consent.[115] With regard to Bulgaria, it was agreed that in the event of an attack upon either party, or of provocation by Sofia of a nature intended to disturb the peace in the Balkans, both sides were to mobilise and dispatch sufficient number of troops to defend each other's territory, and that the commanders of their respective armies were to concert their military operations.[116] While, on the one hand, it was stipulated that the contracting parties would designate through a special convention the forces that each side was to deploy against the common enemy, the Empire and Serbia were at once to engage, should such a contingency prove unavoidable, to mobilize all the land and naval forces at their disposal from the conclusion of the convention onwards.[117] In addition, the two governments should bind themselves not to do anything which might provoke hostilities without their mutual consent, and to act in full accord during the negotiations which would, following a victorious campaign, lead to a peace treaty.[118] Finally, the convention stated clearly that the treaty would remain secret.[119]

This draft convention shed a revealing light on the Porte's view of its own interests. The strongest provisions were directed against Bulgaria; Serbia was offered military support against Austria-Hungary only in the event of Russian intervention; and there was no mention of Bosnia-Herzegovina. Not surprisingly, the Serbs demanded amendments. They proposed that the contracting parties give the utmost importance to the annexation of Bosnia and Herzegovina, and make every effort to find a solution satisfactory to the people of Bosnia-Herzegovina, as well as to Serbia and the Empire, and that, should all their endeavours fail to procure this result, the Porte would undertake to recognize Austro-Hungarian sovereignty over the two provinces only on condition that a strip of territory contiguous to Serbia and Montenegro were ceded to the latter states, either directly or through Ottoman mediation. In addition, the Serbs also suggested that the scope of the convention should cover Ottoman possessions in the Balkans only, as Serbia could not prove useful in defending the Porte's far-flung territories in Asia and Africa.[120] The Grand Vizier apparently received the Serbian counter-proposals without initial objections, and allegedly even said that the Porte would never recognise the annexation, and would demand autonomy for Bosnia and Herzegovina.[121] However, in return for acceptance of Belgrade's amendments, Kâmil Pasha soon came up with a further suggestion to the effect that 'any territory conquered by the allies after a victorious campaign against Bulgaria shall be divided in such a manner that Turkey shall obtain the eastern and Serbia the western portion', and that 'in case a war indemnity is obtained, it shall be divided equally between the two countries', a proposal which soon created a deadlock. Fearing that the Grand Vizier's additional clause implied aggressive intentions towards Bulgaria, the Serbian government thought of appealing to Britain to exert her influence with the Porte.[122] However, second thoughts suggested that the Porte might regard any intervention by the British Ambassador at Constantinople as a breach of confidence, and the Serbs postponed their appeal. As an alternative means of breaking the deadlock, the Serbs put forward a new formula:

Turkey on her part will take into account the wishes of Servia in regard to Bosnia and Herzegovina, and will accept no solution of the status of these provinces which does not either safeguard the fate of the Servian population there or afford territorial compensation to Servia and Montenegro.[123]

The Serbs and the Montenegrins remained anxious for an agreement with the Ottoman Empire. They feared that, if the negotiations failed, Serbia would be left facing a hostile Bulgaria on the one side, and an unfriendly Dual Monarchy on the other.[124] In a bid for further negotiations, Spalaiković, Permanent Under-Secretary in the Serbian Foreign Ministry was sent out to Constantinople, and meanwhile Novaković was instructed to make a declaration affirming the community of interests between the two countries.[125]

However, none of these efforts was likely to budge the Grand Vizier.[126] The negotiations clearly demonstrated that, while the interests of the Ottoman Empire and Serbia were not opposed, they were divergent. For Serbia, and also for its partner Montenegro, the issue of Austria-Hungary's annexation of Bosnia-Herzegovina had absolute priority. For the Porte, by contrast, this was a secondary issue; whether in the short or the long term, the Ottoman Empire's overriding concern was the military threat posed by Bulgaria. In addition, the tactical considerations which had led the Porte to pursue an understanding with Serbia were losing force. The threat of war with Bulgaria had clearly receded, and as early as 12 November Tevfik Pasha had admitted to Lowther that the Porte had been conducting the negotiations with Serbia half-heartedly.[127] In addition, the Entente Powers had by now assured the Porte that there could be no question of compensating Serbia and Montenegro at its expense. Finally, it had become obvious by December that the Porte's demands for pecuniary compensation from Austria-Hungary and Bulgaria would receive the backing of several Powers. In these circumstances, the Grand Vizier could afford to give up the negotiations with Serbia and Montenegro, on the pretext that the latter were not able to sign an alliance of a defensive and offensive nature, that some indiscretions had been committed at Belgrade, and that, as a result, several Powers had become aware of what had been taking place.[128]

The Porte's negotiations with Serbia, as earlier with Greece and Romania, had been undertaken on its own initiative, without prompting from the Entente Powers. However, the Entente Powers were broadly aware of what had been going on. The British were initially somewhat sceptical: they feared that a system of offensive alliances might provoke a war,[129] or at least, that it would push Bulgaria and Romania into the arms of the Dual Monarchy, thereby creating a dangerous polarization in the Balkan peninsula.[130] The British preferred to see a system of defensive arrangements between the Balkan states, from which Bulgaria should not be excluded, and which might then serve to check the Dual Monarchy's influence in the Balkan peninsula.[131] This view was endorsed by the French,[132] who joined the British in urging it upon a CUP delegation which visited Paris and London in November.[133] Not that the British were especially optimistic that an alliance such as they advocated would be achieved; by the end of the year Hardinge had privately admitted that the principal obstacles were the 'inveterate jealousy' among the small Balkan states and 'the secret desire of each of them to eat up Turkey'.[134]

The Russians, too, were warming up to the idea of a general Balkan alliance under the patronage of the Entente. As a counter to Izvolsky's discredited policy of partnership with Austria-Hungary on the basis of mutual compensations, Charykov and the Prime Minister Stolypin floated the idea of a 'Turco-Slavic bloc' in the Balkans, a project which enjoyed enthusiastic support in sections of the Russian press and public opinion. Although Izvolsky never took the idea seriously,[135] public pressure forced him to take steps in that direction, and in a speech to the Duma, on 25 December he declared that 'Bulgaria, Serbia and Montenegro must become imbued with the consciousness of the necessity of moral and political union. Russia's aim is to bring these states together and to combine them with Turkey, through means of common interest for the defence of their national and economic independence.'[136] These sentiments appear to have found no echo at the Porte, which had now abandoned its search for understandings with the Balkan states.

In the meantime, there were hopes, at the beginning of November particularly after mutual demobilization, that Ottoman-Bulgarian relations might lead to an early settlement. The Bulgarian government had despatched its Minister of Trade and Agriculture, Andrey Lyapchev, to Constantinople for formal talks, and empowered him to offer financial compensation in return for recognition of Bulgaria's independence. In principle, the Ottoman government was ready to settle on these terms. From the start, the Porte had indicated that it considered itself entitled to make a number of financial claims upon the basis of international treaties,[137] and Kâmil Pasha had quickly instructed the Minister of Finance and Public Works to enlist the co-operation of the Public Debt Administration in determining how much Bulgaria might be held to owe the Ottoman Empire.[138] By the time the negotiations opened with Lyapchev, the Ottoman demands included: a) the capitalization of the Eastern Rumelian tribute, b) the capitalization of the Bulgarian tribute, which had never been paid, c) Bulgaria's assumption of a share of the Ottoman Public Debt, d) compensation for the nationalization of the Eastern Rumelian railways. As all these claims could be supported by stipulations in the relevant treaties, it appeared that the Porte could demand up to £T.28,000,000, a sum well beyond Bulgaria's ability to pay.[139] Although Kâmil Pasha privately assured Lowther that he was prepared to reduce this demand to T£ 10,000,000,[140] he, nonetheless, emphasized that he had sound political reasons for wishing to burden Bulgaria with as large an indemnity as possible: only thus could she be prevented from spending 'huge sums of money' on armaments, and threatening the Empire in Macedonia. Once more, the Grand Vizier revealed that his overriding preoccupation in relation to Bulgaria was security, not rights or money.

The problem, as Refik Bey had already warned, was that the Bulgarian government took the view that independence was to be won with 'blood', not purchased with 'money'.[141] Lyapchev was prepared to offer compensation for the Eastern Rumelian tribute, and also for the railways, but he adamantly refused to hear of the Bulgarian tribute, or to assume a share of the Ottoman Public Debt. The maximum sum he was prepared to offer was 82,000,000 francs (T£ 3,200,000).[142] He also attempted to raise other issues, demanding that the Bulgarian Exarchate, the supreme leadership of the Bulgarian Orthodox Church, be maintained in Constantinople, and that the Ottoman government give written assurances of the well-being and protection of the Bulgarians in Macedonia.[143] Refik Bey had earlier reported that these demands were made in order to strengthen the position of Malinov's government, and advised that none of these points should be discussed with Lyapchev since they had nothing to do with the Bulgarian declaration of independence.[144]

The Porte proved equally obdurate. It was in no mood to widen the scope of the negotiations; it complained that Lyapchev had been given insufficient powers;[145] it was encouraged by despatches from Refik Bey indicating that domestic opposition to the Bulgarian government's hostile policy towards the Ottoman Empire was growing;[146] and finally it was also encouraged by Britain's declaration that Lyapchev's offer was too small.[147] By the end of November, deadlock had been reached, and Lyapchev returned to Sofia; before leaving, he told the Powers' representatives in the Ottoman capital that 82,000,000 francs remained his maximum offer, and that if the Porte contemplated obtaining a larger sum, it 'ought to go to Sofia to fetch it'.[148] However, Lyapchev's withdrawal did not amount to a formal breaking-off of negotiations, and the Grand Vizier promptly wrote to Prince Ferdinand, assuring him of the Porte's desire for agreement. He explained that he was quite aware that the Powers, when called upon to fix a sum to resolve the dispute, would take into account how much Bulgaria could reasonably be expected to pay, regardless of what the Porte could claim under several headings of international treaties. He hinted that if Bulgaria could go some way further than its initial offer of 82,000,000 francs, a satisfactory settlement might be arranged. Kâmil Pasha added that an independent Bulgaria, deprived of the guarantees she had enjoyed when she was under the Ottoman suzerainty, would need the Porte's friendship more than ever. Finally, he emphasized that the Porte had no intention of resolving the dispute through war.[149]

At the same time, however, the CUP announced that its boycott of Austro-Hungarian goods had been extended to Bulgarian merchandise. The Porte apparently believed that it could afford to wait. For one thing, it enjoyed some support from the Powers. Though the British government had warned that the amount of compensation must be determined by Bulgaria's ability to pay rather than by the letter of the Empire's legal rights, it, nonetheless, insisted that Lyapchev's offer of 82,000,000 francs was inadequate. Its own calculations suggested that Bulgaria should be requested to pay between T£ 5,000,000 and T£ 10,000,000, that is, between 125,000,000 and 250,000,000 francs.[150] The French, with a considerable detailed knowledge of Ottoman and Bulgarian finances, came up with a similar estimate.[151]

For another thing, Refik Bey continued to send optimistic reports from Sofia. These stated that there existed considerable opposition within the Bulgarian parliament, which criticized the Malinov government for having acted with unnecessary haste in declaring independence at a time when the CUP was displaying an unprecedentedly friendly attitude towards Sofia and the Bulgarians in Macedonia,[152] that the pro-Ottoman Allied Committee and other influential persons were stepping up their activities in favour of a *rapprochement* with the Porte, that Prince Ferdinand, disillusioned with the existing government's policy, had approached a prominent member of the Liberal Party, Panchev, about the replacement of Malinov's cabinet, and finally that Panchev, known to be friendly to the Ottoman Empire, had been making plans for a satisfactory agreement with the Porte.[153]

In the event, however, these optimistic predictions were not borne out, and by mid-December there were signs of renewed tension in relations between Constantinople and Sofia. The immediate pretext was an allegedly slighting reference to Prince Ferdinand in the speech with which Sultan Abdülhamid opened the new Ottoman Parliament on 17 December.[154] This prompted the Bulgarian government to issue a strong note of protest to the Porte, and also to the Powers. The note asserted that the Bulgarian declaration of independence was not intended as a hostile act towards the Ottoman Empire, and it complained that the Porte's policy towards Sofia was ambiguous. The trade boycott organized against Bulgarian goods by the CUP after Lyapchev's departure from Constantinople was mentioned as a clear example of the Porte's ambiguity and hostility.[155] Sofia urged the

Powers to take steps to force the Porte to withdraw its 'extravagant' claims.[156] On 26 December the Bulgarian government made a further protest to Refik Bey, this time at the continuation of the boycott, in which, having enumerated several cases where Bulgarian goods had been prevented from being brought to market or from entering Ottoman territory, the Porte was requested to take measures to stop the boycott. Otherwise, the Bulgarian government would hold the Porte responsible.[157] By December Ottoman-Bulgarian negotiations had bogged down.

Though the Porte attempted to restart its stalled negotiations with Bulgaria, nothing concrete came out during December, and the tension between the two countries was rising.[158] To break the deadlock, Kâmil Pasha formally invited, on 7 January, the Bulgarian government to send Lyapchev back to Constantinople. In the meantime, Austria-Hungary had agreed to pay pecuniary indemnity to the Porte for the annexation of Bosnia and Herzegovina, which, it was thought, would in turn open the way for a similar agreement with Bulgaria. From Sofia, Refik Bey reported that the Bulgarians were likely to accede to this request,[159] but in the event the Bulgarian government chose to turn instead to the Powers, explaining to them that it would be pointless to renew negotiations with the Porte without a prior understanding as to the subjects of discussion. Specifically, the Bulgarians warned that they could not raise their offer of financial compensation above the 82,000,000 francs already offered, but added that they would be prepared to discuss an entente or alliance with the Ottoman Empire.[160] The Grand Vizier conceded that the latter suggestion 'mérite de fixer attention', but stressed that Bulgaria must first show a conciliatory spirit by raising her financial offer: once normal relations had been restored, the Porte would be quite willing to consider an alliance with Bulgaria.[161] The British broadly endorsed the Grand Vizier's line, warning the Bulgarians that they must raise their offer of financial compensation,[162] and on 11 January Grey suggested that the moment had arrived for the Entente Powers, perhaps supported by Italy, to inform Sofia that a sum of 125,000,000 francs was the minimum acceptable.[163] However, Izvolsky quickly objected that the figure was too high: to demand more than 100,000,000 francs would risk pushing Bulgaria 'into the arms of Austria and Germany'.[164]

In the meantime, however, the Grand Vizier had come up with a new scheme of his own: if the Bulgarians were unwilling to increase their offer of financial compensation, they might additionally agree to a small rectification of the frontier between the Ottoman Empire and the former Eastern Rumelia. It appears that the Grand Vizier rested his legal case upon the agreement for a frontier revision drawn up in 1886, following the Eastern Rumelia's unification with Bulgaria, and which, he claimed, had never been fully implemented. Practically, he envisaged the cession of a small number of Muslim villages near Cisr-i Mustafa Paşa, whose return to Ottoman control would facilitate communications between Kırcaali and Adrianople. Kâmil Pasha had mentioned the possibility of such a border rectification to Pallavicini in passing on 12 January;[165] he subsequently also mentioned it to the British and Russian Ambassadors, neither of whom appears to have raised any objection.[166]

The Grand Vizier communicated his proposal to the Bulgarian government officially in late December, and in so doing fell into a trap of his own making.[167] Whether because they genuinely feared that the Ottoman government was intending to make substantial territorial demands, and perhaps even revive its earlier demand for Eastern Rumelia's separation from Bulgaria, or whether because they saw an opportunity to discredit the Porte in the eyes of the Powers, the Bulgarians chose to treat the Grand Vizier's proposal as a hostile provocation, and responded by mobilizing the 8th Division of their army, based at Stara Zagora in Eastern Rumelia. They then issued a note to the Powers, accusing the Porte of making military preparations to capture strategic positions on the frontier. There is no evidence to support this accusation in Ottoman records; nonetheless, the result was a fresh Ottoman-Bulgarian war scare, for which the Porte was neither politically nor militarily prepared.

The Bulgarian mobilization came as a complete surprise to Kâmil Pasha's cabinet. Although there was information at the Porte's disposal indicating that the Bulgarian Army had been stockpiling provisions,[168] it does not seem to have been taken seriously. But, as soon as the mobilization commenced, the Ottoman Commission and military personnel in and around Bulgaria began to inundate the Porte with reports on troop movements and other military preparations.[169] The Ottoman Chief of Staff at once warned the Grand Vizier that the Empire was in no position to risk armed conflict with Bulgaria. He conceded that it was not yet clear whether the Bulgarians intended anything 'serious', but he pointed out that the Bulgarian army was capable of mobilizing much more rapidly than the Ottoman army, and that however limited the military measures which Sofia had taken, they nonetheless placed the Empire at a major strategic disadvantage, exposing it to the risk of a Bulgarian first strike. He proposed that a counter-mobilization be ordered, but emphasized that the Empire had nothing to gain by war: it would take a full three years to bring the Ottoman army, and European diplomatic opinion, to a point where the Empire might contemplate war with Bulgaria with a prospect of decisive victory and real political gains. In present circumstances, however, even a successful campaign was most unlikely to produce tangible advantages: defeat would mean disaster.

It is, in all probability, within the bounds of possibilities, that even the Slav governments [Serbia and Montenegro] which have become disillusioned and offended due to the existing conflict with Austria-Hungary would, following the Bulgarian invasion, also hasten to attack the Ottoman Empire in order to obtain the sort of territorial advantages they had sought to gain at the Dual Monarchy's expense from the Ottoman possessions, and it cannot be assumed that Greece would, in such a contingency, keep quiet and stay neutral. Thus it should be deemed certain that the whole situation will result in a disaster, unless Bulgaria and the other aforementioned governments are not prevented from pursuing aggressive policies.[170]

In practical terms, the Chief of Staff proposed two courses: an appeal should be made to the Great Powers for diplomatic assistance, and local alliances should be sought in the Balkans. He suggested that an entente, at least on a defensive basis, be signed with Rumania, and that some kind of military arrangement be concluded with Austria-Hungary with a view to restraining Serbia and Montenegro.[171] The Chief of Staff's advice harmonized with Kâmil Pasha's own inclinations. In a telegram to London, the Grand Vizier instructed Rifat Pasha to impress on the British Foreign Office that his government had conducted itself throughout in accordance with the Powers' advice, and sought a peaceful settlement with Bulgaria through negotiations. He professed no anxiety at the reported Bulgarian military preparations, but warned that any Bulgarian *coup de main* would provoke a general conflagration, with the other Balkan states being drawn in. He drew the British government's attention to reports that the Bulgarian authorities were distributing arms to civilians in frontier districts, thus creating the danger of clashes with civilians on the Ottoman side of the border. As to a solution of the independence dispute, he stressed that his offer to settle for compensation of 100,000,000 francs, with a slight frontier rectification in addition, fell far short of the maximum claims to which the Porte felt theoretically entitled, and he revealed that he had already offered Sofia an alternative: immediate compensation of 100,000,000 francs, with the question of the purchase of the Oriental Railways adjourned for future negotiation. Kâmil Pasha emphasized that Bulgaria's bellicose actions were producing a similarly bellicose reaction on the part of the Ottoman public opinion, and pressed the British government to take the lead in persuading the Powers to force Bulgaria to pay 125,000,000 francs, a sum Grey had suggested all along. As a bait, Kâmil added that he would settle for a down-payment of 100,000,000 francs, with the remainder to be paid later: he was confident that he could defend such an arrangement before the Ottoman parliament, provided that the Powers approved it.[172]

In the meantime the Ottoman government had ordered limited measures of counter-mobilization against Bulgaria.[173] Nonetheless, the Grand Vizier remained anxious above all to avoid war, and continued to address the most urgent appeals for diplomatic intervention to the British government.[174] He assured Lowther that he would be prepared to accept the sum of 100,000,000 francs from Bulgaria as an initial down-payment, on the understanding that Bulgaria should pay a further 25,000,000 francs as soon as she could afford it.[175] He then offered an alternative combination: Bulgaria should pay 100,000,000 francs as an indemnity for her independence, and at a later stage, pay 25,000,000 francs as the purchase price of the Eastern Rumelian railways. Finally, he suggested that if Bulgaria were still unwilling to raise her offer above 82,000,000 francs, the question of compensation might be submitted to the arbitration of the Powers.[176] At the same time Kâmil Pasha informed Lowther that he had assured the Bulgarian government that the Porte had no intention of demanding territory or strategic points: its sole aim was to complete the work of frontier demarcation left unfinished in 1886, preferably in a form which would facilitate communications between the Ottoman district of Kırcaali and Adrianople.[177] These appeals proved effective: on 27 January Grey informed Lowther that he would seek to gather the support of the other Powers for the suggestion that they should jointly settle the amount of compensation which Bulgaria should pay to the Porte.[178]

In the event, however, Grey's proposal for international arbitration was immediately overtaken by a Russian initiative. On 29 January Izvolsky suggested to the British government that the Porte might be offered 125,000,000 francs as compensation for Bulgaria's indepenence.[179] However, he added that this sum need not be paid by Bulgaria directly; instead, Russia would waive, for a period of 15 years, the annual payments due to it from the Porte under the terms of the war indemnity imposed upon the Ottoman Empire following the Ottoman-Russian war of 1877–78. If in need of cash, the Porte might easily arrange with banks for the capitalization of these 15 annual payments representing a total sum of 125,000,000 francs. As to Bulgaria, it would assume a total obligation towards Russia of 82,000,000 francs in the form of a loan, to run for 50 or more years, for which Russia would charge a moderate rate of 4 or 4.5 per cent interest. The burden of the remaining 43,000,000 francs due to the Porte would be assumed by Russia itself. As Izvolsky admitted, the Bulgarians would get off lightly: they would pay no more than the 82,000,000 francs they had held out for, and on considerably easier terms than they would have obtained had they been obliged to raise the sum through a normal commercial loan.[180]

Grey endorsed Izvolsky's proposal with alacrity, and promised to recommend it in Constantinople and in Sofia.[181] The Bulgarian government promptly announced its acceptance of the Russian scheme in principle,[182] much to the annoyance of Aehrenthal, who took this as a major diplomatic setback, and promptly broke off his alliance negotiations with Sofia. The Porte, however, was by no means happy with the Russian proposal, and made plain its dissatisfaction to the British. In the first place, it was not officially approached by Russia until 5 February, long after it had learned of the proposal from other Powers.[183] This led the Porte to suspect that Izvolsky's proposal might have hidden strings attached, possibly including a fresh attempt to open the Straits question.[184] Nor was the Porte impressed with the contents of the Russian proposal. Kâmil Pasha warned Lowther that it would force Bulgaria into permanent dependence on Russia, and that Bulgaria would become the vanguard for a future Russian drive on Constantinople. He also complained that the mild terms imposed upon Bulgaria would leave it free to spend large sums on her army, forcing the Ottoman Empire in its turn to make heavy military outlays.[185]

The British government brushed all these objections aside, however, and insisted that the Porte should accept the Russian proposal.[186] Writing to Lowther on 6 February, Hardinge made no bones about the British goverment's strong support for the Russian proposal.[187] Faced with Britain's uncompromising attitude, the Porte had no choice but to give way, and on 5 February it accepted the Russian proposal in principle. At the same time, however, it indicated that it considered itself entitled to demand more ample compensation: specifically, Russia should agree to waive all the outstanding instalments of the war indemnity, not just 15 years' worth. The Porte noted that Bulgaria would pay no more than 82,000,000 francs, but that several Powers had previously indicated that compensation should amount to as much as 120,000,000 or 150,000,000 francs. A figure in the latter range, the Porte added, would be equivalent to the capitalization of all the outstanding instalments of the war indemnity.[188] Money was evidently not the only consideration. Speaking in his personal capacity, Rifat Pasha explained to Grey that the Grand Vizier's task of reconciling public opinion in the Empire to the settlement of the Bulgarian question, as well as to the results of the negotiations with Austria-Hungary, would be made much easier if what remained as a kind of yearly Ottoman tribute to Russia were entirely remitted, for it would produce an excellent effect morally and politically. Rifat Pasha suggested that Russia should give her consent to a loan being raised on the whole amount of the indemnity, and that the Porte should retain 125,000,000 francs from the amount thus realised, while Russia should receive the remainder.[189] This time Grey's response was sympathetic, though he made no definite commitment.

In the meantime the Porte had also commenced negotiations with Russia on the details of an arrangement to regulate the financial compensation to be paid for Bulgaria's independence. A delegation headed by Rifat Pasha, newly appointed foreign minister, arrived in St. Petersburg on 4 March. The essentials of the settlement were not in dispute: Russia would compensate the Porte by waiving part of the War Indemnity, and the Bulgarians would in turn compensate Russia. However, the Porte remained eager to be freed from the War Indemnity in its entirety, and this prompted Izvolsky to bring forward two essentially political conditions.[190] In the first place, he suggested that the Porte should accept the good offices of Britain and Russia in resolving a long-running Ottoman-Iranian boundary dispute, in which the Russians had a declared interest. In the second, he proposed that the Porte should offer a concession for the construction of a railway linking Serbia with the Adriatic, possibly via the Sanjak of Novi Bazar. Rifat Pasha declared himself willing to consider a settlement of the border dispute with Iran, but refused to be drawn into any engagement in respect of an Adriatic railway: he would do no more than promise to examine the scheme in a friendly spirit at a later date.[191] The financial aspects of an agreement to deal with that portion of the War Indemnity not counted as part of the Porte's compensation for Bulgaria's independence provoked further haggling, in which the British Ambassador to St. Petersburg, Nicolson, offered Rifat Pasha some support. In the event, a compromise was reached: it was agreed that the Porte might offer Russia a down-payment of 125,000,000 francs, to be raised by means of a loan, in lieu of its annual payments for the next 30 to 35 years. Once these 30 or so years had expired, the operation would be repeated, enabling the Porte to liquidate its remaining obligations under the War Indemnity with one single instalment. Nicolson endorsed the compromise, assuring Rifat Pasha that 'in 30 years or so, so much might happen, and even the indemnity might be forgotten'. Rifat Pasha signed the definitive Ottoman-Russian protocol on 16 March.[192]

The Ottoman-Russian protocol was essentially a financial arrangement, and left a number of political issues to be resolved by direct negotiations between the Ottoman Empire and Bulgaria: the questions of Muslim communities and pious foundations in Bulgaria, of posts and telegraphs, the administration of lighthouses and quarantine regulations.[193] The Porte was eager for a quick settlement, possibly because it had obtained a copy of an alleged Russo-Bulgarian treaty of alliance;[194] it quickly asked Sofia to send a delegation to Constantinople to negotiate.[195] Sofia replied that it would send Lyapchev.[196] The Porte appointed Rifat Pasha and Noradonghian Efendi to represent it in the negotiations.[197]

Lyapchev's talks with the Porte began against a background of mounting tension between the CUP and its domestic opponents, and no conclusion had been reached by the time of the '31 March Incident' – the

Constantinople uprising of 13 April which led to the temporary ejection of the CUP from the capital. The newly appointed Grand Vizier, Hüseyin Hilmi Pasha's cabinet fell, and was replaced by one headed by Tevfik Pasha, in which, however, Rifat Pasha retained his previous post as Minister of Foreign Affairs.[198] The Bulgarians quickly sought to turn this situation to their advantage. The Powers were postponing their formal recognition of Bulgaria's independence pending a settlement between Sofia and the Porte: arguing that this latest outbreak of internal instability in the Ottoman Empire threatened to jeopardise the prospects for settlement, Sofia demanded that the Powers recognise Bulgaria's independence immediately.[199] The Bulgarian representative in St Petersburg threatened that otherwise, Bulgaria would mobilize and declare war upon the Ottoman Empire. Izvolsky allowed himself to be carried away by these arguments, and urged Paris and London to agree to early recognition.[200] The French endorsed his proposal,[201] but the British remained firm, dismissing Bulgaria's threats as 'bluff',[202] and insisting that there could be no recognition of Bulgaria's independence before the Porte had consented to it.[203]

Thanks in part to the efforts of Lowther, Rifat Pasha and Lyapchev settled the terms of an Ottoman-Bulgarian protocol on 19 April; the Porte promised to secure early ratification by parliament.[204] This agreement was reached against the background of a fast-changing political situation within the Ottoman Empire. Though ejected from the capital, the CUP had succeeded in rallying support in Macedonia, where units of III Army had been formed into an 'Army of Operations', under the command of Mahmud Şevket Pasha,[205] with the intention of marching upon Constantinople to crush the 'counter-revolutionaries' and overthrow the 'illegal' cabinet of Tevfik Pasha. Alarmed, Lyapchev sent a copy of the 19 April protocol to Shopov at Salonica; Mahmud Şevket Pasha gave Shopov a categorical assurance that he would do all in his power to secure the ratification of the protocol, since both he and the CUP earnestly wished to improve relations with Bulgaria.[206] The Army of Operations duly advanced upon Constantinople; before it entered the capital, the Ottoman Parliament convened under its auspices in the suburbs, under the new title of 'National Assembly'. On 23 April the National Assembly had its first sitting, and immediately ratified the Ottoman-Bulgarian protocol. On the following day the Army of Operations entered the capital, and put down the 'rebellion', restoring Hüseyin Hilmi Pasha's cabinet to office.

The significance of the Ottoman-Bulgarian protocol lay in the fact that it registered the Porte's *de facto* recognition of Bulgaria's independence. Otherwise, its contents were technical. It granted the Muslim population of Bulgaria religious freedom, and stipulated that 'the name of His Majesty the Sultan as the Khalife will continue to be read out in the praying places of the Muslims'. It also stipulated that the problems between the Bulgarian government and the Oriental Railway Company, arising out of Bulgaria's nationalization of the Eastern Rumelian railways should be resolved between Sofia and the Company.[207] The protocol opened the way to international recognition of Bulgaria's independence. Russia was first to recognise Prince Ferdinand as 'Czar of the Bulgarians', and France followed suit.[208] The Porte, however, continued to object to Ferdinand's choice of title, and for the same reasons which it had adduced in October 1908; not until May 1909 did the Porte formally recognize Bulgaria's independence *de jure*, and even then, it insisted upon addressing Ferdinand as no more than 'Roi de Bulgarie'.[209]

From the Ottoman Empire's point of view Bulgaria's independence crisis entailed direct threats to Ottoman security. Naturally enough, for the duration of the crisis, Ottoman attention focused primarily on Bulgarian military movements. Like other governments, the Ottoman Empire was taken by surprise by Bulgaria's declaration of independence. Its unpreparedness was reinforced by the fact that it possessed a new regime which had just come to power as the result of a revolution, a regime, furthermore, which consisted of an uneasy coalition between the CUP, on the one hand, and a cabinet of old regime figures led by Kâmil Pasha, on the other. The new regime had had no time to formulate a clear foreign policy before the crisis overtook it. Kâmil Pasha had brought to office a deep pessimism on the subject of the Empire's relations with Bulgaria. For its part, the CUP had brought with it an anti-Europeanism expressed in a determination to reassert the Empire's independence and dignity in the face of the European Great Powers, and perhaps, too, hopes of reaching a lasting accommodation with Bulgaria. But none of these amounted to a definite diplomatic strategy.

Faced by the outbreak of the crisis, however, Kâmil Pasha was quick to define his priorities. He clearly identified Bulgaria's declaration of independence as an issue more vital from the Empire's point of view than Austria-Hungary's annexation of Bosnia and Herzegovina. This was not because the independence issue possessed greater intrinsic importance, but because Kâmil Pasha had long since identified Bulgarian expansionism as one of the principal threats to Ottoman security. He strove to use the crisis to weaken Bulgaria, by attempting to construct alliances with the other Balkan states, by floating the idea of demilitarising Eastern Rumelia, and by demanding financial compensation so large as to cripple Sofia's capacity for military expenditures. At the back of his mind was the conviction that a war with Bulgaria was inevitable, though not immediately: the Empire needed some three years to prepare.

In sum, Kâmil Pasha pursued a diplomacy of limited aims. He sought to contain the crisis, to forestall potentially hostile demands that other Powers and the Balkan states might make, and to enhance the Empire's long-term security against Bulgaria. In contrast, the CUP's approach to the annexation crisis appears to have been both more ambitious and more hesitant. Unlike Kâmil Pasha, the CUP did talk of alliances, with Austria-Hungary, on the one hand, and with Britain and France, on the other.[210] It also seems likely that the CUP entertained some hopes of a formal alliance with Bulgaria. However, the fact that all these options were explored indiscriminately, and almost simultaneously, is an indication that the CUP was never finally able to make up its mind as to the diplomatic strategy it should follow. It is possible to attribute this hesitancy to the CUP's anti-Europeanism, and also to its lack of any strong preference for any of the Powers. But it is also possible to discern other factors behind the CUP's unsuccessful excursions into grand policy: an inability to fully comprehend the dynamics of Great Power diplomacy, and a marked tendency to overestimate the Ottoman Empire's diplomatic strength. One consequence, it may be suggested, was to render the CUP a less effective influence upon the Empire's diplomacy during the Bulgarian independence crisis than might have been anticipated: the policies pursued from the outbreak of the crisis through to the settlement of principles reached in February and March 1909 were essentially those of Kâmil Pasha. This is not to deny that the CUP made a distinctive contribution to Ottoman policy. All in all, the outcome of the crisis was a success for the Ottoman Empire. Though Kâmil Pasha's Balkan Alliance scheme fell through, it had at least helped to prevent the Balkan states from combining against the Empire. However, there were also some losses. Kâmil Pasha's hopes of fundamentally weakening Bulgaria had been disappointed: the proposed Balkan alliance had come to nothing, the Entente Powers would not hear of territorial or military restrictions upon Bulgaria, and the agreed compensation for independence was not sufficient to curb Bulgaria's military ambitions. The problems of Ottoman-Bulgarian relations, and of the Empire's political and military security in the Balkan peninsula, remained unresolved.

NOTES

1. For a general understanding of Abdülhamid II's foreign policies, see, D. Akarlı, *The Problems of External Pressures, Power Struggles and Budgetary Deficits in Ottoman Politics under Abdülhamid II (1876–1908): Origins and Solutions*, (Unpublished Ph.D. thesis, Princeton, 1976). See, also, F.A.K. Yasamee, *Ottoman Diplomacy: Abdülhamid II and the Great Powers, 1878–1888* (Istanbul, 1996).
2. For a general appraisal of this period, see, L.S. Stavrianos, *The Balkans since 1453* (Holt, Rinehart and Winston, New York, Chicago, 1965), Part IV and V. See, also, B. Jelavich,

History of the Balkans. Eighteenth and Nineteenth Centuries (Cambridge University Press, 1983), I., pp.378–9.

3. In 1880 the Ottoman Empire had a population of 21 millions, while all the other Balkan states put together (Romania, Greece, Bulgaria, Serbia and Montenegro) possessed only a population of less than 11 millions. By 1914, however, the demographic figures had changed considerably. While the Ottoman population decreased to 20 millions, the population of the Balkan states had increased to 22 millions. See, E.J. Hobsbawm, *The Age of Empire, 1875–1914* (London, 1987), p.342, table 1. Although this decline in Ottoman population and increase in that of the Balkan states was partly due to the Empire's territorial losses, it was clear that the populations of the Balkan states were rising rapidly. For details of the Ottoman population from 1880 to 1914, see K.H. Karpat, *Ottoman Population, 1830–1914. Demographic and Social Characteristics* (The University of Wisconsin Press, 1985), pp.18–44, 107–90. This population increase continued in 1930's in the Balkans. See, Stavrianos, op.cit., pp.594–7.

4. See H. Ünal, *Ottoman Foreign Policy During the Bosnian Annexation Crisis, 1908–1909* (hereafter, *Ottoman Foreign Policy*) (Unpublished Ph.D. dissertation, University of Manchester, 1992), pp.27–8; B. Jelavich, *History of the Balkans. Twentieth Century* (Cambridge University Press, 1983), II., pp.440–1.

5. F. Adanır, *Die Makedonische Frage: Ihre Enstehung und ihre Entwicklung bis 1908* (Wiesbaden, 1979) pp.100–3.

6. Adanır, op.cit., pp.88–99.

7. For IMRO, see, Adanır, op.cit., pp.20–209.

8. For details of the Bulgarian armed bands' activities against Ottoman rule throughout Macedonia and Ottoman reaction, see, (Binbaşı) Şemseddin, *Tarihçe-i Devr-i İnkılâb* (Istanbul, 1324–1908), pp.43–51; Adanır, op.cit., pp.179–99; D. Dakin, *The Greek Struggle in Macedonia, 1897–1913* (Thessaloniki, 1966), pp.92–106; T. Uzer, *Makedonya'da Eşkiyalık Tarihi ve Son Osmanlı Yönetimi* (Ankara, 1979), pp.140–60.

9. Ibid. See, also, for all the reform projects imposed upon the Ottoman Empire by the Great Powers and their consequences in Macedonia, A. Gül Tokay, *Makedonya Sorunu: Jön Türk İhtilalinin Kökenleri (1903–1908)* (Istanbul, 1995).

10. H. Ünal, 'Abdülhamit Nasıl ve Ne Zaman Pes Etti?'(hereafter 'Abdülhamit Nasıl'), *Tarih ve Toplum* (Istanbul), Ekim (October) 1993, No.118, pp.43–44.

11. See T.S. Todorova and E.P. Statelova, *Dokumenti po Obyavyavane na Nezavisimostta na Balgaria 1908 godine. Iz Tayniya Kabinet na Knyaz Ferdinand* (Sofia, 1968), no.13.

12. Buchanan to Sir Edward Grey (British Foreign Secretary at the time), 1 August 1908, FO371/544,26786). Buchanan, however, expressed reservations about the whole matter. He thought that Kamil must have come up with such a proposal simply to test Bulgaria's attitude towards what was happening in Ottoman Macedonia. But he conceded that, in the event of Bulgaria's 'assistance' to the Sultan in defeating the Young Turks, he was to have granted Sofia full independence. See, for instance, Buchanan to Grey, 5 August 1908, FO371/545,27961.

13. See, for details, *Documents diplomatiques français, 1871–1914* (Ministère des Affaires Etrangères, Commission de Publication des Documents Relatives aux Origines de la Guerre de 1914 – hereafter *DDF*), 2. série, XI, No.422, note 1, p.732.

14. Sir Gerald Lowther (British Ambassador at Constantinople) to Grey, 10 August 1908, FO371/545,28455.

15. See, H. Ünal, 'Young Turk Assessments of International Politics, 1906–1909' (hereafter 'Young Turk Assessments', op.cit.) *Middle Eastern Studies*, Vol.32, No.2 (April 1996), pp.34–5.

16. Ünal, *Ottoman Foreign Policy*, op.cit., pp.69–70.

17. Yasamee, op.cit., pp.152–3, 219–20, 222–35.

18. H.K. Bayur, *Sadrazam Kâmil Paşa. Siyasî Hayatı* (Ankara, 1954), pp.232–4.

19. Başbakanlık Osmanlı Arşivleri, Yıldız Tasnifi, Yıldız Esas Evrakı, M. Kâmil Paşa Evrakına Ek (hereafter *Y. Kâmil Paşa*), 86/32,3136.

20. See, for these activities, Ünal, 'Young Turk Assessments', op.cit., pp.36–40.

21. T. Vlakhov, *Krizata v Balgaro-Turskite Otnosheniya, 1895–1908* (Sofia, 1977), p.143.

22. According to some Bulgarian press reports, at the outset of the Young Turk revolution the Young Turks even decided to erect monuments in various parts of Macedonia in memory of all the fallen Bulgarian *chetniks* [bandit leaders] who had fought against the previous regime. See, for instance, reports from Refik Bey, Deputy-Ottoman Imperial Commissioner at Sofia, in Bâb-ı Âli Evrak Odası, Eyâlet-i Mümtâze, Bulgaristan Evrakı (hereafter AMTZ), 169/57.

23. Austria-Hungary's Ambassador, Pallavicini, thought that the Ottoman Empire and Bulgaria were drawing close, and that a Balkan League under Ottoman leadership, and friendly to Vienna might be a practical proposition. See Pallavicini to Aehrenthal (Austria-Hungarian Foreign Minister), 12 August 1908, *Österreich-Ungarns Aussenpolitik von der bosnischen Krise bis zum Kriegsausbruch 1914* (ed.) by L. Bittner and Uebersberger (Vienna, 1930) (hereafter *OUA*), I., no.34.

24. For CUP's relations with various Greek groups prior to the Young Turk revolution, see A.J. Panayotopulos, 'Early Relations between the Greeks and the Young Turks', *Balkan Studies*, XXI (Thessaloniki, 1980), pp.89–90. See, also, M. Ş. Bleda, *İmparatorluğun Çöküşü* (Istanbul, 1979), pp.23–5; Dakin, op.cit., pp.377–8.

25. Dakin, op.cit., pp.378–92.

26. There is a great deal of literature on the Bosnian annexation crisis. See, for instance, B.E. Schmitt, *The Annexation of Bosnia, 1908–1909* (New York 1937); M. Nintchitch, *La Crise bosniaque 1908–1909 et les Puissances européennes* (Paris, 1937), 2 volumes; A.F. Pribram, *Austria-Hungary and Great Britain, 1908–1914* (New York, 1951), pp.111–38; F.R. Bridge, *From Sadowa to Sarajevo, 1841–1914: The Foreign Policy of Austria-Hungary* (London, 1972); F.R. Bridge, *Great Britain and Austria-Hungary, 1906–1914: A Diplomatic History* (London, 1972); G.P. Gooch, *History of Modern Europe, 1878–1919* (London, 1924); G.P. Gooch, *Before the War: Studies in Diplomacy: The Grouping of the Powers* (London, 1937).

27. See Ünal, *Ottoman Foreign Policy*, op.cit., pp.78–81.

28. Vlakhov, op.cit., p.155.

29. For instance, on July 21, the Bulgarian agent at Monastir reported that the Young Turks had asked the Greeks to desist from attacking the Bulgarians, a policy that had been favoured and even perhaps fostered by the previous regime. See, for details, Vlakhov, op.cit., pp.143–5.

30. See note 22.

31. Vlakhov, op.cit., pp.147–8.

32. Sir Charles Hardinge (Under-Secretary in the British Foreign Office) to Sir Francis Bertie (British Ambassador at Paris), 30.07.08, Pte. *Bertie Papers* (hereafter *BP*), (FO800/180).

33. P. Goranov, 'Tarnovskiyat Akt ot 5 oktomvri 1908g', in Todorova & Statelova, op.cit., pp.119–21.

34. Goranov, op.cit., in Todorova and Statelova, op.cit., pp.122–3.

35. According to Lowther, the Bulgarian Agent was not invited because he was not a foreign representative but an Ottoman official. See, for instance, FO371/550,31758.

36. Paprikov told the Serbian Diplomatic Agent at Sofia, Svéta Simitch, that the Young Turks' nationalism was to blame for the incident. They wished to manifest the vassal status of Bulgaria. The Young Turks might have done it to simply turn the public attention from internal difficulties to something which, they thought, could enhance their chances before the upcoming elections. See Nintchitch, op.cit., p.263.

37. See, for details of the Incident, Crampton, op.cit., p.310; Bayur, op.cit., pp.259–61; E. Driault and M. l'Héritier, *Histoire Diplomatique de la Grèce, de 1821 à nos jours* (Paris, 1926), V., pp.12–13.

38. Bayur, op.cit., p.261, note 1.

39. Bayur, op.cit., pp.260–261. Later, the Porte also tried to say in vain that, as the banquet was to take place at the Foreign Minister's own house, there was not enough room to invite Geshov because even other Ambassadors were invited on their own (Grand Vizierate to the Ottoman Commission in Sofia, undated, AMTZ, 170/77)

40. See, *Die Grosse Politik der europäischen Kabinette 1871–1914* (hereafter, *Die Grosse Politik*), ed. by J. Lepsius, A. Mendelssohn-Bartholdy and F. Thimme (Berlin, 1922–27)

26/1. nos: 8948–8949.
41. Nintchitch, op.cit., I., p.263. See, also, Geshov to Tevfik Pasha, Ottoman Minister for Foreign Affairs, 13 Sept. 08, AMTZ, 170/77. Although it has been assumed that the Porte responded to Geshov's departure with a tit for tat and recalled its representative in Sofia (Crampton, op.cit., pp.310–12), evidence in the Ottoman Archives suggests that the Ottoman Imperial Commissioner, Kâmil Bey, had in fact been summoned by the new regime before the Geshov Incident occurred possibly due to the part he had played in the Sultan's 'plot' at the outset of the Young Turk revolution to divert attention from the revolutionary movement. Kâmil Bey later in the Young Turk era was put on trial for embezzlement committed while in office in Sofia (Ottoman documents, AMTZ, 175/30; İrâde-i Hariciye, January 1911, No.2621). Ottoman documents do not indicate whether his trial had anything to do with this plot.
42. Crampton, op.cit., pp.310–12.
43. Refik Bey to Kâmil Pasha 15 Sept. 1908, AMTZ 170/77.
44. Crampton, op.cit., p.310.
45. See AMTZ documents dated between 15 and 22 September, 179/77. Pallavicini, the Doyen of the Diplomatic Corps, had at the time complained to the Porte at Geshov's inclusion with other foreign representatives on the occasion of the Sultan's proclamation of the Constitution on 24 July. Geshov had not been invited to the funeral of the British Ambassador who had died in Constantinople in March 1908. Lowther to Grey, 15 Sept. 1908, FO371/32154.
46. Ibid. He also said that he was doing all in his power to keep the press from going to extremes.
47. Refik Bey to Kâmil Pasa, 16 Sept. 1908, AMTZ, 170/77.
48. AMTZ, 170/17, 170/69, 170/70, 171/50.
49. AMTZ, 170/70; 171/17; Crampton, op.cit., p.311.
50. See, for instance, AMTZ, 170/69; 170/70; 170/77; Crampton, op.cit., p.311.
51. Mehmed Şükrü Bey to the General Staff (Umur-ı Erkân-ı Harbiye Dairesi), 22 Sept. 191908, AMTZ, 170/17.
52. The Ministry for Trade and Public Works to the Grand Vizierate, 22 Sept. 1908, AMTZ, 170/69; AMTZ, 170/77; AMTZ, 170/70; Ministry for Trade and Public Works to the Grand Vizierate, 25-26-27 Sept. 1908, AMTZ, 170/50.
53. 'The seizure by the Bulgarian railway administration of the use of the Oriental Railway Company has taken place as a result of a strike and an understanding with the representative of the railway company. Therefore, the restoration of this line to the said company is a question that will be resolved between the government of the Principality and the Oriental Railway Company.' For details of the history of the lines and so forth, see the lengthy note-verbale by the Bulgarian Foreign Office to the Powers and to the Ottoman Vice-Commissioner, Refik Bey, 24 Sept. 1908, AMTZ, 171/50.
54. Ibid.
55. Bayur, op.cit., pp.259–61.
56. Ibid., p.262.
57. Vlakhov, op.cit., pp.172–3.
58. B. Samardziev, 'Great Britain's Policy towards the Declaration of Bulgarian Independence, 1908–1909', Bulgarian Historical Review, Vol.4 (1987), pp.33–4.
59. Samardziev, op.cit., pp.33–4. Kalchov is supposed to have seen Lowther, who allegedly gave full backing to the plan agreed between the former on the one hand and the Young Turks and Kâmil Pasha on the other. However, this should be taken with a grain of salt not least because the whole mission is mentioned neither in British documents (FO371/550-551; Lowther Papers, hereafter LP, FO800/193A-B), nor in the memoirs of Kâmil Pasha and Ahmed Rıza. See, for instance, Bayur, op.cit.; Ahmed Rıza, Meclis-i Mebusan ve Ayan Reisi Ahmet Rıza Bey'in Anıları (Istanbul, 1988).
60. Refik Bey to the Grand Vizierate, 22 Sept. 1908, AMTZ, 170/72.
61. AMTZ, 171/25.
62. Bertie to Grey, 3 Oct. 1908, FO371/550,32245,34247,34248; Lascelles to Grey, 04.10.1908, FO371/550,34261,34274.

63. See, for all these details, Ünal, *Ottoman Foreign Policy*, pp.93–6.
64. The Bulgarian Foreign Minister had already admitted in his instructions to Shopov, who was negotiating with the members of the CUP following Geshov's recall by Bulgaria, that the Sofia government would use the Geshov Incident for a declaration of independence. See, for instance, Vlakhov, op.cit., pp.172–3; Crampton, op.cit., pp.311–12.
65. Crampton, op.cit., p.310.
66. The General Staff to the Grand Vizierate, 30 Sept. 1908 AMTZ,171/32.
67. The General Staff to the Ministry of War, 01.10.1908, AMTZ,171/29; Second Army Corps Deputy-Commander to the General Staff, and the War Ministry to the Grand Vizierate, 23 Sept. 1908, AMTZ, 171/77.
68. General Staff to the War Ministry 27 Sept. 1908; War Ministry to the Grand Vizierate, 5 Oct. 1908, AMTZ, 171/37.
69. General Staff to the Grand Vizierate, 04 Oct. 1908, 171/74; AMTZ, 171/76.
70. Buchanan to Grey, 18 Sept. 1908, FO371/551,32430. Paléologue, French Minister at Sofia, confirmed this information. See Paléologue to Pichon, 29 Sept. 1908, DDF 2ème Série, XI. No.471.
71. Mehmed Şükrü Bey to the General Staff and the General Staff to the Grand Vizierate, 14 Oct. 1908, AMTZ, 171/77.
72. See, for the French text and the Ottoman translation of the letter, Ottoman Foreign Ministry to the Grand Vizierate, 5 Oct. 1908, AMTZ, 171/36.
73. Mehmed Şükrü Bey to the General Staff and the General Staff to the Grand Vizierate 14 Oct. 1908, AMTZ, 171/77.
74. Ali Hilmi Bey, Second Secretary in the Ottoman Commission, to the General Staff, 10 Oct. 1908, AMTZ 171/77. See, also, Commander of the Second Army Corps to the General Staff, and the General Staff to the Grand Vizierate, 3 Oct. 1908, AMTZ, 171/77; Refik Bey to the Grand Vizierate, 3 Oct. 1908, AMTZ, 171/17; the General Staff to the Grand Vizierate 15 Oct. 1908, AMTZ, 171/17.
75. Ali Hilmi Bey, to the General Staff, 10 Oct. 1908, AMTZ 171/77; Commander of the Second Army Corps to the General Staff and the General Staff to the Grand Vizierate, 3 Oct. 1908, AMTZ, 171/77.
76. The British War Office assessments confirmed that the Bulgarian army was capable of striking a knock-out blow at the onset of the war (FO371/551,35118).
77. A.F. Türkgeldi, *Görüp İşittiklerim* (Ankara, 1951), p.12.
78. See, for details, Ünal, *Ottoman Foreign Policy*, pp.121–2.
79. AMTZ, 171/41.
80. Paléologue to Pichon, 7 Oct. 1908, *DDF* No.484.
81. Refik Bey to the Grand Vizierate 15 Oct. 1908, AMTZ, 172/18.
82. Refik Bey to the Grand Vizierate, 23 Oct. 1908, AMTZ, 171/85.
83. Todorova and Statelova, op.cit., no.60.
84. Ibid., No.61.
85. Refik Bey to the Grand Vizierate, 2 Oct. 1908, AMTZ, 172/8; Buchanan to Grey, 5 Oct. 1908, FO371/555,38553.
86. Todorova and Statelova, op.cit., p.129.
87. 'Discours de Faik Bey' in Refik Bey to the Grand Vizierate, 22 Oct. 1908, AMTZ, 171/5; 171/86.
88. 'Déclaration du Comité allié sur nos relations actuelles avec la Turquie', Ibid.
89. For French documents, see despatch from Salonique, 25 Oct. 1908, *Nouvelle Série, Turquie*, 192.
90. Lowther to Grey, 20 Oct. 1908 and 21 Oct. 1908, FO371/553,36535,36536.
91. See FO371/552,35743; FO371/553,36139,36184; FO371/554,37433.
92. Hardinge's minute on the Military Attaché's report in Hohler to Grey, 21 Oct. 1908, FO371/554,37120; Grey to Buchanan, 19 Oct. 1908, FO371/553,36528; cf. Rifat Pasha to the Foreign Ministry, and the Foreign Ministry to the Grand Vizierate, 29 Oct. 1908, AMTZ, 171/77.
93. See minute by Hardinge on Lowther to Grey, 30 Oct. 1908, FO371/554,37763. See also minutes by Hardinge on a similar despatch from the Military Attaché in Constantinople in

172 TURKEY BEFORE AND AFTER ATATÜRK

Hohler to Grey, 20 Oct. 1908, FO371/553,36522.
94. Grey to Lowther, 30 Oct. 1908, and Lowther to Grey, 1 Nov.1908, FO371/554,34877.
95. Grey to Lowther, 3 Nov. 1908, FO371/555,38214. See, also, Hardinge to Lowther, 3 Oct. 1908, Pte. *Hardinge Papers* (hereafter *HP.*); *LP* (FO800/193A).
96. Türkgeldi, op.cit., pp.11–12. Romania immediately consulted Austria-Hungary and subsequently declined to consider the Ottoman proposal. For details, see Szápáry to Aehrenthal, 2 Jan. 1908, *Österreich-Ungarns Aussenpolitik von der bosnischen Krise 1908 bis zum Kriegsausbruch*, ed. by L. Bittner and Uebersberger (Vienna, 1930) (hereafter *OUA*), I., nos: 108–9.
97. See *Y. Kamil Paşa.*, 86/33,3242.
98. Lowther to Grey, 12 Oct. 1908, 13 Oct. 1908, 14 Oct. 1908 and 15 Oct. 1908, FO371/552,35514,35537,35667.
99. *Y. Kamil Paşa*, 86/33,3242.
100. Copy of the Draft Treaty, 10 Oct. 1908, *Y. Kamil Paşa*, 86/33,3242.
101. D. Dakin, *The Unification of Greece, 1770–1923* (London, 1972), pp.149–58, 170–3, 178–9.
102. Driault and l'Héritier, op.cit., pp.13–14. For details of Greek public opinion in the immediate aftermath the Young Turk revolution, see S. Papadopoulos, 'La Révolution des *'Jeunes-Turcs'* et l'Opinion Publique en Grèce', *Balkan Studies*, Vol.27 (1986), pp.129–37.
103. Elliot to Grey, 11 Nov. 1908, FO371/551,35193; Potalis to Pichon, 11 Oct. 1908, *Nouvelle Série, Turquie*, 190.
104. See Elliot to Grey, 11 Nov. 1908, FO371/552, 35235. French documents confirm all this. See, Potalis to Pichon, 11 Oct. 1908, *Nouvelle Série, Turquie*, 190.
105. 'Not only desirous of establishing best friendly relations with the neighbouring Empire, but also desirous of seeing the closest rapprochement between the two countries established'. Elliot to Grey, 14 Nov. 1908, FO371/552,35599.
106. Elliot to Grey, 12 Nov. 1908, FO371/556,40378.
107. Ibid., minute.
108. See H. Noradonghian, *Vers la Guerre balkanique et la Première Guerre Mondiale* (Istanbul, 1950), pp.9–13.
109. Bridge, *From Sadowa to Sarajevo*, pp.277–80.
110. For details of the Serbo-Montenegrin military convention, see J.D. Treadway, *The Falcon and the Eagle, Montenegro and Austria-Hungary, 1908–1914* (West Lafayette, Indiana: Purdue University Press, 1983), pp.30–1; Nintchitch, op.cit., II., pp.83–4.
111. Whitehead to Grey, 27 Oct. 1908, FO371/554,37895. Although the Serbs and the Montenegrins made every effort to assure the Ottoman representative at Belgrade that their convention was not aimed at further spoliation of the Ottoman Empire, it appears that they had every intention to satisfy their ambitions by linking the two countries through the Ottoman province of Sanjak of Novi Bazar. See, for the text of the convention, Nintchitch, op.cit., II., pp.83–4; Treadway, op.cit., p.31.
112. Before his departure for Constantinople, Novaković said that his intention was to conclude an entente with the Porte with a view to putting the question of the annexation on the conference programme and demanding autonomy under the suzerainty of the Sultan and the appointment of a prince nominated by the Powers. See, the despatch from Belgrade in *Nouvelle Série, Turquie*, 27 Oct. 1908, 192.
113. Lowther to Grey, 16 Nov. 1908, FO371/556,40059.
114. See, the copy of the draft alliance dated 5 Nov. 1908, *Y. Kamil Paşa*, 86/33,3242.
115. Article 1 of the Draft Convention, Ibid.
116. Second Clause of the Draft Convention, Ibid.
117. Third Article of the Draft Convention, Ibid.
118. Fourth Clause of the Convention, Ibid.
119. Articles Five, Six and Seven, Ibid.
120. Ibid. cf. Whitehead to Grey, 10 Nov. 1908, FO371/555, 39248 and Whitehead to Grey, 10 Nov. 1908, FO371/555,39856.
121. Whitehead to Grey, 10 Nov. 1908, FO371/555,39856.
122. Whitehead to Grey, 13 Nov. 1908, FO371/555,39596.

123. They asked Britain that until 'the proper moment had arrived' Lowther should refrain from referring to the negotiations in any manner or form (Whitehead to Grey, 25 Nov. 1908, FO371/557,41711).

124. These fears were expressed by the Serbian Military Attaché in Bulgaria to Mehmed Şükrü Bey at the end of November. See Mehmed Şükrü Bey to the General Staff and the Grand Vizierate, 23 Nov. 1908, AMTZ, 173/22.

125. Whitehead to Grey, 2 Dec. 1908, FO371/557,42134.

126. Kâmil Pasha had already told Novaković that the idea of a military alliance had collapsed. Constans to Pichon, 17 Nov. 1908, Nouvelle Série, Turquie, 192.

127. Lowther to Grey, 12 Nov. 1908, FO371/555,39497.

128. Lowther to Grey, 14 Dec. 1908, FO371/558,43731.

129. Lowther to Grey, 26 Oct. 1908, and Grey to Lowther, 28 Oct. 1908, FO371/554,37298, and minutes. On the Porte's approach to Greece, Grey had instructed Elliot to inform the Greeks of the Foreign Office's view that 'in the event of Bulgaria attacking Turkey, the latter should be given moral support' (Elliot to Grey and Grey to Elliot, 28 Oct. 1908, FO371,554,37298, and minutes). In a similar fashion, Whitehead was furnished with instructions to discourage the idea of a defensive and offensive alliance, which might be directed against Bulgaria and even Austria-Hungary, on the grounds that such an Ottoman-Serbian combination would ultimately push Sofia into the arms of the Dual Monarchy. See, Whitehead to Grey, 13 Nov. 1908, and Grey to Whitehead, 14 Nov. 1908, FO371/556, 41617, and minutes; Whitehead to Grey, 10–13 Nov. 1908, FO371/555, 39596,39856. In the same manner, the British endeavoured to dissuade the Montenegrins from seeking an alliance with the Ottoman Empire. See, Lowther to Grey, 16 Nov. 1908, FO371/556,40059; Grey to O'Reilly, 17 Nov. 1908, FO371/556,40059.

130. Ibid. For further information, see, Whitehead to Grey, 25 Nov. 1908, FO371/557,41711; Greene to Grey, 1909 Dec. 1908, FO371/558,43535. For Whitehead's attempts to discourage the Serbs from forming such an alliance, see, Whitehead to Grey, 02 Dec. 1908, FO371/557,42134;FO371/558,43516; Grey to Lowther, 10 Nov. 1908, FO371/555,38062.

131. See Hardinge to Lowther, 1 Dec. 1908, Pte., HP. 11; LP (FO800/193/A). See also M.B., Cooper, 'British Policy in the Balkans, 1908–1909', The Historical Journal, Vol.7, No.2 (1964), pp.275–7.

132. See, 'Jeunes Turcs à Paris', 14 Nov. 1908, Nouvelle Série, Turquie, 193–194.

133. Grey and Hardinge also advised the same delegation to conclude an alliance with the Balkan states, including Bulgaria. See, Grey to Lowther, 14 Nov. 1908, Pte.. GP. (FO800/79); LP (FO800/193A).

134. Hardinge's minute on Greene to Grey, 23 Dec. 1908, FO371/558, 45119.

135. See, for details, Thaden, op.cit., pp.17–21.

136. E.C. Helmreich, The Diplomacy of the Balkan Wars, 1912–1913 (Harvard University Press, 1938), p.20.

137. See, for instance, 'Note des türkischen Botschaftsrates Reschad Hikmet', 7 Oct. 1908, OUA, I., No.173; 'Vom türkischen Botschafter in Berlin Tewfik Pascha am 7 Oktober 1908 dem Stellvertretenden Staatssekretär Stemrich überreicht', 7 Oct. 1908, Grosse Politik., Vol.26/1, No.8973.

138. AMTZ, 172/14.

139. See the memorandum by von Griesinger, 6 Oct. 1908, Grosse Politik., Vol.26/2, No.9289.

140. Grey to Lowther, 26 Oct. 1908, FO371/554,37601.

141. Refik Bey to the Grand Vizierate, 23 Oct. 1908, AMTZ, 171/85.

142. Lowther to Grey, 30 Nov. 1908, FO371/557,41878; Marschall to the German Foreign Office, 26 Oct. 1908 and 30 Oct. 1908, Grosse Politik., Vol.26/2, nos.9290, 9291.

143. Marschall to the German Foreign Office, 4 Nov. 1908, Grosse Politik., Vol.26/2, No.9287.

144. Refik Bey to the Grand Vizierate, 2 Nov. 1908, AMTZ and 5 Nov. 1908, AMTZ, 172/22.

145. See, Todorova and Statelova, op.cit., No.73; Y. Kâmil Paşa., 30 Oct. 1908, 86/33,3268.

146. See, for instance, Refik Bey to the Grand Vizierate, 11 Nov. 1908, AMTZ, 172/34.

147. Minutes on Lowther to Grey, 30 Nov. 1908, FO371/557,41878.

148. Lowther to Grey, 30 Nov. 1908, FO371/557,41878; Marschall to the German Foreign Office, 26 Oct. 08 and 30 Oct. 1908, Grosse Politik., Vol.26/2, nos: 9290, 9291; Constans

to Pichon, 12 Nov. 1908, *Nouvelle Série, Turquie*, 193–4.

149. Kâmil Pasha to Prince Ferdinand, 30 Nov. 1908, *Y. Kamil Paşa.*, 86/33,3268. For the French text, see, Todorova and Statelova, op.cit., No.73.

150. Grey to Nicolson, 13 Nov. 1908, FO371/555,39495.

151. French estimates fixed the sum at T£ 5,680,000 (Bertie to Grey, 17 Jan 1909, FO371/747,2145, and the minutes).

152. See, Refik Bey to the Grand Vizierate, 11 Nov. 1908, AMTZ, 173/34; Refik Bey to the Grand Vizierate, 12 Nov. 1908, AMTZ, 172/53; Refik Bey to the Grand Vizierate, 17 Nov. 1908, AMTZ, 172/55.

153. AMTZ, 172/45; AMTZ, 171/35, 171/46.

154. In this speech allusion had been made to Ferdinand as the Prince of Bulgaria and Governor of Eastern Rumelia, who, having broken his oath allegiance to the Sultan, had, for some reason, declared independence (Lowther to Grey, 17 Dec. 1908, FO371/558,44097).

155. See, for the text of the note, Refik Bey to the Grand Vizierate, 24 Dec. 1908, AMTZ, 173/47.

156. Ibid. See also Refik Bey's comments in his covering letter in the same file, AMTZ, 173/47.

157. See, Refik Bey to the Grand Vizierate, 2 Jan. 1909, AMTZ, 173/60.

158. See, Ünal, *Ottoman Foreign Policy*, op.cit., pp.223–227.

159. Refik Bey to the Grand Vizierate 12 Jan. 1909, AMTZ, 173/67.

160. Grey to Buchanan, 16 Jan. 1909, FO371/748,2051.

161. Grey to Lowther, 19 Jan. 1909, FO371/748,3427.

162. Grey to Buchanan, 16 Jan. 1909, FO371/748,2051.

163. Grey to Nicolson, 11 Jan. 1909, FO371/747,1003.

164. See, all the reports from Nicolson to Grey, 23–24 Jan. 1909, FO371/748,3070,3072,3073. The British Foreign Office thought that it could neither accept nor recommend Izvolsky's proposal to the Porte (Ibid., minutes).

165. Pallavicini to Aehrenthal, 12 Jan. 1909, *OUA*, I., No.880.

166. In a memorandum communicated to Benckendorff, Grey did not seem unfavourable to the Grand Vizier's scheme (Memorandum communicated to Benckendorff, 28 Jan. 1909, FO371/749,3838,3844). Izvolsky equally expressed himself favourable to some very slight frontier rectifications (Nicolson to Grey, 20 Jan. 1909, FO371/748,3148).

167. There is no copy of the Kâmil's letter to Sofia in the Ottoman archives. But his letter is largely summarised in the Bulgarian note to the Powers. See, AMTZ, 174/9.

168. See, reports from the province of Adrianople and the Interior Ministry about these preparations, Interior Ministry to the Grand Vizierate, 4 Jan. 1909, AMTZ 173/73. There is another report from the War Ministry on rumours circulated among the Bulgarian population in Macedonia that Bulgaria was about to move against the Empire. See, War Ministry to the Grand Vizierate, 16 Jan. 1909, AMTZ, 173/88.

169. The Chief of Staff to Kamil Pasha, 25 Jan. 1909, *Y. Kamil Paşa.*, 86/32,3135.

170. The Chief of Staff to the Grand Vizier, 25 Jan. 1909, *Y. Kamil Pasa.*, 86/32,3135.

171. Ibid.

172. *Y. Kamil Paşa.*, 86/34,3351.

173. Ottoman military preparations were of a 'negligible' nature. Although they were made to guard against a possible sudden Bulgarian attack, it seems that even such a small objective might have proved difficult for the Empire to achieve. See *Y. Kamil Paşa.*, 86/32,3135. Neither Lowther nor the British Military Attaché, Colonel Surtees, believed that the Empire's military measures were intended for offensive purposes, nor that the Porte entertained any idea of seizing Bulgarian territory by force. See, Lowther to Grey, 26 Jan. 1909, FO371/748,3466; Lowther to Grey, 27–28 Jan. 1909, FO371/749,3688, 3689; Lowther to Grey together with the British Military Attaché's report dated 19th January, 20 Jan. 1909, FO371/748,3498.

174. See AMTZ, 173/73; 173/77; 173/81; 173/88; 174/1; 174/3; 174/4; 174/5; 174/13; 174/19; 174/55. Kamil Pasha also feared that war with Bulgaria would hold back the Empire's economic development (*Y. Kamil Paşa.*, 86/32,3137).

175. Lowther to Grey, 26 Jan. 1909, FO371/748,3491.

176. Lowther to Grey, 27 Jan. 1909, FO371/749,3688.

177. Ibid.
178. Grey to Lowther, 27 Jan. 1909, FO371/749,3904.
179. Nicolson to Grey, 29 Jan. 1909, FO371/749,3947.
180. For details of the war indemnity, see M.R. Milgrim, 'An Overlooked Problem in Turkish-Russian Relations: The 1878 War Indemnity', *International Journal of Middle Eastern Studies*, Vol.9 (1978), pp.519–37.
181. Grey to Nicolson, 30 Jan. 1909, FO371/749,3947.
182. Buchanan to Grey, 1 Feb. 1909, FO371/749,4340,4341; Buchanan to Grey, 30 Jan. 1909, FO371/749,3953.
183. Lowther to Grey, 1 Feb. 1909, 2 Feb. 1909 and 3 Feb. 1909, FO371/749, 4342,4487, 4587.
184. Lowther to Grey, 30 Jan. 1909, FO371/750,5066; Lowther to Grey, 4 Feb. 1909, FO371/749,4618; Nicolson to Grey, 3–4 Feb. 1909, FO371/749,4584,4762,4770.
185. See, for Kamil Pasha's reservations about the Russian proposal, Lowther to Grey, 1 Feb. 1909, 2 Feb. 1909, 3 Feb. 1909 and 4 Feb. 1909, FO371/749,4342,4618,5066; Lowther to Grey, 5 Feb. 1909, FO371/749,750,4861.
186. Grey to Lowther, 2 Feb. 1909, 3 Feb. 1909, 4 Feb. 1909 and 5 Feb. 1909, FO371/749, 4342,4587,4588,4618.
187. Hardinge to Lowther, 6 Feb. 1909, Pte. *LP*(FO800/193A).
188. 'Reply of the Turkish Government to the Russian Proposal respecting Turkish Claims against Bulgaria' in Lowther to Grey, 6 Feb. 1909, FO371/750,5741.
189. Grey to Nicolson, 12 Feb. 1909, FO371/750,5893; FO371/750,5741; Nicolson to Grey, 15 Feb. 1909, FO371/750,5977, and minutes; Grey to Nicolson, 15 Feb. 1909, FO371/750,6460; Grey to Nicolson, 12 Feb. 1909, FO371/750,5893; Grey to Nicolson, 02 Feb. 1909, Pte. *GP.*(FO800/73); Grey to Poklewski, 12 Feb. 1909, Pte. *GP.*(FO800/73).
190. Nicolson to Grey, 04 March 1909, 07 March 1909, FO371/752,8578,8857.
191. But Izvolsky insisted that Rifat's promise be put in writing. Rifat Pasha objected that he could not do so without consulting his cabinet colleagues. Nicolson to Grey, 4 March 1909 and 5 March 1909, FO371/752,8578,8693; Nicolson to Grey, 8 March 1909, FO371/753,9768.
192. Nicolson to Grey, 7 March 1909, FO371/752,8857; Nicolson to Grey, 15 March 1909, FO371/753,100008; Nicolson to Grey, 8 March 1909, FO371/753,9768.
193. For the text of the protocol, see 'Rifat Pasha to Haridjié' in Lowther to Grey, 18 March 1909, FO371/754,10803.
194. For the text of this alleged treaty, see Lowther to Grey, 18 March 1909, FO371/754,10392.
195. AMTZ, 174/41.
196. Refik Bey to the Grand Vizierate, 21 March 1909, and Hüseyin Hilmi Pasha to Refik Bey, 23 March 1909, AMTZ, 174/41.
197. Türkgeldi, *Görüp İşittiklerim*, pp.13–14.
198. For information about growing domestic tension, see Akşin, *31 Mart Olayı* (Istanbul, 1972).
199. See, for the detailed correspondence between Refik Bey and the Porte regarding Bulgaria's efforts for early recognition, AMTZ, 174/67.
200. He had, in fact, been in favour of early recognition. See AMTZ, 174/67.
201. Nicolson to Grey, 15 April 1909, FO371/757,14199; Buchanan to Grey, 13 April 1909, FO371/757,13945, and minutes.
202. Ibid., Mallet's minute; FO371/757,14324.
203. Grey to Nicolson, 16 April 1909, FO371/757,14199.
204. Lowther to Grey, 14 April 1909, 15 April 1909, 17 April 1909, and 18 April 1909, FO371/757,14034,14122,14176,14188,14192,14199,14414,14490.
205. For Mahmud Şevket Pasha and the 'Army of Operations', see G.W. Swanson, *Mahmud Şevket Paşa and the Defense of the Ottoman Empire: A Study in War and Revolution During the Young Turk Period* (Unpublished Ph.D. thesis, Indiana University, Department of History, 1970), pp.51–73.
206. Lamb to Lowther, 24 April 1909, FO195/2330.
207. See, for the text of the Protocol, K. Strupp, *Ausgewählte diplomatische Aktenstücke zur orientalischen Frage*, X. (Gotha, 1916) pp.245–6.

208. Grey to Buchanan, 21 April 1909, FO371/757,15142; Grey to Nicolson, 4 May 1909, FO371/757,16472; Bertie to Grey, 4 May 1909 and 5 May 1909, FO371/758,16950,17123.
209. Y.H. Bayur, *Türk İnkılabı Tarihi* (Ankara, 1983), I/2, pp.172–3; FO371/758,18450.
210. See, for the CUP's inconsistent and contradictory efforts of diplomacy during the Bosnian annexation crisis, H. Ünal, 'Young Turk Assessments', op.cit.

The Activities of the Union for the Liberation of Ukraine in the Ottoman Empire during the First World War

HAKAN KIRIMLI

Relations between the Ottoman Empire and the Ukrainian people stretch back to the fifteenth century, though various Turkic peoples had been in close contact with the Slavic inhabitants of the lands which constitute the territory of contemporary Ukraine for at least a millennium. However, the Russian annexation of the Zaporozhian lands and other areas inhabited by the 'Little Russians', as well as the collapse of the Crimean Khanate and the consequent Ottoman withdrawal from the areas north of the Black Sea in the course of almost two centuries resulted by the nineteenth century in a sharp break in these relations. It was to take a long time until the beginning of the First World War when the Ottomans would be reminded of the particular identity of the native people of these lands through the Ukrainian national movement actively working via the channels of the Central Powers. The first nationalist organization aiming at the ultimate independence of Ukraine which included the Ottoman Empire in its sphere of activities was the 'Union for the Liberation of Ukraine' (*Soyuz Vyzvolennya Ukrayiny*).

Before the outbreak of the First World War, a number of Ukrainian revolutionaries and nationalists had taken refuge in the Austro-Hungarian Empire, particularly in the Western Ukrainian provinces of East Galicia and Bukovina. The Union for the Liberation of Ukraine (ULU) was formally founded in Lemberg (Lviv) in 4 August 1914 by the most prominent figures among these émigré politicians who cherished hopes of realizing their ideals after the eventual defeat of the Russian Empire. Though it kept close contact with the local (Western) Ukrainians, the ULU was an exclusive organization of the Ukrainians from the Russian Empire. The founders of the ULU were mostly socialists, and they included Andriy Zhuk, Oleksander Skoropys-Yoltukhivs'kyi, Volodymyr Kozlovs'kyi, Mariyan Basok-Melenevs'kyi, Oleksander Semeniv, Peter Bendzia, Mykola Zaliznyak (the leader of the Ukrainian Socialist Revolutionaries; he left the Union soon after and conducted his own activities independently), Dmytro Dontsov (who signed the founding declaration, but soon turned against the Union) and others.[1] The ultimate aim of the Union for the Liberation of Ukraine was stated in its first declaration as follows: 'In this Union all shades of political interests are represented, and these have united in the claim for the political independence of the Ukrainian people. This Union sees the realization of its endeavors through the defeat of the Russian Empire by the United [Central] Powers. The independent Ukraine will be a constitutional and consequently a democratic monarchy, with one legislative body, having all civil, national and other rights and with its own national Church.'[2] To this end, the ULU was to work for winning over the Central Powers who were then fighting against the common enemy for the Ukrainian cause.

Thus, from the very start, the ULU cast its lot with the Central Powers. Based principally in the Austro-Hungarian Empire, apparently, the ULU managed to establish contacts with influencial circles in the Central Powers. The latter at least initially considered the Union for the Liberation of Ukraine and the Ukrainian national factor in general as a potentially useful card to be played against Russia, although both Austria-Hungary and Germany strictly refrained from officially including the formation of an independent Ukrainian state in their war aims. In this manner, the ULU usually received generous support for its activities from the Central Powers. The ULU's projects of large numbers of propagandistic publications, organizational activities, works among the Russian prisoners of war of Ukrainian origin, and even some military ventures were granted sponsorship by the Central Powers, especially by the Austro-Hungarian Empire, during the early months of the war.

The Ottoman Empire was not among the initial participants of the First World War. During the months following the outbreak of hostilities between the two blocs of European Powers, the Ottoman government hesitated to take sides. The recent Tripolitanian and Balkan wars which resulted in humiliating defeats and enormous territorial and other losses had devastated the country. The Committee of Union and Progress (İttihad ve Terakkî Komitesi) which had firmly acquired power since 1913 was looking forward to plenary and quick solutions to the long-accumulated chronic problems of the empire and to repair its prestige under new direction. This is not to say that the ruling Commitee of Union and Progress was unanimous in determining the ways to be chosen in internal and foreign policies; the co-existence of diametrically opposed views on several issues to do with the fate of the country, even among the highest echelons of the Committee, is well known. This indecision and conflicting opinions were clearly reflected in the wavering searches for the most suitable alliance with one of the two blocs of the European Powers. Indeed, either in line with the orientation and symphathies of an individual or a group of influential Union and Progress leaders, or due to the conjunction of circumstances or concerns, Ottoman government circles made approaches to almost all parties in order not to be on the losing side at the end of the Great War.

Still, especially after the outbreak of the First World War in August 1914, the Ottoman orientation toward the Central Powers was to become more and more evident. This, to a great extent, was to do with the pro-German stand of the powerful Minister of War, Enver Pasha, and his supporters, as well as the general frustration with the unsatisfactory responses of the Entente Powers to the previous Ottoman approaches toward them. One the most critical manifestations of this orientation was the secret Ottoman-German Alliance negotiated and signed between Enver Pasha and Hans Baron von Wangenheim, the German Ambassador in Istanbul, on 2 August 1914.[3] This alliance, which would ultimately lead to the Ottoman entry into the war on the side of the Central Powers, was kept strictly secret (only very few people were informed of it, even those in the Ottoman cabinet) and the Ottoman Empire maintained its formal neutrality for the following three months. Only a week after the secret Ottoman-German Alliance, two German men-of-war (*Goeben* and *Breslau*), hotly pursued by the British fleet, took refuge in the Dardanelles and soon the Ottoman government declared that they had been 'purchased' by Turkey. The chief engineer of this 'purchase' was Enver Pasha, who practically imposed it on the rest of the cabinet and the Sultan as a *fait accompli*.

It was during this increasingly pro-Central Powers neutrality of the Ottoman Empire that some joint military projects were secretly discussed and initiated between the Central Powers and the Ottoman political and military leaders. One of these ventures would involve plans for an Ottoman attack on the Russian Ukraine. On 16 August 1914, Enver Pasha called a secret meeting. Among the participants were von Wangenheim, Admiral Souchon (who came to Turkey as the commander of ex-German warship *Goeben* [now *Yavuz*] and then appointed Commander of the Ottoman Navy), General Liman von Sanders (the head of the German military mission in Turkey), German military and naval attachés, and several high-ranking Turkish officers. Apparently, the aim of the meeting was to discuss the possible actions of the Ottoman Empire in case it entered the war. The debate involved choosing between a possible attack on the Suez Canal and a land assault on the Odessa region.[4] The latter plan was advocated by General Liman von Sanders, who thought that a Turkish landing on the coastal area between Odessa and Akkerman would bring considerable relief to the left wing of the Austro-Hungarian eastern front. Liman argued that since the Russian Black Sea Fleet did not seem to be very strong at that time and the Russian troops in the Odessa region were not well trained, such a daring operation could succeed. However, the success of the landed troops would depend on the prior defeat of the Russian Black Sea Fleet. To the dismay of Liman, the majority favoured an attack on the Suez Canal.[5]

Notwithstanding the rejection of Liman's plan, discussion of a possible operation in the Odessa region would appear to have continued for some time. Enver Pasha instructed his German chief of staff, General Bronsart von Schellendorff ('Bronsart Pasha'), to prepare a general plan for the movements of the Ottoman forces were the Ottoman Empire to join the war. In this plan, dated 20 August 1914, a landing operation in Odessa region was considered. The implementation of this project, however, was to be contingent on the prior achievement of naval supremacy in the Black Sea as well as the benevolent neutrality of Romania. Once realized, the timing of the operation would be determined according to the extent of the German and Austro-Hungarian offensive in Russia. Bronsart considered this the best possible military operation to be undertaken against Russia, one whose importance was such that it might even bring the European war to an end.[6]

On the other hand, Russia's impending capture of Lemberg led military circles in Vienna to look desperately for an operation to divert the Russians' attention elsewhere. Thus, on 1 September 1914, just two days before the fall of Lemberg, Joseph Pomiankowski, the Austro-Hungarian military attaché in Istanbul, received a cable from Vienna asking him to urge the Ottomans to organize a landing in Odessa. Pomiankowski had considered Liman's version of an operation against Odessa unfeasible, estimating that no less than two and half months would be needed to transport 50,000 troops from Istanbul to Odessa, during which time the Russians would be capable of destroying such a force without damaging their continuing campaign in Galicia. On that account, Pomiankowski cabled Vienna to the effect that the Turks did not intended to join the war at that time and that, at any rate, such a force was not available to them at that moment.[7]

Margrave Pallavicini, the Austro-Hungarian Ambassador in Istanbul, viewed the matter from a different perspective. As he explained in his cable to Count Berchtold, the Habsburg Foreign Minister, once the defence of the Çanakkale (Dardanelles) Strait was secured, the Ottoman Fleet should organize a sortie in the Black Sea. Such a show of force would cause Romania to enter the war on the side of the Central Powers. Thus, according to Pallavicini, such an outcome was more important than even the result of the landing in Odessa itself.[8]

Admiral Souchon, who in his new capacity as Commander of the Ottoman Navy was supposed to be in charge of amphibious operations, presented a report on the matter on 10 September 1914. He stated that a quick Ottoman naval victory over the Russian Black Sea Fleet was unlikely and the Ottoman naval forces needed better training if they were to undertake any such ventures in the Black Sea. Souchon claimed that it would be very difficult to contain the Russian fleet and that a landing operation in terrain which was so unsuitable and close to the bases of the Russian fleet would be risky. Were such an operation on the Odessa district to succeed, the landing would have to be made as near as possible to the Romanian border.[9]

Russians were already aware of the planned Ottoman-German naval operations on the Black Sea, including that of a landing in the Odessa region. Russian agents had managed to procure the contents of Pallavicini's above-mentioned telegram to Berchtold, and Giers, the Russian Ambassador in Istanbul, informed his government of its contents on 24 September 1914.[10] The Russians already knew about Enver Pasha's prerequisite of Ottoman naval supremacy in the Black Sea before any operations in that region could be launched.[11] The Russians' knowledge of these plans must have been reinforced by other sources too. As Fahreddin Bey, the Ottoman chargé d'affaires in St Petersburg, cabled Istanbul on 25 October 1914, the Russian Foreign Minister Sergei D. Sazonov told a foreign military attaché that his government was aware of Ottoman plans for the Odessa landing supported by the guns of the *Yavuz* (formerly *Goeben*).[12] The Ottoman entry into the First World War was to be triggered by the bombardment by the Ottoman fleet (including *Yavuz* and *Midilli*) of the Russian Black Sea ports of Odessa, Sevastopol (Akyar), Feodosiia (Kefe), and Novorossiisk on 29 October 1914. Within a few days of this 'Black Sea Affair', the Ottoman Empire was officially at war with the Entente in alliance with the Central Powers.

Before the outbreak of the Great War, no contacts between any Ukrainian nationalist organizations and Ottoman circles were known. True, there was an increasing interest among Ottoman intellectual circles in the nationalities problems within the Russian Empire thanks particularly to the presence and activities in Istanbul of several prominent Turkic émigré figures from the Russian Empire. Moreover, there were even renowned Russian revolutionaries, such as Israel Helphand (alias Parvus), who were in close contact with Ottoman intellectuals. Nonetheless, practically speaking, the 'Ukrainian national cause' was still unheard of even among the Turkish intelligentsia prior to the Great War.

Still, the Ottoman Empire seemed to be a promising field for the prospective activities of the ULU, which could also be to the advantage of the Central Powers. The Turkish public had always had a deep-seated animosity and revanchist attitude to Russia and the ever-present apprehension of the Russian threat had always been one of the most critical determinants of Ottoman foreign policy. Therefore, the Turkish public was expected to welcome designs or activities directed against the 'old enemy'. From the point of view of the ULU, the Ottoman Empire appeared to be a crucial ally in its designs for a future independent Ukraine. Not only did the ULU need new bases for its activities in a critical country such as Turkey where there was the possiblilty of serious public and governmental support for the Ukrainian cause, but the prospective Turkish military operations could also directly and concretely involve the Ukrainian factor in the continuing war.

Based initially in the Austro-Hungarian Empire, the ULU soon decided to send its emissaries to other countries which were considered to be potentially sympathetic or operationally useful, and, if possible, to establish representation there. To this end, ULU representatives were dispatched to Germany (Roman Smal-Stocki), Switzerland (Peter Bendzia), Turkey (Mariyan Basok-Melenevs'kyi) and Bulgaria (Lev Hankevych).[13] Basok-Melenevs'kyi, the ULU emissary to the Ottoman Empire, was a Social-Democrat and the leader of the Ukrainian socialist group (Spilka) connected to the Russian Social Democratic Workers' Party.[14] From Vienna, via Bucharest and Sofia he arrived in Istanbul in October, before the Ottomans entered the war. Since the Ottoman entry into the war was considered a foregone conclusion then, he looked to establishing contacts with Ottoman political and military circles. He soon travelled back to Vienna, and returned to Istanbul, where he planned to stay for a long time. In the meantime, his friend Lev Hankevych had settled in Sofia as the representative of the ULU in Bulgaria.[15]

It seems that Basok-Melenevs'kyi was successful in achieving access to a wide range of influential circles in Turkey. One of the first people he met in Istanbul was his old acquaintance from his membership in the Spilka group of Kiev, Parvus. The latter, long established in Istanbul and engaged in business, used his connections to help Basok-Melenevs'kyi organize his propaganda activities. He would also urge the latter to direct action inside Russia in order to incite a rebellion of the Ukrainian peasants.[16] Possibly in return for his services, Parvus was to use his relations with Basok-Melenevs'kyi and the ULU to acquire an Austro-Hungarian passport in November 1914.[17] Parvus was not the only revolutionary whom Basok-Melenevs'kyi met in Istanbul. He was also in close touch with the revolutionaries from the Caucasus, among whom was Trias, the Georgian revolutionary who had led the Georgian legion in the Iranian revolution. Trias had come to Vienna from Switzerland at the invitation of the ULU, and, having visited a number prisoner of war camps in Austria in search of reliable compatriots, travelled to Istanbul. In Vienna and Istanbul the ULU leaders discussed with Trias the possibilities of co-operation between their organizations.[18]

Almost certainly, Basok-Melenevs'kyi was familiar with the previous discussions of an Ottoman landing operation in the Odessa region through his contacts in Vienna and Istanbul. Such schemes must have appealed to him as they provided an excellent opportunity to extend ULU directly into Ukraine by virtue of the Turkish armed forces. He was quick to make acquaintances among the ruling Committee of Union and Progress, governmental and military officials, as well as the press, and it seems that he was received with sympathy wherever he went. According to one source, Ottoman statesmen promised to support the activities of the ULU in the Russian Ukraine as soon as the Turkish forces landed there. Basok-Melenevs'kyi's work in Istanbul was steadily supported by the Austro-Hungarian and German diplomatic missions there.[19] These diplomats of the Central Powers were doubtless of great service to him in his welcome reception by the Ottoman dignitaries.

It was through these channels that, as early as the beginning of October (or late September), the Ukrainian emissaries were involved in a plan considered by Major Süleyman Askerî Bey, the head of the 'Special Organization' (Teşkilat-ı Mahsusa, the Ottoman Secret Service) and a seasoned Union and Progress activist. This plan aimed at instigating revolts in the Caucasus and Kuban regions via sending an expedition by sea. For the initial needs of the operation the Central Powers had to capture a quantity of Russian arms. Therefore, in order to carry on the work of the plan, on 2 October 1914 Pallavicini asked Count Alexander von Hoyos, the Permanent Secretary of the Austro-Hungarian Foreign Office, about the trustworthiness of the Ukrainian emissaries.[20] To this, Hoyos replied, with a request to inform Süleyman Askerî Bey that the Ukrainian emissaries were considered fully trustworthy and co-operation with them was recommended by the Austro-Hungarian government.[21] With his telegram on 9 October 1914 Hoyos informed Pallavicini that the Ukrainian emissaries also planned to incite the Russian Black Sea Fleet to revolt. Turkey would assist such a mutiny by promising to receive mutinous ships in Istanbul and arrange their eventual purchase by the Ottoman government.[22]

It is noteworthy that at the time these plans were being considered the Ottoman Empire had not yet entered the war. The Austro-Hungarians realized the importance of the Ottomans entering the war on the side of the Central Powers. Ottoman military operations on the northern shores of the Black Sea might divert Russia's attention from the critical eastern front of the Central Powers, including hard-pressed Austria-Hungary. The inclusion of Russian Ukraine in the operations, and the partial involvement of the Union for the Liberation of Ukraine, would not only be militarily advantageous but, more importantly, might incite a national uprising among the Ukrainian population in the area. The military feasibility of such projects aside, Ottoman engagement with them could facilitate the participation of the hitherto non-belligerent Ottoman Empire in the war.

Some German diplomats in Istanbul were particularly interested in the subversive consequences of prospective revolutionary or nationalist actions in the rear of the Russian armies. Dr Max Zimmer and his associate Heinrich Nebel had been charged with organizing revolutionary movements in Russia. Zimmer was planning to incite a large-scale revolutionary insurgency in the western Caucasus. He was already working in close co-operation with the Ottoman secret war cabinet led by the like-minded Enver Pasha. To this end, Zimmer sought to establish contacts with dissident groups from the Russian Empire. When he was introduced to Basok-Melenevs'kyi in Vienna in October 1914, he came to the conclusion that the ULU and its agents in the Caucasus could be of use to his designs. Upon the return of both men to Istanbul, they, together with Parvus, began to mull over the project of an uprising by the Caucasian mountaineers as well as the Kuban Cossacks and the Ukrainians.[23] In fact, there was another plan, involving the Georgian revolutionary Trias, to provoke an uprising in the Caucasus with a Turko-German expeditionary force under the command of the Austrian Colonel Count Stanislaw Szeptycki. Basok-Melenevs'kyi must have tried to combine this plan with his own, and to organize a Turkish landing on the shores of the Black Sea, preferably in the Odessa region.[24]

The prospects of participating in the landing on the Ukrainian Black Sea coast together with the Ottoman expeditionary forces prompted Basok-Melenevs'kyi to enlarge the ULU mission in Istanbul. Thus, he established a working group (headed by himself) of nine persons consisting of three ULU members and six associates. He also considered selecting others from among the Russian prisoners of war. The propagandists of the ULU could have been dispatched to Ukraine from this base in Istanbul.[25]

By November 1914 (when Turkey entered the war) the plan of landing a Turkish expeditionary force involving the ULU crystallized and came to be known among the circles of the Central Powers as the 'Constantinople Action' [Konstantinopler Aktion]. The final details of the 'Constantinople Action' were presented to the Austro-Hungarian Foreign Office during the first week of November by Basok-Melenevs'kyi, who then travelled to Vienna. In his private letter to Colonel Hranilovic of 8 November 1914, Count Hoyos summarized the plan and his opinion of it. As explained in this letter, the emissaries of the ULU had discussed with Enver Pasha's representatives in Istanbul Turkish-Ukrainian military co-operation in order to instigate a revolutionary movement in Ukraine by landing on the Russian Black Sea coast a small Ukrainian detachment protected by strong Turkish forces. In conformity with the discussions in Istanbul, the ULU requested from the Austro-Hungarian government an expeditionary corps of 500 Ukrainians, composed of 400 Austro-Hungarian Ukrainian legionaries and 100 Ukrainians to be selected from among the Russian prisoners of war.

Hoyos asked Hranilovic to seek the approval of the Army Supreme Command to implement this plan. Then Colonel Fischer in Bukovina would be entrusted with choosing from among the personnel of the Ukrainian Riflemen [Sichovi Stril'tsi] the 400 legionaries who would necessarily be all volunteers. As for the 100 volunteers from among the prisoners of war, Colonel von Steinitz would authorize their selection. With this in mind, Hoyos suggested establishing a separate prisoner of war camp for the purpose of conducting revolutionary propaganda where suitable elements for the expedition would be selected. An officer of the Ukrainian Riflemen, as well as a representative of the ULU would also go to Bukovina to help select volunteers.[26]

As there was no direct land route between the Central Powers and the Ottoman Empire then (Bulgaria and Romania were still neutral), there was the problem of transporting these volunteers without creating diplomatic complications. The solution proposed by Hoyos was to send them via Romania in civilian clothing and in separate groups of 25 men in each train. The Austro-Hungarians would cover the costs of clothing and travel expenses, while their uniforms and equipment would be supplied by the Ottoman Empire when they arrived in Istanbul. Since the Turkish authorities expected to establish Turkish naval supremacy in the Black Sea within two to three weeks, the expeditionary corps would have to arrive in Istanbul by then. Count Hoyos' expectations from this enterprise were not great, but he still harboured the opinion that the show of courage involved would induce a revolution in the Caucasian border regions of Ukraine which might tie down the Russian forces. He also thought that the outbreak of such revolutionary movements in Russia might help to mobilize Romania, which was apprehensive of the Russian might, on the side of the Central Powers.[27] Accordingly, on 13 November 1914 Hoyos wrote to Colonel Fischer, the Gendarmerie Commander of the District of Bukovina, to brief him on the details of the undertaking. He informed Fischer that the selection of 100 volunteers from among the prisoners of war in the camp in Freistadt (Upper Austria) had been entrusted to a delegate of the ULU. The representatives of the ULU and the Ukrainian National Council would also participate in the recruitment of volunteers from the Ukrainian Riflemen under Fischer's jurisdiction.[28]

While Basok-Melenevs'kyi and Zimmer were in Vienna, they discussed the plan with Hoyos in detail. According to this, the landing was to be in the Kuban region with a Turkish expeditionary force of 50,000, supplemented by the above-mentioned 500 Ukrainian volunteers. The primary aim would be to provoke an uprising among the Kabardians and Kuban Cossacks. Zimmer himself would also take part in the venture, and it was hoped that the presence of the Ukrainian legionaries would be of particular operational use in stirring unrest among their ethnic kinsmen, the Kuban Cossacks. If the operation were a success, a nucleus of the Ukrainian state could be established there, and the Ukrainian movement could be expected to spread toward the west. However, all these plans were yet to be cleared by Turkey. Upon their arrival in Istanbul, Basok-Melenevs'kyi and Zimmer would seek the approval of Liman von Sanders and Enver Pasha. To obtain this, Hoyos asked Pallavicini to contact Enver Pasha and von Sanders. In fact, as Hoyos stated, the Austro-Hungarians preferred a landing in Odessa over an expedition in North Caucasus. The latter option would be acceptable only in the case of a complete abandonment of the Odessa action, or if both operations could be carried out simultaneously.[29] These were, however, not Hoyos' only reservations about the 'Constantinople Action.' He strongly favoured entrusting command of the Turko-Ukrainian expedition to the Austrian General Staff officer Count Szeptycki. For not only would the presence of an Austrian commander have a bearing on further developments in Ukraine (or rather the Kuban region), but it would also demonstrate that his country was not totally reliant on the Germans. Although Hoyos was sceptical about the actions of Germans like Zimmer, who, according to Hoyos, tended to employ incorrect and overhasty methods, he still refrained from outright rejection of the German plans. Such an attitude might have created ill-feeling between the allies, and might have given an awkward impression about the Austrians, and might have made the Germans think that they should do everything alone. Therefore, Hoyos argued, unless their demands were outrageous, the Germans should be listened to in a friendly spirit and given encouragement in order to keep them working for the common cause. After all, Hoyos also believed that only inner unrest could cause the Russian colossus to falter.[30] Apparently, after exerting his influence, Hoyos succeeded in winning the approval of the Austro-Hungarian Army Supreme Commander for the 'Constantinople Action'. The Army Supreme Commander also accepted Hoyos' idea of entrusting the command of the action to Count Szeptycki, provided that he be given unrestricted command over the whole expeditionary corps.[31]

Notwithstanding the euphoria of Basok-Melenevs'kyi, Zimmer, Nebel and the qualified enthusiasm of Hoyos, it soon became apparent that their optimism was premature: Turkey, which was supposed to bear the brunt of the operation, seemed to demur, to say the least. Pallavicini's telegram to Hoyos on 16 November 1914 made it clear that, although Enver Pasha agreed in principle with the idea of landing an expeditionary corps in the Northern Caucasus, this could only occur if control of the Black Sea could be fully secured, and that temporary control would not do. If the 500 Ukrainian legionaries cared to undertake the operation alone, Enver Pasha would be ready to take them to the Black Sea and have them landed in a designated spot; but once landed they would be on their own [*auf eigene Faust operieren*]. General Liman von Sanders was of a similar opinion, that landing a large force before securing total control of the Black Sea would be impractical. Even Pallavicini thought that Turkey should not commit itself to the operation until the position of the Bulgarians became absolutely certain.[32]

Turkey's obvious reluctance to embark on such a daring venture, which entailed so much cost and risk and promised only dubious rewards, put paid to the plan, at least as it had been conceived. Now Hoyos also had to acknowledge that the success of the 'Constantinople Action' depended on Russian Black Sea Fleet being put out of action. Therefore, he decided not to send any Ukrainian legionaries to Istanbul before a decision had been reached on the operation, since keeping them there without any clear duty would serve no purpose.[33] Hoyos reiterated these decisions to Pallavicini and felt it necessary to explicate his previous commitment to the plan, in a somewhat apologetic fashion. He explained that the idea of an expedition had come from Dr Zimmer, who in Vienna had declared that only Colonel of the General Staff Count Szeptycki was suited to lead such an expedition, in which the Circassians and the Kuban Cossacks would join with the landing Turkish troops. At the same time, 'Achari Beg' [Süleyman Askerî Bey] had asked the ULU to dispatch 500 Austrian Ukrainians to Istanbul, where they would be armed and uniformed by the Turks and form the Ukrainian corps of the expedition to the Caucasus. Hoyos had put these plans before the Austro-Hungarian Army Supreme Command and had acquired its consent, provided that the Turkish expedition to the Caucasus were equipped adequately and its command offered to Count Szeptycki with unrestricted power. In his support of Count Szeptycki, Hoyos had thought that the prestige of Austro-Hungary would rise if an Austro-Hungarian officer played a leading role in a Turkish expedition. The 500 Ukrainian legionaries could still be dispatched to Istanbul, but Hoyos would not sanction this without a guarantee that they would be fed and supplied by the Turks and would join a larger Turkish landing force either to Odessa or to the Caucasus. Enver Pasha's proposal to having them land on Kuban was unacceptable to Hoyos. He also had doubts about the commitment of the Ukrainians in these regions and felt that they could be more useful in other areas. The Ukrainian Riflemen (Sichovi Stril'tsi) consisted almost entirely of intelligentsia (students and teachers), who would be needed in Podolia. Hoyos wrote:

> I share your opinion that one should not strive for too much and should be content with a modest benefit. Unfortunately, the hopes of public opinion especially in Germany are very much excited, and

expectations are carried too far especially as far as England is concerned, and the people seem to be almost willing to venture for the great success of *Imperium Mundi*. All this is beyond the *realpolitisch* possibilities, and I share your opinion that we can be very much satisfied if, while maintaining our integrity we and Germany remain the masters in Constantinople.[34]

In the meantime, the Austro-Hungarian Army Supreme Command had already recognized the impracticable nature of the 'Constantinople Action' through its own intelligence sources. Pomiankowski, the Austro-Hungarian military attaché in Istanbul, reported to the Army Supreme Command that the 'plan was totally unknown to the Ottoman government'. His report also included the information that any commitment of the Turkish troops was out of the question.[35] As he stated in his memoirs, Pomiankowski not only had considered the plan unrealistic, but had had difficulty in convincing himself that Vienna had indeed sanctioned such an adventure. For Pomiankowski, the Turks would never accept the sacrifice of 50,000 of their troops under a foreign commander, totally ignoring the incapacity of the Ottoman transportation fleet. Moreover, the Kuban Cossacks, though ethnically related to the Ukrainians, were among the most loyal subjects of the Tsar and they were the very people who had been settled on the lands grabbed from the native Muslims. Not surprisingly they were justifiably regarded as the greatest foes of the Muslims. In view of all this, the Ottoman authorities and the Kuban Cossacks would be most unlikely to accept a plan of an alliance. Pomiankowski cabled Vienna to the effect that even proposing such a plan to the Turks might create a very undesirable reaction in Ottoman circles.[36]

In view of these disappointing developments, on 19 November 1914 the Army Supreme Command had to reverse its recent decision to commission Count Szeptycki to command the operation.[37] As it became clear that Turkish co-operation in the plan was not realistic in the foreseeable future, the selection of volunteers from among the Ukrainian Riflemen was also cancelled. After all, the Ukrainian Riflemen were rendering very good service in the Carpathian passes and the extraction of 500 men from their ranks for a mission which might never take place would be unwise.[38]

Thus, the 'Constantinople Action' remained a unilateral and premature enthusiasm among some ULU members and some officials of the Central Powers. The latter, however, had already gone too far to drop the matter abruptly. This was especially the case for Hoyos.[39] Quite possibly to save face, Hoyos attempted to extract at least some diplomatic concessions from the Turks on the Ukrainian issue. So, he instructed Pallavicini to notify the Ottoman Foreign and War Ministers that their principal goal in the war was the sustained weakening of Russia and that in the event of victory they would initiate the building of a Ukrainian state independent from Russia. The existence of such a state would also greatly suit the interests of Turkey, since Russia's presence on the Black Sea would thereby be dealt a significant, if not mortal, blow. With this goal in mind, all attempts to liberate Ukraine and especially the purposeful activities of the ULU, whose representative in Istanbul was Basok-Melenevs'kyi, had to be strongly supported.[40]

These statements signalled official recognition of the inglorious fate of the 'Constantinople Action'. Many of the officials of the Central Powers (possibly including Hoyos) involved must have realized from the very beginning that such a daring venture was neither feasible nor justifiable. This notwithstanding, at least in the short run, an Ottoman operation somewhere closer to the actual battlegrounds of the Central Powers, especially those of the Austro-Hungarians would have had the immediate effect of relieving the latter's burden to some extent. This would also have had the effect of inflaming revolutionary and nationalist subversion at the rear of Russia with the minimum initial cost to the Germanic Powers.

On the other hand, by committing itself to such an operation, allocating many troops (50,000 men) in a not-so-directly-relevant place far from supply lines, at a time when the immediate defence of other areas (i.e. the Straits, Black Sea, and the Caucasian front, not to mention extremely wide lines of other fronts facing the British and French) was of great urgency, Turkey would have taken an unnecessary gamble. Despite some early talks about landing operations, the actual developments of the Ottoman war from the very beginning of the hostilities were to indicate most clearly that anything of the sort would be out of question. The Ottoman navy could not achieve indisputable supremacy in the Black Sea (until the Russian Revolution), and the Russian Black Sea Fleet continued to be a very serious threat. The urgent transportation of Turkish soldiers and supplies to the critical Caucasian front by the Black Sea could be realized only at great risk and only with the commitment of the best ships in the Ottoman fleet, whose commanders often objected to troop transportation in such numbers. Added to which, the Russian navy would impede the transportation of troops and supplies. Moreover, the calamitous situation on the Caucasian front which followed the Sarıkamış disaster at the end of December 1914, as well as the subsequent military engagements on the Mesopotamian, Suez and Dardanelles fronts throughout 1915 were more than enough to inhibit any adventures like the 'Constantinople Action'.[41]

It is quite possible that the ULU representatives and German diplomats in Istanbul had interpreted the polite reception and expressions of solidarity they had received from Ottoman officials (most of whom must have been subordinates rather than the decision-makers) in an overoptimistic way. There is little evidence to indicate that the 'Constantinople Action' as contemplated by some diplomats and officials of the Central Powers and the ULU had ever been seriously considered by the Ottomans, who at the time had more urgent concerns. However, a landing operation, though only remotely reminiscent of the 'Constantinople Action', indeed took place during the first week of December 1914. This plan (which seemed to be inspired by the early discussions of landing a Turkish force on the shores of Odessa or Akkerman) involved landing 24 Turkish cavalrymen, who spoke Russian and wore Russian uniforms, in Russian Bessarabia. This small force was supposed to reach Romanian territory after destroying the Bender railway and some bridges. As planned, the Ottoman steamboat *Zafer* which carried Russian colours and was protected by the light cruiser *Midilli* (formerly *Breslau*) landed these 24 soldiers, together with their mounts, on Serpent Island to the south of Sulina, at the mouth of the Danube River, on 6 December 1914. Nevertheless, the platoon was soon discovered and captured by the Russians.[42] There is no indication that this abortive attempt was in any way related to the original plan of the 'Constantinople Action' or to the Ukrainians.

Although by the third week of November 1914, the 'Constantinople Action' had been abandoned, the ULU continued to hope to dispatch its propagandists to Ukraine via the Turkish forces. As late as mid-December 1914 the ULU leaders, though with less enthusiasm, were still entertaining the realization of the 'Constantinople Action'. According to them, if any success was to be expected from the operation, it should necessarily be in harmony with the Ukrainian national aspirations. The intelligence gathering and diplomatic contacts of the ULU had laid safe and promising groundwork for the action which not even the most effective secret service could provide. The key for the success of the action lay in the Ukrainians' accepting the enemies of Russia as their friends, and, therefore, the success of the ULU was the prerequisite of the action.[43] As their hopes of ever realizing the original plan waned, the ULU leaders must have desired to obtain the maximum political gain from their efforts. Such gains could be made were some or all of the Central Powers to declare that they would include the independence of Ukraine in their proclaimed war aims and thereby their official and unequivocal commitment to their cause. Of course, the leaders also wanted to see the ULU in a much stronger and secure position *vis-à-vis* the Central Powers. To this end, the ULU leaders stressed that the Central Powers had to support their ultimate aim to establish an independent Ukrainian state. Only in this way could any misgivings about making cannon fodder of the Ukrainian volunteers or abandoning the Ukrainians to their fate after the war be eliminated.[44]

In fact, Austro-Hungary's reservations about the 'Constantinople Action' also coincided with their disenchantment with the activities of the ULU. The frustration of those Austro-Hungarian officials who were involved in the futile engagements of the 'Constantinople Action' might have played a role in this changing attitude. According to Fedyshyn, the Ukrainian movement could be of value to the Habsburg Empire only if Austro-Hungarian troops indeed marched into Russian Ukraine, but at the time the opposite was the case. The Austro-Hungarian government would also not like to see the rise of Ukrainian nationalism in Galicia while promoting revolution in Russian Ukraine. Moreover, the Austrians began to rely increasingly on pro-Polish policies, which would lead them to distance themselves from the Ukrainians, whose national territorial aspirations conflicted with those of the Poles.[45] Thus, on 17 December 1914 Vienna reduced the annual allowance to the ULU by half, and imposed serious restrictions on its activities. Furthermore, the ULU was advised to transfer its headquarters to either Istanbul or Sofia.[46] The ULU leaders were not at all comfortable with the idea of moving their centre of activities to Istanbul. One of the ULU leaders, Skoropys-Yoltukhivs'kyi, argued that such a hasty transfer from Vienna to Istanbul would disappoint the Ukrainian people who hitherto considered the Austrians as their liberators and who would gain the impression that the Austrians were ousting their brothers and would resent their previous symphathies toward Austro-Hungary. Not all the nationally-conscious elements in Ukraine could understand the motives behind such a move, and lend their support in the future. The transfer of the ULU headquarters from Vienna, which had been a very natural centre for Ukrainians, to Istanbul, with which Ukrainians had neither cultural nor national links, would be anathema to Ukrainian intellectuals. Were it to happen, the Russian press could easily impose the idea that the ULU was a group of traitors ready to be sold off to the highest bidder, first to the Germans, and then to the Turks.[47] Skoropys-Yoltukhivs'kyi also claimed that, although the Kuban Cossacks in the Russian army objected to fighting against their brethren within the Austro-Hungarian army on the Galician front, they were not considering every enemy of Russia as their friends yet and stated that they were ready to fight against the real enemy, i.e. the Turks, to defend their country.[48] Eventually, the transfer of the ULU's headquarters to Istanbul did not take place. Though the ULU's relations with the Austro-Hungarian government improved and it was even invited to remain in Vienna for some months, in spring 1915 its headquarters were finally moved to Berlin.[49]

The failure of the 'Constantinople Action' was certainly a matter of frustration for the ULU. Nonetheless, Turkey was still a critical country even without this project. Therefore, the ULU mission in Istanbul tried to make the best use of this important base. Probably with the co-operation of the Ottoman authorities, at least one ULU 'organizer' from Istanbul infiltrated Russian Ukraine in November 1914, and the dispatch of others was under consideration.[50] The activities of the ULU mission in Istanbul on matters of propaganda, however, proved to be much more effective than their plans for military action.

In this respect, relations between ULU representatives and Ottoman statesmen were of special significance. On 9 November 1914 the representatives of the ULU, Mariyan Basok-Melenevs'kyi, Dr Stefan Baran and Longin Tsehels'kyi, were received by Talât Bey (later Pasha and Grand Vizier), the then Ottoman Minister of Interior Affairs and the strongest political leader of the ruling Committee/Party of Union and Progress.[51] In this meeting Talât Bey promised to support Ukrainian efforts to establish an independent state especially during the peace conference. He also stressed that an independent Ukrainian state on the shores of the Black Sea would be in Turkey's interests.[52] Talât Bey's statements were published in *Jeune Turc* (24 November 1914) and thus made public. Talât Bey wrote to the effect that the Porte, Berlin and Vienna had recognized that Ukraine had to be removed from Russian domination, and that the Ottoman government promised the Ukrainian people to support the establishment of an independent state in the event of Russia's defeat.[53] The ULU considered Talât Bey's statements very significant, the first public commitment on the part of one of the Central Powers (which could also be expounded in a way to cover others) to the independence of Ukraine if the war ended in victory. This development certainly attracted attention in Russia too. On 26 November 1914 the Petersburg Telegraf Agency published the news as it appeared in the Ottoman press, and leading Russian papers, such as *Utro Rossii, Novoe Vremia, Rech, Birzhevyie Vedomosti*, and others carried the story.[54]

The ULU mission in Istanbul was particularly keen on propagating its activities and goals through the Turkish press and its own publications. Basok-Melenevs'kyi worked hard to establish contacts in the Turkish press, and thanks to his efforts several articles and news items about Ukraine began to appear in Istanbul papers before Turkey entered the war.[55] It should be noted that before the First World War Ukraine as a political concept, let alone its cause for independence, was virtually unknown to the Ottoman press circles. Therefore, whatever began to appear in these newspapers from October 1914 on were the first pieces of information about the subject Ottoman journalists and their readers ever encountered. The news items in the Istanbul press about the ULU and the Ukraine, particularly before the Ottomans joined the war, were observed with pleasure by the diplomatic missions of Central Powers in Istanbul. When *Tasfîr-i Efkâr (Tasvîr-i*

Efkâr), an influential daily, printed the 'Appeal of the Union for the Liberation of Ukraine to the Turkish Nation',[56] the Austro-Hungarian Embassy in Istanbul was elated, as it considered this an indication of escalating anti-Russian sentiment among the Turkish press as well as in the Muslim population.[57] Such pieces about Ukraine, often containing questionable information of a purely propagandistic nature, continued to appear in the Istanbul press after 1914. A typical example appeared in the semi-official organ of the Committee of Union and Progress, *Tanin*, on 13 December 1914, with the title 'Revolutionary Movements in Ukraine Are Progressing'. In this news item originating from Berlin it was claimed that, although the Russian government had secretly arrested and banished the leaders of the Ukrainian movement and all the Ukraine's press and societies had been closed down, the Ukrainian revolution was progressing every day.[58] Another news item in *Tanin* informed its readers about a congress of the Ukrainians residing in the United States. According to the information, in the congress which took place in New York, the participants expressed their hopes for the disintegration of the Russian Empire, stated their gratitude to the Habsburg Emperor, 'having taken into consideration the liberties which the four million Ukrainians living in the Austro-Hungarian Empire enjoyed'.[59]

The ULU itself was engaged in some publishing activities in Istanbul. First, appeals were printed for the Russian prisoners of war, in both Ukrainian [*Soldate - ozernysy*] and Russian [*Soldatam Russkoi Armii*] languages, 25,000 copies for each language.[60] The 'Appeal of the Union for the Liberation of Ukraine to the Turkish Nation' was also printed in the form of leaflets.[61] In the report on the activities of the ULU until mid-December 1914 it was stated that Longin Tsehels'kyi's booklet entitled 'Russia - Oppressor of Nations' was published in Turkish.[62] The same document also mentions the ULU's intention to publish Turkish translations of Longin Tsehels'kyi's 'How Russia Saved Ukraine?',[63] Lev Hankevych's 'Turkey in the Context of War', a booklet entitled 'Not the Liberator, But the Oppressor of Peoples',[64] and a brochure by Dr Rudnyts'kyi.[65] It seems that none of these was published. Nevertheless, the ULU succeeded in publishing an important collection of articles and documents in Turkish, in 1915. This book, entitled *Ukrayna, Rusya ve Türkiye (Makaleler Mecmuası)* [Ukraine, Russia and Turkey (Collection of Articles)], was the first book in the Turkish language about modern Ukraine and Ukrainian nationalist and revolutionary movements.[66]

The book consisted of eight articles and documents: Longin Tsehels'kyi, 'Ukraine and Turkey'; Mykhailo Hrushevs'kyi, 'A Glance at Ukrainian History in Retrospect'; Volodymyr Doroshenko, 'Political Parties in Russian Ukraine'; Mariyan Melenevs'kyi, 'Cultural Movements of the

Ukrainians'; Andriy Zhuk, 'Russian Ukraine'; 'Appeal of the Union for the Liberation of Ukraine to the Turkish Nation'; 'To the European Public'; and 'Program of the Union for the Liberation of Ukraine'. In the preface, written in December 1914, the editors drew an analogy between the activities and aims of the 'Young Turks' in the past and those of the contemporary Union for the Liberation of Ukraine. They also pointed out the historical ties between the Turks and Ukrainians, and their hopes for the imminent collapse of the 'rotten Russian Empire', with the assistance of the Ottoman Empire.[67]

Among the historical and cultural articles which were originally translated from other publications, Tsehels'kyi's article stood out as the one written specifically for the Turkish reader. Having succinctly surveyed Ottoman-Ukrainian relations in history, Tsehels'kyi wrote:

> The reasons which lead Turkey to consider Ukraine as a defence ditch against Russia in the seventeenth and eighteenth centuries prevail today even more strongly than in the past, as in our times Russia presents such a threat to the Balkans and the Ottoman Empire. Russia's advance to the Straits and Istanbul can come to an end only if either the Straits and Istanbul fall to the hands of the Russians, or the Russians are pushed northwards behind the Ukrainian boundaries. The formation, or rather the re-establishment, of the Ukrainian government, in accord with the designs of the [seventeenth century] Grand Vizier Köprülü Mehmed Pasha, is a direct requirement of Turkey's interests.[68]

In the 'Appeal of the Union for the Liberation of Ukraine to the Turkish Nation', special attention was paid to emphasize the Russian threat to Turkey and to dissociate Ukrainians from the 'fake pan-Slavism of Russia' which had created havoc for the Ottomans in the Balkans. The 'Appeal' also struck another sensitive chord in Turkey, that is, the concern over the fate of Muslims in the Russian Empire. It asserted that while millions of Muslims in the Russian Empire were suffering, it was imperative for the Ottoman Empire to join the fight against Russia, and together with their coreligionist Muslims, Ukrainians and other subjugated peoples of Russia too would welcome the Ottomans.[69] As the Turks and Ukrainians had allied themselves against the common enemy (i.e. Russia) during the times of Hetmans Petro Doroshenko and Filip Orlik, they should renew this alliance; and when Russia was rolled back to its natural borders of the Moscovite world, the free Ukrainian nation would live in alliance with the Ottoman Empire.[70]

There is little doubt that these approaches of the ULU were warmly received in Istanbul, as they reflected the prevailing anti-Russian and nationalistic mood. Nevertheless, the catastrophic progress of the Ottoman military campaigns against the Russian armies soon replaced the initial grandiose hopes of conquest, with serious concerns about recovering great losses, if not finding ways to preserve the very existence of the Ottoman Empire. Under these negative circumstances, both the representatives of the Central Powers and the ULU must have realized that there was little the ULU could expect to accomplish in Istanbul in regard to its initial grandiose hopes and projects. After all, especially after the ULU headquarters were transferred to Berlin, Germany became the pivotal venue of Ukrainian nationalist activities, as by then this country's performance in the war seemed to be the main determinant in the future of the Ukraine. Thus, apparently, Basok-Melenevs'kyi's activities in Istanbul turned rather to lobbying work among the diplomatic corps of the Central Powers, than seeking ways of doing business directly with the Ottoman government. It is known that in May 1915 he visited the German and Austro-Hungarian ambassadors in Istanbul to enquire whether the Central Powers, in view of the progressing spring offensive of their eastern armies, would consider the establishment of a Ukrainian provisional government in the would-be-occupied Ukrainian lands. He asserted that if civil administration were entrusted to such a Ukrainian government and if its legitimacy were recognized even on a portion of Ukraine which could be conquered, this would created a genuine basis for the eventual state-building over the rest of the Ukraine.[71]

Although, in the face of the available evidence, it seems that after 1915 the activities of the ULU in Turkey lost their initial euphoria, this, by no means suggests that the relations between the Ottoman Empire and Ukrainian nationalists were severed. In fact, the energetic Ottoman intelligence service, the 'Special Organizition' (Teşkilat-ı Mahsûsa) or the 'Directorate for Eastern Affairs' (Umûr-u Şarkiyye Müdîriyeti), was always keen on maintaining close relations with, if not directly sponsoring, nationalist movements pertaining to the imperial territories of the enemy powers, especially those of the Russian Empire. Thus, a certain group of Ukrainian nationalists was allowed to live in Istanbul under the auspices of the 'Special Organization'. This group of Ukrainian nationalists is mentioned in contemporary Ottoman documents as the 'Ukrainian Committee' and, for all likelihood, they belonged to the ULU.[72] The evidence suggests that they worked hand in glove with the 'Special Organization', which offered them certain support even beyond the Ottoman boundaries. In this manner, when they needed to travel abroad, they were readily given Ottoman passports.[73] Apparently, such members of the 'Ukrainian Committee' continued to reside in Istanbul at least until the first months of 1918 when they were sent to their country which was then experiencing the turbulent process of the newly declared independence.[74]

Before the Russian revolutions of 1917 and the consequent Ukrainian independence, one more event concerning the Ottoman military and the Ukrainians deserves to be mentioned. In 1916 a large number of Ottoman troops was sent to the Galician front to relieve their allies. This was the first actual appearance of the Ottoman military in a land where Ukrainians lived. The Ottoman troops, whose performance in eastern Galicia were admittedly praised, fought there next to the volunteer Ukrainian Riflemen units of the Austro-Hungarian army.[75] We are not aware of any role the ULU played in establishing contact between the Ottoman troops and the Ukrainian Riflemen there.

The relations between the ULU and the Ottoman governmental institutions and public during the First World War constitute the first instance when the 'Ukrainian national factor' was brought to the attention of the latter and was considered in its foreign policy. Certainly, the activities of the ULU were made possible only within a much broader context of the wartime policies and post-war considerations of the Central Powers as regards the Russian Empire. It was thanks to the German and Austro-Hungarian sponsorship that the ULU was able to operate and find itself in a position to play a crucial role in the future of Ukraine. Similarly, it was again these Central European Powers who introduced the ULU to the Ottomans. As they viewed the ULU primarily as a useful device with which to effect Ottoman policy (before and after the Ottoman entry to the war), Ottoman officials appreciated the intrinsic value of the Ukrainian factor for the future of their own state. To the dismay of both the Germanic empires and the ULU, their initial ambitious, if half-baked, schemes involving the Ottoman Empire proved to be utterly impracticable. It appears that none of the contemplated military operations concerning a joint action of Turkish soldiers and Ukrainian volunteers could be realized. This is not to say that the ULU was left empty-handed in its relations with the Ottomans. The Ottomans too extended their sponsorship to the ULU, and supported its activities clandestinely. On the other hand, the ULU found means to reach out to at least some segments of the Ottoman intellectual public, and received a warm and symphatetic response. The impression created by the ULU in Turkey about Ukraine must have contributed positively to the development of diplomatic relations between the Ottoman Empire and the independent Ukrainian People's Republic following the Treaty of Brest-Litovsk in 1918.

NOTES

1. Andriy Zhuk, 'Soyuz Vyzvolennya Ukrayiny', *Pamyatkova knizhka soyuza vyzvolennya Ukrayiny. Kalendar' na 1917 rik* (Vienna, 1917), pp.367–8; A. Zhukovs'kyi, 'Soyuz Vyzvolennya Ukrayiny', *Entsyklopediia Ukrayinoznavstva* (Munich, 1976), Vol.II/8, pp.2971–72; Roman Smal-Stocki, 'Actions of "Union for the Liberation of Ukraine" during World War I', *The Ukrainian Quarterly*, Vol.XV, No.2, p.170; Oleh S. Fedyshyn, *Germany's Drive to the East and the Ukrainian Revolution, 1917–1918* (New Brunswick, NJ, 1971), pp.30–1.
2. *Der Bund zur Befreiung der Ukraina (Sonderabdruck aus der Nummer 1 der 'Ukrainischen Nachrichten')* (Vienna, 1914).
3. As a matter of fact, the proposals for such an alliance with Germany had been offered by Enver Pasha and Sait Halim Pasha, the Grand Vizier, to the Germans already on 22–23 July 1914, and there must have been negotiations about it preceding these dates. At that time, however, von Wangenheim considered the move premature. Robert J. Kerner, 'Russia, the Straits, and Constantinople, 1914–1915', *The Journal of Modern History* (Chicago), Vol.I (1929), pp.403–4. Only three days after the signing of the Ottoman-German Alliance, Enver Pasha negotiated with the Russian military attaché Leont'ev as to the possibility of an Ottoman-Russian alliance. Akdes Nimet Kurat, *Türkiye ve Rusya* (Ankara, 1970), pp.230–9.
4. Yusuf Hikmet Bayur, *Türk İnkılâbı Tarihi*, Vol.III, part I (Ankara, 1983), p.202; Liman von Sanders, *Türkiye'de Beş Yıl* (Istanbul, 1968), p.41.
5. Von Sanders, p.41.
6. Cemal Akbay, *Birinci Dünya Harbinde Türk Harbi*, Vol.I (*Osmanlı İmparatorluğunun Siyasî ve Askerî Hazırlıkları ve Harbe Girişi*) (Ankara, 1970), p.279.
7. Joseph Pomiankowski, *Der Zusammenbruch des Ottomanischen Reiches. Erinnerungen an die Türkei aus der Zeit des Weltkrieges* (Leipzig, 1928), pp.81–82.
8. 'Pallavicini to Berchtold, 2 September 1914', *Documents Diplomatiques Secrets Russes, 1914–1917. D'Après les Archives du Ministère des Affaires étrangères a Pétrograd* (Paris, 1928), pp.90–1.
9. Akbay, p.84, 455–6.
10. Ibid., pp.203–4; *Documents Diplomatiques Secrets Russes*, pp.90–1.
11. *Documents Diplomatiques Secrets Russes, 1914–1917*, p.94.
12. Kurat, p.241.
13. Smal-Stocki, p.171.
14. Before the First World War, Basok-Melenevs'kyi and his fellow travellers had little to do with Ukrainian nationalist aims. Then, for them, the Ukrainian language could be of importance only so far as it facilitated socialistic propaganda among the Ukrainian peasants. Helga Grebing, 'Österreich-Ungarn und die "Ukrainische Aktion" 1914–18', *Jahrbücher für Geschichte Osteuropas* (Munich), Vol.7, No.3 (1959), 278. In fact, Basok-Melenevs'kyi was the leader of that group of the Ukrainian Revolutionary Party which advocated a general democratization in the Russian Empire and opposed autonomy for Ukraine. After the Congress of the Party, Basok-Melenevs'kyi and his followers split from it, and, under the name *Spilka*, they joined the Russian Social-Democratic Workers' Party. The *Spilka*, which believed that national oppression would become a thing of the past in the general democratization in the Russian Empire, soon dissolved in the Russian organization. Oleh Semenovych Pidhainy, *The Formation of the Ukrainian Republic* (Toronto-New York, 1966), p.27.
15. 'Provisorischer Bericht über die Tätigkeit des Bundes zur Befreiung der Ukraina für die Zeit September–Dezember 1914. Wien, den 14. Dezember 1914', *Ereignisse in der Ukraine 1914–1922 deren Bedeutung und historische Hintergründe*, Vol.I (Philadelphia, PA, 1966), pp.175–177.
16. Jerry Hans Hoffman, 'The Ukrainian Adventure of the Central Powers, 1914–1918', Unpublished Ph. D. Dissertation, University of Pittsburgh, 1967, pp.58–9.
17. Grebing, p.280.
18. Ibid., p.279; 'Provisorischer Bericht über die Tätigkeit des Bundes zur Befreiung der Ukraina für die Zeit September–Dezember 1914. Wien, den 14. Dezember 1914', pp.177–8.

19. 'Provisorischer Bericht über die Tätigkeit des Bundes zur Befreiung der Ukraina für die Zeit September–Dezember 1914. Wien, den 14. Dezember 1914', p.178.
20. 'Pallavicini to Hoyos, 2 October 1914', *Ereignisse in der Ukraine 1914–1922 deren Bedeutung und historische Hintergründe*, Vol.I, p.146.
21. 'Hoyos to Pallavicini, 4 October 1914', ibid., pp.146–7.
22. 'Hoyos to Pallavicini, 9 October 1914', ibid., p.147.
23. Hoffman, pp.59–60.
24. Grebing, p.281. Count Stanislaw Szeptycki was the brother of the Archbishop of the Ruthenian Church in Lemberg (Lviv). Pomiankowski, p.82.
25. 'Provisorischer Bericht über die Tätigkeit des Bundes zur Befreiung der Ukraina für die Zeit September–Dezember 1914. Wien, den 14. Dezember 1914', p.178. As of by mid-Dezember 1914, the ULU group in Istanbul consisted of Mariyan Basok-Melenevs'kyi, Peter Bendzia, Mykola Ryshyi, Peter Dyatliv, Georgii Koval'nyi, Oleksander Pochatok, Isaak Yunak, and Boris Lizovyk. All were originally from the Russian Ukraine. Ibid., p.189.
26. 'Private letter from Hoyos to Hranilovic, 8 November 1914', *Ereignisse in der Ukraine 1914–1922 deren Bedeutung und historische Hintergründe*, Vol.I, pp.144–5.
27. Ibid., p.145.
28. 'Private letter from Hoyos to Fischer, 13 November 1914', *Ereignisse in der Ukraine 1914–1922 deren Bedeutung und historische Hintergründe*, Vol.I, p.150.
29. 'From the Imperial and Royal Foreign Office to Pallavicini, 13 November 1914', *Ereignisse in der Ukraine 1914–1922 deren Bedeutung und historische Hintergründe*, Vol.I, p.153.
30. 'Private Letter from Hoyos to Hranilovic, 14 November 1914', *Ereignisse in der Ukraine 1914–1922 deren Bedeutung und historische Hintergründe*, Vol.I, pp.151–2.
31. 'From Hoyos to Pallavicini, 16 November 1914', *Ereignisse in der Ukraine 1914–1922 deren Bedeutung und historische Hintergründe*, Vol.I, p.154.
32. 'From Pallavicini to Hoyos, 16 November 1914', *Ereignisse in der Ukraine 1914–1922 deren Bedeutung und historische Hintergründe*, Vol.I, pp.154–5.
33. 'Private Letter from Hoyos to Hranilovic, 19 November 1914', *Ereignisse in der Ukraine 1914–1922 deren Bedeutung und historische Hintergründe*, Vol.I, p.156.
34. 'Private Letter from Hoyos to Palavicini, 19 November 1914', *Ereignisse in der Ukraine 1914–1922 deren Bedeutung und historische Hintergründe*, Vol.I, pp.158–9.
35. 'Telegram of the Imperial and Royal army Supreme Command, 19 November 1914', *Ereignisse in der Ukraine 1914–1922 deren Bedeutung und historische Hintergründe*, Vol.I, p.159.
36. Pomiankowski, pp.82–3.
37. 'Imperial and Royal Army Supreme Command, 19 November 1914', *Ereignisse in der Ukraine 1914–1922 deren Bedeutung und historische Hintergründe*, Vol.I, p.159.
38. 'From Hranilovic to Hoyos, 21 November 1914', *Ereignisse in der Ukraine 1914–1922 deren Bedeutung und historische Hintergründe*, Vol.I, p.157.
39. Hoffman, p.62.
40. 'From the Imperial and Royal Foreign Office to Pallavicini and Hohenlohe, 20 November 1914', *Ereignisse in der Ukraine 1914–1922 deren Bedeutung und historische Hintergründe*, Vol.I, p.168.
41. During the first week of November 1914, the principal task of the Ottoman navy was determined as, first, protecting, and keeping open, the Black Sea (Istanbul) Strait, second, securing the naval transportation to Istanbul from Zonguldak (where the main coal mines were located) and from Romania and Bulgaria. So long as these tasks were fulfilled, the bombardment of the Russian shores and harassment of the Russian intercoastal tranportation were also considered. In any case, it was recognized that the Russian Black Sea Fleet could still constitute a serious threat to the Ottoman transportation, and thus any large-scale landing operations on the Russian shores were definitely ruled out. Saim Besbelli, *Birinci Dünya Harbinde Türk Harbi*, Vol.VIII, *Deniz Harekâtı* (Ankara, 1976), p.79.
42. [Hermann] Lorey, *Türk Sularında Deniz Hareketleri* (Istanbul, 1936), p.154; Karl Dšnitz, 'Midilli', in Th. Kraus – Karl Dönitz, *Die Kreuzerfahrten der Goeben und Breslau* (Berlin, 1933), p.170.
43. Skoropys-Joltuchowskyj, 'Über die "Konstantinopler Aktion,' die rolle der ukrain.

Intelligenz in der russ. Ukraine und Stellungnahme zur eventuellen verlegung des Sitzes des Präsidiums des Bundes z. B. d. U. nach Konstantinopel, 20 Dezember 1914', *Ereignisse in der Ukraine 1914–1922 deren Bedeutung und historische Hintergründe*, Vol.I, p.191.
44. Ibid., p.192.
45. Fedyshyn, p.36.
46. Ibid.
47. Skoropys-Joltuchowskyj, pp.194–5.
48. Ibid., p.192.
49. Fedyshyn, p.36.
50. 'Provisorischer Bericht über die Tätigkeit des Bundes zur Befreiung der Ukraina für die Zeit September–Dezember 1914. Wien, den 14. Dezember 1914', p.182.
51. Evhen Onats'kyi, 'Talaat Mehemed Bey', *Ukrayins'ka Mala Entsyklopediia* (Buenos Aires, 1963), p.1873. This source omits the name of Basok-Melenevs'kyi in the ULU delegation received by Talât Bey on 9 November 1914. Nevertheless, since Basok-Melenevs'kyi was the leader of the ULU mission in Istanbul then, and that other sources corroborate the existence of a reception by Talât Bey of Basok-Melenevs'kyi some time in November 1914, almost certainly the latter must be included in the delegation to Talât Bey on 9 November 1914. See, 'From Pallavicini to Berchtold, 1 Dezember 1914', *Ereignisse in der Ukraine 1914–1922 deren Bedeutung und historische Hintergründe*, Vol.I, p.169; and Skoropys-Joltuchowskyj, p.191.
52. Onats'kyi, p.1873.
53. 'La question ukrainienne. Déclarations de Talaat bey', *Jeune Turc* (Istanbul), 24 November 1914. See also, 'From Pallavicini to Berchtold, 1 Dezember 1914 (Supplement)', pp.169–70.
54. Skoropys-Joltuchowskyj, p.191.
55. 'Provisorischer Bericht über die Tätigkeit des Bundes zur Befreiung der Ukraina für die Zeit September–Dezember 1914. Wien, den 14. Dezember 1914', p.177.
56. '"Ukrayna' İstiklâli İçin', *Tasfîr-i Efkâr* (Istanbul), 7 [20] October 1914.
57. 'From Pallavicini to Berchtold, 22 Ekim 1914', *Ereignisse in der Ukraine 1914–1922 deren Bedeutung und historische Hintergründe*, Vol.I, pp.147–148.
58. 'Ukrayna'da Harekât-ı İhtilâliyye Terakkî Ediyor', *Tanin* (Istanbul), 13 Dec. 1914.
59. 'Ukraynalıların Mukarrerâtı', *Tanin*, 29 October 1914.
60. 'Provisorischer Bericht über die Tätigkeit des Bundes zur Befreiung der Ukraina für die Zeit September–Dezember 1914. Wien, den 14. Dezember 1914', pp.178 and 187. The texts of these appeals were published in *Vistnyk Soiuza dlya Vyzvolennya Ukrayiny*, the biweekly organ of the ULU in Vienna. Ibid., p.174.
61. Ibid., p.186. I was unable to locate this booklet in Turkish, if it was ever actually published.
62. Ibid., p.178.
63. Ibid., p.173.
64. Ibid., p.188.
65. Ibid., p.178.
66. *Ukrayna, Rusya ve Türkiye (Makaleler Mecmuası)* (Istanbul, 1915).
67. 'Nâşirler Tarafından', *Ukrayna, Rusya ve Türkiye (Makaleler Mecmuası)*, p.3.
68. Longin Tsehels'kyi, 'Ukrayna ve Türkiye', *Ukrayna, Rusya ve Türkiye (Makaleler Mecmuası)*, pp.12–13.
69. 'Ukrayna Cemiyet-i İstihlâsiyyesi'nin Türk Milleti'ne Hitâbesi', *Ukrayna, Rusya ve Türkiye (Makaleler Mecmuası)*, pp.60–2.
70. Ibid., pp.62–3.
71. Hoffman, pp.89–90.
72. Six (all?) of the members of the 'Ukrainian Committee' residing in Istanbul by early 1918 were identified as such: Yurii Menkin (28, born in Kharkov, electirician), Ivan Mikhailov (33, born in Sevastopol, electrician), Marko Yashin (29, born in Kerç, merchant), Aleksandr Dimo (35, born in Orgiev, agrarian engineer), Yurii Romanenko (31, born in Lodz, agrarian engineer) and Aleksandr Gulotov (31, born in Kiev, agrarian engineer). The Special Organization organized their return to the Ukraine in early 1918. Archives of the Turkish General Staff Directorate of Military History and Strategical Studies, Ankara (hereafter *ATASE* Archives), First World War Collection, K: 332, D: 1332, nos. 3, 3–1, 3–2, 3–3, 3–4,

and 3–5.
73. The presence of two Ottoman passports for Aleksandr Gulotov and Aleksandr Dimo (both issued in Istanbul, in 27 June 1917) in the files of the Ottoman intelligence service testify to this practice. The passports are issued for travel to Stockholm via Bulgaria, Austria and Germany. However, the fact that they do not bear any visa stamps, as well as they still remain among the Ottoman official files, may attest that they were never actually used. *ATASE* Archives, First World War Collection, K: 332, D: 1332, nos. 2–7 and 2–8.
74. *ATASE* Archives, First World War Collection, K: 332, D: 1332, nos. 3, 3–1, 3–2, 3–3, 3–4, and 3–5.
75. V. Oreletsky, 'Ukraine and Turkey', *The Ukrainian Review*, Vol.IV, No.2 (Summer 1957), p.23.

Diplomatic Relations between the Ottoman Empire and the Ukrainian Democratic Republic, 1918–21

HAKAN KIRIMLI

The signing of the Treaty of Brest-Litovsk between the Central Powers and the newly-born Ukrainian Democratic Republic (Ukrayins'ka Narodnia Respublika)[1] on 9 February 1918 was the first step in ending the war on the 'Eastern Front'. This was to be formalized with the following treaty with Soviet Russia, though various forms of military actions on the European parts of the territory of the former Russian Empire went on for over two years. The Ukrainian Treaty of Brest-Litovsk was the first diplomatic recognition of independent Ukraine in modern times. It was to be the subsequent military actions of the Central Powers (particularly those of Germany) in accordance with this treaty which would secure the new independent Ukrainian state from being annihilated by the Bolsheviks. At the time when the representatives of the Ukrainian Democratic Republic signed the Treaty of Brest-Litovsk with the Central Powers, almost all of the territory of the new republic was already under Bolshevik invasion. The treaty of Brest-Litovsk between the Central Powers and the Ukrainian Democratic Republic, which was literally cornered by the Bolshevik invasion of the country, enabled the latter not only to accomplish its first diplomatic relations but virtually to reclaim most of Ukraine thanks to the German and Austro-Hungarian arms.

In fact, the cause of Ukrainian independence had already been introduced to the Central Powers during the initial phase of the First World War, through the activities of Ukrainian nationalist organizations, especially those of the 'Union for the Liberation of Ukraine' (Soyuz Vyzvolennya Ukrayiny). Germany and Austria-Hungary had offered, at times quite generous sponsorship to the activities of the 'Union for the Liberation of Ukraine'. The issue of creating an independent Ukraine was discussed at length by the Germanic Powers, however no clearcut strategy was adopted.[2] Nevertheless, it was with the Treaty of Brest-Litovsk in February 1918 that the independence of Ukraine became a political and diplomatic reality. This process also applied to the Ottoman Empire where the Union for the Liberation of Ukraine, through German and Austro-Hungarian diplomatic circles, had engaged in certain activities especially in 1914–15.

At Brest-Litovsk, at a time when the negotiations with the Bolshevik representatives reached virtual deadlock, the dignitaries of the Central Powers opted to sign a separate treaty with the representatives of the government of the 'Ukrainian Democratic Republic' who represented a country most of which at that time was effectively controlled by the Bolsheviks.[3] Like their allies, the Ottomans too approved the conclusion of a separate truce with the Ukrainians. Apart from vital economic considerations, such as those concerning the grain provisions from the Ukraine, the Central Powers viewed an independent (and, of course, a 'benevolent') Ukraine as a bulwark against the Bolshevik menace, as well as a further device to force intransigent Soviet Russia to accept peace on their own terms.

Having recognized the importance of the factors concerning the Central Powers in general, the Ottoman delegation at Brest-Litovsk headed by the Grand Vizier Talât Pasha had its own notion of the emergence of an independent Ukraine. No doubt, the most important implication of Ukrainian independence for the Turks was that the historical 'Muscovite' threat to the Ottoman Empire was to be effectively removed by such a buffer state, which was expected to be a friendly one. The Ottoman delegation met privately with their Ukrainian colleagues on 17 January 1918. Though the meeting was conducted in a markedly warm atmosphere, the Ukrainian side especially did not have much to say in concrete terms due to the uncertainties surrounding the new and volatile Ukrainian state. At this meeting, the Ottomans expressed special concern about the southern boundaries of Ukraine and the question of the possession of the former Russian Black Sea Fleet. On their part, the Ukrainians brought forward the issue of the free passage through the Turkish Straits, which the Ottomans promised to grant to commercial ships during peace time, though certain restrictions would be imposed in times of war.[4]

Talât Pasha, as he cabled to the Ottoman Generalissimo Enver Pasha on 1 February 1918, hoped that Ukrainian independence would permit the establishment of Muslim governments in the Crimea and the Caucasus. The news which he had received from the Crimean Tatars who had indeed formed a national parliament (*Kurultay*) and a government, encouraged the Grand Vizier to think this way.[5] He was convinced that, their rhetoric notwithstanding, the Bolsheviks intended to recreate the former Great Russia and were trying to prevent the break-away nations from declaring independence, as was proven by the cases of Ukraine and Finland. Talât Pasha also favoured the liberation of the Ukrainian lands from the

Bolsheviks by sending German troops and, for that purpose, the finding of a 'Ukrainian Venizelos' who would call in the Central Powers. He considered the *Rada* Ukrainian representatives who were at Brest-Litovsk 'unfit to take great decisions'.[6]

Consequently, the Treaty of Peace between Ukraine and the Central Powers was signed on 9 February 1918 at Brest-Litovsk.[7] Among other matters, the Treaty called for the commencement of diplomatic relations between the parties, the mutual renunciation of the payment of war costs and damages, the exchange of prisoners, and, of course, the immediate opening and regulation of economic relations, which was the exigent concern of the Germanic Powers. The special paragraph related to the economic relations between the Ottoman Empire and Ukraine read:

> In regard to the economic relations between the Ottoman Empire and the Ukrainian Democratic Republic, these shall, until such time as a definitive Commercial Treaty shall have been concluded, be regulated on the basis of most-favoured-nation treatment. Neither party shall lay claim to the preferential treatment which the other party has granted or shall grant to any other State arising out of a present or future Customs Union, or arising in connection with petty frontier intercourse.[8]

Being the first (and victorious) peace treaty of the exhausting three-and-a-half-year war, the Ottoman parliament (*Meclis-i Mebusân*) acclaimed the Peace Treaty with Ukraine. While reporting on the Treaty, Ahmed Nesîmîı Bey, the Foreign Minister, defended its conditions by pointing out the concomitant economic advantages to the Central Powers. He said, in accordance with the Treaty, starting from that year Ukraine would be 'obliged to sell its surplus [grain] production which was estimated in great numbers as well as several agricultural, industrial and military products such as livestock, coal, and iron to the Allies.' This was a blow to the economic blockade which the Entente was boasting to have imposed on the Central Powers.[9]

As for the Ottoman public and press, in fact, the very concept of an independent country called Ukraine was a novelty. The overwhelming majority of the learned stratum of Ottoman society was virtually oblivious to the presence of a people called Ukrainians as separate from Russians. Still, Ukrainian independence received a warm welcome in the Ottoman Empire. For many, such an occurrence represented the end of the 'Muscovite menace' from the north. At a time when, after an extremely devastating and costly war, the Ottoman front against Russia was in shambles, all of a sudden not only did the Russian Empire collapse, but seemingly great prospects in the north and east emerged from among the ruins of the Russian Empire. *Tanin*, the unofficial mouthpiece of the ruling Union and Progress Committee, applauded this first peace treaty since it would put pressure on both Russia and Romania to conclude peace treaties. *Tanin* saw Ukraine as a potential ally of the Ottoman Empire.[10]

Following the signing of the peace treaty, it did not take long for diplomatic relations between the Ottoman Empire and Ukraine to be forged. The Ukrainian government appointed Mykola Levyts'kyi, a member of the Central *Rada* and the Ukrainian delegate at Brest-Litovsk, as the Ukraine's temporary resident in Istanbul. The Ottoman government was informed of this on 8 April 1918 and it duly recognized his office.[11] Before he came to Istanbul, Levyts'kyi, together with his secretary Mykola Vuchenko, visited the Ottoman Ambassador in Vienna on 17 April.[12] He arrived in Istanbul on 19 April, accompanied by his family and Vuchenko.[13] Three days later he visited Talât Pasha and some other ministers.[14] Levyts'kyi's mission attracted the attention of the Ottoman press. Expressing pleasure at the presence of a representative of independent Ukraine in Istanbul 'as the most vivid and brightest evidence of a great victory which had been won over a centuries-old enemy [Russia]', *Tanin*'s editorial assessed the new geopolitical situation particularly in the context of the issues of the Black Sea and the Straits. Having referred to the long-standing ambitions of Tsarist Russia over the Straits, the editorial pointed out the historical irony that it was due to the successful defence of the Straits by the Turks that the Russian Empire had collapsed and the new Ukraine had been born.[15]

Levits'kyi's arrival in Istanbul coincided with an atmosphere of growing concern among the Ottoman public and press for the fate of the Crimea and the Crimean Tatars. In fact, for a long time, the Ottomans had been virtually oblivious to post-Russian Revolution events in the Crimea. Therefore, the convocation of the Crimean Tatar National Parliament (*Kurultay*),[16] its adoption of a Constitution which declared the principle of the 'Crimean Democratic Republic' and the establishment of its rule over most of the peninsula (except for the Bolshevik-held Sevastopol) throughout December 1917 had all taken place without drawing the attention of the Turkish press. This was the case too with the defeat of the Crimean Tatar troops by the Bolsheviks and the latter's invasion of the Crimea and the accompanying atrocities during the second half of January 1918.[17] It was only from the second half of March 1918 that the Ottoman press, as well as Ottoman officialdom, began to be informed about the nature of the events in the Crimea through the arrival of a few Crimean Tatar refugees, most prominent of whom was Cafer Seydahmet [Kırımer], the Foreign and War Minister (Director) of the Crimean Tatar National Government.[18] From late March, the Ottoman press carried an ever-increasing number of news items and commentaries about the Crimea, most of which called for the adoption of exigent measures to help the Crimean Tatars whose independence the Bolsheviks had violently quashed. The beginning of the German occupation of the Crimea on 19 April 1918, and the arrival of Cafer Seydahmet in Istanbul on 20 April[19] further invigorated the public's pro-Crimean Tatar stand.

Certainly, this current issue proffered a novel but critical dimension to the Ottoman public in its contemplation of Black Sea matters in general and Ukrainian problems in particular. It was obvious that the stance of Ukraine *vis-à-vis* Crimean (Tatar) independence would be crucial. These developments were the first indications that the Crimean factor would be a cardinal issue in determining Turko-Ukrainian relations. This was the political atmosphere which Levyts'kyi encountered on his arrival in Istanbul. It is not surprising that in his very first interview with the Turkish press one of the central questions put to Vuchenko concerned the position of Ukraine in regard to the Crimean events. Vuchenko, understandably, tried to avoid giving a direct answer by referring to the presence of non-Muslims in the Crimea as well as Muslims, and Ukraine's respect for other nationalities. He also stated that Levyts'kyi's mission was a temporary one, in anticipation of the establishment of regular and permanent diplomatic missions.[20] Vuchenko's statements about the Crimea did not satisfy the Ottoman public. *Tanin*'s editorial was politely critical of Vuchenko and 'some new and inexperienced politicians of Ukraine', and expressed hopes of a better understanding and appreciation of Crimean (Tatar) independence among Ukrainian circles.[21]

As a matter of fact, until the end of the First World War the Crimean issue was to remain central to the Ottoman Turkish public in assessing the relations with Ukraine. The newly established government of Hetman Pavlo Skoropads'kyi brought forward claims over the Crimea, which had been under German military occupation from late April 1918. A concrete manifestation of these *démarches* was the Ukrainian Foreign Minister Dmytro Doroshenko's official demand, in early May 1918, to Philip Alfons Mumm Baron von Schwartzenstein, the German Ambassador in Kiev, to annex the peninsula to Ukraine on the grounds of 'economic and maritime necessities'.[22] These claims were vehemently opposed by the Crimean Tatars. The Crimean Tatar National Administration (Millî İdare), which was to use the power of the Kurultay between the latter's sessions and which was allowed by the German occupational regime to handle Crimean Tatar matters, appealed to the Ottoman government and public. For this purpose, Yakup Kemal and Üseyin Badaninskiy, members of the *Kurultay* and leading intellectuals, were sent to Istanbul. The Crimean Tatar representatives arrived in Istanbul on 16 June 1918,[23] and they were received by Enver Pasha on 18 June.[24] Apart from their verbal explanations, they presented a note of protest the full text of which was published by Istanbul papers.[25] Yakup Kemal and Üseyin Badaninskiy also visited the German and Bulgarian ambassadors in Istanbul and brought their cause to their attention and, in all likelihood, presented the note of protest. Apparently they were received with sympathy, though a cautious one, by the diplomats. While Johann von Bernstorff, the German Ambassador, assured them that 'Germany would support the organization of the Crimea as an independent state', the Bulgarian Ambassador stated that, in accordance with the principle of self-determination embraced by Bulgaria, his government would consider the demands of the Crimeans as just.[26]

The Crimean Tatar deputation's presence in Istanbul occasioned renewed vigour in the pro-Crimean stand of the Ottoman press. The influential *Tanin*, among others, strongly condemned Ukrainian ambitions. Its lengthy editorial entitled 'The Crimea and Ukraine' pointed out the irony that while the young Ukrainian state owed its very existence to the principle of self-determination, it denied the application of this principle to other peoples. The editorial stressed that the Ottoman Empire 'certainly could not remain aloof to the destiny of [the Crimean Tatars] with whom we were tied by bonds of race, religion, and history'.[27] The pro-Crimean campaign of the Ottoman press did not go unnoticed by the German press. *Rheinisch-Westfälische Zeitung* cited excerpts from them in its commentary.[28]

On 1 August 1918 Hasan Sabri Ayvazov, a well-known figure in the Crimean Tatar National Movement and the Chairman of the *Kurultay*, arrived in Istanbul in the capacity of 'Diplomatic Representative of the Crimean Government'.[29] Ayvazov's mission was basically arranged by Cafer Seydahmet, who was then the Foreign Minister of the Crimean Regional Government. It was the Ukrainian blockade which prompted the dispatch of a resident Crimean envoy to the Ottoman capital. On his arrival in Istanbul, Ayvazov stated that his aim was to obtain recognition of the independence of the Crimea.[30] Like the previous Crimean Tatar representatives in Istanbul, Ayvazov, already a renowned figure in Ottoman intellectual and political circles, was also received warmly. During his stay in Istanbul he worked assiduously to enlist Ottoman support to prevent a Ukrainian annexation of the Crimea and to end the Ukrainian economic embargo. Apparently, he was on very intimate terms with the Ottoman statesmen, including Enver Pasha.[31] At the same time, Ayvazov made use of the Ottoman press to publicize the Crimean cause.[32]

In early September 1918 Talât Pasha, the Ottoman Grand Vizier, visited Berlin with a full agenda to talk to German statesmen at a time when Ottoman efforts to continue the war were rapidly being exhausted. His visit coincided with that of Hetman Pavlo Skoropads'kyi, who was there to meet the Kaiser. Though the Ottoman and Ukrainian dignitaries did not meet in the German capital, they had certain common issues which they were to discuss with the Germans. The most important was the future of the Crimea (albeit this was by no means a matter of primary concern, especially on the agenda of the Grand Vizier). In fact, Cafer Seydahmet, together with Count V.S. Tatishchev, Crimean Minister of Finance, had already been there for a month. Though the Germans were rather ill at ease with the presence and activities of the Crimean delegation, especially the hand-in-glove relations of Cafer Seydahmet with the Ottoman diplomats and statesmen in Berlin, they were tolerated up to a point, apparently due to this very relationship. On Talât Pasha's arrival, Cafer Seydahmet asked him to help iron out their differences with the German authorities concerning recognition of the independence of the Crimea. Talât Pasha, during his meeting with Paul von Hintze, the German Foreign Minister, raised the issue, but in view of many more urgent matters for the Ottoman Empire he was in no position to push it further.[33] As a matter of fact, neither the Hetman nor the Crimeans nor the Ottomans achieved what they had hoped for the future of the Crimea. Although the Germans refrained from giving a free hand to Skoropads'kyi in annexing the Crimea immediately, during the ensuing months before the end of the war they made it clear that they favoured a union between Ukraine and the Crimea.[34] At any rate, the Crimean question could not be solved in favour of either Ukraine or the Crimean Tatars, as all of these political actors were withdrawn from the scene soon after the defeat of the Central Powers.

Thus, from spring 1918 until the end of the First World War, the question of the Crimean Tatars was a matter of quite sensitive concern on the part of the Ottoman public. These feelings rose high during the Ukrainian-Crimean crisis of summer 1918. Though the Ottoman Empire did not (and could not) take much concrete action in the diplomatic and military field to display its support for the Crimean Tatars, there were cordial relations between the leaders of the ruling Union and Progress and those of the Crimean Tatar National *Kurultay* (many of whom were old acquaintances anyway). Yet, even when the harshest critics of Skoropads'kyi's regime on the grounds of the encroachments against Crimean independence and the economic blockade appeared in the Ottoman press, these critics never went beyond the matter at issue and the indispensability of a firm and enduring friendship between Turkey and Ukraine was always underscored simultaneously. As for the Ottoman statesmen, they considered an independent Ukraine indispensable in the context of a friendly Black Sea region which included equally essential independence for Turkey's ethno/religious brethren in the Crimea and Northern Caucasus. In any case, the prevailing differences of opinion over the Crimean question did not impede the establishment of good relations between the two countries.

A practical issue in Ottoman-Ukrainian relations was the exchange of prisoners of war and internees as required by the Treaty of Brest-Litovsk. Such Ukrainians within the Ottoman Empire had already appealed to Turkish officialdom to be allowed to return to their countries no later than early May 1918[35] (Levyts'kyi should have brought forward the subject to the Ottoman Foreign Ministry too). On 3 June 1918 the Ottoman government resolved that, in accord with the stipulations of the Treaty, the interned Ukrainian civilians would be released and those who desired to return to their homeland would be allowed to do so by ship to Odessa. The Ottoman government was to undertake the transportation expenses of those who did not have the material means to travel.[36] As for the military prisoners of war, as required by the Treaty of Brest-Litovsk, special commissars were to be appointed by both governments to handle their release but these appointments had not been made by mid-August 1918. Also, it was deemed necessary first to examine the reciprocal procedure concerning Ottoman prisoners of war in Ukraine through the Ottoman representatives there.[37] One problem which arose from dealing with the 'Ukrainians' detained in Ottoman Empire was that of authenticating their 'Ukrainianness', as all of them had been interned or taken prisoner as subjects of the former Russian Empire. Therefore, a careful investigation of the 'Ukrainians' was necessary lest non-Ukrainians (i.e. Russians) infiltrated them.

During the final spring and summer of the First World War, Istanbul turned into a very lively centre for lobbying and meeting for many a political figure and diplomat from the territories of the ex-Tsarist empire, especially from the Caucasus, who sought the most advantageous partition of what was left of the former Russian Empire for the peoples they represented. Indeed, several Turkish and foreign circles in Istanbul were constantly discussing the future of the Caucasus, Balkans, Bessarabia, the Crimea, Turkestan, and other lands of the region. Levyts'kyi found himself in the midst of these discussions and lobbies. He became acquainted with many of the men including the Ambassador of Persia in Istanbul to whom Levyts'kyi attributed a special importance. Most likely, this constituted the first official contact between Ukraine and Persia. The representatives of the North Caucasian Muslims or those of the North Caucasian Republic were of particular concern to Levyts'kyi. Apparently, the latter was singularly perturbed by the North Caucasian Muslims' territorial claims including territories as far north as Kuban River which the Ukrainian envoy regarded as belonging to the Kuban Cossacks who were of Ukrainian (i.e. Zaporozhian) stock.[38]

The Ottoman diplomatic missions to Ukraine were established soon after the ratification of the Treaty of Brest-Litovsk. In fact, Fahreddin Bey, the pre-war Ottoman chargé d'affaires to St Petersburg, had already been appointed as the temporary resident to Kiev in June 1918.[39] The establishment of the permanent Ottoman mission in Kiev, however, took place with the appointment of Ahmet Muhtar Bey, an experienced diplomat and the former Ottoman Ambassador in Greece.[40] Having been received by the Sultan on 1 September 1918,[41] Ahmet Muhtar Bey soon set out for Kiev. The arrival of the Ottoman Ambassor in the Ukrainian capital was welcomed by the Ukrainian press, which stressed the importance of Turko-Ukrainian relations.[42] He was ceremoniously received by Hetman Skoropads'kyi on 12 October 1918. In the reciprocal speeches during the ceremony, the historical roots of the Ottoman-Ukrainian friendship and hopes for the future were set forth.[43] Ahmet Muhtar Bey, in his complicated task of establishing the Ottoman mission in Kiev, found an unexpected associate in the person of Abdürreşid İbrahim sometime in late October 1918. The latter, a Siberian Tatar and one of the most important political figures of the Turkic Muslims of the Russian Empire at least during the last two decades of Tsardom, happened to return from Hungary to Istanbul via Kiev, and upon a directive from the Ottoman capital he stayed there to help in the work of the Ottoman mission. Ahmet Muhtar Bey and Abdürreşid İbrahim worked in Kiev under very difficult circumstances, in the midst of a bloody internal turmoil, to defend the rights of the Ottoman subjects there.[44] Apart from the Ambassador, other Ottoman diplomats were appointed to consular missions in three Ukrainian cities. While Ahmet Ferid [Tek] Bey was sent to Kiev as Consul General on 15 July 1918,[45] Eburrıza Namık Bey was appointed Consul General in Odessa on 3 September 1918,[46] and Ruhi Bey Consul (second rank) in Kharkov on 12 August 1918.[47]

Nevertheless, the defeat of the Central Powers and the ensuing chaos in Ukraine did not allow the Ottoman diplomats to stay long. Apparently Ahmet Muhtar Bey could return to Istanbul no earlier than mid-February 1919, after some adventure on the way,[48] while Ahmed Ferid Bey stayed in Kiev a little longer, though he arrived in Istanbul not much later than Ahmet Muhtar Bey.[49] Ahmet Muhtar Bey's diplomatic assignment and the Ottoman mission to Ukraine was officially terminated on 1 April 1919.[50]

Despite the relative brevity of their missions in Ukraine the Ottoman diplomats contrived to acquire an insight into Ukrainian affairs. The circumstantial report of Ahmed Ferid Bey to Istanbul on 5 September 1918 is an example of this. There, he analysed the political, economic and demographic situation in Ukraine. He especially pointed out the organizational and administrative deficiencies of the young Ukrainian state and the conflicting orientations among its rulers. Ahmed Ferid Bey expressed his serious doubts that the Ukrainian state as it was could be viable at a time when its Prime Minister (Fedir Lyzohub) was strongly pro-Russian and made no secret of his desires for the formation of a Russian

Federation, while Ministers of Foreign Affairs (Dmytro Doroshenko) and People's Education (Mykola Vasylenko) were fervent Ukrainian nationalists. According to Ahmed Ferid Bey's observations, many people considered independence a political expedient to escape Bolshevik invasion.[51]

Apart from the diplomats there were some other Ottoman personages who visited Ukraine. Among such men were the famous journalist and writer Celâl Nuri [İleri]. Also, the reopening of the navigation line between Odessa and the Turkish Black Sea ports made a modicum of trade possible between the two countries.[52] It is well known that sometime during the last days of the war, the Ukrainian government, through the Ottoman Consulate General in Kiev, offered to barter certain goods with Turkey. The Ukrainians asked for petroleum, gasoline, naphtha and machine oil, in return for wheat, barley, sugar and iron. Yet the post-armistice diplomatic and political proscriptions, as well as the current circumstances, discouraged the realization of any such economic exchange.[53]

On the other hand, Levyts'kyi was called back by the newly formed Hetman's government in Kiev no later than early June 1918.[54] The resident Ukrainian diplomatic missions were to be established soon afterwards. Initially, in June 1918, the news appeared in the Ottoman press (via Vienna) that Petro Chykalenko would be the first resident envoy of Ukraine in Istanbul.[55] Chykalenko indeed came to Istanbul, but his title was chargé d'affaires; the ambassador was yet to be appointed. In August, for some unknown reason, an improbable rumour spread in the Istanbul press about the appointment of Khristian Rakovskii, the famous Bolshevik of Bulgarian origin who had headed the Bolshevik delegation to Kiev. This obviously annoyed Chykalenko who hurried to deny the rumour to the Ottoman Foreign Ministry on 26 August 1918. He also informed the Ottoman government that Bogdan [?] Kistyakovskii, brother of Igor A. Kistyakovskii, Minister of Interior Affairs, was appointed Ukrainian Ambassador to Istanbul.[56] Kistyakovskii was supposed to travel to Istanbul on 12 October 1918.[57] Yet, he resigned before he arrived to the Ottoman capital.[58]

Finally, the Ukrainian government notified its Ottoman counterpart of the appointment of Mikhail Sukovkin with the title of extraordinary envoy and plenipotentiary minister.[59] The Ottoman government declared its approval of Sukovkin's post as an extraordinary envoy on 9 November 1918.[60] Sukovkin left Kiev for Istanbul on 26 October 1918.[61] The arrival of Sukovkin and his embassy in Istanbul coincided with the Ottoman withdrawal from the war. The defeated Ottoman government signed the Armistice of Mudros on 30 October 1918 and soon occupation forces of the Entente arrived in Istanbul. The new situation, of course, was to affect the Ottoman-Ukrainian relations immediately and radically.

Sukovkin's personality and his activities in Istanbul proved to be most controversial. By origin, he was a Russian. He had worked in the Tsarist bureaucracy as a *gubernator* and before the 1917 revolution he had been the head of the Kievan provincial *zemstvo*. During the early days of the revolution Sukovkin declared himself an adherent of the Ukrainian state, whereupon the Central *Rada* nominated him Regional Commissar (Kraevoi Komissar) of Ukraine to the Russian Provisional Government. Even Myhaylo Hrushevs'kyi praised his devotion to Ukraine in a provincial *zemstvo* meeting.[62] Oleksander Shul'hin, the prominent Ukrainian nationalist and the first Ukrainian Foreign Minister, later characterized him as among the Russians and Tsarist bureaucrats and plutocrats, such as Igor Kistyakovskii, Sergei Gerbel and others, who found a haven in Ukraine and offered their services. According to Shul'hin, these men 'having agreed with the indisposed and unprincipled Skoropads'kyi, thought of rebuilding old Russia on the neck of Ukraine.'[63] In his memoirs, Skoropads'kyi writes, 'I cannot say anything either good or bad about [Sukovkin], [his being sent to Turkey] was the choice of Minister Doroshenko. I do not know Sukovkin.'[64]

In any case, Sukovkin's subsequent activities evinced that he had hardly reconciled himself to the idea of an independent Ukraine and he opted to act more in the interests of a future united (federated) Russia than in those of Ukraine. It is obvious that from the very beginning of his mission Sukovkin made it clear that he favoured the revival of a unified Russia. As a matter of fact, Hetman Skoropads'kyi's edict of 14 November 1918, which read, 'Ukraine must take the lead in the matter of establishment of an All-Russian federation, the final goal of which will be the restoration of Great Russia',[65] was certainly a blessing to Sukovkin. On 15 November 1918, when Sukovkin was not informed of the Hetman's edict yet, he told Ali Merdan Bey Topçubaşı, the Azerbaijani envoy who visited him on the Ukrainian consulate yacht *Velikii Kniaz Aleksandr Mikhailovich*, that Ukraine would not oppose a federal union of the states which had come into being with the disintegration of the Russian Empire. According to him, such a federation could be analogous to that of the United States of America, but a united [*yedinoe*] Russian state as it had been before, would be unthinkable. He also told Topçubaşı that his mission was preparing a memorandum [*zapiska*] which was to illuminate the future position of Ukraine vis-à-vis Great Russia, Poland, and some other countries, and which was to be distributed to all diplomatic missions.[66]

As soon as Sukovkin learned about the Hetman's edict on 21 November 1918, he changed the official language of the Ukrainian mission from Ukrainian to Russian. He also took down the Ukrainian flag on the mast of the consulate yacht *Velikii Kniaz Aleksandr Mikhailovich* and hoisted the flag of St Andrew instead, as he made the crew shout 'hurrah' in celebration of the event.[67] At the same time, probably in accordance with the directives of pro-Russian Georgii Afanas'yev, the Foreign Minister, he notified diplomatic circles and the Ottoman Foreign ministry that Ukraine considered itself part of Great Russia and would willingly be a terrain for the rebuilding of the latter.[68] Sukovkin distributed copies of Skoropads'kyi's edict as well. When more information about its meaning was requested, he sent Prince Tenishev, his first secretary and a Russian, who used to be the dragoman of the Russian Embassy.[69] He replaced General Dr Kobylyans'kyi, the counsellor and Ukrainian nationalist, with Tuholka on the pretext of the former's Polish sympathies. The Russian monarchist émigré circles in Istanbul were Sukovkin's closest companions. He was in close touch with Countess Brasova, the sister-in-law of the last Tsar, Pavel Nikolaevich Miliukov, Sergei Dmitrievich Sazonov, Prince Dolgorukov, Gurko, and other prominent figures.[70]

Sukovkin was received by the Sultan Mehmed VI Vahdeddin on 28 November 1918 and submitted his credentials as the Ukrainian envoy.[71] Notably, during the reception Sukovkin wore a Russian uniform. This was noticed by Mustafa Kemal Pasha (future Atatürk) who happened to be there. When questioned by Mustafa Kemal Pasha as to the reason why he wore a Russian uniform, Sukovkin gave the unconvincing answer that they had not had enough time to order a Ukrainian uniform before they left Kiev.[72]

The defeat of the Central Powers and rising discontent soon led to the downfall of the Hetman's regime. The nationalist and socialist opposition started an insurrection against the Hetman and a 'Directorate' was formed to claim power. The Directorate possessed armed forces and declared Skoropads'kyi a traitor. The Hetmanate collapsed almost the moment the remaining German forces decided to terminate their role as the protectors of Skoropads'kyi and to withdraw. Hetman's meagre military forces were thus reduced to a few Russian officers. The forces of the Directorate led by Colonel Evhen Konovalets entered Kiev on 14 December 1918. Skoropads'kyi fled the city donning a German uniform.

When the information about the insurrection against the Hetmanate and its eventual collapse reached Istanbul, Sukovkin's reaction was characteristic: he spread among the Turkish and foreign circles the false news that the insurrection had an ultra-nationalist and Bolshevik character, and called for the Entente forces to intervene to help the Hetmanate.[73] He also assured the foreign diplomats that no independence movement existed in Ukraine except for the Bolshevik intrigues and revolutionary chaos, and that everything that was civilized and cultured was indeed Russian. He sneered at Kobylyans'kyi whom he called the 'pompous Pole'.[74] When he visited the Ecumenical Greek Orthodox Patriarch of Constantinople, he reiterated that the Russian people and state were one and indivisible. On the occasion of the Patriarch's visit of the Ukrainian Embassy, Sukovkin publicly stated the unity of the Russian and Ukrainian churches.[75] In the meantime, Sukovkin continued the thorough Russification of the Ukrainian Embassy on which he set out after the edict of the Hetmanate. Whenever possible Sukovkin appeared decorated with Russian medals and in the company of officers attached to the embassy in Russian uniforms.[76]

In early January 1919, when the Ukrainian government recalled Sukovkin and ordered him to leave the administration of the embassy to Kobylyans'kyi, Sukovkin not only refused to abide by the order, but also gave a statement to the Ottoman government that the Ukrainian government and its representatives were 'Bolsheviks'.[77] As a matter of fact, he had applied to the Ottoman Foreign Ministry with the request of a loan of 10,000 Turkish Liras. He failed to receive the money. Finally, he informed the Ottoman Foreign Ministry on 3 March 1919 that the Ukrainian Embassy had terminated its activities as of 1 March due to the lack of financial resources.[78]

On the other hand, the Ukrainian government had already appointed, in mid-January 1919, a new extraordinary envoy and plenipotentiary minister to replace Sukovkin. Oleksander Lotots'kyi would be the new Ukrainian envoy in Istanbul.[79] Lotots'kyi was a well-known figure in Ukrainian political circles. A man with a sound clerical and theological education, before 1917 he held high positions in the Ministry of State for the Control of Finance. After the collapse of Tsarism, he had been appointed by the Russian Provisional Government as Governor of Bukovina, and later he had become the Chancellor of State in the first Ukrainian autonomous government in September 1917. In the spring of 1918 he had been appointed State Controller in the Ukrainian government, and had served as the Minister of Religious Cults in the Hetman's cabinet. Upon the latter's edict for a federation with Russia, he had resigned from his post, only to be offered the same post in the succeeding Directorate government. As one of the most renowned experts of canonical law in Ukraine, it was Lotots'kyi who had prepared the law which established the autocephaly of the Ukrainian Orthodox Church on 1 January 1919.[80]

In view of Lotots'kyi's career and experience, he was certainly not a fortuitous choice as envoy to Istanbul. On the one hand, a fervent patriot and dedicated defender of Ukrainian independence, he seemed to be the ideal person to repair the damage done to the prestige and dignity of the Ukrainian state by Sukovkin. On the other hand, the Directorate government considered the recognition of the Ukrainian Autocephalous Orthodox Church by the Ecumenical Patriarch of Constantinople vital. Ukrainian Orthodoxy used to be within the jurisdiction of the Constantinople Church until 1686, when, following the Russian annexation of Ukraine, it had shifted its allegiance to the Patriarch of Moscow. The change of ecclesiastical allegiance in late seventeenth century was a direct result of the altered political subordination. Now, an inevitable component of the political liberation from Russia would be the departure from the ecclesiastical jurisdiction of the Patriarchate of Moscow. The ecclesiastical legitimacy of the Ukrainian Autocephalous Church independent from the Moscow Church could be obtained only through its recognition by, and formal subordination to, the Ecumenical Church of Constantinople. To this effect, Volodimir Chehovs'kyi, the Prime Minister of the Directorate government, considered Lotots'kyi the right man with the necessary religious knowledge and experience, who was, after all, the very author of the autocephaly.[81]

As soon as the news of Lotots'kyi's appointment reached Istanbul, the senior deputy [*starshiy zamestitel'*] Kobylyans'kyi, took over the administration of the Ukrainian embassy. In order to fix the situation with the Ukrainian government Kobylyans'kyi dispatched one of their personnel to Odessa. Through him, Bachyns'kyi, the Ukrainian Deputy Foreign Minister, sent his instructions to the effect that Sukovkin surrender all the mission's work to Kobylyans'kyi, who was to be in charge of the affairs of the embassy until Lotots'kyi's arrival. Thus, after a month's interval, the Ukrainian mission in Istanbul began to function again under Kobylyans'kyi. He informed Ferid Pasha, the Ottoman Foreign Minister, about the resumption of the functioning of the mission.[82] The Ottoman press, which was also notified about the situation, heralded the reopening of the embassy in the second half of April 1919.[83] Yet, the embassy's activities recommenced in theory rather than in practice. Sukovkin not only refused to resign from his post until his salary was paid, but also sent angry letters to the Ottoman Foreign Ministry and the diplomatic missions in Istanbul in which he remonstrated against the reopening of the embassy.[84]

The troubles created by Sukovkin did not come to an end after the arrival of Lotots'kyi in Istanbul via Vienna, Trieste and Venice on 23 April 1919.[85] While he was travelling through Vienna he met Yan (Ivan) Tokarzhevs'kyi-Karashevych, the counsellor of the Ukrainian mission there, and took the latter with him to Istanbul.[86] As soon as he had taken office, Lotots'kyi met Sukovkin and handed him the order of the Directorate. The latter reluctantly gave Lotots'kyi some of the embassy's possessions, though these did not include the commodity inventory and certain important documents and notebooks. When Sukovkin demanded money for his pains, Lotots'kyi asked him to wait until June for the settlement of embassy's financial matters and accounts. Such an inspection of the accounts was to perplex Lotots'kyi. As Lotots'kyi later narrated in his memoirs, Sukovkin had sold several valuable articles from the inventory, including an automobile, credits had been taken from the banks, large sums of indemnities had been paid to the dismissed workers, and the exchange rate of Karbovanets for the Ottoman Lira had been arbitrarily fixed. The overall financial situation of the mission left little place for optimism, and, without finding suitable credits, it would be impossible to run the legation. On the other hand, Sukovkin proved to be very tenacious in demanding his claims immediately. As the embassy was not in a position to pay him straightaway, he appealed again to the Ottoman government and requested that Lotots'kyi not be recognized as the Ukrainian envoy. Sukovkin's open struggle with the Ukrainian mission and his vilifications were not ineffective. After all, he had very close relations with [White] Russian circles (there were even rumours that he wanted to become the representative of the Voluntary Army of General Anton Ivanovich Denikin), who were the masters of the day in Istanbul, and especially with the victorious Entente powers, who put Istanbul under their military occupation and enjoyed a great deal of influence over the affairs of the vanguished Ottoman Empire. Under these circumstances the official recognition of Lotots'kyi by the Ottoman government became all the more complicated. When he considered making a *démarche* to protest at the Ottoman reluctance to recognize him, his Turkish friends asked him to refrain from such an act and told him that the change of the Ottoman government would solve the problem.[87]

The heart of the matter was of course far beyond the individual attitude and policy of this or the other Ottoman government. Under the Entente occupation the weak governments of the Sultan had little space for unconstrained action independent of the will of the occupants. For the Entente Powers, who publicly cast their lot with the anti-Bolshevik 'White' armies, the principle of a 'united and indivisible Russia' was paramount. Therefore, the concept of an independent Ukraine breakaway from Russia, even one fervently and uncompromisingly antagonistic to the Bolsheviks, was not acceptable to the Entente. Hardly any of the post-Mudros Ottoman governments, all of which were built on most delicate political balances, could sturdily confront the seemingly all-powerful Entente on the issue of Ukraine which was obviously not a priority on the overfull Turkish agenda. Otherwise the Ottoman public and political circles were, as before, very sympathetic to the idea of an independent Ukraine.

Thus, from the outset, the persistent efforts of Lotots'kyi to obtain an audience with the Sultan and formal recognition on the part of the Ottoman government were doomed to failure. Though not a factor critical to Ottoman diplomatic decision-making mechanism, Sukovkin's dogged efforts at defamation might have created at least some quandary on the part of the Ottoman diplomats who were in a position to deal with Ukrainian matters. Although Lotots'kyi possessed the *lettres de créance* of his government, the

Directorate had not given a *lettre de rappel* for Sukovkin, considering that in case of a change of government the representatives abroad should leave office unless provided with a written instruction of the new government. This lack of *lettres de rappel* for Sukovkin was exploited by the latter against Lotots'kyi. To clarify the situation before the Ottoman government, the Foreign Ministry of the Directorate sent a letter of explanation to the Grand Vizier on 13 May 1919.[88]

The failure to achieve formal recognition did not thwart Lotots'kyi in establishing good and cordial relations with Ottoman political and diplomatic circles. For instance, Safa Bey, the Ottoman Foreign Minister, displayed a great deal of formal and personal respect to Lotots'kyi to whom on one occasion he paid a home visit. It was such Ottoman diplomats and officials who frankly confessed to Lotots'kyi that their inability to recognize him and arrange an audience with the Sultan was due to their worries of recognizing a state not recognized by the Entente.[89] This being the case however, it is notable that the Ottomans did not object to the presence of the Ukrainian mission in Istanbul and preferred to accept it tacitly as an uninterrupted perpetuation of the purely legitimate Ottoman-Ukrainian relations since Brest-Litovsk.

Formally recognized or not as a *de facto* representative of Ukraine in Istanbul at a most turbulent time for both countries, Lotots'kyi had a manifold set of issues to deal with. At times when most of the territory claimed by the Ukrainian goverment (i.e. the Directorate) was trodden by different parties of warring Russians and other foreigners and the very government itself was for the most part reduced to a peripatetic body with limited power, the continuing presence of a diplomatic legation in Istanbul would testify to the existence of Ukraine as an independent political entity. Therefore, it was imperative to maintain the embassy in the Ottoman capital. Apart from this, there were a number of questions with which such a mission had to deal: the recogniton of the Ukrainian Autocephalous Church by the Patriarchate of Constantinople, the establishment of trade relations between Turkey and Ukraine, the reclamation of certain sea vessels and properties which were then in the hands of the 'White' Russians or the Entente Powers, ordinary consulate services for the several thousands of Ukrainian citizens who had flocked to Istanbul due to the war and disorder at home, providing an outlet to the outside world for the cornered Ukrainian government and offering support for it, including military support, etc.

Not much discouraged by the obvious want of the necessary resources to cope with such complicated tasks, Lotots'kyi set about a thorough reorganization of the embassy. He had little knowledge of the embassy personnel and their disposition toward Sukovkin. Consequently, he retained some of the staff, while he fired others.[90] There were also some functionaries, such as Tokarzhevs'kyi-Karashevych, whom Lotots'kyi brought with him. As far as the work of the mission was concerned, it was virtually in a very disorderly state. There was no longer a place for the embassy and the official address of the legation was presented as the private home of one of the staff. The papers of the embassy were either lost (or had been taken by Sukovkin) or disordered. Only the accounts book and related documents had been kept by the accountant. The staff had not been paid for some time and had to subsist under very difficult circumstances. Lotots'kyi first rented a building for the legation and commenced its work starting with issuing passports and visas. As there were some 40,000 people in Istanbul who had escaped from Odessa and other Ukrainian cities, this was a very urgent matter.[91]

The fate of what was left of the former Russian Imperial Black Sea Fleet had been a long-discussed problem since early 1918 after the collapse of the Tsarist (and soon Bolshevik) Russian power on the Black Sea. The Ukrainian flag had been hoisted on some of the ships which happened to be at the ports under Ukrainian control. The claims of the Ukrainian state were not confined to such military ships formerly belonging to the Black Sea Fleet and extended to those former Russian private merchant vessels which were registered to the ports which later became part of the Ukrainian state. In the aftermath of the First World War some of these vessels were in Istanbul. They were deemed necessary by the Entente Powers who wanted to use them in their assistance to the Russian Volunteer Army. On 26 November 1918 the pro-Russian envoy Sukovkin had agreed certain terms with Vice-Admiral Amet, the High Commissioner of France in Istanbul, about these vessels. According to this agreement, the ships in the Ukrainian ports which the French naval authorities would see fit, the yacht *Aleksandr Mikhailovich* anchored at Istanbul, and the steamers *Koroleva Ol'ga*, *Tigr*, and *Ierusalim*, and all steamers of the Ukrainian Navigation Union, were placed at the disposal of the Entente Powers to be used in the operations in Ukraine.[92] Although in this agreement the French quite explicitly recognized that the vessels in question originally belonged to the Ukrainian state (whose *de facto* existence they thus avowed), the ships were for all practical purposes appropriated by the Entente Powers and, through them, by the Russian Volunteer Army, the irreconcilable foe of the very idea of Ukrainian statehood. Resenting the Sukovkin-Amet deal, Lotots'kyi did his best to reclaim the vessels and to prevent their takeover by Kolchak or Denikin. He was content with their sailing under Entente colours, so long as they transported supplies, goods, arms and troops for the benefit of Ukraine. Yet, to the great dismay of Lotots'kyi, many of these vessels had already been turned to the newly established Russian naval base in Istanbul which was under the command of Kolchak's forces. Lotots'kyi repeatedly appealed to the French High Commission in Istanbul in August and September 1919, but these appeals fell on deaf ears.[93] Having learned about the appeal of the Dutch legation in Istanbul which simultaneously represented Russian interests at the Ottoman capital requesting the return of *Koroleva Ol'ga* to its Russian 'owners', Lotots'kyi wrote to the Ottoman Foreign Ministry to prevent such a transfer and demanded its transfer to its real owners under Ukrainian colours.[94] All such efforts of the Ukrainian mission proved to be in vain. Not even replies were sent to Lotots'kyi or Tokarzhevs'kyi-Karashevych, his successor.

Connected with the prospects of acquiring control over those vessels was the transportation of the would-be Ukrainian soldiers to be recruited from among the prisoners of war. In 1919, there were many ethnic Ukrainian prisoners of war of various origins. A group of them were Galicians and Bukovinians, members of the former Austro-Hungarian army who had been captured on the Western Front. They were held by the French and used by them in a number of duties for the Entente. On 3 July 1919 Lotots'kyi appealed to the French with a memorandum and asked to recruit them into the Ukrainian army which was then fighting the Bolsheviks. He proposed the organization of these prisoners of war into a detachment, supplying them with clothing and ammunition, and their shipment to Southern Ukraine by French vessels. Lotots'kyi could get only a private and verbal reply to the effect that the local military command would look for a solution with the central command. He also appealed to the Romanian embassy on behalf of the Bukovinians to allow their return to their homes. This time he was somewhat more successful and these Bukovinians were indeed sent home. The Galicians were to be shipped much later.[95] In fact, there were different sorts of 'Ukrainian' prisoners of war. In addition to the above-mentioned Galicians and Bukovinians who used to be the subjects of the ex-Habsburg Empire, there were much more numerous 'Russian Ukrainians' who had been captured by the Central Powers as soldiers of the Russian imperial army. To be sure, it was by no means a simple business to determine who could be properly qualified as a 'Ukrainian' as distinct from a 'Russian', since there had been no official documents to indicate their ethnic or national origins at the time of their capture. In 1919 there were some 90,000 prisoners of war of the former Russian (Tsarist) army who were travelling homeward from Germany via France and were taken to Marseille for embarkation. The Ukrainian mission in Istanbul estimated that at least one-third of these men should be counted as Ukrainians and appealed to the French for their safe handover to the Ukrainian authorities. Lotots'kyi also appealed to the British authorities in Istanbul about the Ukrainian ex-prisoners of war, who were then in British hands, though apparently to no avail.[96]

The issue of the return of the ex-prisoners of war was a very pressing concern for Lotots'kyi. Not only did the Ukrainian state (Directorate) desperately need fighters (and particularly those provided by others), but any disembarkation of such ex-prisoners of war to the wrong places carried the dire risk of delivering these men into the hands of the Bolsheviks and thus furnishing the enemy with fresh recruits. Precisely this had taken place in spring 1919 when the Entente navy disembarked some 1,300 such former soldiers of the Tsarist army to Odessa and Ochakov, then under Bolshevik occupation. In his note to the Entente representatives on 8 August 1919, an exasperated Lotots'kyi protested at the event and asked for the adoption of the necessary measures so that it would not be repeated. What had added insult to the injury for the Ukrainian legation was that the transportation of the above-mentioned ex-prisoners of war had taken place on the very ships which had been left to the use of the Entente by the Sukovkin-Amet deal supposedly to provide support for Ukraine.[97] Lotots'kyi also applied to the Ottoman government on 10 August 1919 to receive permission to recruit those Galicians who had been captured by the Entente while serving in the Austro-Hungarian army and who were then detained at the French headquarters. The Ottoman Foreign Ministry was of the opinion that a foreign mission in the Ottoman Empire had the legitimate right to call up its subjects, but it was inadmissible to exert force to summon them and to form any military unit on Ottoman territory. After all, these men were at that time held by the Entente forces which were practically beyond the jurisdiction of the Ottoman government. In consideration of all the complications and delicacies involved, the Ottoman Foreign Ministry decided not to give any reply to the Ukrainian request.[98]

Another issue which preoccupied Ukrainian legation in Istanbul was the printing and circulation of Ukrainian banknotes [karbovantsy] and bonds unauthorized by the Ukrainian government. Such an incident had taken place in Odessa as the Ukrainian Papermoney Emission Bureau continued to operate when the city was under the Entente occupation between November 1918 and April 1919. A telegram of the Finance Minister of Russian (Denikin's) government in Rostov indicated that these banknotes had been printed by them. The Ukrainian Directorate did not know the actual amount of these unauthorized banknotes and securities. In his memoranda to the French and British High Commissioners in Istanbul, on 23 and 25 September 1919 respectively, Lotots'kyi protested against the incident, asked the value of the karbovantsy printed without authorization and the names of those responsible, and declared that his government would not accept these notes as valid, as stated in the ordinance of the Ukrainian Finance Ministry on 27 July 1919.[99] Like his other appeals and protests, Lotots'kyi received no response from the Entente Powers.

Certainly, one of the priorities in the mission of Lotots'kyi was to obtain the official recognition of the Ecumenical Patriarchate of Constantinople (Fener) for the Ukrainian Autocephalous Church. At the time of Lotots'kyi presence in Istanbul, the seat of the Patriarch was vacant and the patriarchal election had been postponed until a definite peace settlement was concluded. The Metropolitan of Bursa, Dorotheos Mammelis had been elected by Fener the acting Patriarch [*locum tenens*].[100] When Lotots'kyi visited the Patriarchate at Fener in July, he was received very warmly by the acting Patriarch and the prelates. Dorotheos returned this visit only the next day at the residence of Lotots'kyi in Tarabya, a suburb of Istanbul. Lotots'kyi and Dorotheos met each other over the following months on religious and personal occasions. On every occasion Lotots'kyi explained his cause to Dorotheos and other dignitaries of Fener. The Ukrainian legation also published and distributed a pamphlet in Greek about 'the historical link of the Ukrainian Church with its mother Church of Constantinople' to win over Fener.[101]

The warm personal and formal relations notwithstanding, the acting Patriarch was in no hurry to accept Lotots'kyi's solicitation for the Ukrainian Autocephalous Church and backed out of the issue at the moment. If nothing else, there was the fact that Lotots'kyi was not the only person in Istanbul who brought the issue before the Ecumenical Patriarchate. Among the tens of thousands of 'White' refugees in Istanbul were several high-ranking Russian and pro-Moscow Ukrainian clergymen. They were actively and effectively lobbying against the recognition of the autocephaly of the Ukrainian Church. The Patriarchate could not simply ignore them. Moreover, there was not much reason for Fener to be convinced that the fall and disintegration of the Russian Empire were irreversible. After all, the military situation during the first half of 1919 was anything but promising for the future of an independent Ukraine. One should also not overlook the extremely full agenda of Fener in 1919. These were the times when under the dynamic and strongly nationalistic Dorotheos, Fener had committed himself more openly than ever to politics and exerted great efforts to bring about a diplomatic solution to the fate of Istanbul in favour of the Greeks, if possible the annexation of the city to Greece or at least the 'internationalization' of it with advantageous rights to its Greek population, in any case its separation from the Turkish rule for good. To bring about the desired outcome, Dorotheos was constantly busy lobbying the Entente authorities in Istanbul, sending delegations to Europe to influence the peace negotiations, and dealing with organizational activities among the Greek population of Istanbul.[102] Therefore, Dorotheos could not commit himself wholeheartedly to the case of the Ukrainian Autocephalous Church which certainly had no priority for Fener, and was not really worth risking other relations and connections with the Entente at such difficult times.

These concerns of Fener were implied in the letter of reply to the Ukrainian government, whose draft was obtained by Lotots'kyi beforehand. There, having expressed the blessings of the Constantinople Church toward the Ukrainian people and the respect for its desire to turn its church into an autocephalous one, the Patriarchate specified three prerequisites for it: independence, the consent of the previously superior Church (i.e. Moscow), and the presence in office of the Ecumenical Patriarch on his seat to make this important decision legitimate. The acting Patriarch recommended the Ukrainians to wait for the election of the new Patriarch so that their request could be answered firmly in the affirmative. These conditions, and especially the first one which questioned the independence of Ukraine caused a great deal of indignation among the Ukrainian mission who sharply protested to the author(s) of the letter. The requirement for the consent of the Moscovite Church, which was the least likely prospect, could only be an expedient on the part of Fener to drag out the issue indefinitely. Moreover, the prevailing vacancy of the seat of the Patriarch had certainly given the acting Patriarch a suitable pretext to avoid offering Lotots'kyi a positive answer. Thus, the contents of the draft letter which were prevented from being sent caused some chill in the relations between the Ukrainian legation and Fener. Subsequently, however, the cordial atmosphere between Lotots'kyi and Dorotheos was restored. Just before Lotots'kyi left Istanbul, an amended letter of reply to the Ukrainian government was penned by Fener. In this letter, dated 9 March 1920, Dorotheos did not make any mention of the previous prerequisites of independence and consent of Moscow, but politely stated that Fener could not confirm the authocephaly of the Ukrainian Church at the moment because of the current vacancy in the Patriarchal see.[103]

The failure to obtain the formal support and sanction of the Ecumenical Church was of course a substantial frustration, if not an intense embitterment, for the Ukrainian mission, particularly for Lotots'kyi who had cherished deep hopes about it. This being the case however, the Ukrainian legation in Istanbul was beset by several complications of much urgent nature which overshadowed its disappointment with Fener. No doubt, the foremost concerns of the legation were the great uncertainties about the future (and of course, the current) situation of Ukraine and its independent government whom Lotots'kyi and his handful of subordinates were supposed to represent and from whom a healthy way of receiving timely information could not be found. What described itself as the Ukrainian government and the armed forces under its command were in the midst of an ongoing struggle against the Bolsheviks, Makhnovites, Whites, and multifarious local bands consisting of simple brigands rather than ideological or political groups, and the sides and alliances in this struggle were subject to sharp changes all the time. Throughout the largest part of 1919 and 1920, the Directorate or the Ukrainian government could hold only on a narrow strip of land in the westernmost part of what it claimed as the territory of Ukraine or it was deprived of even that much as it would be compelled to operate on foreign territory. Certain military achievements which were crowned with the extension of the area controlled by the Directorate to large parts of the country including the capital Kiev, proved to be temporary and rather results of the ebbs and flows of the struggle between the Bolshevik and non-Bolshevik ('White') Russian armies or the Polish army. In brief, as the very state and government which the legation in Istanbul claimed to represent for the most part enjoyed but a nominal existence. This conjuncture, in addition to the fact that the concept of an independent Ukraine (or Ukraine at all) was still a novel one and had been recognized by only a few countries most of whom had to revoke their decisions as a result of their defeat in the war, made the position and status of the Ukrainian mission in Istanbul quite awkward.

The prevailing political situation in Istanbul was no less auspicuous. Istanbul was under the occupation of the victorious Entente Powers who did not hesitate to impose their will on the powerless Ottoman governments and the city overflowed with tens of thousands of 'White' Russian refugees. The latter included numerous political and military figures who were champions of the idea of 'Mother Russia – One and Indivisible' and did not harbour the least sympathy or tolerance for a separate Ukrainian identity, let alone independence. The 'White' Russian movement was, by and large, supported and sponsored by the Entente, who shared the attitude of the former *vis-à-vis* the indivisibility of Russia. Ukrainian independence was never endorsed by Britain or France who, apart from the idea of preserving the territorial integrity of the Russian empire as intact as possible, viewed the Ukrainian Democratic Republic a creation and satellite of Germany. This is not to say that Britain and France had a really concerted policy on matters concerning Russia. They had sharp differences at different times in their approach toward this or the other Russian group. Not even their support of the 'White' armies were unshakable. Still, whether Britain supported one 'White' group and France backed another, or, having exhausted all realistic hopes about the restoration of the old order in Russia, they considered a sort of reconciliation with the Bolsheviks, none of these policies allowed a place for an independent Ukraine. On that account, it would be vain to expect any formal recognition on the part of the Entente Powers of the independence of Ukraine. Yet, as a political and military entity of certain significant power irreconcilably antagonistic to the Bolsheviks, the Ukrainian government had not been totally ignored by Britain and France, who had their unofficial representatives in Ukraine.[104] After all, no matter what its clauses were, the Amet-Sukovkin agreement was in a sense a *de facto* recognition of Ukraine. In any case, the Entente authorities, not to mention the 'White' Russian dignitaries in Istanbul, displayed no intention to co-operate with the Ukrainian legation whose presence there was deemed a nuisance at best.

Thus, the Ukrainian legation had to conduct its duties under severe pressures and harassment. Russian circles in Istanbul, especially that of General Agapiev, the representative of Denikin, effectively propagandized against the presence of a Ukrainian mission. They accused the Ukrainian diplomats of collaborating with the Bolsheviks, Germans, and the nationalist forces of Mustafa Kemal Pasha in Anatolia, as well as of forgery.[105] The Ukrainians were also anxious about their physical safety in the presence of so many intimidating elements. Denikin's intelligence service in Istanbul was constantly watching the activities of the legation and often sent its agents to provide information from within. There were certainly several double agents.[106]

The defamation activities against the Ukrainian legation did not remain ineffective and the Entente authorities initiated police measures against it. First, on 9 September 1919, the Counsellor Kobylyans'kyi and the attaché Rathhaus were subjected to a thorough search by the Interallied police and the sealed baggage of the legation was taken to the British Headquarters.[107] This incident was followed by a more wholesale assault. On 25 September 1919 the Entente police under the command of the British Lieutenant-Colonel Maxwell, together with some Russian civilians, organized a raid on the Ukrainian mission. In reply to protests by Lotots'kyi, Maxwell explained that he acted in accordance with the orders of the British High Commission. They not only minutely searched the mission's office and the private apartments of the envoy and the counsellor, but also temporarily detained the diplomats and functionaries there. Besides the diplomatic and political documents, bank cheques and several private papers were confiscated. The office was sealed off and guards were installed in front of its entrance. Moreover, the bank accounts of the mission at Crédit Lyonnais were frozen. Lotots'kyi subsequently sent notes of protest to the Entente High Commissioners, the Ottoman Foreign Ministry and the diplomatic missions of the neutral states and demanded the return of the confiscated materials, but to no avail.[108] Having been deprived of their income and even their premises, the members of the legation fell into a very difficult financial situation. Lotots'kyi rented a suite at the famous Hotel Pera Palace and began to conduct his meetings there (Soon, however, he had to move due to the overwhelming expenses). A representative of the Ottoman Foreign Ministry visited him at the hotel and explained the regrets of his government about what had taken place and that they were not in a state to extend much support to the Ukrainian mission. So did a representative of the Patriarchate of Constantinople. As the result of the investigations undertaken by the Entente authorities refuted the claims about the Bolshevik connections of 'the persons describing themselves as members of the 'Ukraine Legation', the office of the legation was allowed to be reopened a month later.[109]

All these unfavourable circumstances notwithstanding, the Ukrainian mission tried to continue its work. The inimical attitude of the British and French High Commissions as well as that of the Russian groups could not be changed, but Lotots'kyi and his functionaries did their best to maintain good relations at least with the other diplomatic missions in Istanbul. Good and businesslike relations were established with the representatives of the United States and Romania despite the fact that they too belonged to the Entente, though they did not actively participate in its military operations in Turkey. This was the case too with the diplomatic missions of Sweden, Iran and the newly independent Azerbaijan and Georgia. The fruits of good relations with these foreign representatives and officials were taken when the office of the Ukrainian legation was shut down, as they openly displayed their sympathies with the Ukrainians.[110]

The Ukrainian legation endeavoured to reach out to the European and Ottoman government and public with its own version of the Ukrainian events by issuing many memoranda, notes and declarations. It also worked on publishing a number of pamphlets and leaflets in different languages. One such pamphlet was the above-mentioned one penned in Greek addressing the Patriarchate. Another one was written by Lotots'kyi and published in Turkish, with the title 'Turkey and Ukraine' [*Türkiye ve Ukrayna*]. Lotots'kyi prepared two other pamphlets in French, one entitled *L'Ukraine indépendante* and explained facts about the independent state structure of Ukraine, and the other provided larger information about the same subject and also about the Ukrainian diplomatic missions abroad. Though the first two pamhlets were distributed, those in French were banned by the Entente censorship prior to their distribution. Tokarzhevs'kyi-Karashevych intended to write a long article surveying the past and present of the Ukrainian-Turkish relations in French, but due to the unfavourable circumstances of publication, he could not even complete writing it.[111]

Much more important than these publications were certainly the efforts of Lotots'kyi and his subordinates, most of all Tokarzhevs'kyi-Karashevych, to provide information for the press. This was especially significant since the outside world learned about the events on the territory of the former Russian Empire mostly through sources based in Istanbul, such as the 'White' Russian news agency Rusagen and Osvag. The

Ukrainian legation, whenever the overall politico-military circumstances allowed, received interesting and detailed information from Ukraine, although at times a regular flow of such information proved impossible. Thus, Lotots'kyi and Tokarzhevs'kyi-Karashevych managed to establish good ties with certain Ottoman press circles and news items, commentaries, and interviews about Ukraine and Ukrainians appeared in the Ottoman press occasionally. The Turkish paper which displayed most affection toward the Ukraine was *İfham* (Istanbul), with whose editor Hüseyin Ragıp and Lotots'kyi had become good friends. In this task of illuminating the Ottoman public, Oksana Lotots'ka, daughter of the envoy (and future wife of Tokarzhevs'kyi-Karashevych), played an active role and established warm relations with Turkish women (*İfham* published an interesting interview with her). As in all other matters, the obstructions of the pro-Russian Entente greatly hindered the publication of articles sympathetic to Ukraine in the press and in some cases even any sentences with the word 'Ukraine' would be deleted by the censorship.[112]

A long interview with Lotots'kyi in *İfham* is a good example of his good connections with the Ottoman press. The interview was made at a time when the armed forces of the Directorate initiated a successful offensive against the Bolsheviks and began to recover many parts of the country. Therefore, the spirits of Lotots'kyi and his functionaries were raised. In the interview, having stressed the historical ties of the Ukrainians and Turks and especially their past alliances against the common enemy, i.e. the Russians, Lotots'kyi dwelled on the possibilities of mutually beneficial economic relations. According to him, the two countries indeed produced many commodities which the other needed. For example, Turkey could export lead, asphalt, nickel, sulphur, lime, marble, leather, silk, tobacco, fruits, and cotton, while Ukraine could provide Turkey with especially wheat and sugar, among many other things. He stated that Ukraine was a barrier for Turkey and other smaller states against Russia which would have been able to dominate them if it was not for this barrier. Commenting on Kolchak's refusal to recognize the independence of the breakaway republics until the convocation of the Russian National Assembly, Lotots'kyi said, 'The right to judge and decide upon the fate of Ukraine belongs to the Ukrainians and not to Kolchak. So long as they fight against the Russian Bolsheviks, Denikin and Kolchak can be considered as allies, since we are also fighting against the Soviets. Therefore we wish the success of Denikin and Kolchak. If necessary, we can even help the Volunteer Russian Army to enter Moscow. But if he (Denikin) gives up taking Moscow and marches against Ukraine and refuses to recognize the independence of Ukraine, it is a very different case. So it happened in the past. In 1918, Denikin wanted to subjugate Ukraine and the people rose and forced him out of the border.'[113]

Indeed, *İfham* continued its support for the Ukrainian cause. Upon the controversial information about the capture of Kiev by Petliura's forces or by the Russian Volunteer Army, *İfham* urged its readers to think about the future of this country more seriously as it was a matter of the security of Anatolia. It was preferable to see a small Ukraine in the north of Anatolia, in lieu of a Great Russia.[114]

Apparently, Hüseyin Ragıp, the editor of *İfham*, who was an active member of the nationalist Turkic Hearth Society (Türk Ocakları) also helped Lotots'kyi to get acquainted with Turkish political and intellectual circles. Interestingly, the former Ottoman ambassador Ahmed Muhtar Bey, the ex-Consul General to Kiev, Ahmed Ferid Bey (then, the Minister of State), Müfîde Ferid Hanım, the latter's wife and a well-known figure of the Turkish women's movement, were among the close associates of Lotots'kyi in Istanbul. These respectable figures were harbouring sympathies for the emerging nationalist movement in Anatolia (in fact, they were to take part in and serve the Ankara government in the near future). Thus, Lotots'kyi was able to get regular information about the developments in Anatolia. Through these friends Lotots'kyi established good relations with notables and members of the Ottoman high society, such as Abdülhak Hâmid, the 'Great Master' of Turkish poetry, Ziya Pasha, İzzet Pasha, Ragıp Raif Bey, as well as certain influential members of the local Greek and Armenian community, such as, Peter Mavrokordatos, the Dadyan family, Iosip Azaryan, and others. Lotots'kyi's connection with influential circles in the Ottoman Empire was evident in the admission of his son, Boris, with a special governmental permission to the prestigious Imperial Lycée (Mekteb-î Sultanî) of Galatasaray which was exclusively for the Ottoman subjects.[115]

In the meantime, the military and political accomplishments of the Directorate government back in Ukraine proved ephemeral and the Ukrainian government was forced to retreat to a constantly-diminishing enclave in the westernmost part of the country and to conduct the last efforts of an already lost war. The deteriorating situation in Ukraine naturally affected the functions of the mission in Istanbul which was engulfed in an ever-deepening financial crisis. The number of the functionaries in the legation was steadily decreasing due to their being sent back home since April 1919, and by the autumn of that year only four people remained: the envoy, Counsellor, secretary, and interpreter.[116] Lotots'kyi still firmly believed in the need for the presence of a Ukrainian legation in Istanbul, but the situation was becoming hopeless. Not much could be expected from an unrecognized and penniless legation of a waning state to an impotent government of a country under hostile foreign occupation. Under these circumstances, Lotots'kyi decided to leave Istanbul and hand the business of the mission to the Counsellor Tokarzhevs'kyi-Karashevych who was given the diplomatic title of minister plenipotentiary. Lotots'kyi preferred to tell the Ottoman government that his leave was temporary. He departed on 25 March 1920 and after a long journey arrived in Kamenetsk, the last stronghold of the Ukrainian government which accepted his resignation on 5 May 1920.[117]

After the departure of Lotots'kyi and his daughter Oksana, who used to work as an interpreter, the Ukrainian legation was confined to only two men: Yan Tokarzhevs'kyi-Karashevych and V.P. Prykhod'ko, the secretary.[118] Among the matters which Tokarzhevs'kyi-Karashevych inherited from his predecessor was the Ukrainian request to open consulates in Anatolia and Palestine, namely in Trabzon, Izmir, Adana, Damascus, Beirut, and Jerusalem. This was all the more strange since, with the exception of Trabzon, these cities were under foreign military occupation. Jerusalem, Beirut, and Damascus in which the Ottoman Empire retained all but purely nominal rights of sovereignty until the signing of the peace treaty, had fallen to the British in the course of war in 1917–18, following the Armistice of Mudros Adana and Izmir had been occupied by the French and Greek armies respectively. The stated purpose of these consulates would be to deal with the affairs of a large number of Ukrainians who would be found among the ex-Russian subjects in these regions, while the representatives of Denikin and Kolchak governments had already opened an office headed by a consul in Izmir. The Ukrainian legation had appealed to the Ottoman Foreign Ministry with these requests on 1 February 1920.[119] Apparently, Tokarzhevs'kyi-Karashevych met with Ahmed Reşid Bey, the director of the Political Section in the Ottoman Foreign Ministry during the first half of March 1920. The Ottoman official told Tokarzhevs'kyi-Karashevych that the opening of any consulates in Jerusalem, Beirut, Adana, and Damascus was impossible due to the prevailing military occupations of the Entente there, though provisional functionaries could be sent to Izmir and Trabzon with letters from the Ottoman Foreign Ministry so that they would be treated as representatives of Ukraine by the local authorities.[120] Nonetheless, the Ottoman Foreign Ministry had other concerns as well in rejecting such a request. The Ottoman diplomats had noticed that, unlike Germany and Austria which had been compelled to renounce their Brest-Litovsk Treaties by the Treaties of Versailles and Saint Germain respectively, no conclusive peace treaty was signed with the Ottoman government yet. Moreover, the clauses of the Armistice of Mudros did not contain any reference to the Treaty of Brest-Litovsk. Therefore, the Treaty of Brest-Litovsk was still legally in force between Ukraine and the Ottoman Empire. This being the case, however, any attempt, such as giving permission to open consulates, which would inevitably refer to the Treaty of Brest-Litovsk might remind the Entente Powers of the matter and induce them to exert pressure on the Ottoman Empire to nullify the Treaty. Thus, the Ottoman Foreign Ministry, desiring to let sleeping dogs lie, deemed it wiser to circumvent the issue and avoid giving an affirmative reply to the Ukrainians on the formal pretext of the unnatural state of affairs prevailing both in Ukraine and Turkey and the necessity of waiting for the signing of the peace treaties with the Entente Powers.[121]

In contrast with the period of Lotots'kyi who subsequently wrote and published his memoirs of diplomatic service in Istanbul in detail, we have relatively meager information about the mission of Tokarzhevs'kyi-Karashevych in the Ottoman capital which at any rate lasted more than a year-and-a-half. The latter's mission must have functioned under even more difficult and complicated circumstances than his predecessor. This, if not for anything else, was due to the fact that the independent Ukrainian state practically ceased to exist on the territory it claimed and the power of the Sultan's government which tried to operate under the Entente military occupation hardly went beyond Istanbul, if there at all, and was more and more outshoneby the nationalist government of Ankara. Even under this state of affairs, however, evidence suggests that Ottoman diplomacy did not lose its interest in the independence of Ukraine. The Treaty of Sèvres, which the Ottoman government was compelled to sign on 10 August 1920, explicitly imposed the nullification of the Treaty of Brest-Litovsk. Thereby, of course, the Ottoman recognition of the Ukrainian independence and its official relations with Ukraine would be rendered null and void. Yet the Ottoman Foreign Ministry clearly did not want to revoke its official recognition of Ukrainian independence and looked for a licit way to do so. This attitude was clearly perceptible in its reaction to the request of the Ukrainian Foreign Ministry (then in exile) about the confirmation of Tokarzhevs'kyi-Karashevych as the minister plenipotentiary of Ukraine in Turkey on 30 November 1920. The legal office of the Ottoman Foreign Ministry thought that it would be totally legitimate to confirm the change of a diplomat of a recognized foreign country. The nullification of such a recognition by the Treaty of Sèvres was not effective yet, since that Treaty could be officially in force only after its ratification in Paris. Therefore, even now the legal office recommended to abide by the system of Brest-Litovsk. Nevertheless, a protocol for consulates between the Ottoman Empire and Ukraine was still lacking at the moment and this absence would hamper the recognition of the Ukrainian minister plenipotentiary. Although the Ottoman Foreign Ministry could not confirm Tokarzhevs'kyi-Karashevych's offical position and title immediately, it should state to the Ukrainian side its readiness to sign such a protocol soon.[122]

Tokarzhevs'kyi-Karashevych repeated his government's desire to open a consulate in Istanbul and some other cities, on 28 March 1921 verbally and on 17 July 1921 with a written memorandum.[123] It is not clear why Tokarzhevs'kyi-Karashevych was so insistent in seeking to open consulates for his government now in exile in the territories then onlt nominally attached (in fact, lost by the Treaty of Sèvres) to the Ottoman Empire. Whether what was left of the Ukrainian government in exile would be able to sustain such missions is another question. One can only speculate that by having (or obtaining the right to have) Ukrainian consulates in the Holy Lands Lotots'kyi or the Ukrainian government might have expected better prospects for the settlement of the question of the autocephaly of the Ukrainian Church. Whatever their motives were, the Ottoman Foreign Ministry was not inclined to grant that request, bringing to the fore, first of all, the yet confirmed diplomatic status of Tokarzhevs'kyi-Karashevych. Thus, the legal office of the Ottoman Foreign Ministry recommended to inform the Ukrainian legation verbally that the prior settlement of Tokarzhevs'kyi-Karashevych's diplomatic position would be imperative.[124] In the meantime, the Ottoman Foreign Ministry gave heed to the other diplomatic precedents for the recognition of Ukraine. When the Argentinian government recognized the independence of Ukraine on 5 March 1921, this clearly gratified Ottoman diplomats who received the news through Berlin. The Ottoman Embassy in Berlin was instructed to convey this gratification to the Ukrainian legation there.[125]

Tokarzhevs'kyi-Karashevych stayed in Istanbul until 11 October 1921. This date most probably marks the practical end of the diplomatic mission of the Ukrainian Democratic Republic in the Ottoman Empire. Having left Istanbul, Tokarzhevs'kyi-Karashevych joined the activities of the Ukrainian government in exile in Tarnów, where he was appointed the deputy Foreign Minister.[126] By this time, the Grand National Assembly government in Ankara which had assumed the political leadership of what was left of the Turkish parts of the Ottoman Empire and had effectively halted the Greek advance deep into Anatolia, came more and more to be considered as the real representative of the Anatolian Turks. The Grand National Assembly had already been recognized by some foreign states. The most important among them was Soviet Russia which deemed it expedient to support this new government in Anatolia materially against the Western Powers. Official relations were then established with the Soviet Socialist Republic of Ukraine and the Grand National Assembly of Turkey. On 13 December 1921 a Soviet Ukrainian delegation headed by the famous Marshal Mikhail Frunze in his capacity as member of the Central Executive Committee of the Soviets of Ukraine came to Ankara.[127] A 'Treaty of Peace and Fraternity' was signed between Turkey (Grand National Assembly) and the Soviet Ukraine in Ankara on 2 January 1922. Among other things, article 3 of the treaty stipulated that 'all treaties concluded between Turkey and the former

Russian Empire or between Turkey and Ukraine until 16 March 1921 did not correspond with the real mutual interests of the two parties' and therefore all such treaties were declared null and void.[128] These developments betokened yet another significant step in co-operation between the Grand National Assembly of Turkey and Soviet Russia, which were so crucial especially for the former which desperately needed any support in its ongoing war of independence. To demonstrate the importance the Ankara government ascribed to this treaty, the Grand National Assembly of Turkey decided to dispatch a delegation to Kharkov (then the capital of Soviet Ukraine) headed by the Health Minister and renowned political figure Rıza Nur for the exchange of the ratified texts of the Treaty.[129] The Turkish delegation visited Ukraine in summer 1922. Within half a year after the 'Treaty of Peace and Fraternity' a Turkish mission was established in Kharkov and by a decision of the Central Committee of the Communist Party (Bolshevik) of Ukraine in September 1922 a diplomatic mission of the Soviet Ukraine was opened in Ankara.[130] In the meantime, having inflicted a crushing defeat on the Greek forces and having acquired control of the entire Anatolian peninsula, the victorious Grand National Assembly officially abolished the monarchy which had long been reduced to a nominal existence in the Entente-occupied Istanbul on 1 November 1922.

Important as they were, these relations between Turkey (Ankara) and Soviet Ukraine which was practically not an independent state, in effect, belonged to the general context of the Turko-Soviet co-operation and, therefore, were radically different in nature from the Ottoman-Ukrainian (Ukrainian Democratic Republic) relations. Coincidentally, the latter were terminated almost at the same time as the former came into being. The formally separate relations between Turkey and the Soviet Ukraine did not last long and especially after the victorious conclusion of the Turkish War of Independence in 1922 they were eclipsed by direct Ankara-Moscow relations. In any case, with the formation of the Union of Soviet Socialist Republics in late 1922, the theoretical rights of the constituent Soviet republics to handle foreign relations were delegated to central organs, i.e. to Moscow. The details of the relations between Turkey (Ankara) and the Soviet Ukraine are beyond the scope of the present article. Yet, one may argue that Moscow's choice of inserting the Soviet Ukraine into its close relations with Turkey (Ankara) might have to do with the surviving memories of cordial Ottoman-Ukrainian relations. In spite of the fact that the representatives of Soviet Ukraine had no intention whatever of identifying themselves with the Ukrainian Democratic Republic, many a dignitary and the public in Ankara quite possibly might have had in their minds the image of independent Ukraine after Brest-Litovsk and thought that these new relations were actually a direct extension of the previous relations.

The emergence of an independent Ukraine in the form of Ukrainian Democratic Republic was welcomed by the Ottoman Empire as an historical blessing which would symbolize the end of the centuries-old menace from the north. It was even more significant that this took place in the midst of a badly progressing war and raised the hopes of changing the tide. Turkey, together with its allies, was the first state to recognize the independence of Ukraine and sign the Treaty of Brest-Litovsk. The establishment of diplomatic relations between the two countries followed soon and made headway in a very promising atmosphere. To be sure, certain serious differences arose, such as the question of the future of the Crimea and the Crimean Tatars, as well as some other regional issues. Even then both parties indeed inferred that their common interests prevailed over their differences. A very inauspicious aspect of the Ottoman-Ukrainian relations was the epoch they were initiated. Ukrainian independent statehood had been founded on quite unstable grounds. The Ukrainian state itself could be revived from the brink of destruction thanks to the Treaty of Brest-Litovsk and the armed intervention of the Central Powers. The internal discontent stemming from foreign influence and other intrinsic and deep-rooted problems aside, the removal of the protection of the Central Powers who lost the war left the country exposed to grave threats generated by the intense armed conflicts taking place in the territory of the former Russian Empire. Thus for the greater part of 1919 and 1920, Ukrainian statehood was confined only to a fraction of its claimed territory, its seat of government changed recurrently ending up with the foreign territories, and it had to engage in an almost forlorn struggle with a variety of enemies both from within and from without. As for the Ottoman Empire, its debacle in the First World War and the Armistice of Mudros portended its final breakdown. Now it would rather operate in a capital practically under foreign occupation and with little power and would be reduced to a nominal existence. The real body politic of the Turkish state would slide to Anatolia where a burgeoning nationalist movement ended up with establishing an alternative government which would successfully undertake the consolidation and defence of what was left of the country.

Nonetheless, even under these most unfavourable circumstances when both states and governments barely enjoyed any practical and tangible existence, the diplomatic relations between the Ottoman Empire and Ukrainian Democratic Republic did not come to an abrupt end. On the contrary, Ukrainian diplomatic mission in Istanbul confronting huge difficulties persisted in functioning in the Ottoman capital under Entente occupation and did its best to represent the Ukrainian independence and its interests. It tried to function in a manner as if everything was normal. Among other things, the Ukrainian mission would assiduously work to extract recognition for the Ukrainian Autocephalous Church from the Patriarchate of Constantinople which itself was undergoing tense times. There were even utterly fantastic-looking enterprises of the Ukrainian mission as late as in 1921, when the Ukrainian government had long been in exile, to open consulates in such cities as Jerusalem, Aleppo, Damascus, etc. which the Ottoman Empire had long lost during the war and hardly harboured any hopes of recovering. Equally remarkably, the Ottoman Foreign Ministry also displayed a cautious but sympathetic approach toward the Ukrainian mission there and always looked for legitimate means to maintain its recognition of Ukrainian independence, under the conditions which otherwise forced Turkey to revoke all requirements and consequences of Brest-Litovsk. As both governments waned, their successors, the Grand National Assembly in Ankara and the Soviet Socialist Republic of Ukraine, resumed the relations between the two countries until the latter lost all the trappings of an independent entity with the formation of the Soviet Union. In any case, the nature of the relations between Ankara and Kharkov was assuredly different from those between Istanbul and Kiev (or wherever the seat of the Ukrainian Democratic Republic was) and, in effect, they were rather an integral part of the Turko-Soviet diplomacy. There is little doubt that relations established between the Ottoman Empire and Ukrainian Democratic Republic heralded and provided experience for renewed diplomatic ties between the republics of Turkey and Ukraine some 70 years later.

NOTES

1. The phrase '*Ukrayins'ka Narodnia Respublika*' can be translated into English equally as 'Ukrainian Democratic Republic' and 'Ukrainian People's Republic', the latter being more of a verbatim translation. Throughout this article the form 'Ukrainian Democratic Republic' has been preferred, not only because this form (in French: *République Démocratique Ukrainienne*) was used in many an official Ukrainian document, but also in order to avoid the connotations which the term 'People's Republic' acquired subsequently.
2. For the projects and activities of Germany and Austria-Hungary during the First World War (prior to the Treaty of Brest-Litovsk), see, Jerry Hans Hoffman, 'The Ukrainian Adventure of the Central Powers, 1914–1918', Unpublished Ph. D. Dissertation, University of Pittsburgh, 1967; Oleh S. Fedyshyn, *Germany's Drive to the East and the Ukrainian Revolution, 1917–1918* (New Brunswick, New Jersey, 1971), idem, 'The Germans and the "Union for the Liberation of the Ukraine", 1914–1917', in Taras Hunczak (ed.), *The Ukraine, 1917–1921: A Study in Revolution* (Cambridge, Massachusetts, 1977), pp.305–322; *Pamyatkova knizhka soyuza vyzvolennya Ukrayiny. Kalendar' na 1917 rik* (Vienna, 1917); Roman Smal-Stocki, 'Actions of "Union for the Liberation of Ukraine" during World War I', *The Ukrainian Quarterly*, Vol.XV, No.2, pp.169–174; Helga Grebing, 'Österreich-Ungarn und die "Ukrainische Aktion' 1914–18', *Jahrbücher für Geschichte Osteuropas* (Munich), Vol.7, No.3 (1959), pp.270–296.
3. The representatives of the Ukrainian *Rada* arrived at Brest-Litovsk on 7 January 1918. John W. Wheeler-Bennett, *Brest-Litovsk. The Forgotten Peace. March 1918* (London, 1963), p.166.

4. Selami Kılıç, 'Brest-Litovsk Müzakereleri ve Barışı', Unpublished Ph.D. Dissertation, Atatürk University (Erzurum, 1995), pp.244–245.
5. 'From Talât Pasha to Enver Pasha, 1 February 1918', in Tülây Duran, 'I. Dünya Savaşı Sonunda Türk Diplomasisinin İlk Başarısı Brest-Litovsk Hazırlıkları, III', *Belgelerle Türk Tarihi Dergisi* (Istanbul), No.70 (July 1973), pp.31–32. As a matter of fact, by the time Talât Pasha received an urgent request for help from the Crimean Tatar National Government, the latter had already (during the second half of January 1918) succumbed to the Bolshevik military power and the Crimean peninsula had fallen under the Bolshevik rule.
6. Ibid., p.32.
7. For an English translation of the full text, see, Wheeler-Bennett, pp.392–402. The Turkish text was published in *Takvîm-i Vekâyî* (Istanbul), the official gazette of Ottoman government, consecutively on 23, 24, 25, 26, 28, and 29 September 1918. The Treaty was signed, for the Ottoman government, by Talât Pasha, the Grand Vizier, Ahmed Nesimi Bey, Minister of Foreign Affairs, İbrahim Hakkı Pasha, Ottoman Ambassador in Berlin and the ex-Grand Vizier, Ahmed İzzet Pasha, General of Cavalry and ex-Minister of War, for the government of the Ukrainian Democratic Republic, by Oleksander Sevryuk, Mykola Lyubins'kyi, and Mykola Levyts'kyi, all members of the Ukrainian Central Rada.
8. Wheeler-Bennett, p.399.
9. 'Sulh Meselesi Hakkında Hariciye Nâzırı'nın Beyânâtı ve Müzâkere Cereyânı, ' *Meclis-i Mebusân Zabıt Cerîdesi, Üçüncü Devre-i İntihâbiyye, Dördüncü İctima, 55inci İnikad,* 23 February 1918 (Istanbul), p.898.
10. 'İlk Sulh ve Netâyici', *Tanin* (Istanbul), 11 February 1918.
11. Akdes Nimet Kurat, *Türkiye ve Rusya* (Ankara, 1970), p.390; 'Ukrayna'nın Dersaadet Sefîri', *Tanin,* 9 April 1918; *Takvîm-i Vekâyî,* 30 May 1918.
12. '(Ukrayna)'nın Dersaadet Murahhası', *Tanin,* 19 April 1918.
13. 'Ukrayna Heyet-i Sefâretinin Vürûdu', *Tanin,* 20 April 1918; 'From Pallavicini to Buri‡n, Istanbul, 23 April 1918', *Ereignisse in der Ukraine 1914–1922 deren Bedeutung und historische Hintergründe,* Vol.III (Philadelphia, PA, 1968), pp.619–620.
14. 'Ukrayna Sefîri'nin Ziyareti', *Tanin,* 23 April 1918.
15. 'Türkiya-Ukrayna', *Tanin,* 20 Nisan 1918.
16. The Crimean Tatar nationalists who would spearhead the convocation of the Crimean Tatar Parliament had very good relations with the Ukrainian Central Rada. Leading figures among them, such as Cafer Seydahmet [Kırımer], Dr Ahmet Özenbaşlı, Ayşe İshakova, and others joined the Congress of Representatives of Nationalities, upon the invitation of the Central Rada, in Kiev on 21–8 (8–15 in the Julian calendar) September 1917. The Third Universal Declaration of the Ukrainian Central Rada, dated 20 November 1917, which proclaimed the Ukrainian Democratic Republic, also clearly excluded the Crimea from the territory of Ukraine. Not only did the Central Rada sent its representatives to greet the opening of the Kurultay, but some military cooperation between the Crimean Tatars and the Ukrainians took place in those turbulent months as well. L.P. Garcheva, 'Tsentral'naia Rada i krymskotatarskii Kurultay – Soyuzniki v bor'be s Sovnarkomom Rossii', *Problemy politicheskoi istorii Kryma. Vypusk pervyi* (Simferopol, 1996), pp.17–18; Osman Kemal Hatif, *Gökbayrak Altında Millî Faaliyet* (Istanbul, 1918), pp.66, 83–84; For the English translations of the Third Universal, see James Bunyan – H.H. Fisher, *The Bolshevik Revolution. Documents and Materials* (Stanford, 1934), pp.435–437, and Taras Hunczak (ed.), *The Ukraine, 1917–1921: A Study in Revolution* (Cambridge, Mass., 1977), pp.387–91.
17. In fact, the Crimean Tatar leadership which was at the time literally insulated in the Crimean peninsula was desperately seeking ways to contact the Ottoman delegation at Brest-Litovsk. For this purpose, Colonel (or Major) Dr Osman Bey, a former Ottoman prisoner of war in Russia who managed to come to the Crimea, was secretly dispatched to Brest-Litovsk with a memorandum of the Crimean Tatar National Government. Cafer Seydahmet Kırımer, *Bazı Hâtıralar* (Istanbul, 1993), p.266. It is known that the Grand Vizier Talât Pasha received the memorandum. Kurat, p.205.
18. Cafer Seydahmet, after a very adventurous and perilous journey via Ukraine and the

234   TURKEY BEFORE AND AFTER ATATÜRK

Caucasus,. reached Trabzon during the second half of March 1918. 'From Rauf [Orbay] Bey to Enver Pasha, 26 March 1918', Archives of the Directorate of Military History and Strategical Studies of the Turkish General Staff (*ATASE* Archives), Ankara, First World War Collection, K: 228, D: 946, Fihrist No.14/1; 'Kırım Hükûmeti Hariciye Komiseri İstanbul'a Geliyor', *Sabah* (Istanbul), 24 March 1918.

19. 'Cafer Seydahmet Efendi'nin Vürûdu', *Âtî* (Istanbul), 21 April 1918; 'Kırım Hariciye ve Harbiye Müdiri Şehrimizde', *Tanin*, 21 April 1918.
20. 'İlk Ukrayna Sefareti', *Tanin*, 20 April 1918.
21. 'Ukrayna Hareketi', *Tanin*, 6 May 1918.
22. Fedyshyn, p.202.
23. 'Kırım Mebusları', *İkdam*, 18 June 1918.
24. 'Kırım Mebusları', *İkdam*, 19 June 1918.
25. 'Kırımlıların Protestosu – Kırımlılar Ukrayna'ya Cevap Veriyor', *Tanin*, 30 June 1918; 'Kırımlıların Haklı Bir Mukabelesi', *Vakit*, 30 Haziran 1918; 'Kırım Hakkında', *Sabah*, 30 Haziran 1918.
26. 'Kırım Murahhasları ve Alman, Bulgar Süferâsının Beyanâtı', *Âtî*, 25 June 1918.
27. 'Kırım ve Ukrayna', *Tanin*, 30 June 1918.
28. Edige Kırımal, *Der nationale Kampf der Krimtürken* (Emstedten/Westfälen, 1952), p.228.
29. 'İlk Kırım Sefiri', *Âtî*, 2 August 1918. In fact, Cafer Seydahmet had sent Ayvazov to Istanbul without the consent of the other [especially Russian] members of the Crimean government, who would contest this appointment vehemently upon learning of it later. A. V. Mal'gin, 'Vneshnaia politika Krymskogo Kraevogo Pravitel'stva generala Sul'kevicha', *Krymskii Muzei* (Simferopol), No.1 (1994), p.59.
30. 'Kırım'ın Teşkili – Kırım Vekil-i Resmisiyle Mülâkat', *İkdam*, 5 August 1918.
31. While Enver Pasha was secretly leaving Turkey immediately after the Armistice of Mudros, he called for Ayvazov and asked 40,000 Ottoman Liras back from a sum total of 100.000 Liras which the latter had been given by the Ottoman Generalissimo to be sent to the Crimea. It seems that this was the only sum Enver Pasha took with him when he left Istanbul by a German U-Boat. Muhittin Birgen, 'İttihat ve Terakkı'de On Sene', *Son Posta* (Istanbul), 14 April 1937.
32. Ziynetullah Nûşirevan, 'Kırım Meselelerine Dair Bir Mülâkat', *Sabah* (Istanbul), 10 September 1918.
33. Fedyshyn, p.219.
34. Ibid., pp.219–24.
35. 'Memorandum of the Legal Counsel of the Sublime Porte, 15 August 1918, No.38650', Ottoman Archives of the Turkish Prime Ministry (*T.C. Başbakanlık Osmanlı Arşivi*), Istanbul (Hereafter cited as, *BOA*), Hariciye Nezâreti Hukuk Müşâvirliği İstişâre Odası Evrakı Katalogu, 'Ukraynalı Harp Esirleri', No.54/4–1. Within a few days of the signing of the Treaty of Brest-Litovsk, the Ottoman Foreign Ministry discussed the official status of the Ukrainians residing in the Ottoman Empire and whether they would be treated as subjects of a hostile state any longer. It was resolved that all subjects of the former Russian Empire should be considered as subjects of a hostile state until the Treaty became formally into force, that is, when the ratifications of the Treaty were exchanged in Vienna. 'Memorandum of the Legal Counsel of the Sublime Porte, 3 March 1918, No.38383', *BOA*, Hariciye Nezâreti Hukuk Müşâvirliği İstişâre Odası Evrakı Katalogu, 'Ukrayna Cumhuriyeti – Müteferrik Evrak', No.106/6-1.
36. 'Ukraynalı Üserânın Sevki', *Takvîm-i Vekâyî*, 4 June 1918.
37. 'Memorandum of the Legal Counsel of the Sublime Porte, 15 August 1918, No.38650.' Also, 'Memorandum of the Legal Counsel of the Sublime Porte, 25 September 1918, No.38560', *BOA*, Hariciye Nezâreti Hukuk Müşâvirliği İstişâre Odası Evrakı Katalogu, 'Ukrayna Cumhuriyeti – Müteferrik Evrak', No.106/6-1.
38. Nikolai Nesuk, 'Ukrainsko-turetskie otnosheniia v 1918-1921 gg.', in A. Dergachyov (ed.), *Ukrainskaia gosudarstvennost' v XX veke: Istoriko-politologicheskii analiz* (Kiev, 1996), p.215.
39. 'From Szilassy to Burián, Istanbul, 8 June 1918', *Ereignisse in der Ukraine 1914–1922 deren Bedeutung und historische Hintergründe*, Vol.III (Philadelphia, PA, 1968), p.620.

40. It is known that sometime in May the Ottoman Foreign Ministry thought of appointing Fahreddin Bey, the former chargé d'affaires in St. Petersburg, as the Ambassador to Kiev. For some reason, this choice was changed in favour Ahmet Muhtar Bey. Kurat, p.390. For a biography of Ahmet Muhtar Bey (Mollaoğlu) (1870–1934), see, Hâmid Aral, *Dışişleri Bakanlığı 1967 Yıllığı* (Ankara, 1968), pp.118–119.

41. *Takvîm-i Vekâyı*, 2 September 1918.

42. Kurat cites the lenghty article which appeared in *Nova Rada* on 14 September 1918. Kurat, p.390.

43. Ibid.

44. Abdürreşid İbrahim, 'Türkiye Cumhuriyeti'niñ Vaşington Sefîr-i Kebiri Muhtar Bey'niñ Vefâtı Münasebetiyle', *Yaña Yapon Muhbiri* (Tokyo), No.20 (1934), pp.35–6. Apart from helping the Ottoman diplomats in their work, Abdürreşid İbrahim also gave sermons regularly in the Kiev mosque. He stayed in Kiev for about a month. 'Müslüman Memleketlerinde Beş Sene Seyahat. Abdürreşid İbrahim Efendi'nin Rusya, Sibirya, Türkistan ve Türkistan-ı çinî 'deki Müşâhedâtı', *Tevhîd-i Efkâr* (Istanbul), 6 December 1923.

45. *Takvîm-i Vekâyı*, 18 July 1918.

46. *Takvîm-i Vekâyı*, 4 September 1918.

47. *Takvîm-i Vekâyı*, 14 August 1918.

48. As a matter of fact, the lack of information about Ahmet Muhtar Bey's whereabouts who was known to had long departed from Kiev and had reached Odessa to take a steamer to Istanbul created some apprehension in the Ottoman press. 'Kiyef Sefiri Muhtar Bey Nerededir?', *İkdam* (Istanbul), 13 February 1919.

49. Ahmed Ferid Bey returned to Istanbul on 21 February 1919. Emel Esin, 'Ahmed Ferid Tek (1877–25.XI.1971)', *Türk Kültürü* (Ankara), No.110 (December 1971), p.140. Soon after his arrival in Istanbul, Ahmet Ferid Bey was interviewed by the Ottoman paper *Tasvîr-i Efkâr*. There, the ex-consul general gave brief information about the hard times Ukraine was then living through. He said that then there were several Ottoman citizens who could not return to Turkey since the outbreak of the previous war, as well as some one hundred Ottoman prisoners of war (officers and privates), who had been waiting in Odessa to find some means to go back home. 'Kiyef Başşehbenderinin Avdeti', *Tasvîr-i Efkâr* (Istanbul), 25 February 1919.

50. Aral, p.119. Ahmet Muhtar Bey was soon elected a deputy to the Ottoman Parliament, and upon the dissolution of the latter by the British occupational forces joined the nationalist movement in Ankara, where he served as the acting Minister of Foreign Affairs and in 1922 he was sent to Moscow as the Ambassador of the Turkish (Ankara) government. Kurat, p.391.

51. Kurat, pp.391–4.

52. Ibid., p.395.

53. 'Memorandum of the Legal Counsel of the Sublime Porte, 3 December 1918, No.39340', BOA, Hariciye Nezâreti Hukuk Müşâvirliği İstişâre Odası Evrakı Katalogu, 'Ukrayna Cumhuriyeti – Müteferrik Evrak', No.106/6-1.

54. 'From Szilassy to Burián, Istanbul, 8 June 1918', *Ereignisse in der Ukraine 1914–1922 deren Bedeutung und historische Hintergründe*, Vol.III (Philadelphia, PA, 1968), p.620.

55. 'Ukrayna'nın Yeni İstanbul Sefiri', *Tanin*, 12 June 1918.

56. 'From Chykalenko to the Ottoman Foreign Ministry, Istanbul, 26 August 1918', BOA, Hariciye Nezâreti Evrakı Mütenevvia Kısmı, No.82/34.

57. 'From Emil Egon Prince Fürstenberg to the Imperial and Royal Ministry of Foreign Affairs, Kiev, 11 October 1918', *Ereignisse in der Ukraine 1914–1922 deren Bedeutung und historische Hintergründe*, Vol.III (Philadelphia, PA, 1968), p.620. In September 1918, the Ukrainian government had appealed to the Ottoman Consulate General in Kiev to ask Istanbul whether the Ukrainian mission could travel to the Ottoman capital on an excursion yacht with Ukrainian naval colors. In all likelihood, the mission at issue was that of Kistyakovskii. 'Memorandum of the Legal Counsel of the Sublime Porte, 14 September 1918, No.39137', BOA, Hariciye Nezâreti Hukuk Müşâvirliği İstişâre Odası Evrakı Katalogu, 'Ukrayna Cumhuriyeti – Müteferrik Evrak', No.106/6-1.

58. 'From Ahmed Muhtar Bey to the Ottoman Foreign Ministry, Kiev, 19 October 1918', *BOA*, Hariciye Nezâreti Evrakı Mütenevvia Kısmı, No.82/34.

59. 'From the Ottoman Embassy in Kiev to the Ottoman Foreign Ministry, Kiev, 19 October 1918', *BOA*, Hariciye Nezâreti Evrakı Mütenevvia Kısmı, No.82/34. Tohulka, who had been designated the first secretary in the embassy of Kistyakovskii, resigned and Prince Tenishev replaced him. Also, Chykalenko left his post as he was appointed to another office in Kiev. Yet, he was to come to Istanbul with the Sukovkin embassy to fix his personal affairs there. 'From the Ottoman Embassy in Kiev to the Ottoman Foreign Ministry, Kiev, 27 October 1918', *BOA*, Hariciye Nezâreti Evrakı Mütenevvia Kısmı, No.82/36. See also, 'From the President of the Council of Ministers of Ukraine (*Lettre de créance* of Sukovkin) to the Ottoman Foreign Minister, Kiev, 26 October 1918', and 'From the Hetman of Ukraine to the Sultan, Kiev, 26 October 1918', *BOA*, Hariciye Nezâreti Evrakı Mütenevvia Kısmı, No.82/37.

60. *Takvîm-i Vekâyı*, 9 November 1918. The imperial decree of the Sultan was issued on 7 November 1918. 'From the First Secretary of the Sultan to the Grand Vizier, 7 November 1918', *BOA*, Dosya Usûlü İradeler Tasnifi, No.12 / 1–12 (1–2). Kurat is of course wrong as he assumes that Sukovkin [he read the Ukrainian envoy's name through the Arabic script as 'Sokrokin' or 'Sorokin'] never arrived in Istanbul and the diplomatic relations between Ottoman Empire and Ukrainian Democratic Republic came to an end. Kurat, p.390.

61. 'From Emil Egon Prince Fürstenberg to the Imperial and Royal Ministry of Foreign Affairs, Kiev, 27 October 1918', *Ereignisse in der Ukraine 1914–1922 deren Bedeutung und historische Hintergründe*, Vol.III (Philadelphia, PA, 1968), p.620. This information contrasts with the information of the Ottoman Embassy in Kiev which wired Istanbul that Sukovkin left Kiev on 28 October 1918 and he was supposed to take a steamer to from Odessa to Istanbul on 30 October. 'From the Ottoman Embassy in Kiev to the Ottoman Foreign Ministry, Kiev, 29 October 1918', *BOA*, Hariciye Nezâreti Evrakı Mütenevvia Kısmı, No.82/34.

62. Oleksander Lotots'kyi, *V Tsarhorodi* (Warsaw, 1939), pp.33–34.

63. Alimerdan Topçibaşev, *Diplomaticheskie besedy v Stambule (1918–1919 gg.)* (Baku, 1994), p.121.

64. Pavlo Skoropads'kyi, *Spohadi* (Kiev, 1995), p.266.

65. John S. Reshetar, Jr., *The Ukrainian Revolution, 1917–1918. A Study in Nationalism* (New York, 1972), pp.197–8.

66. Topçibaşev, pp.49–50.

67. Lotots'kyi, p.36; Topçibaşev, p.80.

68. Ivan Tokarzhevs'kyi Karashevich, 'Oleksander Lotots'kyi yak dyplomat', in Bohdan Hoshovs'kyi (ed.), *Lytsar pratsi i obov'yazku. Zbirnyk prysvyachenyi pam'yati prof. Oleksandra Lotots'koho-Bilousenka* (Toronto, 1983), p.58.

69. Lotots'kyi, p.36.

70. Ibid.

71. *Takvîm-i Vekâyı*, 30 November 1918; 'From the Office of the Ottoman Grand Vizier to the Ottoman Foreign Ministry, Istanbul, 27 October 1918', *BOA*, Hariciye Nezâreti Evrakı Mütenevvia Kısmı, No.82/37.

72. Lotots'kyi, p.34.

73. Ibid., p.36.

74. Tokarzhevs'kyi Karashevych, p.58.

75. Lotots'kyi, p.36.

76. Tokarzhevs'kyi Karashevych, p.58.

77. Ibid.

78. Lotots'kyi finds Sukovkin's claim that he had to close down the Embassy on the pretext of the lack of money unconvincing. He argues that Sukovkin had already sent back most of the mission's staff back to Ukraine in January 1919, and the 4,000 Turkish Liras which he drew from the Istanbul branch of the Russian Foreign Trade Bank would have been more than sufficient for the subsistence of the remaining officials and for their travels for a long while to come. According to Lotots'kyi, Sukovkin had paid the January and February salaries of the returned personnel and thus exhausted his resources. Lotots'kyi, p.34.

79. 'From the President of the Directory of the Ukrainian Democratic Republic to the Ottoman Emperor Sultan, Kiev, 17 January 1918', *BOA*, Hariciye Nezâreti Evrakı Mütenevvia Kısmı, No.82/40. For a biography of Lotots'kyi, see, Bohdan Hoshovs'kyi (ed.), *Lytsar pratsi i obov'yazku. Zbirnyk prysvyachenyi pam'yati prof. Oleksandra Lotots'koho-Bilousenka* (Toronto, 1983); Dmitro Doroshenko, 'Lytsar pratsi i obov'yazku (U 40-littya naukovoy ta 45-littya literaturno-publitsystychnoy diyal'nosty prof. Oleksandra Lotots'koho)', *Kalendar-Al'manakh Dnipro na zvychainyi rik 1935* (Lvov, 1935), pp.117–23.
80. Doroshenko, pp.117–21; Boris Lotocki [Lotots'kyi], 'Foreword', in Bohdan Hoshovs'kyi (ed.), *Lytsar pratsi i obov'yazku. Zbirnyk prysvyachenyi pam'yati prof. Oleksandra Lotots'koho-Bilousenka* (Toronto, 1983), pp.11–12.
81. Lotots'kyi, pp.10–11; Evhen Onats'kyi, 'Oleksander Lotots'kyi', *Ukrayins'ka Mala Entsiklopediya* (Buenos Aires), Vol.VI, p.863.
82. Lotos'kyi, pp.34–5. Serhiy Botehyns'kyi, the head of the Ukrainian government and the Foreign Minister, by telegram to the Porte from Odessa on 4 April 1919 informed the Ottoman government that Kobylyans'yi, in the capacity of the chargé d'affaires, was to exercise the functions of the president of the mission in the absence of Lotots'kyi. 'From Serhiy Botehyns'kyi to the Sublime Porte, Odessa, 4 April 1919', *BOA*, Hariciye Nezâreti Evrakı Mütenevvia Kısmı, No.82/39.
83. *İkdam* wrote: 'The Ukrainian embassy which had suspended its functioning due to its failure to receive necessary funds from its government has been reopened for the last couple of days. Until the arrival to our town of Monsieur Lotots'kyi, who has been appointed the Ukrainian ambassador, General Kobylyans'kyi will act as the consul general and deputy ambassador.' 'Ukrayna Sefarethanesi', *İkdam* (Istanbul), 21 April 1919.
84. Lotots'kyi, p.35.
85. Tokarzhevs'kyi-Karashevych, p.59.
86. Lotos'kyi, pp.16–17.
87. Ibid., pp.35–7.
88. Ibid., pp.38–9.
89. Ibid., pp.39–40.
90. Among those who stayed were P. E. Chykalenko (Secretary), V. P. Prykhodko, O. Kovalenko, M. Kovals'kyi, Colonel V. Kedrovs'kyi (military attaché), General Ostafiyiv, V. Radzimovs'kyi (legal adviser), P. Linkevych (courier), and V. Zhelehivs'kyi (courier). Ibid., p.12.
91. Ibid., p.37.
92. Ibid., pp.49 and 155.
93. Ibid., pp.51–4 and 156–7.
94. Ibid., pp.173–4.
95. Ibid., pp.44 and 153–4.
96. Ibid., p.46.
97. Ibid., pp.158–9. The Entente handovers of ex-prisoners of war to Bolsheviks were not always a result of dereliction and carelessness. In return for ex-prisoners of war, Bolsheviks released Entente citizens or Russian nationals who were detained by them. In the above-mentioned event, some 100 such men were taken from the Bolsheviks in Odessa and none in Ochakov. Ibid., p.46.
98. 'Translation of the postscript of the Legal Counsel of the Sublime Porte, 20 September 1918, No.40074.' *BOA*, Hariciye Nezâreti Hukuk Müşâvirliği İstişâre Odası Evrakı Kataloğu, 'Ukraynalı Harp Esirleri', No.154/4-1.
99. Lotots'kyi, pp.159–62. He warned the Ottoman government about the invalidity of such notes then in circulation in Istanbul with a memorandum to the Ottoman Foreign Ministry on 13 February 1920. Ibid., p.161.
100. Alexis Alexandris, *The Greek Minority of Istanbul and Greek-Turkish Relations 1918-1974* (Athens, 1992), p.55.
101. Lotots'kyi, pp.86–8 and 97.
102. Alexandris, pp.54–62.
103. Lotots'kyi, pp.94–8.

238 TURKEY BEFORE AND AFTER ATATÜRK

104. Indeed, during the second half of 1917 both France and Britain endeavoured to monitor the developments in Ukraine by sending their officials there and established direct and friendly contacts with the newly emerging Ukrainian institutions and politicians. These contacts continued and even formalized after the declaration of the Ukrainian national state (though still nominally within the Russian Republic) by the Third Universal. While France appointed General Tabouis as the Commissioner in Ukraine on 29 December 1917, Britain appointed Picton Bagge as the British Representative in Ukraine in January 1918. Upon the Central Rada's joining the peace negotiations at Brest-Litovsk, the frustrated Entente representatives washed their hands of Ukraine. Isidore Nahayewsky, *History of the Modern Ukrainian State 1917–1923* (Munich, 1966), pp.214–16, 251–3.
105. Lotots'kyi, p.66.
106. Ibid., pp.67–70.
107. Ibid., pp.72 and 167.
108. Ibid., pp.72, 168–71.
109. Ibid., p.73.
110. Ibid., pp.77–9.
111. Ibid., pp.110–11. Tokarzhevs'kyi-Karashevych states that they were unable to publish further pamphlets due to the want of money. Tokarzhevs'kyi-Karashevych, p.61.
112. Lotots'kyi, pp.104–10.
113. 'Ukrayna Sefiriyle Mülâkat', *İfham* (Istanbul), 4 September 1919.
114. 'Kiyef'i Kim Aldı?', *İfham*, 10 September 1919.
115. Lotots'kyi, pp.133–6; Tokarzhevs'kyi-Karashevych, p.59.
116. Lotots'kyi, p.138.
117. Ibid., pp.140–2.
118. Yan Tokarzhevs'kyi-Karashevych (1885–1954) was a Podolian aristocrat and a famous historian. See, Evhen Onats'kyi, 'Kn. Yan Tokarzhevs'kyi-Karashevych', *Ukrayins'ka Mala Entsyklopediya*, Vol.XII (Buenos Aires, 1963), p.1910.
119. 'Memorandum of the Legal Counsel of the Sublime Porte, 11 May 1920, No.40613', *BOA*, Hariciye Nezâreti Hukuk Müşâvirliği İstişâre Odası Evrakı Katalogu, 'Ukrayna Cumhuriyeti – Müteferrik Evrak', No.106/6-1.
120. Lotots'kyi, p.172.
121. 'Memorandum of the Legal Counsel of the Sublime Porte, 11 May 1920, No.40613', *BOA*, Hariciye Nezâreti Hukuk Müşâvirliği İstişâre Odası Evrakı Katalogu, 'Ukrayna Cumhuriyeti – Müteferrik Evrak', No.106/6-1.
122. 'Memorandum of the Legal Counsel of the Sublime Porte, 11 April 1921, No.41724', *BOA*, Hariciye Nezâreti Hukuk Müşâvirliği İstişâre Odası Evrakı Katalogu, 'Ukrayna Cumhuriyeti – Müteferrik Evrak', No.106/6-1. The Treaty of Sèvres was never ratified by the Sultan and at any rate the nominal existence of the Ottoman Empire came to an end following the military victory of the Grand National Assembly government in Ankara which had categorically condemned the Treaty of Sèvres in late 1922.
123. 'Memorandum of the Legal Counsel of the Sublime Porte, 22 July 1921, nos. 41718–41940', *BOA*, Hariciye Nezâreti Hukuk Müşâvirliği İstişâre Odası Evrakı Katalogu, 'Ukrayna Cumhuriyeti – Müteferrik Evrak', No.106/6-1.
124. Ibid.
125. 'Memorandum of the Legal Counsel of the Sublime Porte, 27 July 1921, No.41835', *BOA*, Hariciye Nezâreti Hukuk Müşâvirliği İstişâre Odası Evrakı Katalogu, 'Ukrayna Cumhuriyeti – Müteferrik Evrak', No.106/6-1.
126. Onats'kyi, p.1910.
127. 'Ukrayna Heyet-i Mahsûsası Şehrimizde', *Hakimiyet-i Milliyye* (Ankara), 14 December 1921.
128. For the full text of this 'Treaty of Peace and Fraternity between Turkey and Ukraine' in French and Turkish, see, *Traité d'Amitié et de Fraternité entre la Turquie et l'Ukraine signé a Angora le 2 Janvier 1922. Türkiye ve Ukrayna Muhâdenat ve Uhuvvet Muahedenâmesi (Ankara'da 2 Kânûn-u Sânî 1338–1922 Tarihinde İmza Edilmiştir)* (Istanbul, 1923). A quite interesting sign of accommodating political jargon with the Soviets was that the title of Yusuf Kemal Bey was stated not as the 'Foreign Minister' (*Hariciye Vekili*) as it had

been normally the case, but in the form of the 'Foreign Commissar' (*Hariciye Komiseri*).
So was the case in its French translation ('*Commissaire des Affaires Etrangères*').

129. 'Ukrayna Muahedesini Teati İçin Harkof'a Gidecek Heyet Hakkında İcra Vekilleri Heyeti Riyaseti Tezkeresi', *T.B.M.M. Zabıt Ceridesi*, Vol.XVIII (Ankara, 1959), pp.265–70.

130. Stanislav Vladiyslavovych Kul'chyts'kyi, 'Yak vyrishuvalosya "Ukrayins'ke pytannya",' *Polityka i Chas* (Kiev), No.11 (1994), pp.68–9.

The Never-Ending Story:
Turkey and the European Union

MELTEM MÜFTÜLER-BAC

The European Union must make some tough decisions in finding an answer to the ever-present question of 'What to do with Turkey?'. The matter was more or less settled by the Luxembourg summit of the European Council held on 12 December 1997, at which the European Council decided to open accession negotiations with all the applicant countries except Turkey. Turkey's relationship with the European Union is more complicated than that of any other European country seeking EU membership. The complications arise from doubts over Turkey's European identity, whether Turkey is European. Since that question can never be directly raised, the EU explains its rejection on political grounds, i.e. Turkey's shortcomings in upholding the principles of democracy, law and human rights. A serious obstacle to Turkey's incorporation into the EU is, of course, its political system, which provides the EU with a valid reason for rejecting Turkey. The EU position is that since Turkey does not satisfy the democratic requirements of membership, its incorporation is not possible. This essay proposes that Turkey's failure to uphold democracy justifies the EU's rejection but at the same time conceals an aspect of the EU's reservations about Turkey: its perception of Turkey as the Other of Europe.

One factor bound up with Turkey's problems with democracy, making incorporation unlikely, is the perceived cultural differences between Turkey and the rest of Europe. For example, on 4 March 1997 the representatives of the Christian Democratic Party declared that 'the European Union is a civilization project and within this civilization project Turkey has no place'. German Chancellor Kohl's reported claim that the European Union is based on Christian principles and cannot accommodate countries that do not share this identity echoes this argument.[1] These declarations reflect the perceptions in certain quarters in Europe towards Turkey's eligibility for membership of the European Union, and thus as part of the European project. It is tempting to suggest that the issue of Turkey's inclusion into the European Union is determined by the Europeans' perceptions of Turkey as alien. The recent developments seem to reflect Lord Owen's claim that 'You have to clarify about where the boundaries of Europe are; and the boundaries of Europe are not on the Turkish-Iran border'. The paper argues that this critical combination of Turkey's cultural differences and the structural problems in its democracy makes Turkish membership into the EU a distant possibility.

On 12 September 1963 Turkey signed an Association Agreement, the Ankara Treaty, with the European Community and became an associate member of the EC. When this Agreement, which recognized Turkey as eligible for membership, was signed, the then Commission President Sir Walter Hallstein declared that 'Turkey is part of Europe'. Turkey's association with the EC was expanded with the 1970 Additional Protocol that foresaw the establishment of a customs union between Turkey and the EC by 1995. On 14 April 1987 Turkey applied for full membership of the European Community.[2] In response to the Turkish application, the European Commission presented its Opinion (Avis) in 1989, which did not recommend starting accession negotiations, even though Turkey was eligible for membership.[3] Instead of full membership, the Commission suggested the operation of the Association Agreement and the realization of a customs union as foreseen by the 1963 Ankara Treaty and the 1970 Additional Protocol. On 6 March 1995 a Customs Union Agreement (CUA) was signed by Turkey and the European Union, and was put into effect on 1 January 1996,[4] creating a customs free zone between the parties. The Customs Union has demonstrated the Turkish economy's ability to cope with the competitive challenges of free trade in manufactured goods, and the trade, competition and intellectual property components of the EU's *acquis communautaire*, and can therefore be taken as proof that Turkey can fulfil the economic conditions of the Copenhagen criteria for EU membership.

On 12 December 1997 during its Luxembourg summit, the European Council decided not to include Turkey in its enlargement process. The Luxembourg decisions are shaped by the Copenhagen criteria of the European Council and Agenda 2000 proposals of the Commission. During its Copenhagen summit in June 1993, the European Council decided on a set of criteria for EU membership: (i) stable institutions governing democracy, the rule of law, respect for human rights and protection of minorities; (ii) the existence of a functioning market economy and the capacity to cope with competitive pressure; and (iii) the ability to take on the obligations of membership including adherence to the principles of political, economic and monetary union. On 16 July 1997 the Commission President Jacques Santer proposed Agenda 2000 which set the Commission's strategy to widen the Union and suggested that accession negotiations begin with central/eastern European countries in 1998. Santer proposed to open talks with Poland, Hungary, the Czech Republic, Slovenia and Estonia. The 1997 Luxembourg summit ended with the declared objective that these countries' negotiations would begin on 31 March 1998 together with Cyprus. The Commission's position is that even though Turkey would be eligible for membership (this is due to the 1963 Ankara Agreement and the EU's acceptance of Turkey as being part of Europe at that time), the near future prospects for membership are very limited. On 29 April 1997 the EU-Turkey Association Council reaffirmed Turkey's eligibility and confirmed that Turkey would be judged by the same objective standards and criteria as other applicants. However, Turkey is not part of the EU's immediate enlargement plans according to both Agenda 2000 and the decisions of the December 1997 Luxembourg summit of the European Council. In the Luxembourg summit, the EU did not include Turkey among the applicant countries – even though Turkey applied for full membership in 1987 – and based this decision on concerns about human rights violations, Turkey's troops in Cyprus and its tense relations with Greece. The Council instead once again confirmed Turkey's eligibility and offered a Pre-Accession Strategy as well as an invitation to the European Conference.

The Turkish government rejected both of these suggestions and the Luxembourg summit ended as relations between Turkey and the European Union reached crisis point. After the summit, the Turkish Prime Minister, Mesut Yilmaz, accused the EU of erecting 'a new, cultural Berlin Wall' to exclude Turkey and of discriminating against Turkey on religious grounds. The outlook is grim for Turkey's century-old dream to be a part of the European system of states. This paper proposes that there is an interplay of two factors that makes Turkey's membership unlikely: the Turkish political system and Turkish identity.

It is almost impossible to categorize Turkey among a group of states; it is neither a part of Christian Europe nor a part of the Muslim, Arab, Middle Eastern culture. Turks have been a part of Europe since their arrival in Asia Minor in the eleventh century. In the nineteenth century there was a diplomatic and legal acceptance of Turkey's incorporation to the European ranks with the 1856 Paris Conference. Yet throughout history the Turks have never been classified as Europeans. The impossibility of placing Turkey in Europe is part of the European Union's problem of what to do with Turkey. To understand why that is a serious obstacle to Turkey's membership, one has to grasp the binary opposition between European and Turkish identities over centuries. The perception of Turks as the Other of Europe is deeply embedded in the European collective memory, and despite many internal hostilities among the Europeans themselves they can find in Turkey a common Other. 'It was this adversarial identity that ... provided the receptacle for a racial notion of European identity'.[5] Edmund Burke's famous remark that 'Turks are worse than savages' is reformulated with the Christian Democratic Party's declaration on 4 March 1997. Since 'the projections of the European psyche have been and remain, fundamental impediments to cultural encounter and understanding',[6] the perception of Turks as such remains a serious obstacle to Turkey's inclusion in Europe because the Other, i.e. the Turks, is 'marked by an insurmountable particularity, and consequently can never be assimilated into our culture'.[7]

On the other hand, the role of Europe in the construction of Turkish identity is profound.[8] There are two opposing tendencies at work in the construction of Turkish identity. One is based on the modern, secular, Western-oriented discourse, the other is traditional, Islamic and oriental in its formulations. Modern Turkish history is one of continuous struggle between these two tendencies. Modernization in Turkey is perceived to be a process of Europeanization and therefore the critical threshold in defining what the Turkish people will reject, i.e. the non-European elements. One primary goal of modernization is the recognition of Turkey as part of Europe. There is a very strong desire among the Turkish intelligentsia, its bureaucracy and its military to gain acceptance as a European state. One reason for this desire is finally to resolve the clash in favour of the modernizers. Thus, when the new Turkish Republic was established in 1923 out of the ashes of the Ottoman Empire, its political leaders aimed to elevate Turkey to the level of contemporary civilizations and to have Turkey accepted as a European state.

The Cold War presented Turkey with a golden opportunity to gain European status. As a buffer between the Soviet Union and Western Europe, Turkey became a valued pillar of Western security. It was accepted as a member of the Organization for Economic Cooperation and Development (OECD – at that time OEEC) in 1948, the Council of Europe in 1949 and the North Atlantic Treaty Organization (NATO) in 1952. The Cold War structures provided Turkey with a historic opportunity to be accepted as a European state even though the necessary elements were still absent in Turkey. Turkey's place in Europe was granted, albeit reluctantly. Europe accepted Turkey into its ranks in order to contain the Soviets.

In the post-Cold War era, Turkey's position in the European order can no longer be justified by Turkey's function as a buffer state against the Soviet Union. The disappearance of the Red Menace brought into question Turkey's place in European security arrangements, or in any European organization for that matter. The perception is that Turkey's value as a security partner for Europe has diminished. Instead, Turkey's incorporation in Europe will be possible only when the Turkish political system meets European standards. Thus, what the Cold War structures enabled Turkey to hide, its failure in attaining European standards in human rights and the rule of law, can no longer be concealed. The post-Cold War values revolve around the rule of law, protection of human rights and upholding democratic principles.

In the post-Cold War era the European Union acts like a magnet for non-members; a necessary criterion for inclusion is democracy. Article 237 of the Rome Treaty states that any European country that is a democracy and that has a market economy may apply for membership. The 1962 Birkelbach Report of the EC has clear political conditions for membership, a member country should respect all principles of democracy. The Treaty on the European Union (TEU) provides that any European state whose system of government is founded on the principle of democracy may apply to become a member of the Union. Article F of Title I of the TEU states that (i) the Union shall respect the national identities of its member states whose system of government are founded on the principle of democracy and (ii) the Union shall respect fundamental rights, as guaranteed by the European Convention of Human Rights. The 1992 Lisbon Summit of the European Council further emphasizes the importance of a democratic system in a candidate country. In addition, one institution of the European Union (EU) in particular, the European Parliament, is an ardent supporter of democracy in countries aspiring to membership. The Maastricht Treaty has expanded the role of the EP in relations with third parties by requiring the assent of the EP for their accession to the EU (Article O of the Treaty on the European Union). Thus, the assent requirement from the EP put democracy and respect for human rights on top of the agenda for any country aspiring to EU membership. Lastly, among the Copenhagen criteria, political conditions, i.e. democracy, protection of human rights and the rule of law, head the list of requirements for membership. Thus, the European Union has a very clear position on membership: democracy is a must.

To top it all, the end of the Cold War reintroduced the Central and Eastern European countries to the European order. Since 1991 the European Union has developed various schemes to bring the Central and Eastern European countries into its orbit. The 1991 Europe Agreements established associations between the EU and the Visegrad countries. In July 1997 three of these countries – Poland, Hungary and the Czech Republic – signed accession agreements with NATO as a further step towards their integration into the European order, and the European Council of December 1997 decided to open negotiations with these countries in March 1998 for their accession into the EU.

The end of the Cold War was unfortunate for Turkey because first the dismantling of Cold War structures decreased Turkey's strategic importance and eroded the *raison d'être* for Turkey's incorporation into the European order. Second, since post-Cold War Europe is shaped along such values as rule of law and democracy, Turkey is left to face its own shortcomings in its political system. Third, Turkey fell behind the Central and Eastern European countries in its bid for membership of the EU.

Given the absence of a systemic factor paving the way towards EU membership, Turkey faces the unenviable task of reforming its political system. The immediate issues involve Turkey in a continuing process of adaptation to post-Cold War values which in turn necessitates changes in the Turkish socio-political structure. The July 1997 report of the Commission states that Turkey falls well below EU standards on human rights. This does not mean, however, that Turkey is not going to be accepted into the EU just because of its political system. There are many other reasons why the European Union member states are opposed to Turkey's membership. Turkey is too large, too poor, too populous, with high inflation and unemployment rates; it has an enduring rivalry with Greece, and a pending Kurdish problem. According to various statements from EU officials, Turkey's membership is determined by Turkey's efforts to improve democracy, respect for human rights, its treatment of the Kurdish population, and to resolve the Cyprus problem and the ongoing dispute with Greece. In 1997 the Commission suggested that Turkey should allow the International Court of Justice at the Hague to arbitrate in disputes between Turkey and the EU member states – i.e. Greece – and that the Cyprus question should be resolved prior to any negotiations between Turkey and the EU. It seems likely that as long as disputes with Greece and the Cyprus problem continue, Turkey's chances of membership are slim. Furthermore, were it to gain membership, Turkey would threaten the European states with an influx of people and would be a net recipient of the Union's structural funds. Given all these objections, the EU concludes that membership negotiations with Turkey cannot be opened, despite its eligibility. However, certain groups in Turkey claim that the real reason for the rejection lies in Turkey's cultural differences and its religion and that the EU is a Christian club, ill disposed to admit a Muslim country.

While the EU members are becoming increasingly sceptical about Turkey's membership, Turkish policy-makers tend to regard the European Union as the ultimate manifestation of European identity. Therefore, closer ties with the Union are perceived to be a stamp of approval for Turkey's 'Europeanness'. The final step in this bid towards Europeanness seems to be Turkey's full membership of the EU. Europeanness, however, has a number of prerequisites one of which is 'democracy'. Turgut Özal, the Turkish Prime Minister between 1983 and 1989 and president until his death in April

1993, summarized this view in his declaration: 'If Turkey wants to be in the European Community, there has to be democracy in Turkey'.[9]

During the negotiations for the Customs Union, the importance of Turkey's political situation in forging any kind of relationship with the EU became clearer. Under the Maastricht Treaty the assent of the EP by an absolute majority is required before the Customs Union can be operational. The EP appointed Carlos Carnero Gonzales as the EP's *rapporteur*, whose report formed the basis of the EP's decision on 13 December 1995.[10] The report identified the major areas requiring attention, such as the 1982 Constitution, improving the position of Turkish MPs from the Democracy Party, the Anti-Terrorist Law, improving the country's human rights record, and finding a political solution to the Kurdish issue. The basic conclusion of the report was that Turkish democracy falls far short of European standards, echoing the conclusions of earlier reports: the 1985 Balfe report and 1988 Werner reports of the European Parliament.[11] Since the CUA demonstrated Turkey's ability in both satisfying the economic conditions of membership and adapting to the Community's *acquis communautaire*, Turkey's upholding of democratic values emerges as the most important criterion on which the EU will judge Turkey's eligibility in the future.

The EU's objections to Turkey's membership are summarized by the statement of Luxembourg's Prime Minister, Jean Claude Juncker, that a Turkey in which torture persists cannot 'sit at the table of the European Union'. The British Foreign Secretary, Robin Cook, also repeated the major arguments against Turkey concerning its human rights record and its treatment of the Kurdish population. Since these problems seem to constitute visible obstacles blocking Turkish membership, one should look at the structural problems in Turkish politics and analyse the incompatibilities between Turkey and the rest of Europe.

The Turkish political system is a puzzling sight to the foreign analyst. The years 1996 and 1997 turned out to be highly interesting for Turkish politics. In some circles Turkey is said to be the only Muslim country that is a secular democracy. This statement is, however, highly dubious if one takes into account the omnipresent and omnipotent role of the Turkish military, the rise of political Islam and the cloud surrounding Turkey's human rights record. Thus, since Turkey is neither a democracy nor secular the only certainty in that statement is that it is Muslim.

In the period that followed the 24 December 1995 general elections, three different coalition governments were formed, charges of corruption became commonplace, political Islam emerged as a force to be reckoned with and the presence of the Turkish military is increasingly felt in everyday politics. A key development in this period is the notorious Susurluk incident – the coincidental discovery of an illegal formation within the state apparatus – the so-called 'state, mafia and *aşiret* [tribe] triangle'– when a parliamentarian, a police commissioner and a fugitive hitman wanted by Turkish police were discovered to have been sharing a car involved in a traffic accident. This incident had various aftershocks; first it demonstrated state involvement in clandestine activities, second, that the security forces acted as a party to these activities, and third, it showed the state's weakness insofar as various governments failed to explain the connection between these three men.

An ever-present question in Turkish politics is whether Turkey will ever complete its transition to democracy or whether it will revert to more authoritarian forms of government. Turkey's problems with the process of democratization are derived, first, from the enduring role of the military in politics, second, from the rise of radicalism, and third, from structural problems exemplified by the Anti-Terrorism Law, 'thought crime', and the Devlet Guvenlik Mahkemeleri (DGMs) – the State Security Courts.

The first problem is the role of the Turkish military in politics, which constitutes a major obstacle to the process of democratization in Turkey. The Turkish military acts as the 'guardian' of the Turkish state and Kemalist reforms. Therefore any threat to Kemalism meets with a severe reaction from the military. It is within this context that the military opposes the rise of political Islam, which threatens laicism, and the actions of Kurdish separatists which threaten Turkey's territorial integrity. Since the transition to multi-party rule in 1946, Turkish democracy has been interrupted three times by military interventions, in 1960, 1971 and 1980. In each case, the military intervened to 'clean up the mess created by the politicians' and then left the stage to the civilians. Turkey has never had long periods of uninterrupted military rule such as the military dictatorships of Spain, Portugal and Greece. The Turkish military interventions of 1960, 1971 and 1980 are explained as 'moderating coups' in that they did not lead to the establishment of military juntas. The problem in the 1990s is no longer the danger or possibility of a military take-over, but the omnipresent role of the military in civilian politics. The Turkish Chief of Staff's declaration one day before the 24 December 1995 General elections that 'the Turkish Armed Forces are the most effective guarantor of the Turkish Republic which is a secular, social and lawful state' succinctly clarifies the military's position in Turkey. The 1990s have witnessed the integration of the Turkish military into everyday political affairs through the National Security Council (NSC), which acts as a supervisory body where the president, prime minister, various ministers and the Commanders of the Turkish Armed Forces meet routinely to discuss political problems and issues. The NSC has a special role under the 1982 Constitution in the formulation and implementation of national policies and the Council of Ministers gives priority to its recommendations and decisions. The developments of 1997, specifically in administration and educational reform, while intended to deal with the threat of political Islam, stress the particular role of the military through the National Security Council in Turkey. The NSC and its role as a supervisory body is not accepted by the EU, since in liberal democracies the military should be under the control of civilian power and not in a position to guide civilian authority. In Turkey, the power of the Generals through the NSC indicates that the military is in a position of highest command. For example, on 28 February 1997, during an NSC meeting, the Generals were adamant on reforming the education system and asked the government to prepare an educational reform. The NSC announced on March 1 1997 that it expected the government to take measures to strengthen secularism and that failure to do so might result in military intervention. The inability of the government in power – the coalition between the True Path Party and Welfare Party – to pass an educational reform became one of the factors that led to its downfall in June 1997. The EU opposes this omnipotent military presence in politics and cites it as concrete proof that Turkish democracy is far behind the European standard. One interesting note, however, is that the military in Turkey is the institution most trusted by the public at large.

Second, Turkish democracy suffers from the growing strength of radicalism in the 1990s. A major challenge to Turkish democracy in the nineties comes from the incorporation of these radical parties/movements into mainstream Turkish politics, the incorporation of political Islam and two types of nationalism – Kurdish and Turkish – into the Turkish political system, or to put it another way, the taming of radicalism. The rise of radicalism results from a number of developments in Turkey. First, since 1980 Turkey has been experimenting with extensive economic restructuring which has led to the economic marginalization and alienation of lower middle urban classes and fixed income groups. Political Islam and ultranationalist movements find fertile ground in times of economic hardship. Second, the rapid pace of socio-economic change in the 1980s and 1990s resulted in the erosion of some traditional values. This, in turn, led to a search for a new source of legitimacy: some found it in Islam, some others in nationalism. Third, the state's failures in coping with people's demands and needs led to a decreased legitimacy and trust in the governments and increased the search for alternatives. Pro-Islamic parties stepped in to improve people's everyday living conditions by providing food, healthcare, education, services which led to an increase in their popular support. The growing role of radicalism in Turkish politics can be better understood by looking at party politics in Turkey.

The mainstream of Turkish politics – comprising the major centre-right, centre-left and centrist splinter parties – steer clear of radical ideology.

Mainstream Turkish politics during the 1990s are represented by the major centre-leaning parties; the Motherland Party, the True Path Party, the Democratic Left Party and the Social Democratic Party/Republican People's Party. The centrifugal parties are, first, the pro-Islamic Welfare Party (WP) led by Necmettin Erbakan, who was the founder and leader of the pro-Islamic National Salvation Party during the seventies; the Nationalist Action Party (NAP) – the ultranationalists, and finally, the Kurdish oriented parties: People's Labour Party (HEP), later succeeded by the Democracy Party (DEP), which was succeeded by People's Democracy Party (HADEP) in June 1994.

In the 1995 elections, WP received 21.4 per cent of the national vote, the ultranationalists in the Nationalist Action Party had 8.2 per cent of the vote and HADEP, which represents the Kurdish vote, had 4.2 per cent. Even though neither NAP nor HADEP could go over the national threshold of 10 per cent of the national vote and therefore could not gain seats in parliament, the results demonstrated that the three parties 'did boost the combined extremist vote share to one-third and raised the possibility that Turkish democracy is facing a systemic challenge'.[12] Of these parties, the strongest party is the pro-Islamic party – the Welfare Party. The first time mainstream Turkish politicians as well as the EU became aware of any threats to Turkish democracy from WP was when the party received 18.6 per cent of the national vote in the local elections of 27 March 1994. The Welfare Party received one quarter of the votes in the two major metropolises in Turkey, Istanbul and Ankara, whose mayors since then have all belonged to the Welfare Party. In the December 1995 general elections the Welfare Party emerged from the ballot box as the leading party. Necmettin Erbakan, the leader of WP, is able to manipulate the decreased levels of trust among the public. For example, he claimed that with the Welfare Party in power Turkey would cease to be a 'guardian state' but instead would become a 'waiter state'. It seems the pro-Islamic movements present a major challenge to the consolidation of democracy in Turkey. The WP throughout 1996 and 1997 engaged in a number of acts which demonstrated that they are not committed to the preservation of Turkish democracy as a secular state. Various WP officials insulted the basic principles of the Turkish Republic. Especially noteworthy is the February 1997 Sincan incident where the mayor of Sincan – a small town near Ankara – organized a pro-Islamic rally and delivered a speech in which he described how an Islamic government would be established in Turkey. In response, the Turkish military sent its tanks to Sincan, the mayor, Bekir Yildiz, was arrested, and the incident demonstrated that Turkey's major domestic headache is the rise of Islam. The Welfare Party is currently under the investigation by the Turkish Constitutional Court in response to an appeal made for its closure.

The case against WP is based on Article 68/4 of the Turkish Constitution which states that political parties cannot engage in acts that threaten the Turkish Republic and its founding principles, and Article 69/6 which states that the Constitutional Court can decide the closure of a political party accused of such acts. The WP's file is pretty heavy with accusations of violating the Article 68/4. The WP is the modern-day reflection of the continuing struggle between the two tendencies in Turkey – modernizers and religious reactionaries. The fact that their struggle still goes on rings alarm bells for the EU. Turkey, with its militant Islamism, does not look like a kindred spirit. The rise of political Islam in Turkey seems to indicate that Turkey's political stability and its secular character are increasingly at stake.

Another aspect of the rise of radicalism in Turkey is related to the Kurdish problem. The governments' capabilities in handling the Kurdish problem constitute a testing ground for judging the government's commitment to democratization. In Turkey, there is an estimated population of about 12 million people of Kurdish origin constituting about one-fifth of Turkey's population. Problems basically centre around the recognition of the separate cultural identity of the Kurdish population and the use of the Kurdish language.[13] The Kurdish problem was militarized by the establishment of a Kurdish terrorist organization – Partiya Karkeren Kurdistan, Kurdistan Workers' Party (PKK), led by Abdullah Öcalan, which had began its separatist activities in Southeast Turkey in 1984. The Turkish government does not recognize Kurds as a separate minority; and views the problem as being one of military conflict. The Turkish military's position is that the Kurdish problem is one of separatist terrorism the cause of which is the PKK that has to be smashed militarily.

The Turkish government's approach to the Kurdish issue began to change in the 1990s. First, under Turgut Özal the Kurdish problem was placed on the public agenda for debate. In 1991, Özal pushed the Cabinet to revise the laws that banned the public use of the Kurdish language. Second, during the TPP-SHP coalition which ruled Turkey from October 1991 to December 1995, a number of changes were enacted. One of the coalition partners, the Social Democratic Party (SHP), allied itself with the Kurdish oriented People's Labour Party (HEP) in the October 1991 general elections. HEP constituted a quarter of SHP's parliamentary strength: of the 82 MPs SHP had in the parliament formed following the 1991 elections, 22 were HEP members.

SHP was the first party to associate itself with the Kurdish issue and it was highly sensitive to issues relating to the Kurdish problem. The then SHP leader, Erdal İnönü, the deputy prime minister between October 1991 and June 1993, stated on a number of occasions that 'the Kurdish citizens' cultural identity must be recognized in full'.[14] In line with such developments, a separate Kurdish identity was more or less officially recognized and the use of the Kurdish language, with the exception of broadcasting and publishing in Kurdish, was legalized. In June 1993, HEP was closed by a constitutional court decision, but its members resigned before the court decision and formed the Democracy Party (DEP). In March 1994 a turning point for Turkish democracy arrived. The Turkish Parliament (TBMM) voted to lift the immunities for six Democracy Party parliamentarians as well as an independent pro-Islamic Member of the Parliament, and placed them under arrest. The Turkish parliament's decision was based on the suspicions that centred around the six DEP members for supporting the PKK and its terrorist activities. Since the decision to lift the immunities was taken by the Turkish Parliament – the people's elected representatives – the action was defended as not being a violation of the democratic practices accepted in Turkey. The lifting of immunities followed a major economic downfall in Turkey and it preceded the 27 March 1994 local elections. One explanation for the arrests was that in an attempt to divert people's attention from sky-rocketing inflation and faltering economic policies, the then Prime Minister Tansu Çiller found in DEP an easy target to stir national sentiment one of her favorite arguments was that she was going to 'cleanse the Parliament of the PKK'.

Reactions from various European institutions to the arrests were very severe. In line with a report prepared by an MEP from Holland, Eric Jurgens, the European Parliamentary Assembly decided to condemn the Turkish Parliament's decision to lift the immunities DEP members based on the argument that they had used their right to free speech that was protected by the Turkish Constitution and the European Human Rights Convention. The European Parliament immediately passed a resolution on the issue[15] and on 28 March 1994 the EP declared a freeze on the activities of the EU-Turkish Joint Parliamentary Committee. The crisis deepened when the Constitutional Court in June 1994 decided to close the Democracy Party, which had 13 members, six of them already in custody since March. The stated reason for closing DEP was that the party had contravened the Turkish Constitution and the Political Parties Law. When HEP was closed in July 1993, all members with the exception of Fehmi Işıklar retained their parliamentarian status because they resigned before the Constitutional Court decision and became members of DEP; however, with the closure of DEP in June 1994, the DEP members lost their parliamentarian status under Article 84 of the 1982 Constitution. On 26 October 1995 the Turkish Supreme Court decided to release two of the DEP parliamentarians. The four MPs who are still in jail took their case to the European Court of Human Rights which passed a decision in November 1997. The Court decided that the Turkish government was guilty with respect to the arrest procedures of these parliamentarians and the period for which they were held in custody. The decision delivered a blow to the standing of the Parliament in Turkey and that of Turkey in the international community was damaged.[16]

The Kurdish question seems to be a major challenge for Turkey in its process of democratization. The Turkish government's handling of the problem is used as the yardstick by which Turkish democracy is judged, and there is increasing pressure on Turkey to improve the situation. For example, the European Parliament passed a number of resolutions condemning Turkey for the bloodshed. In July 1996 European parliamentarians met in Bonn for a 'peace conference' and accused the Turkish government of state terrorism and pleaded for international legal action against Turkey.[17] During the July 5–9 1996 meeting of the OSCE's parliamentary assembly, a resolution was adopted on the Kurdish problem that criticized the Turkish government for mishandling the situation. Finally, in September 1996 the EP decided to suspend all financial aid to Turkey except that to be used to restore democratic practices.[18]

The closing down of political parties and lifting the parliamentarians' immunities, therefore, are not only domestic issues but have direct repercussions for Turkey's EU membership. The immediate issue is recognizing a separate Kurdish identity which in turn may lead to granting the Kurdish people some form of cultural autonomy. On a number of occasions the EU has called on the Turkish government to lift the state of emergency in the Southeast and to enter into a dialogue with the Kurdish people with a view to a peaceful solution safeguarding the rights of the Kurds.[19] In addition, the European Parliament and the Commission cite the DEP case as a further proof irreconcilable differences between Turkey and the European democracies and require their release as a precondition for accession negotiations. The EU has been influential in making the Turkish government realize that Turkey's future within the European order is largely determined by maintaining democratic practices for all and that therefore there is a necessity to find a political solution to the Kurdish problem, not only a military solution because the problem goes much deeper. For example, the Turkish government's treatment of its Kurdish people is stated as one major reason for Turkey's non-inclusion in the enlargement process of the EU in the years 2000. 'Danielle Mitterrand, widow of the late French president François Mitterrand, wrote to all 15 EU leaders to ask that Turkey be rejected on the grounds of its treatment of the Kurds. Some 3,185 Kurdish villages have been destroyed and 3 million Kurds displaced, she wrote; 'Must I remind you how many journalists, writers ... are in prison or disappeared?'[20] Thus, in the European Union, Turkey's position is increasingly determined by its handling of the Kurdish problem, and that by itself became the measure of the success of the process of democratization in Turkey.

Turkey's worsening human rights problem is not making the picture any brighter. Such incidents as the murder of a journalist, Metin Göktepe, by a group of police officers and the ever increasing number of people who have 'disappeared' while in police custody are major indicators of this deterioration. Added to which, the corruption charges haunting the leading politicians raise doubts about the accountability of various governments. The most prominent figure in this is the leader of TPP, Tansu Çiller, whose troubles really began in March 1996 when she was accused of corruption, notably $6.5 million appropriated from the government slush fund just before she left office. The discovery of a close friendship between some parliamentarians, police officers and mafia figures in autumn 1996 – the Susurluk incident – did not make life any easier for her. It seems that in the last years of the 1990s the government has to engage in a cleansing process similar to the one that took place in Italy. This requires effective political leadership. However, this seems to be lacking in Turkey when it is most needed.

The 1990s are witnessing a fragmentation of Turkish politics reminiscent of the seventies. The promising picture of the second half of the eighties began to deteriorate speedily in the 1990s. The general elections of 20 October 1991 and 24 December 1995 both resulted in the formation of coalition governments. The Welfare Party won the December 1995 elections, with the TPP and MP trailing by a small margin. The governments formed after December 1995 elections were: first, a coalition government between the TPP under Tansu Çiller and MP under Mesut Yilmaz that lived only five months, second, a coalition government between TPP under Çiller and WP under Necmettin Erbakan and, third, a coalition between MP under Mesut Yilmaz, DSP under Ecevit and DTP-Democratic Turkish Party under Cindoruk.

Of these coalition governments, the most ironic is that of Çiller and Erbakan. Çiller's alliance with Erbakan was prompted by her desire to escape a cloud of accusations. Throughout 1994 and 1995 Tansu Çiller campaigned in Europe and in Turkey for support against the pro-Islamic Welfare Party. She even convinced the European Union that failure to sign the Customs Union Agreement with Turkey would bring the Islamists to power. During the negotiations for the Customs Union Çiller claimed that such a union with the EU would strengthen her hand against religious reactionaries. Similarly, the French President, Jacques Chirac, claimed that 'If we dissuade Turkey from being European, we will strengthen the religious revivalists'. Thus, it seems that both Çiller and the EU members thought that a new tie between Turkey and the EU, i.e. the Customs Union, would damage the cause of political Islam in Turkey. Her strongest argument was that support for her would stop the Welfare Party. The day before the 1995 general elections, Çiller declared to the Turkish public that 'tomorrow, you will choose between civilization and darkness', darkness denoting the Welfare Party and political Islam. But when she could not get enough votes to form a government by herself, and when she could not find other partners, she made an alliance with Necmettin Erbakan, the leader of the Welfare Party. She allied with the very person she labelled the major enemy of Turkish democracy, the 'bogeyman'. A similar level of hypocrisy was also witnessed among the ranks of the Welfare Party. Çiller claims she represents the Western-oriented, secular and 'modern' segments while Erbakan represents the Islamic-oriented, conservative reactionaries. Their political marriage was one of convenience. They ruled Turkey together from 28 June 1996 to 12 July 1997, one of the oddest couples in Turkey. Their partnership was an exemplar of the oddities that have gripped Turkey in the nineties. Çiller's strategies, unfortunately, seriously harmed Turkey's reputation in European quarters since her claims as protector of the Turkish Republic as a democratic, secular state did not match her actions while she was in office.

Despite this grim picture, several efforts were made to strengthen Turkey's democracy and bring it into line with European standards. For this purpose, in the 1990s various Turkish governments adopted 'democracy packages'. On 14 November 1991 the TPP-SHP coalition introduced a 'democratization package'. One of the elements of the package is the Criminal Court Procedural Law (CCPL) introduced in April 1992 which brought new regulations for common criminals in custody. The amendment of the CCPL was an important part of the 'judicial reform', the 'democratization package' of the TPP-SHP coalition government.[21]

The reform efforts gained momentum in the interim period between the signing of the Customs Union Agreement on 6 March 1995 and the European Parliament's vote of assent on 13 December 1995. An important step was taken in summer of 1995 when an absolute majority of the Turkish parliament agreed more than 20 amendments to the 1982 Constitution. The 1995 democracy package preceded the vote in the European Parliament for the Customs Union. In addition, in September 1995 the Turkish parliament revised the Anti-Terrorist Law of April 1991 and its most notorious provision, Article 8, aimed at 'thought crime'. The Anti-Terrorist Law seeks to curb separatism in Turkey and does so by restricting freedom of expression and freedom of speech. The amendments of September 1995 to Article 8 of the Anti-Terrorist Law have lightened only some of its aspects. Under the MP-DSP-DTP government, a number of political reforms have been underway since July 1997. One of its first acts was to release various newspaper editors imprisoned on charges of 'thought crime'. Second, in summer 1997 the government engaged in an educational reform by replacing the five-year compulsory education with one of eight years which restricted the religious schools in Turkey – the *imam hatip lycées* – responsible for socializing the youth in political Islam. Third, the government accepted a package on human rights on 8 December 1997. This package dealt directly with conditions of custody and torture and aimed to eliminate the widespread use of torture and 'disappearances' while under custody. According to the EU, the persistent cases of torture, disappearances and extra-judicial executions illustrated the government's inability to monitor and control the activities of the security forces. In November 1997 this government decided to lift the parliamentarians' immunities in order to deal with corruption charges. Even though this attempt failed, on 10 December 1997, the government was able to lift immunities for two parliamentarians; Sedat Bucak – who was the parliamentarian involved in the Susurluk incident – and Mehmet Agar, the former director of police in Istanbul and former minister of the interior. This decision was taken in order to shed light on the Susurluk incident which threatens the Turkish state's legitimacy both at home and abroad.

Thus, under the present Turkish government, there are a number of developments in Turkish democracy. The pressures from the EU (the stick) and potential membership of the EU (the carrot) have been influential in bringing about some of these changes. The Turkish problems in human rights, the treatment of the Kurds, the rise of political Islam and the role of the military justify the European Union's position that Turkish democracy is well below that of the 15 members of the EU. The Turkish government accepts that Turkish democracy is far from ideal and claims to take the necessary measures to restructure its political system. The increasing strength of Turkish civil society and the growing demands from the people for more democratic government are also influential in this restructuring. Unfortunately, by accepting such countries as Bulgaria and Romania – which also have dubious human rights records and unstable and uncertain political systems and economies – as applicant countries, the EU has damaged its credibility as an unbiased institution.

This paper has argued that there are problems in Turkey with respect to human rights, upholding democratic principles and protection of minorities which justify the European Union's rejection of Turkey's pleas for membership. Such political conditions present themselves as a visible, valid cover concealing the unspoken reservations about Turkey – whether Turkey is European or not. As long as the political objections remain valid, the

Turkish government cannot effectively bargain with the EU.

The EU has clear requirements for membership; democracy, market economy, ability to adapt the Community's *acquis communautaire*. Turkey's success in satisfying the requirements of the Customs Union Agreement of 1995 demonstrated that Turkey would not have too much trouble in adjusting to the economic conditions of membership. The real obstacle seems to lie in Turkey's democracy. The structural problems in Turkey's democracy are valid grounds against opening negotiations with Turkey for membership of the European Union. The EU is increasingly concerned about the rise of radical movements in Turkey: Islamic militant fundamentalism and Kurdish terrorism which is controlled only by the Turkish army – hardly a democratic force itself. The magnitude of Turkey's political problems is such that the EU is unable to tackle them. The new challenges to Turkish democracy are now coming from the urgent necessity to solve the Kurdish problem, to which the EU is specifically sensitive, and the incorporation of the pro-Islamic Welfare Party into mainstream Turkish politics. The Turkish political system is passing through hard times in the 1990s due to the rise of radicalism and abuses of human rights. Turkish officials, the military as well as the civilian government are aware that a new Europe is in the making and that if they are not fast enough, Turkey will not be included. One can observe an adaptation process in Turkey to the Union's political norms and values. The main motive behind these processes is that membership of the European Union implies a constant reconciliation of national interests and standards,[22] since all countries aspiring to membership have to bridge the gap between their political systems and EU standards.

The European Union demands that the pursuit of democratization in Turkey should be accompanied by a firm commitment to resolve a number of problems in the region. The EC-Turkey Association Council of 29 April 1997 suggested that tensions in the Aegean could be overcome only by settling the dispute between Greece and Turkey in accordance with international law, even through the International Court of Justice, as well as through good neighbourly relations and the rejection of the threat or use of force in accordance with the UN Charter. Moreover, Turkey is expected to contribute actively to a just and lasting settlement of the Cyprus question in accordance with the relevant United Nations resolutions. Thus, membership is possible only if these conditions are met, Turkey's democracy must be satisfactory, disputes between Turkey and Greece must be resolved and the Cyprus issue should be settled. With the exception of the democracy requirement, the EU's conditions are vague and controversial and overlook the fact that in many cases Greece was blocking the settlement of disputes.

The closer ties between Turkey and the European Union under the

Customs Union Agreement coupled with the Turkish desire for membership of the EU have provided an additional stimulus to Turkey's democratization process. An emerging pattern in Turkey's society and political system is, however, to resist the pressure for democratization coming from the EU. The Welfare Party criticizes the influence of Europe and presents the European Union as a Christian club. The declaration from the Christian Democratic Parties in March 1997 that Turkey would never be accepted as a full member of the European Union[23] helped the cause of the Islamists. In addition, the Luxembourg summit decisions left Turks angry and bitter. In Turkey the slogan 'Go to hell, Europe!' reflects the popular mood. In response to the EU rejection, the Turkish government decided to suspend all political dialogue between the EU and Turkey, thereby eliminating the external stimuli for Turkey's process of democratization.

The EU's credibility is questioned because it treats Turkey and the rest of the applicant countries differently. Central and Eastern European nations are invited in and the EU discusses whatever problems they have, and these problems are addressed jointly, with the EU's help. On the other hand, Turkey is told that it will have to put its political house in order before the EU will reconsider its position. The mixed messages coming from the EU unfortunately undermine its legitimacy, thereby decreasing Turkish trust and weakening the pro-European and pro-democratic arguments of the modernizing, Western-oriented forces in Turkey. Thus, religious reactionaries are gaining over modernizers by arguing that since Europe is so hostile to Turkey, Turks should reconsider their Western orientation. After the Luxembourg summit Erbakan declared that the Turkish government had received a roasting in Europe and that all ills that had befallen Turkey had been caused by the modernizing elite's Western aspirations. Thus, the pressure exerted by the EU may be counter-productive: on the one hand it presses for democratization in Turkey and on the other it pushes Turkey out to the periphery of Europe, thereby strengthening the hands of authoritarian movements such as political Islam.

NOTES

1. Barry Schweid, 'Turkey's Leader Denounces Kohl', Associated Press, 18 December 1997.
2. See Meltem Müftüler-Bac, *Turkey's Relations with a Changing Europe* (Manchester: Manchester University Press, 1997).
3. The Commission Opinion (18 December 1989) presented a number of factors that made Turkey's accession almost impossible; these were the expansion of political pluralism, the poor state of democratic government, the persistence of disputes with a Member State, namely Greece, the lack of a viable solution to the Cyprus problem, relative economic backwardness compared to EU members, the Kurdish problem and human rights abuses.
4. Following the implementation of the Customs Union, total EU-Turkey trade increased from 22 billion ECUs in 1995 to an estimated 27 billion ECUs in 1996 with an estimated EU

surplus of 9 billion ECUs. The CUA encompasses financial support to Turkey in compensation for its trade deficit: 375 million ECUs in special aid and 750 million ECUs in EIB loans. These payments have been blocked for political reasons.

5. Gerard Delanty, *Inventing Europe: Idea, Identity and Reality* (London: Macmillan Press, 1995), p.37.

6. Kevin Robins 'Interrupting Identities: Turkey/Europe', in Stuart Hall and Paul du Gay (eds.), *Questions of Cultural Identity,* (London: Sage, 1996), pp.61–86.

7. Robins, p.66.

8. See Meltem Müftüler-Bac, 'Through the Looking Glass: Turkey in Europe', *EastWest Journal*, forthcoming.

9. Istanbul daily *Hurriyet*, 18 September 1987.

10. European Parliament, Report by Carnero Gonzales for the Committee on Foreign Affairs, Security and Defense Policy on the fact-finding mission to Turkey, 13-16 September 1995, Doc Pe. 214.242.

11. The two reports were written by members of the European Parliament in 1985 and 1988. They recommended that the Turkish political system had to become more compatible with European democracies.

12. Ergun Özbudun, 'Turkey: How Far from Consolidation?', *Journal of Democracy*, Vol.7, No.3 (1996), p.129.

13. See Nimet Beriker-Atiyas, 'The Kurdish Conflict in Turkey: Issues, Parties and Prospects', *Security Dialogue*, forthcoming December 1997 and Meltem Müftüler-Bac, 'Negotiating Kurdish Separatism in Turkey', in Marc Ross and Jay Rothman (eds.), *Theory and Practice in Ethnic Conflict Management* (New York: Macmillan, forthcoming).

14. FBIS, 17 December 1991.

15. European Parliament, Resolution on the trial of the members of the TGNA, Doc.Pe 182.023, 28 March 1994.

16. *Briefing*, Turkey, 7 March 1994, issue 980, p.3.

17. As reported in the Turkish daily *Cumhuriyet*, 8 July 1996.

18. European Parliament, Resolution on the political situation in Turkey, Doc.Pe 252.050, 19 September 1996.

19. Raymonde Dury, European Parliament Session Documents, Report of the Committee on Foreign Affairs and Security on EC-Turkey relations, DOC-EN/RR/208559, 21 May 1992, p.7.

20. Anne Swardson 'European Union Excludes Turkey From Expansion Plans', *Washington Post*, 13 December 1997, P.A24.

21. Ömer Faruk Genckaya, 'Consolidation of or Resistance to Democracy: Redemocratization and the Turkish Grand National Assembly', in Lawrence D. Longley (ed.), *Working Papers on Comparative Legislative Studies* (Appleton, Wisconsin: IPSA, 1994), p.323.

22. Andrew Mango, 'Turkey's Vocation', in Erol Manisalı (ed.), *Turkey's Place in Europe* (Istanbul: Logos Publications, 1988), p.9.

23. *Yeni Yüzyıl* (Turkish daily), 7 March 1997.

Double-Faced State: Political Patronage and the Consolidation of Democracy in Turkey

METİN HEPER and E. FUAT KEYMAN

Turkey has had a strong state tradition in the sense that, from the time of the Ottoman Empire to the present, there has always been a particular category of elite, who acted in the name of the state by assuming virtually complete autonomy from other groups in the polity, including the political elite. In the Ottoman Empire, the state elite was particularly preoccupied with the problem of reforming the Ottoman military and government along Western lines.[1] In the Republican period (from 1923 to the present), the state elite, including 'the intellectual-bureaucratic elite' and military, has been instrumental in introducing Westernizing reforms in government and society. The state elite has always acted primarily as the defender of the reforms, in particular secularism.[2] It also played a dominant role in socio-economic life.

However, since the transition to a multi-party democracy in 1945, Turkish modernization also involved the pursuit of the strategy of political patronage, with respect to the way in which the political elite approached socio-economic problems.[3] With the exception of the 1961–65 and 1983–87 periods, almost no effort has been made to develop coherent socio-economic policies; instead, the political elite tended to be overly responsive to the demands of particularistic socio-economic issues. What passed as 'policies' on such matters were, on the whole, no more than slipshod decisions essentially motivated by a desire to garner votes.

Thus, politics has not revolved essentially around the pros and cons of socio-economic policies; political patronage became the basic strategy of obtaining votes, in which religion was frequently used for political purposes. This led to a confrontation between the state elite and the political elite. When the state elite perceived a serious threat to such republican values as secularism, democracy was discontinued, for a limited period, because of the state elite's commitment to Westernization and, therefore, to democracy.

This essay elaborates on this double-faced quality of the state in Turkey – strong and weak – and on the adverse effects of the weak state and the strategy of political patronage for democracy. It also addresses the question of whether, in the near future, Turkey can attain a healthy combination of a strong state (prudence) and a weak state (responsiveness), which, of course, is a prerequisite for a viable democracy.

As noted, in the pre-1950 period, Turkey was ruled under a single-party regime. During this era, the founders of the Republic, Atatürk and İnönü, emerged as the defenders of the long-term interests of the community and, thus, as the proponents of a strong state. Consequently, the socio-economic policies they pursued were strongly coloured by their 'high politics.' For instance, İnönü governments insisted on balanced budgets in order not to be dependent on foreign aid. These governments were engaged in a major railroad construction project so that, in time of war, personnel and equipment could be transferred quickly from one part of the country to another. The government started extensive educational programmes in order to educate new generations of Turks to believe in the virtues of the new Republican regime.[4] Along the same lines, the socio-economic dimension of populism, as it emerged during the War of Independence, emphasized the necessity of improving the living standards of the people by the application of modern science and technology to the achievement of national progress.[5] Also, İnönü always stood firm against those who tried to use political office for economic gain; he always started legal proceedings against officials and politicians suspected of having been engaged in corruption.[6]

Consequently, relatively coherent socio-economic policies could be devised during this era. In the 1920s a liberal economic policy was adopted. Soon, this approach to the economy proved to be less than satisfactory, because there was a lack of private capital and vigorous and experienced private entrepreneurs. Also, the economy did not have the basic infrastructure. Moreover, at the end of the decade, the 1929 Great Depression hit the world economy. Thus, there was a shift to pragmatic etatism. The state took upon itself an active entrepreneurial role out of necessity rather than for ideological reasons.[7] The state actively became involved in a number of economic activities, including the establishment of exchange controls, major public investments in manufacturing, the nationalization of foreign and local companies delivering public services, and the imposition of import duties and quotas to protect industry. Private manufacturing started to develop under the tutelage of the state.[8] Capital began to be accumulated through contracts with the state.[9] In the single-party period in question, the groundwork was successfully completed for Turkey's later rapid industrialization.

The process of capital accumulation through contracts with the state was the beginning of the formation of vertical links between the state and society at the expense of effective horizontal links among members of the same social classes. Individual entrepreneurs became successful due to special protections granted to them by the state. During the single-party decades, the state tended to extend the scope of such special protections in order to create the necessary requirements of economic modernization. The state elite did not consider such protections as a means of political patronage to obtain political support. It was rather an integral part of their commitment to Westernization.

The exercise of political patronage in return for votes became paramount only with the coming to power of the centre-right Democrat Party (DP) in 1950 and the successor centre-right political parties to the DP – the Justice Party (AP) and the True Path Party (DYP). Later other political parties, including those on the left, also followed suit. During the DP government, the earlier state-centred polity began to move in the direction of a political party-centred polity; the political elite began to replace the state elite as the major public policy-makers. The state elite, themselves, maintained veto powers, as it became apparent with the three military interventions and with the fall of the Erbakan-Çiller government in 1997. For their part, the political elite remained as unresponsive to civil society as the state elite concerning the general 'policies' they pursued.[10] Instead, in order to garner votes they formed links with leading economic interest group associations and some key persons such as local notables and others who could mobilize votes for them.

In the multi-party democracy of post-1950 Turkey, several factors contributed to the flourishing of patronage politics. For one thing, the traditionally strong state quickly found its adversaries among the new political elite. The latter presented themselves as the proponents of the 'national will' against the 'state's will', and as the protectors of the masses against the state elite. This was an instinctive reaction on the part of the new political elite against the state elite who for long dominated the polity and society as well as towards those bureaucrats, whose self-designated mission of safeguarding the Republican norms was far more important than administrative merit – efficient and effective implementation of policies adopted by the new political elite.[11] The new political elite also tried 'to protect the people against the corrupt and tyrannical government officials'.[12] Many did need such a protection because, as a consequence of the rapid socio-economic change from 1950 onward, the traditional webs of protection had begun to crumble,[13] while the ethics of belonging, solidarity and intimate relations, as opposed to individualism, continued to be salient.[14] Consequently, elected representatives needed to be direct personal representatives of the people.[15] In the process, the party system became extremely responsive to the localized and particularistic demands of its constituencies.[16] Also, a highly unequal distribution of income placed many in need of special favours;[17] the multi-party system created incentives to use the resources of the state to win political competition;[18] and the increased scope of the public sector facilitated to meet the localized and particular demands of the constituencies through political patronage.[19]

On the other hand, in the making of policies, political responsiveness to, let alone regular consultations with, organized interests have remained alien to the Turkish scene.[20] In formulating policies, the political elite, not unlike the state elite, perceived nothing wrong in depriving themselves of the benefits of close consultation and cooperation with the business groups.[21] Therefore, there has emerged in Turkey neither an effectively functioning Social and Economic Council, within the framework of which representatives of the government, private sector and labour could confer and determine certain targets, nor interest group associations that could efficaciously impinge on governments.[22]

From 1950 onward, the political parties in Turkey increasingly resembled ventures established to promote solely their members' economic interests.[23] As noted, the origins of such party structures in Turkey harked back to the DP of the 1950s, which emerged as a political machine – an organization interested less in political ideals and more in securing and holding office for its leaders and distributing income to those who ran it and worked for it through patron-client networks and to those who voted for the party through pork-barrel grants such as roads, schools, electricity, mosques, and the like.[24] Based essentially on a myriad of patron-client relations, the DP was bound to lack elements of political institutionalization, including autonomy and coherence.[25] Without the latter characteristics – the DP and its successor parties, as well as other political parties, could hardly develop rationally formulated public policies. In any case, political parties have remained indifferent to rational policy-making. They did not have research bureaux let alone think-tanks for this purpose.[26] Also, they hardly paid attention to carefully prepared and debated policy proposals by independent research foundations and think-tanks.[27] As a result, politicians made promises which were not based on a careful analysis of the situation; in fact, they often made decisions on the spot.[28] It was not, therefore, surprising that, for instance, the decade of the 1950s was characterized by 'careless and uncontrolled high growth rates'.[29]

As a result of this state of affairs, the party programmes in Turkey turned out to be nothing more than window dressing. They, in fact, very much resembled each other, consisting of long lists of promises with no mention of how those promises were going to be fulfilled.[30] A recent study has found that in the formation of coalition governments, in twenty countries with well-established democracies, if the political regime was threatened, all system parties tended to pool their resources together and tried to deal with that problem. If the political milieu had a left-right divide the political parties on either side of that divide attempted to form governments within their own camp. If neither of these two situations obtained, the political parties were often attracted to those parties with similar policy lines.[31] In Turkey, none of the above conditions played a significant role in the formation of coalition governments. Instead, agreements among the political parties in Turkey were almost always based on short-term and tactical matters; the parties were preoccupied with trying to prevent other political parties from making electoral gains through exercising patronage powers and not with attempting to convince the electorate about the merits of their policies and programmes.[32]

This was because, as noted, politics in Turkey has not revolved around the pros and cons of political parties' policies and programmes. Parliamentary activities in Turkey have tended to be based on grand spoils operations; there was little concern with other functions. Individual parliamentarians felt under constant pressure to repay their 'debt' to their narrowly defined constituencies; they were not interested in debate, deliberation and policy-making. In any case, they were not expected to make such contributions.[33] Those parliamentarians, who were skilled in developing benefit networks, came to have an advantage over those who had a strong background in policy-making.[34] Skill in personal relations was more valued than expertise.[35] Wealth was also important; those party members who could finance party activities at the local level thought they deserved to be, first, the chairpersons of local party organizations and, then, parliamentarians.[36] One study has listed the typical characteristics of a parliamentarian in Turkey as follows: being wealthy, having a large network of acquaintances, the ability to make promises in a persuasive tone even if the parliamentarian has no intention of delivering what is promised, skill in bargaining, maximizing one's own interests rather than those of the people, and the like.[37]

In turn, party leaders were not in need of new ideas and programmes to keep their places.[38] In ministers, on the whole, loyalty rather than merit was sought. They were not expected to have independent opinions of their own, for the Councils of Ministers was dominated by the Prime Minister.[39] Since 1950 the bureaucracy therefore has been increasingly politicized.[40] Political parties were not interested in positive contributions the bureaucracy could make to the formulation of policies. Rather, they tried to curb the power of the bureaucracy for their own purposes – being able to pursue their particular aims without any interference from the bureaucracy.[41]

During the 1950s, however, the state elite was very critical of some of the economic measures of the DP governments. They opposed granting foreign companies the right to search for oil and providing incentives to foreign investors. They also opposed the 'anti-secularist' policies of the DP governments. The state elite also emphasized the need for (indicative) planning in order to render economic decision-making more rational.[42] Moreover, when DP governments began to run out of resources to distribute to their supporters and they began to use religion to garner votes, the clash between political and state elites occurred. Consequently, the DP governments resorted to authoritarianism and this move triggered the 1960 military intervention.

The 1961 Constitution was an effort to re-institutionalize the State in Turkish politics with (1) the National Security Council, comprised of some ministers and the members of the High Command, (2) the Constitutional Court, (3) the State Planning Organization, (4) the autonomous State Radio and Television Agency and universities, and (5) the Council of State (the Turkish version of France's Conseil d'Etat), with additional powers. The 1961 Constitution was also a 'programmatic' constitution; it spelled out government's economic goals to be achieved through planning.

The first group of planners in the early 1960s insisted that the political elite should not interfere with socio-economic planning. Within the coalition governments, formed during the 1961–65 period between the pro-state Republican People's Party (CHP) on the one hand and such anti-state parties as the AP and the New Turkey Party on the other, politicians from both camps became engaged in intense conflict on the issue of planned versus unplanned economy. Still, during this period there was a relative lull in patronage politics. Planning instead of patronage, industrial growth instead of populism, and an urban, polished universalism instead of rural parochialism were emphasized.[43]

With the coming to power of Süleyman Demirel's AP – the successor party to the DP – clientelism returned to Turkish politics. In addition to the DP tradition that the AP inherited, Demirel's personality characteristics and his political philosophy were also conducive to the re-emergence of patronage politics in Turkey. Demirel came from a small village in western Turkey. For many, he was the image of the people's man; Demirel himself enjoyed having that image. He was in favour of the exercise of 'the national will' unhindered by the state elite. This led him to embrace a populist and majoritarian conception of democracy, with non-mediated mass political participation. Demirel, thus, had a strong commitment to improve the lot of the masses; in the absence of a political tradition of competing to come up with better policies this led him to adopt distributive policies.[44]

Consequently, in the post-1965 period, patronage politics resurfaced in earnest.[45] It is true that economically the AP was more liberal than the DP, yet, just as in the DP period,[46] the state economic enterprises – a major means of political patronage – continued to flourish. Demirel tried to please everybody, including business and labour at the same time.[47] This was a difficult task to fulfil particularly in the post-1965 period. The 1961 Constitution had not only re-institutionalized the state but it had also expanded the scope of basic rights and liberties. The primary motive behind the expansion of basic rights and liberties was that of protecting the state elite against the 'tyranny of the majority'. However, the new Constitution also made possible the development of ideologies on the Left and the Right and, thus, the gradual crystallization of a class conflict. The economic independence of the peasants was also increased, while their dependence on the meager resources of the merchants decreased; as a result, the bargaining power of the voter *vis-à-vis* the government grew.[48]

These developments took place at a time when Turkey faced a structural trade deficit, which steadily deteriorated over time due to the stagnation of exports and the expansion of necessary imports[49] and when the 1974 and 1979 world-wide oil crisis occurred. What needed to be done was to persuade labour to accept income policy the corporate capital to seek accommodation with labour. However, the government, controlled by the political elite, was not coherent enough to force a new consensus that required such mutual concessions.[50] Steeped in patronage politics and, thus, having had vertical relations with individual members of the nascent social classes and having a condescending and dominant attitude toward civil societal groups, the political elite could not exercise social control, that is 'the successful subordination of people's own inclinations of social behaviour or behaviour sought by other social organizations in favour of the behaviour prescribed by state rules',[51] to bring about the consensus in question.

The result was the escalation of the clash between the armed Left-Right groups and also, at times, sectarian confrontations. The crises both in 1971 and 1980 were defused by the military that either temporarily became the real power behind an 'above party' government formed at its behest, as in the 1971–73 'coup by communiqué', or took power directly into its hands, as in the 1980–83 intervention. Throughout the 1960s and 1970s the military remained the most coherent and professional institution. After purging the radicals amongst its ranks, the military, acting as the state elite, could live with patronage-oriented governments but not with the extreme polarization in the polity and society that, in their view, threatened Westernizing reforms – in particular secularism – and the national unity and the territorial integrity of the country.

In 1983 the three-year interregnum after the 1980-military intervention ended and the Motherland Party (ANAP), under Turgut Özal, became the governing party which ruled the country until 1991. From 1980 onward, Özal played a key role in the liberalization of the economy and in the shift from import substitution to export orientation in Turkey. It is true that these shifts in the economic policy were the products of a 'forced decision', following the acute economic crisis of the late 1970s.[52] However, the fact that these and related decisions could be taken at all was significant in itself, for they were important steps toward a strong state, *vis-à-vis* the economy.

Özal emerged as a leader with a vision. He placed emphasis on economic rationality. Thus, in the early Özal period, economic decisions tended to be responsive to market signals,[53] they were not dictated by clientelist demands, and, relatively speaking, they were not the products of slipshod political or bureaucratic decisions. Entrepreneurial activity began to be appreciated and market values such as efficiency gained much salience. The boundaries of what business could expect from the government were quite clearly set: progressively, the government was to have less control over private sector, to reduce protection from imports and enhance export orientation, thereby opening Turkish economy to world market.[54]

This reorientation in economic policy had some positive results. The exports/GDP ratio grew from 4.9 per cent in 1979 to 20.9 per cent in 1985, while the annual economic growth rate averaged 5.3 per cent between 1981 and 1986.[55] Inflation, which was 108 per cent in 1980, dropped to 29.6 per cent in 1986. Similarly, while in 1980 the growth rate of GNP was -1.1, in 1986 it rose to 8.1.[56] Between 1980 and 1990 the value of exports increased from US$2.9 billion to US$13.0 billion and, in the same period, the share of manufactured goods in total exports increased from 29 to 79 per cent.[57]

It is true that the economic success story of the early part of the 1980s in Turkey was given a boost by the fact that between 1980 and 1983, the military brought major restrictions to trade union rights and labour's bargaining power. However, even after the transition to multiparty politics in November 1983, considerable restrictions over labour's bargaining power continued to be a major feature of the system.[58] One reason why the ANAP governments could keep the lid on demand was the fact that until 1987 the political patronage-oriented political cadres of the pre-1980 period were barred from participating in active politics. In addition, Özal focused his attention on the economy; since successful economic performance was dependent on political stability, Özal pursued a policy of reconciliation and harmony in areas other than the economy. Among other things, he refrained from engaging in debate on critical issues and tried to improve Turkey's relations even with such neighbouring countries as Iran and Syria with whom, for a long time, Turkey had not had friendly relations. Also critical here were Özal's related efforts to de-emphasize ideology in Turkish politics. Özal explained the *raison d'être* behind his founding the ANAP as that of bringing under one roof the four political tendencies represented in the pre-1980 period by the (centre-right) AP, the (centre-left) CHP, the (religiously oriented) National Salvation Party and the (ultra-right) Nationalist Action Party. He thought of the ANAP as a catch-all party.[59]

The ANAP was going to 'catch all' not through patronage politics but through well-formulated and clearly explained policies. ANAP had weak links to the localities,[60] probably on purpose. Özal chose to reach the voters directly, through regular appearances on television, and explain in simple language the dynamics of the economy, the constraints his governments faced, and the measures they were going to take. He proved to be quite persuasive.[61]

Despite the fact that the ANAP under Özal had adopted a novel approach to the economy, the style of rule during this period also evinced some continuities with the previous decades and this state of affairs facilitated the return to patronage politics from the second part of the 1980s onward. It is true that, as compared to such previous leaders as Menderes and Demirel, Özal seems to have consulted others more frequently before making decisions.[62] This was only to be expected, because Özal had a grand project the achievement of which dictated that he act according to a set of market rules. However, Özal used others basically as suppliers of data; otherwise, he made all the critical decisions himself.[63] Such extreme centralization of policy-making did not help to develop the institutionalization of collaboration between the state and business. Consequently, it proved difficult to obtain concessions from business where it was necessary. Some powerful and well-organized groups in the economy continued to show effective resistance to extensive tax reform or, at least at the time, to a widespread privatization programme. Also, during this period, there was a reluctance to delegate authority to the managers of state economic enterprises, while the overall weight of the public sector in the economy continued and even increased.[64] In 1979 the share of the public sector in total fixed investment was 50 per cent and its total fixed capital investment represented 22 per cent of GNP; in 1987, those figures were 54 and 24 per cent, respectively.[65] The annual inflation rate, which averaged 33 per cent in the early 1980s, reached 75 per cent in 1988.[66]

Furthermore, as noted, in the bureaucracy there were only 'pockets of efficiency'; otherwise, the Özal government had been unable to 'outgrow the narrow and weakly-rooted universalism of the bureaucracy and to transform it into a socially-grounded industrial (bourgeois) universalism'.[67] For instance, in 1987, when the ANAP government was criticized in Parliament for having signed the Council of Europe's Convention against Torture rather late, the then Foreign Minister Mesut Yılmaz heaped the blame primarily on the inefficiency of the bureaucracy.[68]

Following the 1984 local elections in which, as compared to the 1983 general elections, the ANAP's votes decreased, particularly with the return of the previous political leaders to active politics and the relaxation of constraints in trade union activity in 1987, virtually full-scale patronage politics returned.[69] As ANAP could not survive in this new (old) game of politics by pursuing its previous policies, it, too, drifted to patronage politics.[70] While the percentage increase in staff positions in the Civil Service was 2.4 in 1985 and 3.0 in 1986, it jumped to 10.0 in 1987.[71] More generally, after a downward trend observed from 1982 to 1988, current public expenditure increased from 34.5 per cent in 1988 to almost 50.0 per cent in 1990. This was basically due to wages and salary increases granted to public employees in 1989.[72] While in 1983 and 1984, the resources devoted to agricultural producers hovered little over ten per cent of the round value of their crops, in 1987 it rose to 30 per cent and in 1991 to 40 per cent.[73]

Patronage politics further increased in the post-1991 period[74] and reached its peak in 1996–97. The rise in political patronage in the 1991–95 period was due to the return of Demirel and his cadres to government and to the fact that Demirel's new party DYP basically represented the 'losers' in the 1983–87 structural adjustment programme of ANAP. These included large industrial groups with a predominantly internal market orientation, agricultural interests, and a large component of wage- and salary-earners.[75]

Demirel spent the first three months of his stay in power by 'receiving delegates from his party's local branches, giving speeches, listening to their demands, and making promises'.[76] His favourite line was, 'My workers, my villagers, my civil servants'. He was everybody's 'father'. Meanwhile Tansu Çiller, the minister responsible for economic affairs in the DYP-Social Democratic People's Party (SHP) coalition government led by Demirel, came up with her 'National Dynamic Equilibrium Model' that aimed at lowering interest rates and inflation, boosting the stock exchange, and starting a major reform of state economic enterprises. This was a pet project of Çiller herself; in preparing it she had not consulted the Undersecretariat of Treasury and Foreign Trade, the Central Bank, and/or the State Planning Organization.[77]

During the early years of the DYP-SHP coalition, Çiller presented herself as a proponent of discipline in the economy. For instance, she protested against 'the appointment of 100 persons to state economic enterprises every day'.[78] Demirel, however, gave assurances that the government was going to provide 'work for everybody'.[79] On another occasion Demirel said, 'The rights that had been usurped [by the past governments] will be returned to their true owners.'[80] In an economic reform programme, enunciated in January 1992, the government aimed at ambitious goals: lowering inflation and keeping it at low levels, bringing increases in production, improving the distribution of income, seeing to it that the market functioned in a healthy manner, achieving an integration of the Turkish economy with the world economy, expanding ownership in Turkey, and, more generally, raising people's welfare.[81] Leaving aside the fact that it is always very difficult, if not impossible, to realize all of these goals at the same time, the policies pursued aimed only at pleasing *all* major social groups: industry was supported by a low tax burden, as well as low input costs to compensate for rising wages; labour was compensated by high wage increases; and farmers were given high prices for their agricultural products. In 1993 almost the whole of the government's budgetary funds were allocated to current expenditures (mainly wage and salary payments – 34.9 per cent), interest payments on domestic and external debt, and the transfer payments, leaving very little for public investment – only 11.0 per cent.[82]

Demirel's weak state caused Turkey to drift towards the economic crisis of April 1994. There had been a rapid increase in expenditures without a parallel increase in tax revenues. A growing current account deficit could only be covered by inflows of primarily short-term capital. The large current account deficit, in turn, was the outcome of a real appreciation of the exchange rate that undermined the growth of the export sector while, at the same time, encouraging a rapid increase in imports. To make things worse, in response to the growing disequilibrium in the economy the two major international credit rating institutions reduced the country's credit rating, which led to a crisis of confidence on the part of the investors and resulted in a significant outflow of short-term capital.[83] The newspapers began reporting astonished people mumbling, as early as summer 1992, 'Father, what have you done to us?'[84] Despite the growing cries of protest from 'Demirel's workers', 'Demirel's villagers' and 'Demirel's civil servants', those representing the strong state – the military – did not lift a finger because the economic crisis in question only indirectly threatened the vital interests of Turkey.

In 1993 Demirel became president. With his withdrawal from the day-to-day running of the government, Turkey lost its last political leader with vision. It is true that Demirel was quite responsive to particular demands but, at the same time he had great ideals for Turkey. In post-Demirel Turkey, prime ministers had either narrow visions (as was the case until recently Mesut Yılmaz, leader of the ANAP, twice prime minister for brief periods before July 1997), or they had few ideals (e.g. Tansu Çiller, of the DYP, Prime Minister in 1993–95 and Deputy Prime Minister in 1996–97), or or again they were utopian (Necmettin Erbakan, then leader of the now defunct religiously-oriented Refah Party (RP), Prime Minister in 1996–97). It has been claimed that in recent years politics in Turkey has been conducted almost completely with a view not only to narrow party interests but also to sheer material interests[85] and that the resources at the disposal of governments have been seen by both politicians and bureaucrats as nothing more than booty to be distributed among themselves.[86]

There may be exaggerations in these claims; at least, they are too sweeping. On the other hand, they seem to be not too wide off the mark. The 1996–97 coalition government between Erbakan's RP and Çiller's DYP was based on entirely instrumental motives: Erbakan wished to join the government in order to further legitimize his religiously oriented RP in the eyes of the state elite, and Çiller wanted to avoid legal proceedings because of the allegations of wrongdoing and corruption on her part while Prime Minister.[87]

In the Erbakan-Çiller coalition, although Çiller's DYP controlled most of the economic ministries, she could not prevent the RP from having a considerable role in the conduct of the economy. Erbakan's economic policy based on the notion of a Just Order was utopian; the party did not even pretend to implement it.[88] Nevertheless, the RP came up with several economic packages, each of which contained exaggerated promises to different social groups, although the government had hardly any funds for this purpose.[89] Consequently, Erbakan's statements on the economy began to be reported in the media as 'fairy tales for adults'.[90] The managers of the leading holding companies such as Koç and Sabancı,[91] as well as interest group associations representing business and labour,[92] directed pointed criticisms at the government and wanted discipline in the economy. Çiller could not do anything about these developments because of her personal liability.[93]

Faced with the prospect of not delivering on the economic front, Erbakan increasingly tolerated the rising voices of militant Islam in his party. What made things even worse was Erbakan's visits to such militant Islamic states as Libya and Iran. Erbakan's RP, which at least to some people in the past, had given the impression of being a party that aimed at making Turkish society more Muslim rather than rendering the Turkish state an Islamic one,[94] now seemed to many, most critically to the military, as a party longing for an Islamic state. This time, however, the military chose not to make an overt intervention.[95] At the 28 February 1997 meeting of the National Security Council, at the behest of its military members, the Council recommended to the government that it should take stern measures against further Islamization of the state and society.[96] One of those measures included scrapping the middle school section of the Prayer Leader and Preacher Schools, thus, in effect, making an eight-year secular education compulsory for every pupil. When the DYP-RP government did not act on these recommendations in any great hurry, they were repeated at subsequent meetings of the Council, and the General Staff held a series of 'briefings' with members of the media, selected higher civil servants, and university administrators 'about the security threat some Islamic activities posed for the state'. These pressures on the government by the military were coupled with protests 'by the secularists' in the country[97] – every night for ten minutes they turned off the lights in their premises – and the influential secularly oriented media and interest group associations representing big business, small producers and both the moderate and militant wings of labor directed sharp criticisms at the government.

For a while, the government seemed to give no heed to the increasing pressure. However, it seems that when talk began to circulate that a military intervention was imminent Çiller persuaded Erbakan that she 'the secularist' should be the Prime Minister, in order to avert a possible military take-over. Erbakan resigned in favour of his coalition partner.[98] However, President Demirel did not appoint Çiller but designated Mesut Yılmaz, the leader of ANAP, as Prime Minister, despite the fact that, at the time, Erbakan and Çiller together commanded a majority in Parliament. Demirel explained that his appointment of Yılmaz was a political (read, 'prudent') rather than a 'democratic [read 'numerical'] choice'. It soon proved to be a numerical choice, too, because, in the event, the Yılmaz government obtained a vote of confidence, thanks to resignations from both Erbakan's RP and particularly Çiller's DYP. This confidence was due to the fact that many groups in the polity and society, including parliamentarians, were convinced that the state's weakness on issues not concerning the secular and democratic regime had the potential to pose a critical threat for the country.

Will Turkey be able to break the vicious circle of a weak state (in the economic sphere) giving rise to developments that invite the strong state (vis-à-vis the political regime) to take over completely or at least intervene indirectly in politics and, when things are normalized, will the weak state return to the scene and try to make up for the losses some groups experienced during the strong state period and, therefore, re-start the whole circle again? The fact that Turkey could not break this vicious circle since the transition to multi-party politics more than 50 years ago, during which time many hard core authoritarian regimes elsewhere have made significant progress toward consolidating their democracies, may make one pessimistic about the future of democracy in Turkey.

On the other hand, there are also grounds for being optimistic. In the course of the last ten years, patronage politics reached new highs and, at least on the surface, there was a concomitant rise of political Islam – they were both related and autonomous from each other – yet the military did not take power directly into its hands. The military acted as only one of the several pressure groups, though without doubt, the most critical one since in the last analysis only it could apply immediate and effective sanctions if the Erbakan-Çiller team insisted on staying in power. The military's not taking power into its hands was extremely useful, in that it gave a chance to the political elite to figure out where they went wrong and what to do to deal effectively with the difficult problems, confronting Turkish political, economic and social life.

It was also significant that in the months leading to the fall of the Erbakan-Çiller coalition, the military made several pleas to the political elite that, this time around, the government, and not the military, should cope with the 'threat the rising political Islam posed for the secular and democratic regime in Turkey'. Consequently, many 'secularists', including some leftists who in the past had bitterly opposed the military, had praise for the military for its patience, and urged the political elite to put their house in order. This, too, may oblige the political elite to think carefully over how democracy in Turkey can be improved.

In all probability, whether the political elite strives to make that improvement will continue to be monitored not only by the media but also by other elements of civil society. For the first time in Turkish politics, civil societal groups actively joined forces with the state elite to deal with the problem of the weak state in Turkey. Thus, there is reason to think that in the near future there will be in Turkey, a judicious combination of a weak state and a strong state, or political responsiveness and political prudence. These norms, which are, in combination, the indispensable dimensions of a consolidated democracy, may be internalized by the political elite so that in the future there may not be a need for the military to act even as a critical pressure group. Such a development would also have important implications for the healthy functioning of the executive branch, Parliament, and the bureaucracy, over and above its favourable impact upon the consolidation of democracy in Turkey.

Joel S. Migdal has seen a close link between the degree of social control a state exercises and the strength of that state. He has suggested that extensive societal dislocations and/or social disturbances resulting from war and/or revolution and massive migration weaken the state's social control and transform a strong state into a weak state.[99] In Turkey the state became weaker not because of extensive societal dislocations and/or social disturbances but because the political elite, largely as a reaction to the dominance of the state elite, began to pursue non-prudent and incoherent economic policies. Only at times of complete or partial depolitization of the political milieu (1923–45, 1961–65 and 1983–87 periods), selected political leaders (İsmet İnönü and Turgut Özal) pursued more prudent and coherent economic policies. Because of their basic commitment to democracy, the state elite did not act even when they thought that the economic policies were incoherent and irresponsible. They moved only when in their perception the Republican regime had come under a serious threat, as a consequence of other political developments, such as the armed Left-Right confrontation or the rise of political Islam. Concerning the Republican regime the state in Turkey remained strong; *vis-à-vis* the socio-economic sphere the state in Turkey more often than not evinced characteristics of a weak state. Because of the overall (and increasing) commitment of the state elite to democracy, although from time to time the phenomenon of the weak state led to political crises (such as short-term military interventions), it did not lead to regime crises (such as the establishment of a long-term authoritarian regime).

NOTES

This is a revised version of a paper presented at the Seventeenth World Congress of the International Political Science Association, Seoul, South Korea, August 1997. We are grateful to İzak Atiyas of the World Bank and Sabancı University, Ankara and Selçuk Sancar of the State Planning Organization of Turkey who made invaluable comments on the earlier version; we, of course, absolve them of any responsibility for the final product.

1. See Metin Heper, *The State Tradition in Turkey* (Walkington: The Eothen Press, 1985), Chapter Two. On military schools, see Bernard Lewis, *The Emergence of Modern Turkey* (London: Oxford University Press, 1961), p.181.
2. Heper, *The State Tradition in Turkey*, Chapters Three and Four.
3. İlkay Sunar, 'Populism and Patronage: The Demokrat Party and Its Legacy in Turkey', *Il Politico*, Vol.60 (1990), pp.745–57.
4. Metin Heper, *İsmet İnönü: The Making of a Turkish Statesman* (Leiden: E. J. Brill, 1998), Chapter Six. With the exceptions of 1939 and 1949, surpluses were recorded in the budget in the 1933–1949 period, which made possible the importation of intermediate goods. Therefore, there was an impressive average growth rate of 3.6 per cent during this period, which included the World War II years. See Devlet Planlama Teşkilatı, *Ekonomik ve Sosyal Göstergeler* (Ankara: Devlet Planlama Teşkilatı, 1977), p.20.
5. Kemal H. Karpat, 'The Republican People's Party, 1923–1945', in Metin Heper and Jacob Landau (eds.), *Political Parties and Democracy in Turkey* (London: I. B. Tauris, 1991), p.54.
6. Heper, *İsmet İnönü: The Making of a Turkish Statesman*, p.175.
7. Ziya Öniş, 'The State and Economic Development in Contemporary Turkey: Etatism to Neoliberalism and Beyond', in Vojtech Mastny and R. Craig Nation (eds.), *Turkey Between East and West: New Challenges for a Rising Regional Power* (Boulder, Colorado: Westview Press, 1996), pp.157, 158.
8. İzak Atiyas, 'Uneven Governance and Fiscal Failure: The Adjustment Experience in Turkey', in Leila Frischtak and İzak Atiyas (eds.), *Governance, Leadership, and Communication: Building Constituencies for Economic Reform* (Washington, D C: The World Bank, 1996), p.287.
9. Öniş, 'The State and Economic Development in Contemporary Turkey', p.157.
10. Metin Heper, 'The State, Political Party and Society in Turkey', *Government and Opposition*, Vol.25 (Summer 1990), pp.321–33.

11. Leslie L. Roos and Noralou P. Roos, *Managers of Modernization: Organizations and Elites in Turkey* (Cambridge, Mass.: Harvard University Press, 1971), pp.168ff.
12. Sabri Sayarı, 'Political Patronage in Turkey', in Ernest Gellner and John Waterbury (eds.), *Patrons and Clients in Mediterranean Societies* (London: Duckworth, 1977), p.106.
13. Ergun Özbudun, 'Turkey: The Politics of Political Clientelism', in S. N. Eisenstadt and René Lemarchand (eds.), *Political Clientelism, Patronage and Development* (Beverly Hills and London: Sage, 1981), p.252.
14. Ayşe Güneş-Ayata, 'Roots and Trends of Clientelism in Turkey', in Luis Roniger and Ayşe Güneş-Ayata (eds.), *Democracy, Clientelism and Civil Society* (Boulder, Colorado and London: Lynne Rienner, Publishers, 1994), p.61.
15. Ibid., p.53.
16. Atiyas, 'Uneven Governance and Fiscal Failure: The Adjustment Experience in Turkey', p.284.
17. Öniş, 'The State and Economic Development in Contemporary Turkey', p.169.
18. Atiyas, 'Uneven Governance and Fiscal Failure: The Adjustment Experience in Turkey', p.287.
19. Özbudun, 'Turkey: The Politics of Political Clientelism', p.253.
20. Ayşe Buğra, *State and Business in Modern Turkey: A Comparative Study* (Albany: State University of New York Press, 1994).
21. İlkay Sunar, 'The Politics of State Interventionism in "Populist" Egypt and Turkey', in Ayşe Öncü, Çağlar Keyder and Saad Eddin Ibrahim (eds.), *Developmentalism and Beyond: Society and Politics in Egypt and Turkey* (Cairo: The American University in Cairo Press, 1994), p.98.
22. İzak Atiyas and Şerif Sayın, *Siyasi Sorumluluk, Yönetsel Sorumluluk ve Bütçe Sistemi: Bir Yeniden Yapılanma Önerisine Doğru* (Istanbul: Türkiye Ekonomik ve Sosyal Etüdler Vakfı, 1996), p.27 and Metin Heper, 'Interest-Group Politics in Post-1980 Turkey: Lingering Monism', in Metin Heper (ed.), *Strong State and Economic Interest Groups: The Post-1980 Turkish Experience* (Berlin and New York: Walter de Gruyter, 1991), pp.163–76. In Turkey, there is an Economic and Social Council, but it is no more than an advisory body and not much attention is paid to its advice.
23. Kamran İnan, *Siyasetin İçinden* (Istanbul: Milliyet Yayınları, 1995), p.35.
24. Sayarı, 'Political Patronage in Turkey', p.260; Ayşe Güneş-Ayata, 'Roots and Trends of Clientelism in Turkey', pp.54, 55ff.
25. Sayarı, 'Political Patronage in Turkey', p.265.
26. Atiyas and Sayın, *Siyasi Sorumluluk, Yönetsel Sorumluluk ve Bütçe Sistemi: Bir Yeniden Yapılanma Önerisine Doğru*, p.29.
27. Gökhan Çapoğlu, *Türkiye'de Siyasi Tıkanıklığı Aşmak İçin* (Ankara: Stratejik Araştırmalar Vakfı, 1994), p.18.
28. Ibid., pp.27, 43.
29. Öniş, 'The State and Economic Development in Contemporary Turkey', p.159. The growth rates of 12.8, 11.9 and 11.2 per cent were recorded in 1951, 1952 and 1953, respectively.
30. İnan, *Siyasetin İçinden*, p.36.
31. Ian Budge and Hans Keman, *Parties and Democracy: Coalition Formation and Government Functioning in Twenty States* (New York: Oxford University Press, 1990).
32. Metin Heper and Selçuk Sancar, 'Is Legal-Rational Bureaucracy a Pre-Requisite for a Rational-Productive Bureaucracy?: The Case of Turkey', *Administration and Society*, Vol.30 (May 1998), pp.143–65.
33. İlter Turan, 'Stages of Political Development in the Turkish Republic', in *Perspectives on Democracy in Turkey*, Üstün Ergüder, Ersin Kalaycıoğlu, Ergun Özbudun and İlter Turan, contributors (Ankara: Turkish Political Association, 1988), p.91 and İzak Atiyas, 'The Effect of the State's Presence in the Economy on Politics: Notes on the Reform of the State', a Paper presented at the 'Fifth National Conference on Quality in General and Political Quality in Particular', 13–14 November 1996, Istanbul.
34. Atiyas, 'The Effect of the State's Presence in the Economy on Politics: Notes on the Reform of the State', p.338.
35. Atiyas and Sayın, *Siyasi Sorumluluk, Yönetsel Sorumluluk ve Bütçe Sistemi: Bir Yeniden*

Yapılanma Önerisine Doğru, p.28.
36. Çapoğlu, *Türkiye'de Siyasi Tıkanıklığı Aşmak İçin*, pp.54–5.
37. Erdoğan Yıldırım, *Türkiye'de Siyaset Süreci ve Profesyonel Siyasette Benliğin Kurulması: SHP Örneği* (Ankara: Ark Yayınevi, 1995), pp.130–6.
38. Gökhan Çapoğlu, *Yepyeni Bir Türkiye İçin* (Ankara: Anadolu Stratejik Araştırmalar Vakfı, 1997), p.38.
39. İnan, *Siyasetin İçinden*, pp.42–4.
40. Heper, *The State Tradition in Turkey*, Chapter Five.
41. Güneş-Ayata, 'Roots and Trends of Clientelism in Turkey', p.59; Metin Heper, 'Negative Bureaucratic Politics in a Modernizing Context: The Turkish Case', *Journal of South Asian and Middle Eastern Studies*, Vol.1 (1977), pp.65–84.
42. Heper, *The State Tradition in Turkey*, Chapter Five.
43. Sunar, 'The Politics of State Intervention in "Populist" Egypt and Turkey', p.101.
44. Feride Acar, 'The True Path Party, 1983–1989', in Metin Heper and Jacob Landau (eds.), *Political Parties and Democracy in Turkey*, pp.190–5.
45. In the post-1965 period, except the early 1970s when its then leader Bülent Ecevit had its charisma at its peak, the CHP, too, gradually adopted patronage politics, as a consequence of its repeated failures at the polls. See Sayarı, 'Political Patronage in Turkey', p.111.
46. For the DP period, see John Waterbury, 'Export-Led Growth and the Center-Right Coalition in Turkey', *Comparative Politics*, Vol.24 (January 1992), p.129.
47. Avner Levy, 'The Justice Party, 1961–1980', in Heper and Landau, *Political Parties and Democracy in Turkey*, pp.141, 142.
48. Güneş-Ayata, 'Roots and Trends of Clientelism in Turkey', p.54.
49. Öniş, 'The State and Economic Development in Contemporary Turkey', p.159.
50. Sunar, 'The Politics of State Intervention in 'Populist' Egypt and Turkey', p.104.
51. Joel S. Migdal, *Strong States and Weak States: State-Society Relations and State Capabilities in the Third World* (Princeton: Princeton University Press, 1988), p.22.
52. Ziya Öniş, 'International Context, Income Distribution and State Power in Late Industrialization: Turkey and South Korea in Comparative Perspective', *New Perspectives on Turkey* (Istanbul), Vol.13 (Fall 1995), p.26.
53. Üstün Ergüder, 'The Motherland Party, 1983–1989', in Heper and Landau, *Political Parties and Democracy in Turkey*, p.156.
54. Atiyas, 'Uneven Governance and Fiscal Failure: The Adjustment Experience in Turkey', p.292.
55. Sabri Sayarı, 'Political Parties, Party Systems, and Economic Reforms: The Turkish Case', *Studies in Comparative International Development*, Vol.31 (Winter 1996/97), p.35
56. Cevat Karataş, 'Public Debt, Taxation System and Government Spending Changes in Turkey, 1980–1992', *Journal of Economics and Administrative Studies* (Istanbul), Vol.6 (1992), p.47.
57. Atiyas, 'Uneven Governance and Fiscal Failure: The Adjustment Experience in Turkey', p.293.
58. Ziya Öniş, 'Globalization and Financial Blow-Ups in the Semi-Periphery: Perspectives on Turkey's Financial Crisis of 1994', *New Perspectives on Turkey*, Vol.15 (Fall 1996), p.7.
59. Ergüder, 'The Motherland Party, 1983–1989', in Heper and Landau, *Political Parties and Democracy in Turkey*, pp.155ff.
60. Işın Çelebi, Aykut Toros and Necati Aras, *Siyasette Kilitlenme ve Çözüm* (Istanbul: Milliyet Yayınları, 1996), p.15.
61. If one of the authors may be allowed a personal note: in those years, Heper once asked a shopkeeper if he liked Özal. The shopkeeper told Heper that he did not like Özal because Özal often took too stern measures in the economy. Then, the shopkeeper paused for a moment and then added: 'But Özal may make a speech on the TV tonight and I would in all probability change my mind.'
62. İnan, *Siyasetin İçinden*, p.102.
63. Sabri Sayarı, 'Politics and Economic Policy Making in Turkey', in Tevfik F. Nas and Mehmet Odekan (eds.), *Economics and Politics of Turkish Liberalization* (Bethlehem, PA: Lehigh University Press, 1992).
64. Öniş, 'The State and Economic Development in Contemporary Turkey', p.160, 166 and

276   TURKEY BEFORE AND AFTER ATATÜRK

idem, 'International Context, Income Distribution and State Power in Late Industrialization: Turkey and South Korea in Comparative Perspective', p.29.
65. Waterbury, 'Export-Led Growth and the Center-Right Coalition in Turkey', p.134.
66. Sayarı, 'Political Parties, Party Systems, and Economic Reforms: The Turkish Case', p.39.
67. Sunar, 'Populism and Patronage: The Demokrat Party and its Legacy in Turkey', p.756.
68. Betül Uncular, İşte Böyle Bir Meclis, 1983-1991 (Ankara: Bilgi Yayınevi, 1991), p.154.
69. Çelebi et al, Siyasette Kilitlenme ve Çözüm, pp.15-16.
70. Ergüder, 'The Motherland Party, 1983-1989', in Heper and Landau, Political Parties and Democracy in Turkey, p.165.
71. Atiyas, 'Uneven Governance and Fiscal Failure: The Adjustment Experience in Turkey', p.296.
72. Karataş, 'Public Debt, Taxation System and Government Spending Changes in Turkey, 1980-1992', p.70.
73. Atiyas, 'Uneven Governance and Fiscal Failure: The Adjustment Experience in Turkey', pp.298-9.
74. Çelebi et al., Siyasette Kilitlenme ve Çözüm, p.16.
75. Ziya Öniş, 'The Political Economy of Export-Oriented Industrialization in Turkey', in Çiğdem Balım, Ersin Kalaycıoğlu, Cevat Karataş, Gareth Winrow and Feroz Yasamee (eds.), Turkey: Political, Social and Economic Challenges in the 1990s (Leiden: E. J. Brill, 1995), p.123.
76. Güneş-Ayata, 'Roots and Trends of Clientelism in Turkey', p.58. Later it was reported that during his first 500 days in office Demirel shook hands with 113,117 persons! Milliyet (Istanbul daily), 15 April 1993.
77. Cumhuriyet (Istanbul daily), 12 December 1992. Çiller could not get along with the key higher civil servants, too. She could not put up with those civil servants who disagreed with her openly. There were also claims that at times she asked civil servants to 'doctor' some figures in order to show the performance of the government in a more positive light. She removed a number of civil servants from their posts; some others resigned.
78. Hürriyet (Istanbul daily), 4 March 1992.
79. Milliyet (Istanbul daily), 23 December 1992.
80. Bayram Gazetesi (newspaper published on religious holidays), 12 June 1992. Here Demirel referred to the pre-1987 period when the trade unions faced some legal constraints.
81. Cumhuriyet, 19 January 1992.
82. Öniş, 'Globalization and Financial Blow-Ups in the Semi-Periphery: Perspectives on Turkey's Financial Crisis of 1994', p.10.
83. Ibid., pp.10-11.
84. See, for instance, Milliyet, 8 July 1992.
85. Atiyas and Sayın, Siyasi Sorumluluk, Yönetsel Sorumluluk ve Bütçe Sistemi: Bir Yeniden Yapılanma Önerisine Doğru, p.29.
86. Çapoğlu, Yepyeni Bir Türkiye İçin, pp.26-7.
87. Earlier Erbakan's Refah Party had proposed a parliamentary investigation concerning the allegations about Çiller; they voted against their own proposal once they came to power. Before Çiller had agreed to enter a coalition with Erbakan, the other party leaders had turned down Erbakan.
88. According to this policy, profit was permitted but not interest, monopolies were to be eliminated completely, and the income tax was to be replaced by a production tax. See David Shankland, 'The Demise of Republican Turkey's Social Contract', Government and Opposition, Vol.31 (Summer 1996), p.315.
89. It was reported that the costs to the economy of the first round of promises made by Erbakan was half a quadrillion Turkish lira. Hürriyet, 2 July 1996.
90. Milliyet, 23 March 1997.
91. Hürriyet, 21 September 1996; Milliyet, 19 July 1996; Sabah, 13 May 1997.
92. Yeni Yüzyıl (Istanbul daily), 7 August 1996; Hürriyet, 16 April 1997; Sabah (Istanbul daily), 13 May 1997.
93. At the time, Çiller was Deputy Prime Minister and Foreign Minister. She spent most of her time trying to hold her party together because many members of her party had begun to be

disgruntled about the developments in question. She also tried to make Turkey a full member of the European Union but she was not successful in bringing about any progress in that direction. One reason was that she had lost the confidence of Western leaders; in the past she had promised many things to them but had not delivered. Particularly critical here was her statement in the past that for Turkey the Refah Party was a greater threat than the separatist Kurdish organization PKK and then her decision to enter a coalition government with that party. At some point Çiller even could say that 'politics was at the disposal of religion' (*Hürriyet*, 21 February 1997).

94. See, for instance, Metin Heper, 'Islam and Democracy in Turkey: Toward a Reconciliation?' *Middle East Journal*, Vol.51 (Winter 1997), pp.32–45.

95. The view that, in the Third Turkish Republic (from 1980 to the present), the military became increasingly reluctant to take power once more into its own hands is supported by a recent study of the memoirs and statements of the last three chiefs of general staff. See Metin Heper and Aylin Güney, 'The Military in the Third Turkish Republic', *Armed Forces and Society*, Vol.22 (Summer 1996), pp.619–42.

96. Turkey's 1982 Constitution stipulates that governments are obliged to give priority to the recommendations made by the National Security Council.

97. At the December 1995 national elections, 21 per cent of the voters cast their votes for the Refah Party. According to a survey carried out in 1994, only one-third of the voters of the party voted for that party because the party was a religiously oriented party and there is little doubt that only a small percentage of this group of voters longs for an Islamic state. For an elaboration, see Heper, 'Islam and Democracy in Turkey: Toward a Reconciliation?' pp.35–38.

98. Earlier, Erbakan and Çiller had agreed that this office of prime minister should rotate and that in summer 1998 Çiller should succeed Erbakan.

99. Migdal, *Strong Societies and Weak States: State-Society Relations and State Capabilities in the Third World*, pp.259ff.

Notes on Contributors

E. Burak Arıkan is in the Department of Political Science, Bilkent University, Ankara.

Meltem Müftüler-Bac is in the Department of Political Science, Bilkent University, Ankara.

Gavin D. Brockett is a doctoral student in the Department of Near Eastern Languages and Civilizations at the University of Chicago.

Christopher Clay is a professor in the Department of Historical, University of Bristol.

Metin Heper is a founding member of the Turkish Academy of Sciences and Dean of College of Administrative Sciences and Economics at Kog University, Istanbul.

M. Asım Karaömerlioğlu is in the Department of History, Ohio State University.

E. Fuat Keyman is in the Department of Political Science, Bilkent University, Ankara.

Hakan Kırımlı is in the Department of International Relations, Bilkent University, Ankara.

Mustafa Turkeş is Associate Professor in the Department of International Relations, Middle East Technical University, Ankara.

Hasan Ünal is Assistant Professor of International Relations at the University of Bilkent, Ankara.

Syed Tanvir Wasti is Professor of Engineering at the Middle East Technical University, Ankara.

Index

Books of Related Interest

Turkey
Identity, Democracy, Politics

Sylvia Kedourie *(Ed)*
With a Foreword by **W M Hale**

'... *enlightening historical and political essays* ...'
International Affairs

Elie Kedourie wrote of the 'mixed fortunes of constitutional and representative government in the Turkish Republic' as 'the outcome of one hundred and fifty years of tormented endeavour to discard the old ways, which have ceased to satisfy and replace them with something modern, eye-catching and attractive' Whether this has been wholly successful is being constantly put to the test in Turkey.

This volume covers a variety of topics, all of which shed light on puzzling issues. The discussions range over national and international politics, democracy and freedom of the press, voting patterns, official control of indigenous music, and conditions in industrial estates. It is essential reading for a broader understanding of Turkey, a country which is trying hard to become part of the European Community.

256 pages   1996
0 7146 4718 7   cloth
0 7146 4447 1   paper (1998)
A special issue of the journal Middle Eastern Studies

FRANK CASS PUBLISHERS
Newbury House, 900 Eastern Avenue, Newbury Park, Ilford, Essex, IG2 7HH
Tel: +44 (0)181 599 8866 Fax: +44 (0)181 599 0984   E-mail: info@frankcass.com
NORTH AMERICA
c/o ISBS, 5804 NE Hassalo Street, Portland OR 97213 3644
Tel: 800 944 6190 Fax: 503 280 8832 E-mail: cass@isbs.com
Website: www.frankcass.com E-mail: sales@frankcass.com

The Kurdish Question and Turkey
An Example of a Trans-state Ethnic Conflict

Kemal Kirişci and **Gareth M Winrow,**
Bogazici University, Istanbul

> '*Kirişci and Winrow's courageous and timely account is unquestionably the single most important study to date on the intricacies and difficulties of Turkey's Kurdish question.*'
> **Middle East Quarterly**

> '*Kirişci and Winrow's book should be purchased by all university, college, and large urban libraries.*'
> ***Choice***

This book provides a comprehensive examination of the Kurdish question in Turkey, tracing its developments from the end of the Ottoman Empire to the present day. Unlike many other works which have focused on the Kurds, the authors develop their argument by defining and making use of terms such as nation, ethnic group, civic nationalism, ethnic nationalism, minority rights and self-determination. Many commentators agree that ethnic conflict should be resolved by a 'political' rather than a military solution; but what would a political solution to the Kurdish question in Turkey actually entail? A number of possibilities are examined including: secession, federal schemes, the granting of various forms of autonomy, the provision of special rights and further democratization.

256 pages   1997
0 7146 4746 2   cloth
0 7146 4304 1   paper

FRANK CASS PUBLISHERS
Newbury House, 900 Eastern Avenue, Newbury Park, Ilford, Essex, IG2 7HH
Tel: +44 (0)181 599 8866 Fax: +44 (0)181 599 0984   E-mail: info@frankcass.com

NORTH AMERICA
c/o ISBS, 5804 NE Hassalo Street, Portland OR 97213 3644
Tel: 800 944 6190 Fax: 503 280 8832 E-mail: cass@isbs.com

Website: www.frankcass.com E-mail: sales@frankcass.com

The Great Powers and the End of the Ottoman Empire

Marian Kent *(Ed)*

In the final decades of its existence the Ottoman Empire was a focus of international rivalry among European Great Powers. Historians of the foreign policy, especially the Turkish policy of these Great Powers, have come together to address some of the important questions posed by the fall of the Ottoman Empire, following the First World War, to the victorious Allied Powers and to the forces of militant nationalism led by Kemal Atatürk. This collection is the fruit of their researches, presented for the first time in one unified volume.

238 pages   1996
0 7146 4154 5 paper

FRANK CASS PUBLISHERS
Newbury House, 900 Eastern Avenue, Newbury Park, Ilford, Essex, IG2 7HH
Tel: +44 (0)181 599 8866 Fax: +44 (0)181 599 0984 E-mail: info@frankcass.com
NORTH AMERICA
c/o ISBS, 5804 NE Hassalo Street, Portland OR 97213 3644
Tel: 800 944 6190 Fax: 503 280 8832 E-mail: cass@isbs.com
Website: www.frankcass.com E-mail: sales@frankcass.com